Gospel of disunion

Gospel of disunion

Religion and separatism
in the antebellum south

Mitchell Snay

THE UNIVERSITY OF NORTH CAROLINA PRESS
Chapel Hill and London

First published by The University of North Carolina Press in 1997

© 1993 by Cambridge University Press

Manufactured in the United States of America

The paper in this book meets the guidelines for permanence and
durability of the Committee on Production Guidelines for
Book Longevity of the Council on Library Resources.

Library of Congress Cataloging-in-Publication Data

Snay, Mitchell.
Gospel of disunion: religion and separatism in
the antebellum South / by Mitchell Snay.
p.   cm.
Originally published:
New York: Cambridge University Press, 1993.
Includes bibliographical references and index.
ISBN 0-8078-4687-2 (pbk.: alk. paper)
1. Southern States—Church history.
2. Secession—Southern States.
3. Southern States—Intellectual life.
4. Southern States—Civilization—1775–1865.
I. Title.
[BR535.S63   1997]
277.5'081 — dc21   97-13941
                                           CIP

01 00 99 98 97   5 4 3 2 1

To my parents

Contents

Acknowledgments

Although it often seemed like a solitary endeavor, the creation of this book was nurtured by many individuals and institutions. It is a pleasure here to acknowledge and thank them as *Gospel of Disunion* is brought to completion.

The research and writing of this book was made possible by financial support from several institutions. An Irving and Rose Crown Fellowship from the Graduate Program in the History of American Civilization at Brandeis University provided me with the priceless free time to begin my education in Southern history and with the resources to research extensively throughout the South. Most of this book was written during a residence at the Virginia Center for the Humanities in Charlottesville, which provided an unusually collegial and stimulating atmosphere for scholarship. Denison University not only funded a research summer in Boston but also granted me a Joyce Junior Faculty Fellowship, which gave me a vital semester off teaching to complete the writing of the manuscript.

Though they are too numerous to mention individually, the many librarians and archivists who guided me through their collections deserve my deep respect and gratitude. The Denison University Library was most helpful in the writing of this book. The interlibrary loan staff, particularly Emily Hoffmire, was cheerful and efficient in making accessible necessary primary sources. And for keeping an eager if pesty reader supplied with the most recent books, Carol Lukco and Mildred Charron merit at the least a nod in the acknowledgments.

The writing of this book was helped immeasurably by the comments and criticisms of many fellow historians. As members of my dissertation committee, David Herbert Donald and Morton Keller helped direct my initial thinking about turning the dissertation into a book. Bertram Wyatt-Brown and Michael O'Brien gave generously of their time and insights by reading the entire dissertation and offering suggestions for revisions. Their continual interest and support over the years have been of great value in the development of this book. The reviews of Robert M.

Calhoon and the anonymous reader for Cambridge University Press were extremely helpful in the final revisions of the manuscript. I owe a special debt of gratitude to Eugene D. Genovese. Critically commenting on several conference papers and the final draft of the manuscript, he forced me to refine my arguments and saved me from many factual errors. He also provided a greatly appreciated voice of support at a discouraging moment in the book's history. By listening to my ideas or reading parts of the manuscript, the following people have undoubtedly improved the quality of this book: Harriet Amos, Edward L. Ayers, David T. Bailey, Alan Brinkley, Stanley M. Elkins, William W. Freehling, Drew Gilpin Faust, Stuart Henry, Samuel S. Hill, Jr., Michael F. Holt, James Kloppenberg, Donald G. Mathews, Cynthia Maude-Gembler, John M. McCardell, James H. Moorhead, Leonard Richards, James H. Smylie, Kenneth M. Startup, and J. Mills Thornton III. The contributions of all these historians have convinced me that the ideal of a scholarly community can indeed be realized.

Other communities of historians contributed to this book in less tangible but no less important ways. My fellow members of the History Department at Denison have been friends as well as colleagues. Their own commitment to history, expressed in a rich variety of ways, and their care for me as a scholar, teacher, and person made this book much easier to write. An NEH Summer Institute held at the University of Connecticut in June 1989, "Classic Texts in Early American History," helped shape my thinking about words and ideology. Richard D. Brown, one of the Institute's instructors, has continued to be a valued teacher and an encouraging mentor.

To James Oliver Horton goes much of whatever credit or blame that may eventually be attached to my becoming a Middle Period historian. As my undergraduate teacher at the University of Michigan, he exposed me to the rich complexity of antebellum America and fostered my budding interest in becoming a historian. His infectious enthusiasm for history and his demanding standards of scholarship continue to shape my career. Lois Horton has always been there asking the good questions and proffering support. Raymond Arsenault and Stephen J. Whitfield, other members of our Brandeis clique, have been valued friends and colleagues for a long time.

I am particularly grateful for the friendship and intellectual companionship of three colleagues I met during graduate school. Alan Melchior always had the keen insight to ask the penetrating but necessary questions while never wavering in his faith and respect that I could answer them. Ruth Friedman was patient with my enthusiastic forays into moral philosophy, insistent in reminding me to read things written after the nineteenth century, and steadfast in her encouragement. Jama Lazerow and I have spent many stimulating and pleasurable years talking about religion, society, and politics in nineteenth-century America. As both mentor and protegé, he has been indispensable in my education as a historian. To all my other friends who have over the years understood the importance of history in my life, I offer my deepest thanks for their loyalty and support.

My greatest intellectual debt in writing this book goes to Marvin Meyers. He guided this project with interest and respect from its beginnings as a dissertation through the revisions into a book. His tough questions forced me to clarify confused thoughts and develop my own arguments. Although it took me a long time to realize, his constant probing, whether through conversation or through scribbled drafts of chapters, taught me how to think like a historian. I sincerely hope that whatever merit this book possesses begins to repay my gratitude to this great scholar and gentleman.

My thanks go to several people associated with Cambridge University Press, who skillfully and promptly helped turn the manuscript into final form as a book: executive editor Frank Smith, production editor Eric Newman, and copy editor Shirley Covington.

The north side of Chicago in the 1950s and 1960s was a world far removed from the plantations and churches of the Old South. Although I can never fully fathom nor explain the connection, I have no doubt that my upbringing there somehow shaped why and how I sought to understand the role of religion in the formation of Southern separatism. What I recognize more clearly, however, are the ways in which my parents contributed to the making of this book. They instilled in me the empathy to dispassionately understand people whose experiences and values differed greatly from my own, the ability to accept criticism without losing confidence, and the persistence necessary to undertake and finish a project. For all their love and support, *Gospel of Disunion* is dedicated with respect and affection to them.

INTRODUCTION

Religion and the search for Southern distinctiveness

At noon on February 18, 1861, the Rev. Basil Manly, pastor of the Baptist church in Montgomery, rode to the capitol in a carriage with Jefferson Davis, Alexander H. Stephens, and their military escort. He delivered a prayer later that afternoon that spoke directly to the event – the inauguration of the president and vice-president of the Confederate States of America. "Thou hast provided us a man," Manly proclaimed, "to go in and out before us, and to lead thy people." He also invoked God's blessing for the new born Southern nation: "Put thy good spirit into our whole people, that they may faithfully do all thy fatherly pleasure,..." Manly called further for truth and peace in the administration of government and righteousness for the people. He concluded, finally, by asking God to "turn the counsel of our enemies into foolishness."[1]

Present at Manly's benediction were the politicians who had brought the South to the brink of separate nationhood. Taken together, they embodied the wide spectrum of antebellum Southern politics. William L. Yancey, the fire-eater from Alabama and the leading orator of the secessionist cause, and Robert Barnwell Rhett, the vociferous Southern nationalist from South Carolina and the voice behind the radical Charleston *Mercury*, were the extremists who had pushed Southerners toward political revolution. Although not as radical as Rhett or Yancey, Davis himself had been a strong advocate of Southern rights as a senator from Mis-

---

1. "Diary of Basil Manly: January 1, 1858–1878," Manly Collection, Special Collections, Samford University Library (Microfilm), p. 37. For a brief biographical sketch of Manly, see Samuel S. Hill, ed., *Encyclopedia of Religion in the South* (Macon, Ga.: Mercer University Press, 1984), p. 442. Davis's inauguration is covered in Hudson Strode, *Jefferson Davis: American Patriot, 1808–1861* (New York: Harcourt, Brace, 1955), pp. 406–12; William C. Davis, *Jefferson Davis, The Man and His Hour: A Biography* (New York: HarperCollins, 1991), p. 307; John M. McCardell, *The Idea of a Southern Nation: Southern Nationalists and Southern Nationalism, 1830–1860* (New York and London: W. W. Norton, 1979), pp. 334–5; William E. Dodd, *Jefferson Davis* (Philadelphia: George W. Jacobs & Company, 1907), pp. 223–5.

sissippi during the 1850s. The moderates were represented by Stephens, a former Whig who only a few months before had opposed separate state secession, and fellow-Georgian Howell Cobb, a Unionist in the early 1850s who had only recently joined the Georgia secessionists.[2]

By joining together Yancey and Rhett with Stephens and Cobb, the inauguration of Jefferson Davis signaled a momentary political consensus that had made disunion a reality. The Rev. Basil Manly's place on the steps of the capitol was equally significant. Not only did his prayer call for divine sanction on the Confederacy, but his participation symbolically acknowledged the role religion played in the growth of Southern distinctiveness. For religion contributed much to the origins of Southern separatism. It invested the sectional controversy over slavery with moral and religious meaning, strengthening those elements in Southern political culture that made secession possible.

I

The development of antebellum Southern sectionalism centered on the issue of slavery and evolved primarily in the arena of national politics. The Missouri crisis of 1819–20 first laid bare the potential danger of Northern politicians who heeded to the belief that slavery was wrong. The ensuing decade witnessed the emergence of a states' rights philosophy and proslavery argument that would safeguard the South throughout the antebellum era. The nullification controversy in South Carolina, Nat Turner's slave revolt in Virginia, and the appearance of immediate abolitionism brought slavery to the center of Southern consciousness during the 1830s. In 1846, Pennsylvania congressman David Wilmot introduced his fateful proviso banning slavery from all territories acquired during the Mexican War. Southerners grew increasingly vociferous during the 1850s about their rights and honor. By 1860, the sectional conflict had escalated to the point at which Southerners saw themselves as a distinct people. A year later, eleven slave states seceded from the Union and created their own new Confederate nation.[3]

2. For brief accounts of the politics of these Southern statesmen, see William J. Cooper, Jr., and Thomas E. Terrill, *The American South: A History* (New York: McGraw-Hill, 1991), pp. 338, 345. On Cobb, see Avery O. Craven, *The Growth of Southern Nationalism, 1848–1861* (Baton Rouge: Louisiana State University Press, 1953), p. 370.

3. Two older studies remain perhaps the best introduction to the course of the South to secession: Charles S. Sydnor, *The Development of Southern Sectionalism, 1819–1848* (Baton Rouge: Louisiana State University Press, 1948), and Craven, *Growth of Southern Nationalism.* They must now, however, be supplemented by William W. Freehling, *The*

The sectional controversy over slavery touched almost every facet of Southern life. The search for a distinctive Southern identity was expressed in the commercial conventions aimed at promoting Southern economic growth, the establishment of such Southern schools as the University of the South at Sewanee, and in the Romantic fiction of William Gilmore Simms. Yet perhaps nowhere outside the realm of politics can the growth of Southern separatism be seen so clearly as in the religious sphere, which acted both as a sensitive barometer of mounting sectional pressures and a decisive influence on a developing Southern identity. There are three compelling reasons to turn to religion in order to understand the origins and nature of Southern separatism.[4]

First, religion was central to the culture and society of the antebellum South. Spurred on by the Cane Ridge Revival in 1800, evangelical Protestantism came to dominate the religious life of most Southerners. Repentance of sin and conversion to a career of holiness, the central message of evangelicalism, gave order and meaning to the lives of all but a few Southern men and women, black as well as white. Christianity and the Bible were the moral foundations of Southern public order as well. The reading of slaveholders included the Bible and other religious tracts. For these men and women, religion sanctioned a hierarchical and particularistic approach to human relations. Proslavery sociologists, political economists, and judges grounded their secular theories in Scripture. If religion was so paramount in a society that was forging a distinctive sectional identity, it is likely that it played a strong role in this process. Donald G. Mathews, in an illuminating study of Southern religion, suggests such a relationship: "During the years when the Southern ideology was taking shape, ... Evangelicalism became in the view of many Christian theorists one of the distinguishing marks of what it meant to be a Southerner."[5]

Road to Disunion, Vol. 1: Secessionists at Bay, 1776–1854 (New York: Oxford University Press, 1990).

4. John M. McCardell's *Idea of a Southern Nation* provides the most recent synthesis of antebellum Southern nationalism. This book is especially valuable in exploring sectional manifestations in economics, politics, literature, religion, and education.

5. Eugene D. Genovese, *The Slaveholders' Dilemma: Freedom and Progress in Southern Conservative Thought, 1820–1860* (Columbia: University of South Carolina Press, 1992), p. 4; Donald G. Mathews, *Religion in the Old South* (Chicago: University of Chicago Press, 1977), p. 246. Emory Thomas draws the connection even further: "Perhaps Southern churches are the best place to look for the origins of cultural nationalism in the Old South. There the Southern mind, conditioned by reverence for the concrete and characterized by assertive individualism, blended with a unique religious tradition to mold intellectual and cultural life." *The Confederate Nation, 1861–1865* (New York: Harper & Row, 1979), p. 21. Antebellum Southern religion has become a prolific and vibrant field in Southern

Another reason to search for the development of Southern separatism in religion is the strongly religious character of the sectional controversy over slavery. The earliest Northern attacks on slavery in the 1830s were religious and moral ones. Abolitionists condemned slavery as a sin. In response, Southern clergymen defended the morality of their "peculiar institution" through an elaborate scriptural defense of human bondage. As the antislavery message penetrated the evangelical consciousness of the North, the South continued to rely on Christianity as a necessary sanction of their slaveholding order.[6]

history. On the origins and nature of evangelicalism, see John B. Boles, *The Great Revival, 1787–1805: The Origins of the Southern Evangelical Mind* (Lexington: University Press of Kentucky, 1972); Robert M. Calhoon, "The Evangelical Persuasion in the South," in Peter J. Alberts, ed., *Religion in a Revolutionary Age* (forthcoming); and especially Mathews, *Religion in the Old South*. The place of religion in the lives of white Southerners can be gleaned from Jan Lewis, *The Pursuit of Happiness: Family and Values in Jefferson's Virginia* (Cambridge: Cambridge University Press, 1983), chap. 2; James Oakes, *The Ruling Race: A History of American Slaveholders* (New York: Knopf, 1982), chap. 4; and most recently, Elizabeth Fox-Genovese, *Within the Plantation Household: Black and White Women of the Old South* (Chapel Hill and London: University of North Carolina Press, 1988), pp. 16–20. On Southern women and religion, consult Jean E. Friedman, *The Enclosed Garden: Women and Community in the Evangelical South, 1830–1900* (Chapel Hill: University of North Carolina Press, 1985). On the centrality of religion to social theory, see Eugene D. Genovese and Elizabeth Fox-Genovese, "The Religious Ideals of Southern Slave Society," *Georgia Historical Quarterly* 70 (Spring 1986): 4–5 and Robert M. Calhoon, *Evangelicals and Conservatives in the Early South, 1740–1861* (Columbia: University of South Carolina Press), p. 176.

Besides religion, honor was another central component of the ethical system of the Old South. The major works establishing this tradition are Bertram Wyatt-Brown, *Southern Honor: Ethics and Behavior in the Old South* (New York: Oxford University Press, 1982); Edward L. Ayers, *Vengeance and Justice: Crime and Punishment in the Nineteenth-Century American South* (New York: Oxford University Press, 1984); and Kenneth S. Greenberg, *Masters and Statesmen: The Political Culture of American Slavery* (Baltimore and London: Johns Hopkins University Press, 1985). For a discussion of the relationship between honor and evangelicalism, see Bertram Wyatt-Brown, "God and Honor in the Old South," *Southern Review* 25 (April 1989): 283–96; and Edward R. Crowther, "Holy Honor: Sacred and Secular in the Old South," *Journal of Southern History* 58 (November 1992): 619–36. In Chapter 4, I suggest that religion reinforced the importance of honor in sectional politics.

6. Of the many works on the religious dimension of the antebellum controversy over slavery, see David Brion Davis, "The Emergence of Immediatism in British and American Antislavery Thought," *Mississippi Valley Historical Review* 49 (September 1962): 209–30; Anne C. Loveland, "Evangelicalism and 'Immediate Emancipation' in American Antislavery Thought," *Journal of Southern History* 32 (May 1966): 172–88; John R. McKivigan, *The War Against Proslavery Religion: Abolitionism and the Northern Churches, 1830–1865* (Ithaca and London: Cornell University Press, 1984); David T. Bailey, *Shadow on the Church: Southwestern Evangelical Religion and the Issue of Slavery, 1783–1860* (Ithaca, N.Y.: Cornell University Press, 1985); Elizabeth Fox-Genovese and Eugene D. Genovese,

Finally, the intimate ties between religion and nationalism in early America suggest that religion played a major role in the formation of a Southern national identity. Between the Revolution and the Civil War, American religious nationalism was expressed primarily through the tradition of "civil religion." Secular and religious motifs were woven into the belief that America had a unique role in bringing the Kingdom of God to this world. Millennialism fused with the political ideology of republicanism, convincing Americans that their social and political institutions had a providential destiny to serve as a model for all humankind. Because Southern sectionalism was forged in a period when the issue of American national identity was particularly acute, we might expect that Southern Protestants turned naturally toward civil religion as they created their own version of nationalism.[7]

The centrality of religion in the Old South, the strongly religious flavor of the slavery controversy, and the close affinity between religion and American nationalism suggest, then, the importance of religion in the formation of antebellum Southern distinctiveness. Although several recent efforts at linking religion and sectionalism have been made, the connection between the two has not yet received the comprehensive examination it deserves. *Gospel of Disunion* is an attempt to explore the relationship between religion and the origins of Southern separatism. It examines the ways in which religion adapted to and shaped the development of a distinctive Southern culture and politics before the Civil War, adding depth and form to the movement that culminated in secession.[8]

The term *separatism* most accurately describes the sectional consciousness and growing distinctiveness of Southerners before the Civil War. It encompasses both sectionalism, the loyalty to a set of values and interests associated with a geographical region, and Southern nationalism, the belief that sectional interests would be best served in a separate nation. *Sectionalism* is too narrow a term here, for it excludes the religious advocacy of a Southern nation that flowered during the first few months of the Confederacy. Similarly, the use of the term *nationalism* would be mis-

"The Divine Sanction of Social Order: Religious Foundations of the Southern Slaveholders' World View," *Journal of the American Academy of Religion* 55 (Summer 1987): 211–34.

7. For good introductions to civil religion in nineteenth-century America, see Ernest Tuveson, *Redeemer Nation: The Idea of America's Millennial Role* (Chicago: University of Chicago Press, 1968), and Sacvan Bercovitch, *The American Jeremiad* (Madison: University of Wisconsin Press, 1978).

8. C. C. Goen, *Broken Churches, Broken Nation: Denominational Schisms and the Coming of the Civil War* (Macon, Ga.: Mercer University Press, 1985), and Calhoon, *Evangelicals and Conservatives in the Early South, 1740–1861*, are the best and most thorough attempts to link religion and politics in the South.

leading, for few clergymen advocated a separate Southern nation in the antebellum period.[9]

II

The relationship between religion and politics can be examined from several angles. They have intersected on a variety of levels throughout American history, such as the familiar conflict between church and state and the association between religious affiliation and patterns of voting behavior. It is in the subtle and complex interaction between religious beliefs and public values and activities, however, that the connection between religion and Southern separatism can best be studied.[10]

Religion in the antebellum South functioned simultaneously as an institution, a theology, and a mode of discourse. It shaped an emerging sectionalism in all these ways. Moreover, the relationship between religion and sectionalism was reciprocal. Religion worked as an active agent translating the sectional conflict into a struggle of the highest moral significance. At the same time, the slavery controversy sectionalized Southern religion, creating separate sectional institutions and driving theology further toward orthodoxy.

The relationship between religion and Southern separatism can be most efficiently and reliably traced through the thoughts and actions of the Southern clergy. The minister in nineteenth-century America was generally considered the articulate consciousness of society, sensitively attuned to the problems of his time and aware of his persuasive role as moral steward. In the antebellum South, the authority of the clergy was high.

9. For a brief and useful discussion of these terms, see McCardell, *Idea of a Southern Nation*, p. 5.

10. Mark A. Noll, ed., *Religion & American Politics: From the Colonial Period to the 1980s* (New York and Oxford: Oxford University Press, 1990), pp. 3–4. The relationship between religion and politics during the era of the American Revolution suggested useful lines of inquiry. Particularly helpful were Alan Heimert, *Religion and the American Mind: From the Great Awakening to the Revolution* (Cambridge, Mass.: Harvard University Press, 1966); Nathan O. Hatch, *The Sacred Cause of Liberty: Republican Thought and the Millennium in Revolutionary New England* (New Haven, Conn.: Yale University Press, 1977); Harry S. Stout, "Religion, Communications, and the Ideological Origins of the American Revolution," *William and Mary Quarterly* Third Series 34 (October 1977): 519–41; William G. McLoughlin, "Enthusiasm for Liberty: The Great Awakening as a Key to the Revolution," in Jack P. Greene and William G. McLoughlin, *Preachers and Politicians: Two Essays on the Origins of the American Revolution* (Worcester, Mass.: American Antiquarian Society, 1977); and especially Bernard Bailyn, "Religion and Revolution: Three Biographical Studies," *Perspectives in American History* 4 (1970): 83–169.

Ministers enjoyed status in their pastorates. They were the voice of moral authority and powerful molders of public opinion. Southern clerics exerted their influence not only through the pulpit but through their positions as editors and educators. The clergy thus had an attentive audience through which they could fashion the sectional identity of the South.[11]

The ministers most actively engaged with the sectional controversy over slavery tended to come from a group that one historian has aptly termed the "Gentlemen Theologians" of the Old South. They were the elite of the Southern clergy – well-educated, urbane clergymen with comfortable pastorates among the middle and upper classes of the cities and towns of the Old South. Their ministerial careers were active and varied, usually involving religious journalism or some kind of college teaching. Whether Methodist, Baptist, Presbyterian, or Episcopalian, they had a strong sense of denominational identity and were active in building the institutions necessary for the growth of their churches. Above all, they represented the professionalization of the clergy, seeking status, influence, and power in their society. This study thus relies heavily on the published writings of the Gentlemen Theologians. To seek a broader sample of religious thought on sectional issues, denominational newspapers and the records of church assemblies have been used to recover the ideas of less elite clerics and less prominent congregations.[12]

---

11. On the authority of the clergy in antebellum America, see the quotation by Alexis de Tocqueville in Noll, *Religion & American Politics*, p. 6. On the influence of the Southern clergy, see Genovese, *Slaveholders' Dilemma*, p. 14; Drew Gilpin Faust, *The Creation of Confederate Nationalism: Ideology and Identity in the Civil War South* (Baton Rouge and London: Louisiana State University Press, 1988), p. 22; and Cooper and Terrill, *American South*, pp. 265–6. Important studies of the Southern clergy include Anne C. Loveland, *Southern Evangelicals and the Social Order, 1800–1860* (Baton Rouge and London: Louisiana State University Press, 1980); E. Brooks Holifield, *The Gentlemen Theologians: American Theology in Southern Culture, 1795–1860* (Durham, N.C.: Duke University Press, 1978); James Oscar Farmer, Jr., *The Metaphysical Confederacy: James Henley Thornwell and the Synthesis of Southern Values* (Macon, Ga.: Mercer University Press, 1986).

12. Holifield, *Gentlemen Theologians*, chap. 2. On the professionalization of the antebellum American clergy, see Donald M. Scott, *From Office to Profession: The New England Ministry, 1750–1850* (Philadelphia: University of Pennsylvania Press, 1978), and Daniel H. Calhoun, *Professional Lives in America: Structure and Aspirations, 1750–1850* (Cambridge, Mass.: Harvard University Press, 1965), pp. 88–177. The connection I am drawing here does not mean to suggest that all of Holifield's 100 elite were active in sectional politics or that each minister who appears in this book should be included on his list. Still, the association between the "Gentlemen Theologians" and sectional politics is significant. Larry E. Tise substantiates this claim with a much more systematic study. *Proslavery: A History of the Defense of Slavery in America, 1701–1840* (Athens and London: University of Georgia Press, 1987), especially pp. 163–70.

In using the clergy as the voice of Southern religion, it is important to recognize that the Southern clergy was anything but monolithic. Ministers in the South were distinguished by denomination, region, and class. Episcopalians and especially Presbyterians placed a heavy emphasis on a learned clergy. Their ministers were usually the products of theological seminaries and were hence more likely to emphasize doctrinal preaching and spend more time on sermon preparation. Methodists and Baptists, on the other hand, focused more on their "calling" from God to legitimate their ministry. They were truly evangelicals, more interested in awakening and saving sinners through emotion rather than doctrine. Although they lagged behind the Presbyterians, Baptists and Methodists steadily improved their educational efforts during the antebellum decades. There were significant differences in the ways denominations structured their ministries. Presbyterian clergymen tended to have established pastorates, most often catering to the upper and middle classes in the towns and cities of the Old South. Methodists adopted a system of itinerancy to reach their following in widely scattered rural areas. Baptists used what was called the once-a-month system, in which a church was supplied by a minister who came once or twice a month to preach. Considering all these differences, it is misleading then to speak of *the* Southern clergy.[13]

Yet in terms of their views on slavery and sectional politics, there was a conspicuous consensus among Southern clergymen. The major denominations in the South – Baptist, Methodist, Presbyterian, and Episcopalian – differed little in their approach to such sectional issues as slavery, abolition, and the protection of Southern rights. In other words, denominational distinctions were not really a determinant of sectional thought. Some differences, however, did exist. Presbyterian ministers tended to be more literate and prolific in their sectional writings. From their authoritative positions as educators and editors, they exerted an influence disproportionate to their relatively small numbers. With a theology and church structure geared toward conversions, the Methodists took the lead in the religious mission to the slaves. Regional variations within the South accounted for the more significant differences between the sectional views of Southern clerics. Ministers most often followed the sectional extremism or moderation of their respective states. Keeping these points of diversity in mind, we can be reasonably confident about the underlying unity of Southern clerical thought on sectional issues. This unanimity was essential in helping mold a moral consensus that could unite the South behind secession.[14]

13. Loveland, *Southern Evangelicals and the Social Order*, pp. 45–8. Chapter 2 of this book provides a useful overview of the Southern ministry in the antebellum period.

14. Genovese and Fox-Genovese, "Divine Sanction of Social Order," p. 227. A similar difficulty regarding social role should be mentioned. Clergymen in the antebellum South

III

To incorporate the variety of ways in which religion shaped the growth of Southern separatism, this book has been arranged chronologically, topically, and thematically. It follows in rough outline the progressive course of the South to secession. Chapter 1 explores the role of the Southern clergy and churches in an early episode of the sectional conflict, the abolitionist crisis of 1835. Chapters 2 and 3 probe the crucial relationship between Southern religion and slavery. The material presented here represents the entire time span of the sectional controversy. Chapter 4 moves to the middle of the antebellum decades, examining the denominational schisms in the Presbyterian church in the late 1830s and in the Baptist and Methodist denominations in the mid-1840s. Finally, Chapters 5 and 6 focus on the period between the late winter of 1860 and the summer of 1861, when Southern clergymen justified secession and created a Confederate national identity.

Within this chronological context, the book is also arranged thematically. Considering the variety of ways religion and politics intersect and the difficulties of establishing causal relationships, it is useful at the outset to sketch out the major themes that best illuminate the points of interaction and lines of influence between religion and sectionalism.

The Southern clergy and the problem of religion and politics

What emerges most often in the sectional writings of Southern clergymen is the persistent effort to clarify and define the proper boundaries between religion and politics. It shaped almost every public discussion of slavery, informed political sermons delivered on public occasions, and even infused private diaries and correspondence. It remained a consistent concern from the 1830s through the secession crisis, occupying clergymen of all denominations and regions of the South. There is a seeming paradox in the way Southern clergymen wrote about this issue. On the one hand, they vigorously accepted the principle of separation of church and state

were Democrats and Whigs, slaveholders and nonslaveholders, Virginians and South Carolinians, but always churchmen and Southerners. These various personas complicate the task of understanding the role of religion in the creation of Southern separatism. It is difficult to know precisely the factors and roles that determined the sectional thought of Southern clergymen. This problem is met largely by focusing on the public statements of the Southern clergy in their self-proclaimed role as clergymen. These are easily accessible in the denominational newspapers that served the South and in sermons delivered at public events. The private writings of clergymen most often reflected their public statements.

and insisted that slavery and abolition were political questions that lay outside the realm of religion. But at the same time and often from the same voices, Southern ministers maintained that slavery and abolition involved moral issues that were the rightful domain of the clergy. They vehemently objected to abolitionist preaching from Northern pulpits while they freely defended slavery from their own. This contradictory approach can be partially, if not fully, resolved through carefully reconstructing the distinctive way Southern clergymen understood the role of religion in sectional politics.

The ideas of Southern clergymen on the boundaries between religion and politics depended first on how they defined politics. They condemned clerical involvement in the political sphere when pragmatic questions of policy or especially party were involved. In these cases, politics was deemed particulary unworthy of Christian consideration. Yet if a political issue was perceived as possessing any kind of moral significance, Southern clerics claimed that it fell within their realm and justified their attention. The Rev. James A. Lyon, a Presbyterian minister from Mississippi, clearly explained this conception of the issue. Political questions, he maintained, "I leave to the politician, except when politics cross the line into the domain of Christian morals, and invade the territories of religion: then I will discuss so called politics, since it thereby becomes a question of morals, and a legitimate subject for the pulpit." Southern clergymen followed this reasoning throught the antebellum period. They endowed the sectional conflict with religious significance by extracting and articulating the moral dimension of political issues.[15]

Southern clerical thinking about the proper relationship between religion and politics was also directly related to the slavery controversy. What clergymen really objected to was a specific mixture represented by the abolitionist assault on slavery. Southern clerics believed that slavery contained two distinct realms, the civil and the religious. The existence of slavery itself was considered a political, or civil, question. Within the institution of slavery, however, were certain moral issues, such as the relationship between master and slave, that properly fell within clerical

15. James A. Lyon, *Christianity and the Civil Laws: A Lecture on Christianity and the Civil Laws by Rev. James A. Lyon, D. D. of Columbus, Mississippi* (Columbus: *Mississippi Democrat* Print), p. 11. There were, of course, exceptions to the general disinclination of ministers to engage in politics. William Winans, a Methodist clergyman from Mississippi, was a vociferous supporter of the Whig party. Jesse Mercer, a Methodist elder, of Georgia also had a yearning for politics. He was a member of Georgia's constitutional convention of 1798 and ran for the state Senate in 1816. See Ray Holder, *William Winans: Methodist Leader in Antebellum Mississippi* (Jackson: University of Mississippi Press, 1977), especially pp. 132–34, and Charles D. Mallory, *Memoirs of Jesse Mercer* (New York: Printed by John Gray, 1844), p. 54.

jurisdiction. By questioning the existence of slavery, a political issue, the abolitionists had wrongly pushed religion into the political realm.

In addition, Southern clergymen drew a careful distinction between their roles as minister and private citizen. They generally condemned political participation from the office of the ministry but maintained that clergymen had a right as individuals to their political views. This understanding, which was generally accepted among the Southern clergy, was succinctly set forth by Robert Lewis Dabney of Virginia, soon to be a military aide to Stonewall Jackson. "My conviction has all along been," explained the Presbyterian pastor, "that we ministers, when acting ministerially, publicly, or any way representatively of God's people as such, should seem to have no politics." Yet Dabney insisted that he had his "politics personally, and at the polls act on them."[16]

The way Southern clerics understood the relationship between religion and politics is key to understanding the role of religion in the development of Southern separatism. Southern ministers invested the sectional conflict with religious significance, legitimating their participation in the political realm. They sanctified slavery with an elaborate scriptural justification of human bondage, a slaveholding ethic to guide the conduct of Christian masters, and a program to bring the Gospel to the slaves. They transformed the meaning of the sectional controversy into a larger struggle between orthodoxy and infidelity. Through clarifying the boundaries between religion and sectional politics, Southern clergymen essentially translated the political conflict into religious terms.

The "Americanness" of Southern clerical thought

The growth of Southern distinctiveness was part of the American quest for a national identity that was particularly acute between the Revolution and the Civil War. Nationalism and sectionalism should therefore not be seen as mutually exclusive phenomena but as complementary processes of American self-definition. Discussing the nature of Southern nationalism, historian David Potter recognizes that antebellum Southerners considered themselves both Southern *and* American. He explains that "southern loyalties to the union were never obliterated but rather were eclipsed by other loyalties with which, for a time, they conflicted." Other histo-

16. Thomas C. Johnson, *The Life and Letters of Robert Lewis Dabney* (originally published 1903; Edinburgh and Carlisle: The Banner of Truth Trust, 1977), p. 221. For similar views, see Elizabeth H. Hancock, ed., *Autobiography of John E. Massey* (New York and Washington: Neale Publishing, 1909), p. 27, and H. P. Griffith, *The Life and Times of Rev. John G. Landrum* (Philadelphia: H. B. Garner, 1885), pp. 198, 160.

rians have argued along similar lines that American values and institutions were instrumental in the formation of Southern separatism. Republicanism, for example, the common ideological heritage of the American Revolution, was a staple in Southern political rhetoric devoted to the defense of slavery and states' rights.[17]

The sectional thought of Southern clergymen fit this pattern. They drew naturally upon American intellectual resources to fashion a distinctive sectional ideology. The Bible was the center of their defense of slavery. Moral philosophy provided the terms for delineating the ideal Christian relationship between master and servant. The tenets of evangelicalism and the discourse of American civil religion furnished the rhetoric for the religious justification of secession. In these ways, antebellum Southern distinctiveness was a legitimate if ironic product of American thought.

In important ways, however, the sectional views of Southern clergymen were distinctive products of the Southern soil. Slavery was the foundation of antebellum Southern civilization. The master–slave relationship and the paternalism that defined it lay at the foundation of antebellum Southern civilization. Not surprisingly, slavery shaped Southern theology in a profound way. The organic and hierarchical social philosophy of the Southern clergy was intimately related to the paternalistic and particularistic view of human relations indigenous to a slaveholding society. The sectional thought of Southern clergymen was thus both Southern and American. It was grounded in the material and social realities of slavery and fashioned by the larger discourse of American religion.[18]

The dialogue between the Southern clergy and an antislavery North

Southern religious separatism was forged in the context of an ongoing dialogue between North and South. Specifically, the sectional ideas of

17. David Potter, *The South and the Sectional Conflict* (Baton Rouge: Louisiana State University Press, 1968), p. 78; McCardell, *Idea of a Southern Nation,* pp. 336–8. For the influence of republicanism on Southern political thought, see especially Robert Shalhope, "Thomas Jefferson's Republicanism and Antebellum Southern Thought," *Journal of Southern History* 42 (November 1976): 529–56, and Michael F. Holt, *The Political Crisis of the 1850s* (New York: Wiley, 1978).

18. For studies that emphasize this argument, see Jack P. Maddex, "The 'Southern Apostacy' Revisited: The Significance of Proslavery Christianity," *Marxist Perspectives* (Fall 1979): 140, and Fox-Genovese and Genovese, "Religious Ideals of Southern Slave Society," p. 2. The larger issue here of course is the debate between the liberal/capitalist and traditional/paternalist interpretations of the Old South. For a good and succinct examination of this important historiographical problem, see Drew Gilpin Faust, "The Peculiar South Revisited: White Society, Culture, and Politics in the Antebellum Period,

Southern clergymen were in large measure shaped by the specific debate with Northern abolitionists over the morality of slavery. Abolitionism began in the 1830s as a religious movement based on the premise that slavery was a sin. It was in response to this attack on the rectitude of slavery that the Southern clerical defense of slavery and criticism of abolitionism were initially framed. The dynamic of call and response between North and South continued throughout the antebellum sectional controversy. During the denominational schisms, the constitutional arguments of Southern churchmen were again specific defenses against the antislavery actions of Northerners. In the winter and spring of 1860-1, Southern clergymen escalated their debate with the North from the issue of the morality of slavery to the relative merits of free and slave society.

The North was critical in another way to the growth of Southern religious separatism, by providing a negative reference point by which Southern ministers could assure themselves of their own political and religious orthodoxy. The dangerous closeness Southern clerics saw between abolitionism and infidelity reaffirmed the position of the South as the bastion of religious conservatism. The aggressive political preaching from Northern pulpits suggested that the North was perverting the sacred office of the ministry. The North had become, in the eyes of Southern clerics, a subversive threat to American values and institutions.

The relationship between religious and political discourse

The role of religion in the development of Southern separatism can also be measured through the interaction between religious and political discourse. Southern sectionalism was primarily a political phenomenon played out in the annals of Congress, the halls of state legislatures, and the columns of the political press. It was the politicians who pioneered and maintained the defense of Southern rights. Secession itself, the culmination of antebellum Southern separatism, was essentially a political act. To assess the reciprocal influence between religion and Southern sectionalism, then, the points of connection between religious and political thought and language are crucial. The relationship between the spheres of religion and politics was symbiotic. At certain times and on certain issues, politicians borrowed from the clergy. The scriptural justification of human bondage became a staple in secular proslavery writings. The lessons

1800-1860," in John B. Boles and Evelyn Thomas Nolen, eds., *Interpreting Southern History: Historiographical Essays in Honor of Sanford W. Higginbotham* (Baton Rouge and London: Louisiana State University Press, 1987), pp. 79-86.

taught by the denominational schisms of the 1840s became valuable to politicians forced to defend the rights and honor of the slaveholding South. Conversely, Southern clergymen took many of their political ideas from the politicians. Essentially, Southern politics and Southern religion took separate but intersecting roads to secession.

Counterthemes

Religion worked in different ways and on various levels to move the South toward disunion. Yet its influence did not always flow in the direction of separatism. At the same time that religion encouraged sectionalism, it also had the potential to inhibit the drive toward a separate sectional identity. The comments of historian Bernard Bailyn on the role of religion in the coming of the American Revolution aptly applies in this case:

> For religion was no singular entity in eighteenth-century American culture and it had no singular influence on the Revolutionary movement: it was in itself both a stimulus and a deterrent to revolution, brought to different focuses in different ways by different men.[19]

Religion acted in several ways as a counterforce to the development of Southern separatism. It could have divided Southerners, impeding the drive for internal unity. It could also have frustrated the movement toward Southern separatism by acting as a cohesive force that bound together North and South in a common nationality. Finally, the very means through which religion acted as a separatist force contained the possibility to thwart this movement. Implicit in the Christian doctrine of slavery, for example, was the acknowledgment that the slave was a spiritual being. This could have exacerbated the inherent contradiction of slavery – the identity of the slave as both person and property – and possibly have weakened the peculiar institution. The existence of these counterthemes does not negate the very real contributions religion made to the growth of Southern separatism. They may instead point accurately to its very essence. Religion in fact highlights the "incompleteness" of Southern nationalism in 1861. The South was not a monolithic unit but a diverse society with conflicting interests. The decision for secession was not uniform and clear-cut but characterized instead by division, drift, and doubt. Southerners retained strong identities as Americans. The fact that religion simultaneously encouraged and undercut the movement toward Southern

---

19. Bailyn, "Religion and Revolution: Three Biographical Studies," p. 85. This short article remains one of the most perceptive and incisive discussions of the role of religion in the Revolution.

separatism serves as a reminder of the inevitable ambiguities and conflicts involved in attempting to create a separate sectional identity in antebellum America.[20]

IV

Religion was instrumental in the formation of a distinctive sectional identity in the three decades before the Civil War. It invested the political conflict between North and South with profound religious significance, helping to create a culture that made secession possible. It established a moral consensus on slavery that could encompass differing political views and unite a diverse and disharmonious South behind the banner of disunion. The role of religion in the development of Southern separatism began in earnest in the summer of 1835 when a political maelstrom came sweeping down from the North, striking with fearful accuracy at the heart of Southern society.

20. See the relevant comments in Craven, *Growth of Southern Nationalism, 1848–1860*, p. 390, and James G. Randall, *Lincoln the Liberal Statesman* (New York: Dodd, Mead, 1947), p. 46.

PART ONE

Religion and sectional politics

1

The abolitionist crisis of 1835:
The issues defined

In May 1835, the American Antislavery Society announced its intention to "sow the good seed of abolition thoroughly over the whole country." Lewis Tappan, prominent evangelical abolitionist from New York and member of the society's executive committee, devised the plan to flood the nation with antislavery pamphlets, kerchiefs, medals, and even blue wrappers around chocolate. The names of 20,000 Southerners appeared on Tappan's mailing list. Targeting the South, suggested the antislavery newspaper *Emancipator*, would force Southerners to show "their real views and feelings."[1]

These words proved prophetic. On July 29, 1835, the steam packet *Columbia* arrived in Charleston from New York with thousands of antislavery tracts in its hold. No sooner had the boat arrived than a group of angry citizens snatched these mail bags from the post office. The next evening 3,000 Charlestonians gathered at the Parade Ground and watched as this antislavery literature, along with effigies of Tappan and two other leading abolitionists, was burned. The bonfires that night in the summer of 1835 provided unmistakable evidence of the "real views and feelings" of the South. The abolitionist crusade to end slavery would be met by swift and stiff resistance by the slaveholding states.[2]

By confronting the South with an assault on the morality of slavery, the

1. Bertram Wyatt-Brown, "The Abolitionists' Postal Campaign of 1835," *Journal of Negro History* 50 (October 1965): 228–30; Leonard Richards, *"Gentlemen of Property and Standing": Anti-Abolition Mobs in Jacksonian America* (New York: Oxford University Press, 1970), p. 52.
2. This description is based on Wyatt-Brown, "Abolitionists' Postal Campaign of 1835," p. 230; William W. Freehling, *Prelude to Civil War: The Nullification Controversy in South Carolina, 1816–1836* (New York: Harper & Row, 1965), pp. 340–1; and Charles S. Sydnor, *The Development of Southern Sectionalism, 1819–1848* (Baton Rouge: Louisiana State University Press, 1948), p. 232. See also Frank Otto Gatell, ed., "Postmaster Huger and the Incendiary Publications," *South Carolina Historical Magazine* 64 (October 1963): 193–201.

postal campaign of 1835 created a political crisis that drew Southern ministers into sectional politics. Their first important confrontation with Northern abolitionists prefigured the ways in which religion would help shape antebellum Southern distinctiveness. It revealed the dynamics of call and response between abolitionism and Southern religion. It also forced Southern clergymen to articulate their moral defense of slavery and to divest abolitionism of religious authority. The antebellum debate between Northern abolitionists and Southern clergymen over the morality of slavery would follow the lines set forth in 1835. In their response to abolitionism, Southern clergymen spoke most often about the relationship between religion and politics. They emerged from the crisis of 1835 with a particular understanding of this relationship, one that would profoundly shape their thinking throughout the sectional conflict.

I

The Southern clergy faced the abolitionist crisis of 1835 with an ambivalent and somewhat contradictory legacy toward slavery. Historians have traditionally argued that the early 1830s marked a decisive shift in Southern thinking toward a defense of slavery as a positive good. According to this interpretation, the liberal Jeffersonian acceptance of slavery as a necessary evil crumbled under the combined weight of the Nat Turner rebellion, the debates over slavery in the Virginia legislature, the nullification controversy in South Carolina, and the emergence of immediate abolitionism marked by the publication of William Lloyd Garrison's *The Liberator* in 1831.[3] Although this interpretation is clearly credible and compelling, much evidence suggests that among Southern clergymen and denominational groups, proslavery emerged far earlier than the 1830s. Throughout the seventeenth and eighteenth centuries, Southern churches accepted slavery and attempted to Christianize slaveholders. These efforts persisted during the eighteenth century, despite increasing attacks on slavery after the American Revolution. By 1835, then, the Southern clergy had ample precedence for choosing either to defend or challenge human bondage.

With their insistence upon human brotherhood, spiritual equality, and benevolence, Quakers provided the earliest and strongest religious con-

---

3. For a succinct statement of this view, see Allan Nevins, *Ordeal of the Union: Fruits of Manifest Destiny, 1847–1852* (New York: Scribner's, 1947), pp. 149. The abandonment of Jeffersonian liberalism for the defense of slavery is also the theme of Clement Eaton, *The Freedom-of-Thought Struggle in the Old South* (New York: Harper & Row, 1964).

tribution to early American antislavery. Southern Quakers were speaking out against slavery by the mideighteenth century. In 1758, the Virginia Yearly Meeting directed its members to avoid both the importing or holding of slaves. Quakers in Maryland, Virginia, and North Carolina petitioned their legislatures for exemptions from restrictions on manumissions. Quaker emancipation was practically complete in Maryland and Virginia by 1788, although the process was a little slower in North Carolina. Quakers continued their antislavery activities during the early nineteenth century. For example, they dominated the North Carolina Manumission Society formed in 1816. Yet the Quaker thrust toward antislavery was blunted in the Southern slaveholding environment. The Western Quarterly, for example, a subdivision of the North Carolina Yearly Meeting, advised its members in 1768 not to buy or sell slaves "in any case that can be reasonably avoided." Other Quaker governing bodies in the South sought to distance themselves from manumission and antislavery.[4]

It was the secular ideology of the American Revolution that really sparked the growth of antislavery sentiment in the late eighteenth-century South. What historian Bernard Bailyn has termed the "contagion of liberty" brought into sharp focus the inconsistency of human bondage in a republican society. The Lockean emphasis on natural rights and the republican insistence on liberty led logically to a questioning of slavery. Virginia Baptists, for example, stated in 1789 that slavery was "a violent deprivation of the rights of nature and inconsistent with a republican government." The influence of Revolutionary ideology on religious antislavery is more fully illustrated in a public letter written by the minister David Barrow in 1798 explaining his decision to leave Virginia. A native of Virginia, Barrow freed his own slaves in 1784 and later moved to Kentucky, where he became an antislavery preacher. Barrow's religious antislavery views reflected Enlightenment liberalism and republicanism. He stressed the natural equality of man and argued that liberty was "the unalienable privilege of all complexions, shapes and sizes of men." Ac-

4. Mary Locke, *Antislavery in America from the Introduction of African Slaves to the Prohibition of the Slave Trade (1619–1808)* (originally published 1901; New York: Johnson Reprint Company, 1968), pp. 21–2; ibid., p. 36; Lester Scherer, *Slavery and the Churches in Early America, 1619–1819* (Grand Rapids, Mich.: William B. Eerdsman Publishing, 1975), p. 131; Patrick Sowle, "The North Carolina Manumission Society, 1816–1834," *North Carolina Historical Review* 42 (Winter 1965): 47; David Brion Davis, *The Problem of Slavery in the Age of Revolution, 1770–1823* (Ithaca, N.Y.: Cornell University Press, 1975), p. 221. On the antislavery tradition of the Quakers, see Davis, *Problem of Slavery in the Age of Revolution,* pp. 213–55, and Stephen B. Weeks, *Southern Quakers and Slavery: A Study in Institutional History* (Baltimore, Md.: Johns Hopkins University Press, 1896).

cordingly, he argued that slavery was "contrary to the laws of God and nature." Appealing to the clash between slavery and the ideals of the Revolution, Barrow suggested that slaveholders "may consider how inconsistently they act, with a Republican government, and whether in this particular, they are *doing, as they would others should do to them!*"[5]

Evangelicalism was an equally potent source of antislavery sentiment in the late eighteenth-century and early nineteenth-century South. Originating in the First Great Awakening and reinforced by the great revivals of the 1790s and early 1800s, the logic of evangelical thought could and often did lead to a conflict between professed religious creeds and the holding of slaves. This was first made manifest by Baptists in pre-Revolutionary Virginia who welcomed black slaves into spiritual fellowship, further antagonizing the class conflict between these poorer farmers and their gentry neighbors. The evangelical ideal of a true community of believers and the insistence that the conversion experience was open to all people, regardless of race or sex, had profound egalitarian implications. "Christ has shed his blood for all nations," suggested one Virginian in 1774, "and therefore why should we counteract the kind intentions of heaven, by enslaving and making them miserable, and thereby putting an effectual bar in the way of their conversion?" Drawing upon the evangelical emphasis on spiritual freedom and equality, the Presbyterian David Rice claimed that the slave was "a free moral agent legally deprived of free agency." In 1823, the Jefferson Branch of the Manumission Society of Tennessee declared that blacks and whites were equal before God. In addition to its implicit egalitarian message, the evangelical commitment to a life of holiness, signified by the conversion experience, also led some Southern Protestants to free their slaves.[6]

5. Bernard Bailyn, *The Ideological Origins of the American Revolution* (Cambridge, Mass.: Belknap Press of Harvard University Press, 1967), pp. 232–46; Donald G. Mathews, *Religion in the Old South* (Chicago: University of Chicago Press, 1977), p. 69; Carlos Allen, Jr., "David Barrow's Circular Letter of 1798," *William and Mary Quarterly* 20 (July 1963): 440–1, 447, 445, 450. For additional studies on the contradictions between slavery and the ideals of the Revolution, see Duncan Macleod, *Slavery, Race and the American Revolution* (London, and New York: Cambridge University Press, 1974); Edmund S. Morgan, "Slavery and Freedom: The American Paradox," *Journal of American History* 59 (June 1972): 5–29; and Winthrop Jordan, *White over Black: American Attitudes Toward the Negro, 1550–1812* (Chapel Hill: University of North Carolina Press, 1968), pp. 269–311.
6. Rhys Isaac, "Evangelical Revolt: The Nature of the Baptists' Challenge to the Traditional Order in Virginia, 1765–1775," *William and Mary Quarterly* 31 (July 1974): 345–68; Elhanan Winchester, *The Reigning Abominations, especially the Slave Trade, considered as Causes of Lamentation: being the Substance of a Discourse delivered in Fairfax County, Virginia, December 30, 1774* (London: H. Trapp, 1788), p. 25; Mathews, *Religion in the*

Antislavery sentiment in the post-Revolutionary South was often channeled into support of colonization, the program aimed at sending freed
slaves back to Africa. Founded in 1816, the American Colonization Society (ACS) received support from such prominent Americans as James
Monroe, John Marshall, and Henry Clay. The colonization movement
had widespread appeal in the 1820s. It seemed to be a viable solution to
the problem of slavery, it appealed to the prevailing belief that blacks
were essentially not assimilable into white America, and it even appeared
to be a means of Christian benevolence toward blacks. Not surprisingly,
colonization was backed by church leaders across the nation. Within the
first five years of its existence, the ACS program was adopted by the
General Assembly of the Presbyterian Church, the Methodist General
Conference, the Baptist General Convention, and the General Convention of the Protestant Episcopal Church.[7]

Most Southern churchmen with humanitarian proclivities joined the
American Colonization Society. All Virginia religious denominations
gave this organization their official approval. The Presbyterian Synod of
Virginia resolved that "this enterprise, if conducted with proper discretion, will produce the happiest effects, particularly in aiding to communi-
cate the glad tidings of the gospel to an interesting quarter of the globe;
and to meliorate the condition of a degraded portion of our population,
while it promises the means of alleviating evils which our own country has
reason to deplore." Denouncing slavery as "one of the most tremendous
evils that ever overhung a guilty nation upon earth," the Episcopalian
Bishop William Meade of Virginia was an ardent worker for the American Colonization Society. Although it was never as strong as in Virginia,
colonization did receive support from religious groups outside the Old
Dominion. The New Orleans *Observer* sought to interest Presbyterians in
the activity of the Mississippi Colonization Society. The Rev. Christopher
Gadsen, rector of St. Philip's Church and later Episcopal Bishop of South

Old South, p. 66, 73; David Rice, "Slavery Inconsistent with Justice and Good Policy," in
Charles S. Hyneman and Donald S. Lutz, eds., *American Political Writing During the
Founding Era, 1760–1805* (Indianapolis: Liberty Press, 1983), p. 862; James B. Stewart,
"Evangelicalism and the Radical Strain in Southern Antislavery Thought During the
1820s," *Journal of Southern History* 39 (August 1973): 382; Mathews, *Religion in the
Old South*, p. 70.

7. James B. Stewart, *Holy Warriors: The Abolitionists and American Slavery* (New York:
Hill & Wang, 1976), pp. 29–30; John R. Bodo, *The Protestant Clergy and Public Issues,
1812–1848* (Princeton, N.J.: Princeton University Press, 1954), pp. 119–20. For fuller
treatments of colonization, see P. J. Staudenraus, *The African Colonization Movement,
1816–1865* (New York: Columbia University Press, 1961), and the important analysis in
George Fredrickson, *The Black Image in the White Mind: The Debate on Afro-American
Character and Destiny, 1817–1914* (New York: Harper & Row, 1971), pp. 1–43.

Carolina, pledged $50 to the American Colonization Society. The two vice-presidents of the North Carolina Society were clergymen. William Winans of Mississippi and James Osgood Andrew of Georgia, who were to become proslavery spokesmen in the Methodist Church, served as vice-presidents of the American Colonization Society in 1839.[8]

The message of the Quakers, the ideology of the American Revolution, and evangelicalism clearly gave rise to antislavery sentiment and support for colonization in the late eighteenth- and early nineteenth-century South. Yet the extent and significance of Southern religious antislavery feeling in the period before 1835 should not be overstated. The number of Quakers in the South remained small. Their influence was limited to small areas in Virginia and the North Carolina piedmont. The "contagion of liberty" unleashed by the Revolution never spread so far as slavery in the South was concerned. Southerners acknowledged the contradiction between liberty and slavery but pleaded helplessness in its face. To further avoid the antislavery implications of Whig ideology, they blamed the British for the existence of slavery in the colonies, cited their own inalienable rights of property, and suggested that blacks were really not part of humanity. Similarly, the evangelical potential for abolition was difficult to maintain in a society becoming increasingly dependent upon slavery. The social soil of the South simply could not nourish the seeds of radical emancipationism implicit in the evangelical ethos. In the words of one historian, the evangelical attack on slavery between 1750 and 1800 "was as shallow as it was short-lived."[9]

At the same time that Southern religion was nourishing antislavery sentiments, some ministers and denominational groups were giving significant support to slavery. This can best be explained as a process of the accommodation of religious institutions to a slaveholding society. With both the established Anglican Church and the growing evangelical sects of Baptists and Methodists, the need for denominational growth required acquiescence to slavery. The religious support for slavery in the colonial South often took the form of Christianizing both slaves and slaveholders. The result of these efforts was to move Southern denominations and clergymen in the direction of becoming defenders rather than critics of slavery.[10]

8. *Virginia Evangelical and Literary Magazine* 2 (October 1819): 580; Eaton, *Freedom-of-Thought Struggle in the Old South*, p. 294; Staudenraus, *African Colonization Movement*, p. 71; Bodo, *Protestant Clergy and Public Issues*, pp. 122, 147.

9. Sherer, *Slavery and the Churches in Early America*, pp. 108–10; Jon Butler, "Enlarging the Bonds of Christ: Slavery, Evangelism, and the Christianization of the White South, 1690–1790," in Leonard I. Sweet, ed., *The Evangelical Tradition in America* (Macon, Ga.: Mercer University Press, 1984), p. 110.

10. Butler, "Enlarging the Bonds of Christ," p. 111.

Anglican attitudes toward slavery were closely connected to the growth of the church in the Southern colonies. In the seventeenth century, the Anglican Church lacked a solid institutional foundation. The absence of a legal establishment to support religion and the settlement patterns of early Chesapeake society worked against the formation of strong parishes and organized religion. During the late seventeenth century, Anglican authorities in England began to reassert their authority in the Southern colonies to invigorate the church. Significantly, this paralleled the growth and entrenchment of slavery in the Chesapeake region during those same years. Anglican missionaries inadvertently strengthened slavery as they sought support among colonial slaveholders. They helped ease the concern that Englishmen could not hold baptized Africans in captivity and presented the emerging slaveowning class with a doctrine of slave obedience.[11]

James Blair, an Anglican commissary sent to Virginia in 1689, suggests how even the Christianization of slavery capitulated to the social and political pressures of the time. Blair recognized that the success of the church depended on an acceptance of slavery and an alliance with slaveholders. With a blend of humanitarian and pragmatic motives, he recommended to the General Assembly of Virginia in 1699 a plan "to endeavour the good instruction and Education of their Heathen Slaves, in the Christian faith." The plan was never adopted. The Christianization of slavery continued in the eighteenth century through the work of Dr. Thomas Bray and his associates, who began a missionary program in 1729. Schools for black children were later established under their auspices in Williamsburg and Fredericksburg. In these ways, the Anglican Church established itself in the Southern colonies partly through adapting itself to the needs of a slaveholding society.[12]

A similar process of denominational accommodation to slavery can be seen in the experience of Methodists in post-Revolutionary Virginia. Southern Methodists inherited a strong antislavery heritage. Both John Wesley, the founder of Methodism in England, and Francis Asbury, the key leader in American Methodism, were strongly opposed to slavery. The organizing conference of American Methodism in 1784 enacted legislation disapproving of slavery. In 1785, Virginia Methodists petitioned the General Assembly for the emancipation of slaves. The quick and hos-

11. Michael Anesko, "So Discreet a Zeal: Slavery and the Anglican Church in Virginia, 1680-1730," *Virginia Magazine of History and Biography* 93 (July 1985): 252; Butler, "Enlarging the Bonds of Christ," pp. 89-91, 93-7, 99-104.
12. Anesko, "So Discreet a Zeal," pp. 263-5; George M. Brydon, *Virginia's Mother Church and the Political Traditions Under Which it Grew* (Richmond: Virginia Historical Society, 1947-1952), p. 274. See also the important discussion in Butler, "Enlarging the Bonds of Christ," pp. 97-108.

tile response they encountered – even among Methodists – demonstrates the limits of antislavery potential in the Southern churches. Thomas Coke, an English Methodist touring Virginia in 1785, wrote that his opposition to slavery "provoked many of the unawakened to retire out the barn ... and to combine together to flog [me] ... as soon as I came out." Counterpetitions by proslavery Methodists, arguing that slavery was authorized in the Bible and stressing the dangers of manumission, quickly circulated. By 1793, Methodists already saw the inherent conflict between antislavery and the success of their denomination. "We thought it prudent to suspend the minute concerning Slavery," Coke recalled, "on account of the great opposition that had been given it, our work being in too infantile a state to push things to extremity."[13]

These denominational retreats from the antislavery implications of evangelicalism and republicanism did not necessarily signify the acceptance of slavery as a positive good. Early scriptural defenses of slavery, however, do constitute compelling evidence of religious proslavery before the 1830s. In his *Sermon on the Duties of Servants* (1743), the Anglican clergyman Thomas Bacon of Maryland anticipated the central themes of later religious defenders of slavery. Using the metaphor of the family to describe slavery, he justified inequality and hierarchy, arguing that God makes "some kings, some masters and mistresses, some tradesmen and working people, and other servants and slaves." Proslavery petitions presented to the Virginia legislature during the 1780s were filled with an extensive scriptural defense of human bondage. Residents of Amelia County, for instance, maintained in 1785 that "under the Old Testament Dispensation, Slavery was permitted by the Deity himself." Even Christ and his Apostles, believed Virginians in Brunswick County, "hath not forbid it." Full and elaborate scriptural defenses of slavery had emerged by the 1820s. Two important and influential tracts were written by Charleston clergymen in the wake of the Denmark Vesey slave revolt of 1822: Richard Furman's *Exposition of the Views of the Baptists, Relative to the Coloured Population of the United States* (1822) and Frederick Dalcho's *Practical Considerations Founded on the Scriptures, Relative to the Slave Population of South Carolina* (1823).[14]

13. Walter B. Posey, *The Development of Methodism in the Old Southwest, 1783–1824* (Tuscaloosa, Ala.: Weatherford Printing Co., 1933), pp. 92–4; Albert Mathews, "Notes on the Proposed Abolition of Slavery in Virginia in 1785," *Publications of the Colonial Society of Massachusetts* 6 (February 1900): 373, 377.

14. *Charleston Gospel Messenger and Protestant Episcopal Register* 7 (November 1830): 228, 336; Fredrika Schmidt and Barbara Wilhelm, "Early Proslavery Petitions in Virginia," *William and Mary Quarterly* 30 (January 1973): 133, 139, 144. Both the Furman and Dalcho sermons are discussed in Larry E. Tise, *Proslavery: A History of the Defense of Slavery in America, 1701–1840* (Athens and London: University of Georgia Press, 1987), pp. 61–2.

Although it is difficult to determine its beginnings with exact precision, religious proslavery clearly existed before the abolitionist postal campaign of 1835. By the 1820s, the movement of Southern religion toward the defense and Christianization of slavery had been confirmed. This shift toward proslavery can be illustrated in the changing views of John Holt Rice. An important leader of the early Presbyterian Church in the South, Rice had argued for the eventual abolition of slavery in 1817. His opinions were already changing by 1819, when he published "Thoughts on Slavery" in his *Virginia Evangelical and Literary Magazine*. Rice still believed that slavery was "the greatest political evil which has ever entered the United States." He warmly supported colonization and the religious instruction of slaves. Yet Rice backed away from advocating abolition. Immediate emancipation, he argued, was "out of the question." Even eventual emancipation of the slaves in the United States "will always be impracticable." By 1826, Rice had moved far enough along to publish a proslavery article in his journal, although he continued to support colonization.[15]

Religious voices against slavery persisted into the 1830s. "We believe that the interests of the country, as well as those of humanity," admitted the *North Carolina Baptist Interpreter* in 1834, "require an eventual, and, as far as practicable, a speedy emancipation." The *Religious Herald* of Richmond also clung to remnants of the "necessary evil" argument. Some clerics spoke out against the internal slave trade and called for the amelioration of slavery's worst abuses. As late as 1840, one Baptist newspaper in North Carolina declared its desire not "to see this system perpetuated." This antislavery sentiment seemed limited to the upper South, especially North Carolina and Virginia. It did not reflect the majority of Southern clerical opinion after the abolitionist crisis of 1835.[16]

The growing proslavery turn of Southern religion was undoubtedly reflected in and was in turn influenced by the growing sectionalism of the 1820s. During the early national period, the South became increasingly devoted to a slave economy and society as the phenomenal increase in cotton production propelled migration southwestward into Alabama, Mississippi, and Louisiana. The Missouri Controversy of 1819–20 was

15. William Sumner Jenkins argues that the "positive good theory was an outgrowth of the twenties." *Proslavery Thought in the Old South* (Chapel Hill: University of North Carolina Press, 1935), p. 77; *Virginia Evangelical and Literary Magazine* 2 (July 1819): 292, 295–9; Louis Weeks III, "John Holt Rice and the American Colonization Society," *Journal of Presbyterian History* 46 (1968): 34.
16. *North Carolina Baptist Interpreter*, October 4, 1834; *Religious Herald*, September 28, 1835; John S. Bassett, *Slavery in North Carolina* (Baltimore, Md.: Johns Hopkins University Press, 1899), p. 63; *Southern Baptist and General Intelligencer*, April 17, 1835; *Biblical Recorder and Southern Watchman*, May 9, 1840.

the first political crisis that awakened Southerners to the threat posed to slavery by a Northern antislavery majority. In addition, John Marshall's nationalist decision in *McCulloch* v. *Maryland* (1819) further strengthened the states' rights school of such Virginians as Judge Spencer Roane. In South Carolina, the Denmark Vesey revolt and agitation over the federal tariff significantly contributed to the rise of Southern sectionalism in the 1820s.[17]

Finally, it is important to recognize that there were regional distinctions within Southern religious views on slavery. In general, religious antislavery seems to have made more headway in Virginia than elsewhere in the South. The support of colonization was stronger in Virginia than in other Southern states. The persistence of antislavery in Virginia might be explained by the lingering liberal influence of Thomas Jefferson and the decreasing importance of slavery in the state's economy. The sale of Virginia's surplus slaves helped populate the new cotton states of the southwest. In contrast, religious proslavery took firmer root in the lowcountry of South Carolina. A large slave population and dependence on the staple crops of rice and cotton made slavery there more of an essential part of the social and economic fabric, which provided a receptive setting for a proslavery interpretation of the Bible.[18]

II

Southern churches and clergymen faced the abolitionist crisis of 1835 with a complex and often contradictory legacy of antislavery, colonization, and proslavery. This mixed heritage nonetheless gave the Southern clergy ample precedents and even impetus for attacking abolitionism and defending slavery. Because of its strongly religious flavor, the abolitionist assault on slavery triggered for ministers a conflict between the cause of religion and their commitment to defend Southern institutions. Their response to abolitionism was paradoxical. Southern ministers argued that slavery was a political issue that lay outside the province of religion. Yet

17. On the Missouri Compromise, see Glover Moore, *The Missouri Controversy, 1819–1821* (Lexington: University of Kentucky Press, 1953), and Don E. Fehrenbacher, *The South and Three Sectional Crises* (Baton Rouge: Louisiana State University Press, 1980), pp. 9–24. On the growth of states' rights associated with *McCulloch*, see the essays collected in Gunther Barth, ed., *John Marshall's Defense of McCulloch v. Maryland* (Stanford: Stanford University Press, 1969). For the South during the 1820s in general, see Sydnor, *Development of Southern Sectionalism.*

18. Staudenhaus, *African Colonization Society*, p. 106. Good on South Carolina sectionalism in the 1820s is Freehling, *Prelude to Civil War*, chaps. 1–4.

simultaneously, they entered the political arena to attack abolitionism and defend slavery. The rise of abolitionism thus forced the Southern clergy to clarify the relationship between religion and politics. It set the patterns that would guide their thoughts and actions throughout the sectional controversy.

The abolitionist postal campaign of 1835 represented the change in American antislavery from gradualism to immediatism. The emergence of immediate abolitionism in the early 1830s was a complex phenomenon rooted in religious and social change. The profound unrest unleashed by economic transformation and rapid social and geographic mobility in the early Republic created fertile soil for a series of religious revivals that became known as the Second Great Awakening. Evangelicalism signified a casting off of sin and a consequent commitment to a life of holiness. To the young men and women converted by the revivals of the 1820s, slavery came to symbolize the host of ills troubling the young Republic. As one historian explains: "Immediate abolition was at heart a theological conception that united the image of the sin of slavery with the basic evangelical conception of Christian duty toward sin." Abolitionism provided a generation of young ministers with a new role and vocation in which they could channel their evangelical impulse to eradicate sin.[19]

The beginnings of an organized abolitionist movement closely followed the emergence of immediatism, a development facilitated by a relatively sophisticated network of benevolent agencies created as a result of the Second Great Awakening. In January 1831, the publication of William Lloyd Garrison's *The Liberator* in Boston gave immediate abolitionism a voice that would be heard. The American Antislavery Society, established in Philadelphia in December 1833, joined New England abolitionists such as Garrison with New York evangelicals Lewis and Arthur Tappan. Quickly, these new abolitionist institutions attacked colonization and began to spread the gospel of immediatism.

Abolitionists at first sought to spread their message through Northern churches and denominations. The American Antislavery Society urged its members in 1835 to call on their respective denominations "to pass resolutions condemning slavery as a sin, and to take such other measures as are proper to effect its speedy removal." Yet the Northern clergy and churches proved unreceptive to the abolitionist message. "I have been almost as cruelly opposed," argued Garrison, "by ministers of the Gospel

---

19. Donald M. Scott, *From Office to Profession: The New England Ministry, 1750–1850* (Philadelphia: University of Pennsylvania Press, 1978), p. 91. Scott provides a most insightful portrait of the ways in which abolitionism emerged out of the strains and ideas of evangelicalism. See especially pp. 76–95.

and church members as by any other class of men." The more conservative evangelical clergymen argued that abolitionism perverted the clerical role of public guardianship, trampled on the boundaries between religion and politics, and threatened to undermine public order. The strong religious dimension of early American abolitionism is essential to understanding the response of the Southern clergy to the postal campaign of 1835. Although Southern clerics recognized that the conservative clergy of the North opposed abolitionism, they nonetheless remained haunted by the intimacy between religion and the attack on slavery.[20]

The postal campaign of 1835 and the growing abolitionist threat provoked worry in the South. "Let them see how their associations are growing with the rapidity of a rolling snow ball," advised the Richmond *Whig,* "and how their audacity of design and influence wax with their increasing strength!" Governor John A. Quitman of Mississippi warned that the antislavery movement "has assumed a character which will no longer permit us to be silent or inactive." The Mobile *Daily Commercial Register and Patriot* cautioned that "the Abolitionists are prosecuting their plans, so widely, with such system, and with such energy." Southerners recognized the sophistication and resources of the emerging abolitionist movement. The abolitionists, resolved citizens of Surry County, Virginia, "are formidable both from the means which they appear to command, and the activity with which they employ them."[21]

Alarmed by this growth, Southerners called public meetings during the fall of 1835 to denounce abolitionism. Clergymen were active in these meetings gathered to denounce abolitionism, often assuming a leadership role. At a meeting of citizens in Mecklenberg County, North Carolina, the Rev. R. H. Morrison was chosen chairman. The Rev. John J. Triggs led a similar gathering in Waynesboro, Georgia. At another antiabolitionist assembly in Athens, the Rev. James Shannon introduced a resolution urging legislators to pass a law prohibiting distribution of antislavery literature in the South. The citizens of Beaufort, South Carolina, heard a scriptural defense of slavery by the Rev. Thomas Young.[22]

20. John R. McKivigan, *The War Against Proslavery Religion: Abolitionism and the Northern Churches, 1830–1865* (Ithaca, N.Y.: Cornell University Press, 1984), p. 41; quoted in Bodo, *Protestant Clergy and Public Issues,* p. 137; Scott, *From Office to Profession,* pp. 95–105; Bodo, *Protestant Clergy and Public Issues,* pp. 139–40.

21. Richmond *Whig* quoted in *Georgia Journal,* August 4, 1835; Woodville *Republican,* January 16, 1836; Mobile *Daily Commercial Register and Patriot,* August 12, 1835; Richmond *Enquirer,* October 13, 1835. For further evidence of the alarm over abolitionism, see the *Religious Herald,* July 31, 1835, and the report of the meeting in Campbell County in the Richmond *Enquirer,* September 29, 1835.

22. Raleigh *Register and North Carolina Gazette,* September 22, 1835; *Georgia Journal,* October 27, 1835; idem, September 15, 1835; Charleston *Mercury,* September 11, 1835.

Religious bodies initiated their own protests against the abolitionists. Their response was widespread and indignant. Presbyterian synods, Baptist associations, and Methodist conferences passed resolutions condemning abolitionist agitation. The South Alabama Presbytery resolved that "the inculcation of Incendiary Papers and Pamphlets deserves the reprobation of this community as destructive to the comfort of the Slave population the interest of the church and the Stability of established Institutions." The Concord Presbytery in North Carolina deprecated "the interference of men in other states with the civil institutions and domestic relations of our Southern country." The Baptist state convention in the same state thought abolitionism "uncalled for, intrusive, and pernicious, and that as such they have our most unqualified disapprobation." In Alabama, the Tuscaloosa Presbytery labeled the Northern reform "wicked and fanatical." Typical of the sentiments of the major Southern denominations, the East Hanover Presbytery in Virginia resolved to "unequivocally & entirely disapprove of & condemn the principles, plans, and efforts of the Abolitionists, as impolitic, unscriptural, & cruel."[23]

The secular press applauded these religious denunciations of abolitionism. "Every patriot," the Charleston *Mercury* proclaimed, "must be pleased at observing the decided manner in which our Clergy are coming forth in defense of truth and Southern institutions." The *Western Carolinian* voiced its pleasure with the antiabolitionist resolution passed by the Synod of North Carolina. The Charleston *Courier* observed that ministers enhanced a protest meeting there by "lending their sanctions to the proceedings, and adding, by their presence, to the impressive character of the same." This gratitude contained the hope that religion would be a strong defense against Northern aggression. The Charleston *Mercury* believed that "our most efficient champion against the machinations of the zealot, is the reflecting, prudent, meek Christian." Denominational bodies endorsed this view. "Firm, decided and scriptural movements in reference to our misguided friends at the North," observed the Edgefield Baptist Association in South Carolina, "may have a tendency with the divine blessing to arrest the progress of their fanatical course." A Methodist conference in Virginia agreed, arguing that religious opposition to the abolitionists "is one of the strongest evidences that the South is pursuing

23. "Minutes of the South Alabama Presbytery, vol. 4: 1835–1840," Historical Foundation of the Reformed Presbyterian Church, Montreat, North Carolina (hereafter cited as "Montreat"); "Records of Concord Presbytery, 1825–1836," Montreat; *Proceedings of the Fifth Annual Meeting of the Baptist State Convention, of North Carolina* (Newbern: Recorder Office, 1835), p. 8; Walter B. Posey, *The Presbyterian Church in the Old Southwest, 1778–1838* (Richmond, Va.: John Knox Press, 1952), p. 80; "East Hanover Presbytery Minutes, vol. 2, 1835–1843," Montreat, p. 10.

the proper course, in a spirited resistance to Northern interference." Religion, then, added respectability and a divine blessing to the fight against antislavery.[24]

It also provided a powerful critique of abolitionism. During the crisis of 1835, Southern clerical and political writers correctly recognized that the antislavery crusade was to a large extent inspired and sustained by religion. This belief helped propel Southern clergymen into the political arena to discredit abolitionism by destroying its claims to religious credibility. Not unlike their conservative Northern counterparts, Southern ministers portrayed abolitionism as a fanatical crusade that wantonly politicized and perverted religion.[25]

Is abolitionism "merely a political question?" asked a Methodist newspaper in Virginia: "We venture to assert that, however it may be considered by Southern Christians, it derives its whole strength from the religious influence of the North. It is to all intents and purposes a question of religion." This view was echoed throughout both the religious and secular South. The tendency of abolition, according to the Richmond *Whig,* was "to band together religious and political fanaticism in a crusade against the Southern States." The Bethel Presbytery of South Carolina deprecated "the efforts of Northern fanatics to identify abolitionism with the cause of religion." Citizens in Beaufort, South Carolina, viewed "with unutterable disgust and loathing, the names of Religion and Philanthropy prostituted to the purposes of the INCENDIARY." At a public gathering in Halifax, Virginia, citizens believed that abolitionism was presented "under the garb of philanthropy, and in the sacred name of religion." The connection between religion and abolition was made explicit in the U.S. Senate by William C. Preston of South Carolina:

> The cause of religion is made identical with religion, and men and women are exhorted by all that they esteem holy, by all the high and exciting obligations of duty to man and to God by all that can warm the heart or inflame the imagination, to join in the pious work of purging the sin of slavery from the land.

Northern ministers came under particular attack. It could not be denied, argued the influential Richmond *Enquirer,* that "the Evil has been fomented by the Fanaticism of some of the Northern Ministers." Simi-

24. Charleston *Mercury,* October 1, 1835; Raleigh *Register and North Carolina Gazette,* November 10, 1835; Charleston *Courier* quoted in Woodville *Republican,* September 5, 1835; Charleston *Mercury,* September 25, 1835; *Minutes of the Edgefield Baptist Association* (Charleston, S.C.: James S. Burges, 1835), p. 5; Richmond *Enquirer,* November 10, 1835.
25. This will be covered in further depth in Chapter 2.

larly, at a public meeting in Wellington, Georgia, citizens blamed Northern missionaries for spreading abolitionist doctrine under the guise of
Christianizing the South.[26]

Insisting that abolitionism had important religious support, church
leaders in the South sought to divest it of its moral legitimacy by portraying the movement as un-Christian. The Alabama Baptist state convention
found the efforts of abolitionists to be "inconsistent with the gospel
of Christ." Presbyterians in Georgia censured "the impolitic and un-
Christian conduct of that infatuated people called Abolitionists." They
argued that the movement was "in entire opposition to, both the letter
and spirit of the Gospel." A more direct identification of abolitionism
with paganism came from a Mississippian, who insisted "that those fanatics who are endeavoring to interfere with our slaves, possess the very
same spirit that those fanatics did who accused Christ of being a Sabbath
breaker, and murdered him upon the cross."[27]

Abolitionists also used religion hypocritically, masking their real purposes with religious intentions. "They profess to be men of high-toned
religious feelings," complained a Macon, Georgia, newspaper, "Philan-
thropists who could humanely seek the good of mankind – that they
are God's Apostles, laboring in his vineyard." A Mississippi journal concurred, suggesting to its readers that abolitionists "have thrown around
them the sacred mantle of religion – seized hold of the horns of the
altar – profaned the sanctuary of the church, and made it the citadel
of their strength and safety." Abolitionism, according to the citizens of
Crawford County, Georgia, labored "under the false pretense of religious
philanthropy and moral obligations." The precepts of religion, some Virginians agreed, were being "studiously perverted and profanely invoked."
Abolitionism, concluded the *Georgia Journal*, was "rendered odious in the
extreme, by its hypocritical religious pretense."[28]

In elaborating on the ways in which abolitionism perverted religion,

26. *Virginia Conference Sentinel*, September 23, 1836; Richmond *Whig* quoted in *Georgia Journal*, August 4, 1835; "Records of the Presbytery of Bethel, 1824–1849," Montreat, p. 195; Richmond *Enquirer*, October 16, 1835; Edgefield *Advertiser*, April 19, 1936; Richmond *Enquirer*, November 6, 1835; *Georgia Journal*, November 13, 1835. For another suggestion of Northern religious complicity in abolitionism, see "Jabez" in *Georgia Messenger*, November 19, 1835.

27. *Minutes of the Twelfth Anniversary of the Alabama State Convention* (Greensborough, Ala.: Smith and DeWolf, 1835), p. 7; "Records of Flint River Presbytery, Vol. 1," Montreat, p. 56; *Georgia Messenger*, November 10, 1835; Woodville *Republican*, October 29, 1835.

28. *Georgia Messenger*, August 6, 1835; *Mississippi Free Trader and Natchez Gazette*, August 25, 1835; *Georgia Messenger*, October 15, 1835; Richmond *Enquirer*, September 29, 1835; *Georgia Journal*, October 27, 1835.

Southern clergymen in 1835 developed a view of the Northern cause as both religiously and philosophically unsound. The Edgefield Baptist Association, for example, regretted the "unscriptural course" of the abolitionists. To South Carolina Methodists, abolitionism originated "in a false philosophy overreaching or setting aside the scriptures through a vain conceit of a higher moral refinement." A Presbyterian newspaper in Virginia maintained "that the great doctrine on which the whole system rests, is unauthorized and unsupported by the precepts given on the subject by the Apostles." Behind these remarks lay the belief that abolitionism was symptomatic of a subversive social philosophy that undermined religion. The Bethel Baptist Association of South Carolina thought that abolitionism reflected "the tendency which exists in man to abandon the clear and stable principles of justice and religion, for the extravagance of an ill-regulated imagination." The Charleston *Mercury* called it a fanaticism that threatened to remove social equalities ordained by God, and a Baptist paper in the same city decried its tendency toward ultraism. The dangerous cultural upheaval revealed by abolitionist agitation was summed up by Senator Preston: "The bosom of society heaves with new and violent emotions." Underlying these comments was a nascent assault on the equal rights philosophy and religious liberalism that would later find fruition in an elaborate critique of abolitionism.[29]

There are significant similarities between the Southern clerical attack on abolitionism and that of the conservative Northern evangelicals who opposed the abolitionists. Both feared the disruption to public order and the threat to traditional boundaries between religion and politics. Both argued that slavery was essentially a political and not a religious question. The rise of abolitionism did cause a predicament for conservative Northern clergymen, but the pressures from their society pushed them away from proslavery. They sought to find what they considered legitimate and less threatening forms of Christian action against slavery. The rise of abolitionism divided the Northern clergy into two polar factions: the abolitionists who saw the churches as the "bulwarks of slavery" and the more conservative clergy who shrank from the activist implications of evangelicalism. In the South, on the other hand, the appearance of

29. *Minutes of the Edgefield Baptist Association, convened at Mount Pleasant, S.C. on the 17th and continued to the 19th of October, 1835* (Charleston: James S. Burges, 1835), p. 4; *Minutes of the South Carolina Conference of the Methodist Episcopal Church for the Year 1836* (Charleston: J. S. Burges, 1836), p. 20; *Southern Religious Telegraph*, October 23, 1835; *Minutes of the Bethel Baptist Association* (n.p., 1835), p. 6; Charleston *Mercury*, August 10, 1835; *Southern Baptist and General Intelligencer*, October 2, 1835; Edgefield *Advertiser*, April 14, 1836.

abolitionism produced a striking unanimity among the clergy vehemently against Northern interference with slavery.[30]

The close association between Northern ministers, religion, and abolitionism heightened planters' preexisting suspicion of Southern clergymen. Clerical ties with national ecclesiastical organizations that had been critical of slavery and the belief that religious slaves were the most rebellious ones were the basic reasons planters distrusted Southern clergymen. Many ministers felt that abolitionism had jeopardized their standing in society and the cause of religion in the South. Even the religious critique of abolitionism in part reflected the attempt of ministers to differentiate Southern religion from that of Northern reformers. The need of ministers to defend themselves led them to separate religion from the political issue of abolition.

Even before the abolitionist controversy of 1835, clergymen often were suspected by the public of antislavery sympathies. Whitemarsh Seabrook, in an address to the Agricultural Society of St. John's, Colleton, South Carolina, argued that clergymen were dangerous persons, unaware or unconscious of the value of property. Part of this distrust stemmed from the association between religion and the slave revolts of the period. Investigations into the Denmark Vesey revolt of 1822 and the Nat Turner insurrection of 1831 revealed that many of the participants were church members. When the Presbyterian minister John B. Adger tried to establish religious missions to the slaves in Charleston during the 1840s, his efforts were hindered by the fears and distrust provoked by the Vesey revolt. The fact that antislavery tracts in 1835 were sent to clergymen in the South heightened this suspicion of clergymen. Both the *Mercury* and Alfred Huger, postmaster of Charleston, pointed out that the clergy were special targets of antislavery literature. "A truly pious man," warned a planter in the Richmond *Whig*, "may from entertaining political visions, distinct from his Gospel duties, be a dangerous teacher, tho' in other respects a good man." Citizens in Sumterville, South Carolina, asked the churches and courts not to allow a minister with antislavery leanings to speak in nearby churches.[31]

30. Scott, *From Office to Profession*, pp. 95–102, 106–8, 109.
31. Freehling, *Prelude to Civil War*, p. 75; Anne C. Loveland, *Southern Evangelicals and the Social Order, 1800–1860* (Baton Rouge and London: Louisiana State University Press, 1980), p. 194; John B. Adger, D. D., *My Life and Times, 1810–1899* (Richmond, Va.: Presbyterian Committee of Publication, 1899), p. 55; Gatell, "Postmaster Huger and the Incendiary Publications," p. 194; Freehling, *Prelude to Civil War*, p. 340; Richmond *Whig* quoted in Charleston *Mercury*, August 5, 1835; Charleston *Mercury*, September 12, 1835.

In this atmosphere, suspicion often produced intimidation. In Benton, Alabama, the Rev. James A. Butler was found in possession of a religious journal that contained an article on emancipation. Butler was summoned before Benton's Committee of Vigilance and Safety, where he convinced more than 200 citizens that he opposed abolitionists. His integrity having been questioned by an anonymous writer to the Charleston *Mercury*, Aaron G. Brewer, pastor of the Methodist Protestant Church of Charleston, felt obliged to offer proof of his advocacy of "Southern Institutions." In Laurensville, Georgia, the Rev. John S. Wilson was suspected of antislavery connections. Three clergymen, each representing one of the major denominations, had to testify at a public meeting that Wilson "had uniformly and at all times when conversing upon the subject, censured and disapproved of the conduct of the Abolitionists." Only after this testimony was Wilson safe.[32]

Clergymen were painfully aware of the suspicion generated by the abolitionist affiliation with religion. "We regret," announced the Baptist Goshen Association in Virginia, "that in consequence of having certain incendiary publications addressed to us, without our knowledge or consent, our ministry should be censured and suspected in some degree as aiding and abetting the Northern fanatics in their nefarious designs." A Baptist newspaper in Charleston worried: "We know not who can be safe, when even the open advocates of slavery are denounced as abolitionists." The problem for clergymen was well articulated by the Charleston *Observer:*

> The whole Ecclesiastical Connexion to which they belong has to bear the odium of their conduct. Men are emboldened to revile the whole Ministry, from the fact that now and then one has justly incurred their indignation; and suspicion is apt to be fastened upon the innocent as well as the guilty.[33]

Religious leaders saw that this suspicion had extended beyond clergymen to include the cause of religion in general. A group of Mississippi Methodists believed that abolitionism "militates directly, and with wide sweeping effect, against the interests of religion in the slaveholding States." They feared that their fellow Southerners would not discriminate "between reli-

32. Mobile *Daily Commercial Register and Patriot*, October 7, 1835; Charleston *Mercury*, August 7, 1835; *Georgia Journal*, November 17, 1835.
33. Richmond *Enquirer*, September 29, 1835; *Southern Baptist and General Intelligencer*, October 9, 1835; Charleston *Observer*, October 10, 1835. See also *Minutes of the Tyger River Baptist Association, convened at Head of Tyger Church, Greenville District, S.C., October 30, 1835* (n.p., 1835), p. 2.

gion itself and the mischievous companion which has been thus forceably intruded upon her." The Bethel Baptist Association was concerned that abolitionism tended to "weaken the affections of the people toward the Christian religion, in so far as they may be led to suppose that these doctrines are sanctioned by the Bible." Because it involved direct contact with slaves, the religious mission to plantations was particularly disrupted by the distrust of ministers. "In every period of her [the Methodist Church's] history," explained the *Virginia Conference Sentinel*, "she has directed her efforts to the promotion of their salvation, and was in the full career of usefulness and success when her course was stayed by the interference of Abolitionists." The Charleston *Observer* argued similarly that "the tendency of these Abolition Measures is to check the efforts of those who would improve their character, by importing to them religious instruction, and their condition, by giving them as many privileges as are compatible with their general good." In Mississippi, recalled the Rev. John G. Jones, Methodists came under such suspicion that ministers often lost their access to slaves.[34]

The assumed complicity of religion with abolitionism forced Southern clergymen to disavow any connection with the movement. Religious groups objected to being the recipients of antislavery propaganda. Students at Columbia Theological Seminary in South Carolina resolved "no longer [to] submit to the imposition so long practiced upon us, of being made the receivers of Publications, which though professedly devoted *solely* to the cause of religion, are in reality the advocates of Abolition." Mississippi Methodists also declared that they "indignantly protest against being favored with any gratuitous supply of *such* publications and prints." Denominational bodies throughout the South disavowed any sympathy with the abolitionists. The Presbytery of Georgia resolved: "That our beloved Zion may calm their fears in regard to their ministers and Elders – they reject the *tenets* and doctrines of Abolitionism and solemnly declare for themselves and their churches, that they never were and cannot be Abolitionists." A group of students at the Evangelical Lutheran Seminary in Lexington, South Carolina, assured the public that "They [the abolitionists] may expect no countenance or support from us, but that their cause meets with our decided and unqualified disapprobation." These denials were undoubtedly aimed at neutralizing the prevail-

34. Woodville *Republican*, December 5, 1835; *Minutes of the Bethel Baptist Association*, p. 6; *Virginia Conference Sentinel*, October 14, 1836; Charleston *Observer*, July 11, 1835; John A. Jones, *A Complete History of Methodism as Connected with the Mississippi Conference of the Methodist Episcopal Church, South*, vol. 2 (Nashville, Tenn.: Publishing House of the Methodist Episcopal Church, South, 1908), p. 346.

ing prejudice against the church. They attest to the seriousness of the ministerial predicament.[35]

The problems abolitionism created for ministers and religion in the South led them to divorce religion from the political issue of abolitionism, contrary to their other statements connecting the two. To extricate religion from this particular political issue, Southern clergymen drew upon the Christian distinction between the spiritual and secular realms. "We regard the question of the abolition of slavery," maintained South Carolina Methodists in 1836, "as a *civil one*, belonging to the State, and not at all a *religious one* or appropriate to the church." The Charleston *Southern Baptist and General Intelligencer* argued: "It is vain to present the matter in a religious dress; its bearings under any garb will be *political*, for it strikes at the foundation of our domestic institutions." Methodists in Mississippi also were careful, when discussing abolitionism, to confine their attention to its bearings on religious interests. The Synod of Virginia warned its members to limit themselves "strictly to their proper province of inculcating upon masters and slaves, the duties enjoined upon them respectively in the sacred scriptures."[36]

This reasoning was based in part on the Revolutionary principle of separation of church and state. "As it has always been one of the happiest features of our government, to keep the Church and State entirely distinct," explained the Tuscaloosa Presbytery in Alabama, "so we wish them to continue and as this subject is one which we consider entirely political, we are resolved to leave it in the hands of our Legislative & Judicial tribunals." A Presbyterian paper in South Carolina offered its support to any denominational journal that "will raise their voice against that unholy alliance of church and state, of religion with the cause of abolition, which threatens to deluge the country in blood." The *Southern Religious Telegraph* of Richmond warned that religious involvement in politics could corrupt American Christianity. An aversion to ministerial participation in politics followed logically. The Bethel Presbytery in South Carolina deprecated the discussion of abolitionist doctrine in the pulpit, regarding it as a lamentable prostitution of the sacred office. A secular newspaper in Mississippi warned that "when a clergyman is sunk to the

---

35. Charleston *Mercury*, September 17, 1835; Woodville *Republican*, December 5, 1835; "Records of the Presbytery of Georgia, 1821–1840," Montreat, p. 219; Charleston *Mercury*, September 7, 1835. See also Loveland, *Southern Evangelicals and the Social Order*, p. 196.

36. *Minutes of the South Carolina Conference of the Methodist Episcopal Church, for the year 1836*, p. 20; *Southern Baptist and General Intelligencer*, October 2, 1835; Woodville *Republican*, December 5, 1835; *Southern Religious Telegraph*, October 30, 1835.

character and conduct of a political scavenger and brawling demagogue, he forfeits all claim to respect and confidence."[37]

III

The confrontation with the abolitionists in 1835 forced Southern clergymen to carefully delineate the boundaries between religion and politics. Their conduct during this crisis and their conception of the relationship between religion and politics that emerged from this controversy raise several important questions. If Southern clergymen accepted the general rule of avoiding political controversy, why did they get involved in 1835? What about this crisis propelled them into the political arena? Was there an inconsistency in their condemnation of Northern abolitionists for dragging religion into politics while they simultaneously entered the political fray themselves? If so, how can this apparent paradox be explained? A brief examination of Southern clerical assumptions about the relationship between religion and politics held by Southern clergymen will begin to help answer these questions.

In the decades before 1835, several key factors fostered a strong separation between religion and politics and discouraged ministers from political participation. With the revivals of the 1790s and the early 1800s, evangelicalism became the dominant mode of religious expression in the South. During the early nineteenth century, Southern evangelicals took little interest in politics. The logic of evangelical thought was inclined away from involvement in such worldly affairs as politics, because the primary concern of the evangelical was the salvation of souls. Sin was viewed as an individual rather than as a social problem. The Christian struggle took place within the human soul, not in society. In addition, evangelicalism stressed the helplessness of the moral individual to alter social arrangements.[38]

The formal separation between church and state reinforced the evangelical aversion to politics. During the colonial era, the Anglican Church was the established church in the Southern colonies, supported by political

37. "Records of the Tuscaloosa Presbytery Constituted February 1835," Montreat, p. 28; *Southern Christian Herald*, March 2, 1836; *Southern Religious Telegraph*, December 24, 1835; "The Records of the Presbytery of Bethel, 1824–1849," Montreat, p. 145; Woodville *Republican*, January 23, 1836.
38. See the discussion in John B. Boles, *The Great Revival 1787–1805: The Origins of the Southern Evangelical Mind* (Lexington: University Press of Kentucky, 1972), pp. 165–74; Mathews, *Religion in the Old South*, p. 56.

authorities. The growth of such evangelical dissenting sects as the Baptists and Methodists during the eighteenth century hastened the decline of the Anglican establishment. It was the ideology of the American Revolution that eventually institutionalized the Enlightenment ideal of religious freedom in America. Disestablishment took place in North Carolina in 1776 and in Georgia a year later. Thomas Jefferson and James Madison led Virginia toward disestablishment in 1785, and by 1790 South Carolina had also abolished the state-supported church. Southern clergymen generally accepted disestablishment. Many religious leaders harbored bad memories of the established church and welcomed the formal separation of church and state.[39]

The firm boundaries between church and state in post-Revolutionary America were further strengthened by the formal disenfranchisement of clergymen to run for public office. The South Carolina constitution of 1778, stating that "the ministers of the gospel are by their profession dedicated to the service of God and the cure of souls, and ought not to be diverted from the great duties of their function," barred clergymen from holding office. The North Carolina constitution of 1776 and Georgia's constitution of 1777 also denied the minister a formal role in politics. This practice spread into the newer states of the southwest. Tennessee, Louisiana, and Mississippi, for example, all had constitutional provisions barring ministers from holding public office. By 1850, reported the Presbyterian *Watchman and Observer,* nine Southern states prohibited clergymen from office holding.[40]

Despite strong adherence to the formal separation of church and state, Southern clergymen maintained that religion still had a vital role to play in public life. They accepted the voluntary establishment of religion that was embraced by Protestants throughout the nation during the early Republic. One historian has described this vision as "a conception of the relation of religion to society that accepted the American commitment to freedom and the voluntary principle in church–state relations without making sacrifice of the precious conception that religion was the essential ingredient of the public weal." Religion was considered vital to the maintenance of virtue and order essential to the survival of the republic. In 1803, Henry Holcombe, editor of the *Georgia Analytical Repository,* argued that "no consistent friend to this country can be indifferent, much

39. Mathews, *Religion in the Old South,* pp. 56–7; Boles, *Great Revival,* p. 182.

40. Francis Newton Thorpe, editor and compiler, *The Federal and State Constitutions, Colonial Charters, and the Organic Laws of the States, Territories and Colonies now or heretofore forming the United States of America* (Washington, D.C.: Government Printing Office, 1909), vol. VI, p. 3253; vol. V; p. 2793; vol. II, p. 785; vol. VI, p. 3420; vol. III, p. 1384; vol. IV, p. 2044; Loveland, *Southern Evangelicals and the Social Order,* p. 120.

less opposed, to the interests of Religion." It was evident, he said, that "without Religion there can be no virtue, there can be no liberty." Furthermore, the emerging American nationalism of this era was inextricably interwoven with religion. Patriotism to a Protestant commonwealth became a form of secular worship. "The Christian has passions as other men," explained one writer in a Charleston religious journal, "and he is no Christian who is not a lover of his country." The *Virginia Evangelical and Literary Magazine* agreed that our "first duty is to him who created and redeemed us; our next to our country. We rejoice that these are not inconsistent."[41]

The understanding Southern clergymen had of the proper relationship between religion and politics on the eve of the sectional conflict may be summarized as follows: Ministers accepted the formal separation of church and state. They generally eschewed clerical involvement in politics, especially when politics referred to pragmatic questions of policy or especially party. However, if any political issue was perceived as possessing any kind of moral or religious significance, Southern clergymen claimed that it fell within their realm and justified their attention. Morality thus became the main criterion for determining religious involvement in politics.[42]

These guidelines help explain why Southern clergymen chose to enter the political arena in 1835 and how they legitimized their attack on abolitionism and defense of slavery. To the clergy, slavery had two distinct but related realms – the civil and the religious. The existence of slavery itself, the idea and practice of holding slaves, was considered a civil or political question. Yet within the institution of slavery, certain moral and religious issues were involved, such as the relationship between master and slave and the spiritual welfare of the latter, which invited the attention of the clergy. Southern clerical objections to abolitionism must be understood in this context. The Northern attack on slavery, according to Southern ministers, was wrong in two ways. First, it was ill-founded. By the mid-1830s, the Southern clergy agreed that slavery was sanctioned by the Bible and justified by natural law. It did not, therefore, violate any moral or religious principle. Second, by attacking the existence of slavery itself – a civil matter – the abolitionists had pushed religion into the political realm where it did not belong. Abolitionism thus falsely forced religion into the

41. Loveland, *Southern Evangelicals and the Social Order*, pp. 110–20; Scott, *From Office to Profession*, pp. 100–1; *Georgia Analytical Repository* I, no. 5 (January-February 1803): 230; *Charleston Gospel Messenger and Protestant Episcopal Register* IV (November 1827): 321; *Virginia Evangelical and Literary Magazine* I (January 1818): 7.
42. This interpretation must be qualified by the fact that there did exist Southern ministers who ran for public office. See the evidence in the Introduction, note 15.

civil sphere, compelling Southern clergymen to enter the political arena to defend both the morality of slavery and the integrity of religion.[43]

The assumptions that guided the conduct of Southern clergymen can be clarified by looking briefly at a political controversy they chose *not* to become involved with – the nullification controversy in South Carolina. The decision of South Carolinians to nullify the federal tariffs of 1828 and 1832 culminated a dramatic contest between majority and minority rights that brought the nation close to disunion in the early months of 1833. South Carolina clergymen interpreted nullification differently from the abolitionist controversy of 1835. They saw nullification as a question of party and policy rather than one of morality and religion. South Carolina clergymen focused their attention on the political turmoil that deeply divided the citizens of the Palmetto state and diverted their attention from religion. The nature of the nullification controversy reinforced the inclination of the clergy to keep the spheres of religion and politics separate.

At the same time Gov. Robert Y. Hayne recruited a brigade of mounted minutemen to defend Charleston from threatening federal forces, he also sought divine protection. In January 1833, he proclaimed a fast day for South Carolina, imploring the Almighty to help "in restoring and perpetuating the liberty and prosperity of our native state." Yet Governor Hayne's call for a fast day generally went unheeded. Although the Charleston *Mercury,* a leading voice of the nullifiers, suspended publication on this day, one angry opponent of nullification announced in the unionist Charleston *Courier* that he would not "attend any place of worship on that day." Hardly any other newspaper in South Carolina reported either the proclamation or observance of the fast day. The fact that only three sermons from this fast day are extant is further evidence of the unenthusiastic response to Gov. Hayne's proclamation. All this suggests that South Carolinians were not inclined to involve religion in the contest over nullification.[44]

In fact, the nullification controversy brought forth among South Caro-

43. These ideas are explored more fully in Chapters 2 and 3.
44. Freehling, *Prelude to Civil War,* p. 2; Charleston *States Rights and Free Trade Evening Post,* January 29, 1833; Charleston *Courier,* January 30, 1833. The fast day sermons are Thomas Goulding, *A Fast Day Sermon, for Thursday, January 31st, 1833* (Columbia: *Telescope* Office, 1833); Richard P. Cater, *A Discourse delivered in the Presbyterian Church at Pendleton Village, on the 31st January, 1833: A Day of Fasting, Humiliation and Prayer Appointed by the Convention of the Site of South Carolina* (Pendleton: *Messenger* Office, 1833); and S. G. Bulfinch, *The Benefits and Dangers Belonging to Seasons of Public Excitement: A Discourse, delivered in the Unitarian Church at Charleston, S.C. on the Day of Humiliation and Prayer, January 31, 1833* (Charleston: J. S. Burges, 1833). Of the three, only Cater, a Presbyterian minister from Calhoun's home district of Pendleton, supported nullification.

linians in general and South Carolina ministers in particular a strong aversion to religious involvement in political affairs. The participation of ministers in politics was considered anathema to some. "One of the most contemptible scenes that my eyes have ever witnessed," wrote a citizen of Camden in 1833, "I saw yesterday at Church – It was nothing more nor less than a Minister of the Gospel with a Blue Cockade [signifying support for nullification] in his hat." The Baptist Bethel Association of Union District did not think ministers should "mix subjects of political controversy in their pulpit discourses" except when liberty of conscience was at stake. The *North Carolina Baptist Interpreter* warned that enlisting Christian sympathies in the nullification controversy was "not only unwise in itself and mischievous in its tendencies, but is an actual violation of the precepts and spirit of the gospel." The use of the Bible to support political positions offended many religious leaders. "There is no feature in the political contests of the day," wrote the editor of the Presbyterian Charleston *Observer*, "so revolting to our own feelings or propriety, as the references which partizan writers make to the Sacred Scriptures in proof of the correctness of their respective creeds." A writer to the Charleston *Observer* agreed, arguing that when politics are introduced into the church, "both cannot dwell together."[45]

The general discord and divisiveness engendered by the nullification contests also alienated ministers. Elections between Nullifiers and Unionists during the fall of 1832 were particularly volatile. The issue was debated everywhere – even children were said to have taken sides – and fights were not uncommon. As could be expected, the conflict seeped into the churches. Thirty members from the Purity Church in Chester District seceded because of disagreement over nullification. The Charleston *Observer* lamented the bitterness that politics seemed to produce: "We deprecate it because it produces divisions in families – it arrays neighbor against neighbor – it strikes the very root of social order – it separates very friends – it creates discord in Society – it fosters envy and jealousy and other hateful passions."[46]

Clergymen feared as well that political excitement distracted attention

---

45. Camden *Journal*, February 2, 1833; *Minutes of the Bethel Baptist Association; At the Forty-First Anniversary Meeting, Convened at Cane-Creek Church, Union District (So. Carolina) October 2d, and continued till October 5th, 1830* (n.p., 1830), p. 3; *North Carolina Baptist Interpreter* (February 1833): 44; Charleston *Observer*, January 26, 1833; idem, September 1, 1832.

46. Thomas J. Kirkland and Robert M. Kennedy, *Historic Camden, Part Two: The Nineteenth Century* (Columbia, S. C.: The *State* Company, 1926), p. 86; George Howe, *A History of the Presbyterian Church in South Carolina, Vol. II* (Columbia: Duffie and Chapman, 1870–83), p. 502; Charleston *Observer*, December 29, 1832.

from religion. John Witherspoon, pastor of the Presbyterian church in Camden, was aware that "a dark cloud is gathering over our country and the church must for a season be overshadowed by the same." A Methodist minister confronted difficulties in his spiritual endeavors, because the political fervor had "neutralized to a great extent all religious feeling." And J. M. H. Adams found his fellow citizens in York District "so deeply immersed in politics, that but a very small portion of their time and attention is given to Jesus' cause." The power of politics to disrupt religious progress was evident in a revival meeting in Yorkville, where, according to one woman, there were "8 faithful days of preaching and not a single convert... nothing but quarreling." South Carolina clergymen saw nullification as nullifying their own efforts.[47]

The reaction of South Carolina clergymen to the nullification controversy illustrates from a reverse angle the Southern clerical understanding of the relationship between religion and politics. They steered clear of involvement in nullification because in their minds it was a question of party and policy. There were neither vital moral nor religious principles at stake. Other differences between this political controversy and the abolitionist crisis of 1835 help explain why Southern ministers chose to get involved in the later conflict. Nullification pitted one Southern state against the federal government over tariff policy and states' rights. Moreover, South Carolina was isolated from other Southern states because of her radical stance. In contrast, the abolitionist postal campaign of 1835 touched the deepest Southern concern over slavery and the social order in a more immediate and significant way than did nullification.[48]

Several factors help explain why Southern clergymen made the decision to get involved in the sectional controversy as defenders of slavery. One

47. John Witherspoon to John McDowall, November 26, 1832, Simon Gratz Collection, Historical Society of Pennsylvania, Philadelphia; William Wightman to Whiteford Smith, February 27, 1833, William Wightman Papers, South Caroliniana Library, University of South Carolina, Columbia; Margaret Burr Deschamps, "Union or Division? South Atlantic Presbyterians and Southern Nationalism, 1820-1861," *Journal of Southern History* 20 (November 1954): 484–98.

48. In *Prelude to Civil War,* perhaps the most influential interpretation of the nullification controversy, William Freehling argues that the crisis was largely an expression of the South's growing sensitivity to the Northern attack on slavery. Freehling's evidence and interpretation have been questioned by J. P. Ochenkowski, "The Origins of Nullification in South Carolina," *South Carolina Historical Magazine* 83 (April 1982): 121–53. The response of South Carolina clergymen suggests that Freehling's emphasis on slavery as the underlying issue in nullification might be misplaced. For further thinking along these lines, see Paul Bergeron, "Tennessee's Response to the Nullification Crisis," *Journal of Southern History* 39 (February 1973): 23–44, and Richard E. Ellis, *The Union at Risk: Jacksonian Democracy, States' Rights and the Nullification Crisis* (New York: Oxford University Press, 1987).

major reason was the intimate association between Northern religion and abolitionism. It was this connection that compelled ministers to enter the political arena to discredit the abolitionists' use of religion, to defend their own religion from the taint of antislavery, and to prove their own loyalty to slavery. Another factor was the deepening entrenchment of slavery in the Southern social, political, and economic order. The phenomenal growth of cotton production in the decades between 1790 and 1830 fueled the spread of white Southerners, blacks slaves, and the plantation into the southwest. The Missouri controversy, the slave revolts of Denmark Vesey and Nat Turner, nullification, and the Virginia debates over emancipation made Southerners by the 1830s morbidly sensitive to any questioning of their peculiar institution. In view of these trends and considering the dependent nature of religious institutions on secular society, the Southern clergy were under tremendous pressure to become advocates of slavery.

Finally, the institutional growth of Southern religion probably facilitated the Southern clergy's involvement in the sectional controversy in 1835. For instance, the governing bodies of the major denominations in the South, well in place by the 1830s, promoted cooperative action among Southern Protestants. Presbyterian synods and presbyteries had long been established in the South Atlantic states; the Synod of Mississippi and South Alabama was formed in 1829. Baptist state conventions were founded in South Carolina in 1821, in Georgia a year later, and in Mississippi in 1823. Because their ecclesiology was based on a system of itinerancy, the Methodists lacked the more formal structure of these other two denominations. Yet by 1830, the Methodists had conferences in Virginia, South Carolina, Georgia, and Tennessee and a system of districts, circuits, and class meetings to organize local church members. All these organizations were quite important in 1835, for they furnished the formal resolutions of their denominations' condemning abolitionism and affirming their loyalty to slavery.[49]

Perhaps more important in formulating and influencing opinion among Southern Protestants was the growth of the religious press. The earliest religious journals in the South, the *Georgia Analytical Repository* and

49. Ernest Trice Thompson, *Presbyterians in the South, Vol. I: 1607–1861* (Richmond: John Knox Press, 1963), p. 177; Robert Baker, *The Southern Baptist Convention and Its People*, pp. 130, 132, 138. Methodist church organization can be pieced together from several state histories, such as Albert D. Betts, *History of South Carolina Methodism* (Columbia: *Advocate* Press, 1952), and William Warren Sweet, *Virginia Methodism: A History* (Richmond, Va.: Whittet and Shepperson, 1955). Alfred M. Pierce has a good summary of Methodist church structure. *A History of Methodism in Georgia, February 5, 1746–June 14, 1955* (Atlanta: Georgia Conference Historical Society, 1956), pp. 59–61.

the *Virginia Religious Magazine,* appeared at the turn of the century, although their existence was short-lived. Weekly denominational newspapers proliferated in the 1820s. By the mid-1830s, Southern Baptists were informed by the *Religious Herald* (Virginia), the *Christian Index* (Georgia), and the *Biblical Recorder* (North Carolina). The *Virginia Literary and Evangelical Magazine* and the *Southern Religious Telegraph* served Presbyterians in Virginia, whereas those in the lower South were influenced by the *Charleston Observer,* established in 1827. The first Methodist journal, the *Wesleyan Journal,* began in 1825 and was followed by the *Georgia Christian Repository* and the *Christian Sentinel* (Richmond). Significantly, the major Methodist journal in the South, the *Southern Christian Advocate,* was established in Charleston in 1837 "in view of the peculiar political aspects of the times." By carrying resolutions of denominational bodies and interpreting political events through editorials, the religious press of the South was instrumental in promoting and easing involvement in the sectional controversy.[50]

IV

The response of the Southern clergy to the events of 1835 prefigured the role religion would play in the ensuing decades of sectional strife. The conception of the relationship between religion and politics that was articulated during this conflict set the framework in which Southern clergymen would think and act about slavery, the denominational schisms, and secession. Moreover, the crisis of 1835 previewed the dynamic of call and response between Southern clergymen and Northern abolitionists and underscores how the growth of sectionalism in Southern religion took place within this context of a dialogue between North and South. Beginning in the 1830s, the Southern clergy engaged in a long and elaborate debate with Northern abolitionists over the morality of slavery. The religious proslavery argument was fundamentally an extended reply to the abolitionist contention that slavery was a sin. The crisis of 1835 also reveals the common goal of the Southern clergy and conservative Northern clergymen to stop the onslaught of abolitionism and stem the tide of sectional agitation. Presbyterians in particular would share similar social, political, and theological views with Old School Presbyterians in the North. Fi-

50. Robert A. Baker, *The Southern Baptist Convention and Its People, 1607–1972* (Nashville, Tenn.: Broadman Press, 1974), p. 85; Thompson, *Presbyterians in the South, Vol. I,* p. 290; Baker, *Southern Baptist Convention and Its People,* p. 146; Thompson, *Presbyterians in the South, Vol. I,* p. 291; Henry Smith Stroupe, *The Religious Press in the South Atlantic States: An Annotated Bibliography with Historical Introduction and Notes* (Durham, N.C.: Duke University Press, 1956), pp. 9, 108.

nally, the Southern clerical critique of abolitionism explicitly if subtly suggested the idea that it was the North that was revolutionizing and subverting religious and political doctrine. This notion would later merge with and help shape a basic tenet of Southern nationalism: the belief that the North had departed from American values and institutions.[51]

The abolitionist crisis of 1835 also reveals the reciprocal relationship between religious and political discourse in the Old South. In some ways, the clerical response to abolitionism closely mirrored that of Southern politicians. Both argued that the Northern attack on slavery was an unwarranted perversion of religion to political means. Both also feared that abolitionism might lead to disunion. The preservation of the Union was of paramount importance in the resolutions passed at public meetings in Greensboro and Athens, Georgia, in 1835. The *Mississippi Free Trader and Natchez Gazette* worried that the rise of abolitionism was a call "to rally the south against the north and ultimately *divide the Union.*" There was a similar response in the religious realm. "If the principle of *interference* is not abandoned – if the South is not left to the exercise of its own discretion in regard to its domestic institution," warned the Methodist *Virginia Conference Sentinel* in a dramatic editorial, "then farewell to the brilliant hope of an enduring confederated republic; farewell to the prosperity of our favored country; farewell to all the glory of the American name." Baptists in Alabama worried similarly that abolitionism would "alienate the people in one State from those in another, thereby endangering the peace and permanency of our happy republic."[52]

The most conspicuous difference between the clergy and secular statesmen was that, although both condemned abolitionist infidelity and its threat to disunion, the political response to abolitionism focused on the constitutional issue of states' rights. This doctrine was carefully formulated in the 1820s by such Old Republicans in Virginia as John Randolph of Roanoke, John Taylor of Caroline, and Judge Spencer Roane. It was radicalized by South Carolinians like Thomas Cooper in the late 1820s and was used by John C. Calhoun to contest against the delivery of antislavery mail. The states' rights philosophy was the bulwark of the Southern political defense of slavery during the 1830s. "It is to this

---

51. Bodo, *Protestant Clergy and Public Issues*, pp. 139–40. This is essentially the argument of James McPherson, "Antebellum Southern Exceptionalism: A New Look at an Old Question," *Civil War History* 29 (September 1983): 220–44.

52. *Georgia Journal*, September 15, 1835 and October 6, 1835; *Mississippi Free Trader and Natchez Gazette*, August 18, 1835; *Virginia Conference Sentinel*, October 14, 1836; *Minutes of the Twelfth Anniversary of the Alabama Baptist State Convention, Held at Oakmulgee Meeting House, Perry County, Alabama, commencing on Saturday the 7th November, 1835* (Greensborough: Printed by Smith and De Wolf, 1835), p. 7. See also "Records of the Presbytery of Georgia, 1821–1840," Montreat, p. 218.

STATE RIGHT," proclaimed the *Georgia Journal*, "that Georgia and all her sisters of the South are now to look for safety." The *Edgefield Advertiser* of South Carolina elaborated: "Ours is a Union of separate, independent, Republican States, each possessing the attributes of Sovereignty perfect within itself, with the exception of the small portion which was delegated, when they formed the Federal Union." Citizens in Fredricksburg, Virginia, maintained that slavery was "a domestic institution – belonging exclusively to the citizens of these States – and that the people of no other State have any right to attempt to change the relation therein existing between master and slave." One Mississippi newspaper labeled the doctrines of the abolitionists "*anti-republican*" because they "would lead the people of one state to interfere with the domestic governments or reserved rights of any other state." The fact that the states' rights argument did not appear in the resolutions of denominational bodies can probably be explained by the fact that a discussion of constitutional issues was considered a political issue and outside the purview of religion. Southern clergymen recognized that they had to restrict themselves to those dimensions of abolitionism that were moral and religious.[53]

In the 1835 crisis, then, religious and political discourse joined at the crucial junction of portraying abolitionism as infidelity, yet political language remained autonomous in its emphasis on states' rights. In this case, clergymen contributed religious vocabulary to the political discussion, adding emotional charge to the Southern defense against the assault of abolition. The paths of religion and politics would cross again during the 1840s, and this time religious leaders would borrow constitutional arguments from the political sphere during ecclesiastical controversies. Over the course of the antebellum decades, both Southern religion and Southern politics would become increasingly sectional and radical. Their relationship would be complex and symbiotic, at times converging on and borrowing from each other and at other times taking different but complementary paths toward the same goal.

V

One night in 1836, the Baptist minister Iveson L. Brookes awoke from a terrible dream. "The substance is that in some twenty or thirty years," the

53. On states' rights, see Sydnor, *Development of Southern Sectionalism*, pp. 135–6, 177–82, 244–8; *Georgia Journal*, August 11, 1835; *Edgefield Advertiser*, April 21, 1836; *Richmond Enquirer*, September 29, 1835; *Mississippi Free Trader and Natchez Gazette*, December 4, 1835. See also the resolutions of a citizens' meeting in Greensboro, Georgia, in *Georgia Journal*, October 6, 1835.

South Carolinian confided to his wife, "a division of the Northern and Southern states will ensue between the Yankees & Slaveholders." The experience of Brookes and his clerical brethren during the abolitionist postal campaign reveals how religion would help incite and shape his nightmare, a civil war between the North and South. By formulating a working understanding of the relationship between religion and sectional politics, establishing an association between abolitionism and religious infidelity, and demonstrating the various ways in which religion and sectionalism would interact, Southern clergymen in 1835 had taken the first step toward secession and separate nationhood. Their next was to place slavery, the South's peculiar institution and the basis of antebellum Southern separatism, on a firm moral foundation of religion.[54]

---

[54] Iveson L. Brookes to Sarah Brookes, February 25, 1836, Iveson Lewis Brookes Papers, William R. Perkins Library, Duke University, Durham, N.C.

PART TWO

Religion and slavery

2

Slavery defended:
The morality of slavery
and the infidelity of abolitionism

On a lazy Sunday afternoon in New Orleans, Marie St. Clare, the fictional slaveholding mistress from Harriet Beecher Stowe's *Uncle Tom's Cabin*, sits down to dinner after returning from church. She describes to St. Clare and Miss Ophelia, their Vermont cousin, the "splendid sermon" she had heard:

> The text was, "He hath made everything beautiful in its season;" and he showed how all the orders and distinction in society came from God; and that it was so appropriate, you know, and beautiful that some were born to rule and some to serve, and all that, you know; and he applied it so well to all this ridiculous fuss that is made about slavery, and he proved distinctly that the Bible was on our side, and supported all our institutions so convincingly.

Stowe's readers, whether antislavery Northerners or proslavery Southerners, would have recognized in this passage a fundamental fact of the antebellum sectional controversy – that the Southern church was usually a bulwark of slavery. From the 1830s through the secession crisis, religion took on a major role in the proslavery crusade. When Northern abolitionists contended that slavery per se was a sin, Southern clergymen responded that the institution was a moral one. In response to this antislavery attack, Southern clerics forged an impregnable union between religion, morality, and slavery.[1]

Proslavery Christianity occupies a pivotal place in this study. It illuminates two themes that shaped the relationship between religion and the development of Southern separatism. First, it vividly illustrates the important dynamic of response and reaction between North and South. The

---

1. Harriet Beecher Stowe, *Uncle Tom's Cabin* (New York: Viking Penguin, 1981), p. 279.

53

religious defense of slavery was formulated in the context of the debate between the Southern clergy and Northern abolitionists over the morality of slavery. Proslavery ministers had two essential and inseparable objectives in this debate: to establish the righteousness of slavery and destroy the credibility of abolitionism. The morality of slavery and the infidelity of abolitionism became the twin pillars of religious proslavery orthodoxy.

The second theme, closely related to the first, is the use of shared American values and ways of thinking in the creation of a distinctly sectional ideology. In their debate with Northern abolitionists over the morality of slavery, Southern clergymen drew upon the most common intellectual resources of their time – the Bible and natural law – to demonstrate the rectitude of slavery and the infidelity of abolitionism. They were essentially seeking political legitimacy through a sectional adaptation of national discourse.

Proslavery Christianity established a firm moral foundation for the South's peculiar institution. By investing the sectional conflict with profound religious significance and helping to convince Southerners that a deep and irreconcilable moral chasm divided North and South, it became the most visible and one of the most essential contributions religion made to the cause of Southern separatism.

I

The scriptural justification of slavery was the central pillar in the proslavery argument. The Baptist minister Iveson L. Brookes maintained that "the Biblical argument in support of slavery must be considered the most important defense of that institution." His fellow South Carolinian John Bachman, a Lutheran clergyman and respected scientist, similarly regarded the teachings of the Bible as "the most effective weapons" in defending slavery. Biblical authority was employed perhaps more often than any other single argument in the proslavery arsenal.[2] The debate over the morality of the slavery that pitted Southern clergymen against

2. Donald B. Touchstone, "Plànters and Slave Religion in the Deep South," Ph.D. diss., Tulane University, 1973, p. 97; William Sumner Jenkins, *Proslavery Thought in the Old South* (Chapel Hill: University of North Carolina Press, 1935), p. 207. Historian Arthur Y. Lloyd notes that the scriptural justification of slavery played "an important part in the establishment of the new philosophy of slavery among the Southerners." *The Slavery Controversy, 1831–1860* (Chapel Hill: University of North Carolina Press, 1939), p. 166. For other studies of the biblical defense of slavery, see Jenkins, *Proslavery Thought in the Old South*, chap. 5, and H. Shelton Smith, *In His Image, But ... Racism in Southern Religion, 1790–1910* (Durham, N.C.: Duke University Press, 1972), chap. 3.

Northern abolitionists centered on the Bible. At the heart of the new abolitionist creed of the 1830s was the conviction that slavery was a sin. The abolitionists had "spiritualized" the antislavery movement, redefining the slavery controversy as a religious and moral one. They had thus brought the Bible to the center of the slavery controversy, forcing Southern clergymen to defend the morality of slavery. To effectively show that slavery was not a sin, proslavery clerics demonstrated that the Bible – as God's Word the standard of morality – did not condemn slaveholding per se as a moral wrong.

The abolitionist interpretation of the Bible is well illustrated in a sermon delivered in 1834 by the Rev. James T. Dickinson before the Second Congregational Church of Norwich, Connecticut. Dickinson's main argument was that slavery "is a system of oppression, and therefore is regarded by the Bible as sin." He explained that the laws of slavery force the slaveholder to be an oppressor, "and consequently to break the laws of God." Dickinson succinctly spelled out the basic abolitionist logic to his parishioners. The Bible "is against oppression and injustice in *every form,* and surely it condemns injustice so flagrant. And whatever it condemns as wrong, it requires should be *immediately* repented of." Immediate abolitionism was thus predicated on the belief that slavery was a form of oppression denounced by the Word of God. Slavery was a sin, argued David Root of New Hampshire, because the Scriptures "condemn every species of oppression."[3]

Southern clergymen emphatically countered that slavery was sanctioned in the Bible. In an early and important defense of slavery written in 1822, the Rev. Richard Furman of Beaufort, South Carolina, insisted that the right to hold slaves was clearly recognized in the Holy Scriptures. On no other subject, agreed a Virginian in 1836, "are its instructions more explicit, or their salutary tendency and influence more thoroughly tested and corroborated by experience than on the subject of slavery." The influential *Quarterly Review* of the Methodist Episcopal Church, South, asserted that slavery "has received the sanction of Jehovah" throughout the historical era covered in the Bible. "If the Scriptures do not justify slavery," a South Carolina Presbyterian concluded, "I know not what they do justify." The secular South agreed. The radical Charleston *Mercury* endorsed the clerical opinion that "Slavery as a system has been sanctioned both in the Old and New Testament." A writer to the Macon

3. James T. Dickinson, *A Sermon, delivered in the Second Congregational Church, Norwich, on the fourth of July, 1834, at the Request of the Anti-Slavery Society of Norwich & Vicinity* (Norwich, Conn.: Published by the Anti-Slavery Society, 1834), pp. 4, 11, 34; David Root, *A Fast Day Sermon on Slavery, delivered April 2, 1835, to the Congregational Church & Society in Dover, N.H.* (Dover: Printed at the *Enquirer* Office, 1835), p. 6.

Georgia Messenger in 1835 similarly insisted that there was no conflict between the moral laws of the Bible and slavery.[4]

Proslavery clergymen began their biblical defense of slavery with the Old Testament. Many writers first cited Genesis 9:25, Noah's curse on Ham, the father of Canaan: "Cursed be Canaan; A servant of servants shall he be unto his brethren." Not only was this passage intended to show that God – and not man – had inaugurated slavery, but that Noah's curse applied specifically to blacks. "From Ham," explained a Georgian in 1844, "were descended the nations that occupied the land of Canaan, and those that now constitute the African or negro race." J. B. Thrasher of Mississippi added that blacks "are the lowest and most degraded of the descendants of Canaan."[5]

The Old Testament also demonstrated that God sanctioned slavery in the Mosaic law that He gave to His chosen people, Israel. The Methodist *Quarterly Review* believed that the Mosaic law contained "the most emphatic endorsement and sanction of the right of property in man." The passages most commonly cited to support this particular argument were Leviticus 25:44–6, which authorized the buying, selling, holding, and bequeathing of slaves as property. A historical precedent for slaveholding from biblical Israel had a powerful appeal to antebellum Americans, who saw themselves as uniquely favored by God. A Baptist minister from Georgia, for instance, assured his readers that "the Jews, up to the time of their national dispersion, were as emphatically a slaveholding people, as we Georgians are."[6]

4. Richard Furman, *Rev. Dr. Richard Furman's Exposition of the Views of the Baptists, Relative to the Coloured Population in the United States in a Communication to the Governor of South Carolina* (1822; reprint ed., Charleston: A. E. Miller, 1833), p. 6; S. Taylor, *Relation of Master and Servant, as Exhibited in the New Testament* (Richmond, Va.: T. W. White, Printer, 1836), p. 6; *Quarterly Review* 6 (January 1857): 31; Ferdinand Jacobs, *The Committing of Our Cause to God. A Sermon, preached in the Second Presbyterian Church, Charleston, South Carolina on Friday, 6th of December* (Charleston: Edward C. Councell, 1851), p. 20; Charleston *Mercury*, August 11, 1835; *Georgia Messenger*, November 19, 1835. For further evidence among clerics, see *Southern Christian Herald*, May 20, 1836, and the sermon by E. W. Warren printed in *Christian Index*, February 13, 1861. For other examples of this view in the political press, see *Georgia Messenger*, November 19, 1835, and the *Sumter County Whig*, quoted in James B. Sellers, *Slavery in Alabama* (University: University of Alabama Press, 1950), p. 340.

5. Smith, *In His Image*, p. 130; [Patrick Hues Mell], *Slavery. A Treatise, Showing that Slavery Is Neither a Moral, Political, nor Social Evil* (Penfield, Ga.: Benjamin Brantly, 1844), p. 15; J. B. Thrasher, *Slavery A Divine Institution: A Speech Made before the Breckinridge and Lane Club, November 5th, 1860* (Port Gibson, Miss.: *Southern Reveille* Book and Job Office, 1861), p. 18.

6. *Quarterly Review* 11 (January 1857): 35; Jenkins, *Proslavery Thought in the Old South*, p. 202; *Quarterly Review* 11 (January 1857): 35; *Christian Index*, February 13, 1861.

The fact that several Old Testament prophets held slaves was additional proof that God sanctioned human bondage. The Methodist Samuel Dunwody from South Carolina, an early defender of slavery, pointed to Genesis 14:14 to show that Abraham held slaves. The Rev. Alexander McCaine, in an address before the Methodist Protestant Church in 1842, added Jacob, Isaac, and Job to the list of slaveholding prophets, arguing that "these few instances may suffice to show, that some of the most eminent of the Old Testament saints were slaveholders." On the eve of Lincoln's election, one Mississippian carried this argument to a curious extreme. Not only did Isaac own slaves, J. B. Thrasher explained in a speech to the Lane and Breckinridge Club in Port Gibson, but because Isaac lived on roughly the same latitude as did Southern Americans, he could be considered a "Southern" slaveholder.[7]

Northern abolitionists and antislavery clergymen did attempt to refute the credibility and relevance of the scriptural testimony on behalf of slavery. Joseph P. Thompson of New York, for example, considered Noah's curse on Ham "of questionable authority." Abolitionists argued that the domestic servitude practiced by the Patriarchs was different from chattel slavery. They tried to undermine the power of the Mosaic code to support human bondage. One argued that "the whole system of American slavery, which originated in kidnapping, and is maintained only by the law of force, which is the essential element of kidnapping," clashed with Mosaic law, which made kidnapping a crime. Another line of argument, expressed by the Connecticut theologian Horace Bushnell, was that the ordinances supporting slavery were "permissive statutes" that would be superseded by the advance of moral sentiment.[8]

"The teachings of the New Testament in regard to bodily servitude accord with the Old," asserted the Methodist *Quarterly Review*. Because slavery was not explicitly sanctioned in the New Testament, Southern clergymen were forced to argue that the absence of condemnation signified approval. As the influential Methodist journal explained: "In the absence of such an injunction, are we not warranted in saying that the apostle did *not* so regard it, but, contrariwise, deemed the relation in itself

7. Samuel Dunwody, *A Sermon Upon the Subject of Slavery* (Columbia, S.C.: S. Weir, 1837), p. 4; Alexander McCaine, *Slavery Defended from Scripture, against the Attacks of the Abolitionists* (Baltimore: Wm. Woody, 1842), pp. 5–7; Thrasher, *Slavery a Divine Institution*, p. 10. See also Jacobs, *The Committing of Our Cause to God*, p. 11.

8. "Slavery and the Bible," *New Englander* 15 (February 1857): 104–5; ibid, 106; Caroline Shanks, "The Biblical Anti-Slavery Argument of the Decade, 1830–1840," *Journal of Negro History* 16 (April 1931): 143. For a contemporary effort to refute the proslavery biblical argument, see "Slavery and the Bible," pp. 102–8. See also the evidence assembled in Shanks, "The Biblical Anti-Slavery Argument," pp. 138–44, and Lloyd, *The Slavery Controversy*, pp. 172–4.

a moral and lawful one, and therefore undertook to regulate the recipro-
cal duties of the Christian master and Christian slave?" The arguments
from the New Testament most commonly cited to defend human bond-
age can be found in a series of letters on slavery written by George D.
Armstrong, pastor of the First Presbyterian Church in Norfolk, Virginia.
Armstrong pointed out that the Apostles received slaveholders into the
Christian Church and spoke on the relative duties of master and slave.
He also reminded his readers that Paul sent back the fugitive slave
Onesimus to his owner Philemon. These cases clearly demonstrated, Arm-
strong concluded, that slaveholding "is not a sin in the sight of God, and
is not to be accounted an 'offense' by his Church."[9]

As they had done with proslavery evidence from the Old Testament,
Northern abolitionists countered these assertions. They questioned, for
example, whether Onesimus was really a slave. They suggested further
that the instructions given to servants were duties incumbent on all
Christians. Most important, they insisted that the system of slavery was
repugnant to the whole tenor and spirit of the Bible. Albert Barnes, a New
School Presbyterian and antislavery minister, argued that if fairly applied,
the principles of the New Testament would lead toward the abolition of
slavery.[10]

The logic of proslavery ministers still seemed unassailable. Because the
Bible was the Word of God and God was morally supreme, anything
sanctioned in the Bible had to be moral. To anyone who acknowledged
that slavery was authorized in the Old and New Testaments, the implica-
tion was clear. "If the Divine Author sanctioned slavery," concluded the
Methodist *Quarterly Review,* "it *cannot be* an absolute and universal evil
– a moral wrong, per se." David Ewart, a Baptist from Columbia, South
Carolina, reasoned that if God propounded laws for the relation between
master and slave in the Old Testament, slavery itself must be a "moral
relation." The logic behind the biblical justification was well summarized
by Samuel Dunwody of South Carolina:

> Thus, God, as he is, infinitely wise, just, and holy, never could author-
> ise the practice of moral evil. But God has authorized the practice of
> Slavery, not only by the bare permission of his Providence, but the
> express provision of his word. Therefore, Slavery is not a moral evil.

9. *Quarterly Review* 11 (January 1857): 37; George D. Armstrong, *Letters and Replies on
   Slavery* (Philadelphia: Joseph M. Wilson, Publisher, 1858), p. 5. For more on the New
   Testament vindication of slavery, see Thornton Stringfellow, *A Brief Examination of
   Scripture Testimony on the Institution of Slavery* (Washington, D.C.: *Congressional Globe*
   Office, 1850), p. 10, and S. Taylor, *Relation of Master and Servant,* p. 19.
10. Shanks, "The Biblical Anti-Slavery Argument," pp. 148–54; "Slavery and the Bible,"
    p. 119.

Endowing the Bible with such moral supremacy and universality allowed Southern clergymen to invest the biblical justification of slavery with an authority that would be impregnable.[11]

The debate over the scriptural view of slavery inevitably raised the issue of the moral authority of the Bible. To Southern proslavery clergymen, the Bible – as God's revealed Word – embodied the highest standard of moral rectitude. The Methodist Bishop William Capers of South Carolina held "the Scriptures to be the rule, and the only rule, for determining what is and what is not moral evil." These ministers emphasized the constancy and supremacy of the Bible as *the* source of moral authority. The *Southern Dial,* a short-lived proslavery organ edited in part by some Alabama clergymen, saw the Bible as "the immutable and authoritative standard, which God has established for the creed and conduct of mankind." A Whig newspaper similarly considered the laws of God "eternal and unchangeable." Even when sound philosophy and revelation clashed over issues of morality, the Scriptures were to be considered supreme. "Man may err," explained the Southern theologian James H. Thornwell, "but God can never lie."[12]

To Southern clerics, the religious argument against slavery drifted dangerously close to infidelity. Repudiating direct scriptural testimony that sanctioned slavery could appear as an attack on the literal authority of the Bible itself. In an atmosphere of secularization and heightening sectional tensions, the defense of slavery could easily become the guard for religious orthodoxy as well.

II

On the eve of secession, the *Southern Presbyterian* of South Carolina affirmed that there was "a *religious* character to the present struggle. Anti-Slavery is essentially infidel. It wars upon the Bible, on the Church of Christ, on the truth of God, on the souls of men." The image of abolitionism as infidelity grew naturally out of the scriptural defense of slav-

11. *Quarterly Review* 11 (January 1857): 36; *Southern Baptist,* March 21, 1849; Dunwody, *Sermon Upon the Subject of Slavery,* p. 10.

12. Harmon Smith, "William Capers and William A. Smith, Neglected Advocates of the Pro-Slavery Moral Argument," *Methodist History* 3 (October 1964): 27; *Southern Dial* (November 1857), p. 11; Sellers, *Slavery in Alabama,* p. 340; Jenkins, *Proslavery Thought in the Old South,* p. 233. See also Robert J. Breckinridge, *Fidelity in our Lot. The Substance of a Discourse preached by the Appointment of the General Assembly of the Presbyterian Church, at their Annual Meeting in the City of Nashville, Tennessee, in May, 1855* (Philadelphia: Board of Missions, 1855), p. 24.

ery. Slavery, in the minds of Southern clergymen, was clearly and unequivocally sanctioned in the Bible. An assault on slavery was thus an
attack on the Bible and an implicit challenge to the moral supremacy of
God. Abolitionism then became a dangerous form of religious infidelity
that threatened not only slavery but the basic fabric of Western civilization. The Southern clerical critique of abolitionism was an essential and
substantial component in religious proslavery literature.[13]

The debate between Southern clergymen and the abolitionists over the
source of ultimate moral authority revolved around conflicting interpretations of the role of the conscience. According to proslavery ministers, the
abolitionists made the conscience the highest source of moral authority.
To J. B. Thrasher of Port Gibson, Mississippi, Northern critics of slavery
were guided by an "inward monitor claimed to reside in their own unbal-
anced craniums." The *Central Presbyterian* of Richmond suggested further that the abolitionists "made their own consciences right and wrong,
not only for themselves, but for all others." Making the individual conscience the supreme moral arbiter challenged the authority of religion in
the realm of ethics. Following the views of Southern moral philosophers,
the *Southern Methodist Itinerant* of Virginia believed that the conscience
should always be in harmony with the Bible. Among abolitionists, however, the conscience had "usurped the throne of judgment" and hence
they had "disregarded the word of God."[14]

In responding to the argument that the conscience was the highest
source of moral rectitude, Southern clergymen acknowledged the conscience as a moral sense but circumscribed the authority given to it by
the abolitionists. The Southern position was well explained in an article
published in 1853 in the influential *Southern Presbyterian Review* by
Samuel J. Cassels of Georgia. In disputing the supremacy of the conscience, Cassels separated the problem into two parts. He argued first that
the conscience was not supreme among faculties of the human mind. Like
any mental enterprise, a moral judgment, Cassels explained, was a complex act that involved several mental powers, such as the will, memory,
reason, and the conscience. Because the separate mental faculties worked
together, no one faculty could be permanently sovereign. Cassels thus
concluded that all "we can mean by the authority of a mental power, is
simply its precedence over the rest in any one action."[15]

The second aspect of the problem, the authority of the conscience in

13. *Southern Presbyterian*, December 15, 1860.
14. Thrasher, *Slavery a Divine Institution*, p. 21; *Central Presbyterian*, February 25, 1860;
    Southern Methodist Itinerant, February 27, 1861.
15. Samuel J. Cassels, "Conscience – Its Nature, Office and Authority," *Southern Presbyte-
    rian Review* 6 (April 1853): 455, 465–6, 467.

relation to revelation, directly challenged the abolitionist argument that the conscience was the highest source of moral rectitude. Cassels insisted that the conscience was subordinate to divine revelation. "God is our only true moral governor," the Presbyterian minister maintained, "and his will is our only supreme law." He argued further that the "very moment we set up conscience as a sort of rival to Jehovah, that moment we become idolators." A secular proslavery writer, John Fletcher of Virginia, shared the belief that man must look to a higher source – God's moral law – to confirm the judgment of the conscience.[16]

Closely related to the dispute over the power of the conscience was the question of the role of reason in religion. Again, the issue of ultimate moral authority was at stake. To Southern clergymen, rationalism did not signify solely a rational mode of thought. Rather, it represented an exaltation of the potential of human reason at the expense of divine revelation. The Southern clerical conception of the issue of reason was clearly described by the Rev. S. W. Stanford in an article in the *Southern Presbyterian Review*. "The great intellectual battle of the age," he began, "is that which is now going on between Scripturalists and Rationalists." In accord with most orthodox Southern clergymen, Stanford described rationalism as "that system which so exalts human reason, as to deny the necessity, or destroy the authority, of the Divine Revelation." Scripturalists, on the other hand, received "the Scriptures of the Old and New Testaments, as the inspired word of God, and as an infallible rule of faith and practice." Essentially, then, rationalism was seen as an attack on the authority of the Bible.[17]

Predictably, Southern churchmen accused the abolitionists of rationalism, arguing that Northern reformers sought to replace divine revelation with reason. "One ground of error, into which the anti-slaveholders have fallen," suggested the Rev. Samuel Dunwody of South Carolina, "is, that of substituting a train of metaphysical reasonings, for the plain letter of the word of the Lord." He contended further that no system of reasoning could replace the Scriptures. The *Biblical Recorder* of North Carolina also believed that the "principles of interpretations" adopted by such

16. Cassells, "Conscience," pp. 467–8; Jenkins, *Proslavery Thought in the Old South*, p. 235.
17. S. W. Stanford, "Scripturalism versus Rationalism," *Southern Presbyterian Review* 5 (October 1851): 274. On reason and Southern religion, see E. Brooks Holifield, *The Gentlemen Theologians: American Theology in Southern Culture, 1795–1860* (Durham, N.C.: Duke University Press, 1978), pp. 50–72, and James H. Smylie, "Clerical Perspectives on Deism: Paine's *Age of Reason* in Virginia," *Eighteenth Century Studies* 6 (Winter 1972): 202–20. For the European background that shaped Southern religious thought on reason, consult Gerald R. Cragg, *Reason and Authority in the Eighteenth Century* (Cambridge: Cambridge University Press, 1964).

reformers as abolitionists "strike directly and fatally at the root of divine revelation." The *Carolina Baptist,* drawing this reasoning to its logical conclusion, argued that the abolitionists "presume to know and teach more of the will of God towards man than the sacred Scriptures teach." By placing human ability equal to or above God, rationalism posed essentially the same threat to divine moral supremacy as did the conscience doctrine of ultimate truth.[18]

As they had done with the issue of conscience, Southern clergymen acknowledged the value of reason in religion while emphasizing its limitations. "In this controversy," wrote the Rev. Thomas Smyth of Charleston, "we maintain ... the absolute necessity of reason to every opinion which man holds, and to every action man performs." S. W. Stanford, affirming a role for reason in religion, argued that "the Bible submits its credentials to be judged of by reason." Southern clergymen thus accepted the use of reason but condemned the exclusive reliance placed upon it. The Rev. W. J. Sasnett, a Methodist minister from Oxford, Georgia, explained that "true evangelical religion" rested on both reason and revelation "in right combination and adjustment." He warned that the "presence of reason without faith gives rationalism or infidelity." Man could not rely solely on reason because it was unable to comprehend those religious truths attainable only through revelation. Man is a finite being, explained Sasnett, "and there is consequently a sphere of knowledge whose premises are necessarily outside of his reason, and which if he ever embraces, it must be upon evidence extrinsic to itself." Thomas Smyth argued similarly that reason was "finite, limited and imperfect" and that there were "things supernatural" which lay beyond the reaches of our senses. An Alabama Methodist concurred that matters of revelation "lie beyond the comprehension of the loftiest powers of the human intellect."[19]

Behind Southern clerical opposition to the exclusive reliance placed on the conscience and the exaltation of reason lay the more fundamental concern that the individual was replacing God as the center of the moral universe. Abolitionism was portrayed as part of a dangerous apotheosis of the individual. The spirit of abolitionism, warned the *Southern Baptist* of South Carolina, "is the setting up of individual notions of justice and

18. Dunwody, *Sermon Upon the Subject of Slavery,* p. 17; *Biblical Recorder,* September 6, 1845; *Carolina Baptist* (December 1845): 88.
19. Thomas Smyth, "The Province of Reason, Especially in Matters of Religion," *Southern Presbyterian Review* 7 (October 1853): 276–7, 288; Stanford, "Scripturalism versus Rationalism," p. 275; W. J. Sasnett, "German Philosophy," *Quarterly Review* 12 (July 1858): 328–9; Smyth, "The Province of Reason," pp. 289–91; *Quarterly Review* 4 (April 1850): 193, 187.

humanity, against the morality of the Bible." The Presbyterian theologian James H. Thornwell agreed that the abolitionists believed in "the perfection of the individual as the ultimate end of his existence, while the Scriptures represent it as a means to a higher and nobler end, the glory of God." The threat individualism posed to religion was neatly summarized by the *Central Presbyterian* of Richmond:

> The intense individualism alluded to that makes each man a higher law unto himself, judging even the Bible by his own uncontrolled reason, generates that morbid self-reliance that prevents the adoption of any settled code of opinions, and ignores the established faith of the church, that has been handed down from generation to generation.[20]

In attacking the morality of slavery – by questioning the Bible and hence the moral omnipotence of God – abolitionism was clearly a form of infidelity. As early as 1835, the Alabama Baptist State Convention declared the efforts of the abolitionists "inconsistent with the gospel of Christ." Iveson L. Brookes similarly denounced the abolitionists for their "mad disregard" of the Bible. In a Thanksgiving Day sermon delivered in 1856, a Georgia Presbyterian expressed the thinking of most Southern clergymen by labeling abolitionism as "diametrically opposite to the letter and spirit of the Bible, and as subversive of all sound morality, as the worst ravings of Infidelity." The attempts by abolitionists to replace the Bible with another source of moral authority, one more closely attuned to their antislavery principles, further qualified them as infidels. Stephen Elliott, an Episcopal bishop from Georgia, denounced the abolitionists as "infidels – men who are clamoring for a new God, and a new Christ, and a new Bible." The New School Presbyterian minister F. A. Ross from Huntsville, Alabama, argued similarly that the abolitionists were "seeking, somewhere, an abolition Bible ... and an abolition God."[21]

20. *Southern Baptist,* October 23, 1850; Paul Leslie Garber, "The Religious Thought of James Henley Thornwell," Ph.D. diss., Duke University, 1939, p. 267; *Central Presbyterian,* December 29, 1860.
21. Benjamin F. Riley, *History of the Baptists of Alabama* (Birmingham: Roberts and Son, 1895), p. 98; Iveson L. Brookes, *A Defense of Southern Slavery Against the Attacks of Henry Clay and Alexander Campbell by a Southern Clergymen* (Hamburg, S.C.: Robison and Carlisle, 1851), p. 8; A. N. Pratt, *Perils of a Dissolution of the Union; A discourse, delivered in the Presbyterian Church of Roswell, on the Day of Public Thanksgiving. November 20, 1856* (Atlanta: C. R. Hanleiter & Co., Printers, 1856), p. 16; Stephen Elliott, *Address of the Rt. Rev. Stephen Elliott. D. D., to the Thirty-Ninth Annual Convention of the Protestant Episcopal Church in the Diocese of Georgia* (Savannah: Power Press of John M. Cooper & Company, 1861), p. 10; F. A. Ross, *Position of the Southern Church in Relation to Slavery* (New York: John A. Gray, 1857), p. 11.

The disagreement between Southern clergymen and Northern abolitionists over biblical testimony on slavery revealed contrasting approaches to interpreting the Scriptures. Abolitionist ministers tended to
argue that it was the spirit rather than the letter of the Bible that was
antislavery. "The scriptures specify few crimes," explained David Root of
New Hampshire: "They advance general principles from which we are to
gather lessons of duty." A Massachusetts minister similarly stressed the
"principles of the Gospel of Christ" in his antislavery address. To the
Garrisonian Adin Ballou, the Bible should be construed "according to the
evident *spirit* of its text, rather than the mere *letter*."[22]

The logic of the antislavery interpretation of the Bible led easily toward
a fundamental questioning of its moral authority. If the Bible did contain
direct mention of slavery, and if slavery was an unmitigated and unqualified sin, then perhaps the error in morality was in the Bible. The
radical abolitionist and former minister Henry C. Wright expressed this
extreme position in a speech before the New England Antislavery Convention in 1850. Denouncing the biblical sanction of slavery, Wright pronounced "shame on such a God. I defy him, I scorn him, he is not my
God." Critics of the abolitionists seized on this reasoning to discredit
the movement. They claimed that the abolitionists taught that "the Bible
is an unintelligible book" and that "'the writing upon the wall, may be
from God, but the impression is, according to their confidence in the
interpreter.'" It is true that some abolitionists, usually those radicals associated with William Lloyd Garrison, did entertain these views. Nathaniel
Peabody Rogers, for example, claimed the Bible was "useful" only as
much as it appealed to "human understanding." Another Garrisonian,
Charles B. Stearns, argued that private judgment could overturn the authority of the Bible. During the late 1830s, articles rejecting the divine
inspiration of the Bible could be found in the columns of *The Liberator*. Garrison himself repudiated certain biblical passages "as contrary to
God's true intent." These views, really confined to the small left wing of
the antislavery movement, emerged not only from the logic of abolitionist
thought but also from the disillusionment that plagued abolitionists in the
1830s when they had failed to convert the Northern church and clergy to
abolition.[23]

22. Root, *A Fast Day Sermon on Slavery*, p. 9; Daniel Foster, *An Address on Slavery, de-
livered in Danvers, Mass.* (Boston, Mass.: Bela Marsh, 1849), p. 6; Lewis Perry, *Radical
Abolitionism: Anarchy and the Government of God in Antislavery Thought* (Ithaca and
London: Cornell University Press, 1973), p. 243.
23. Quoted in Lloyd, *The Slavery Controversy*, p. 191; John R. McKivigan, *The War Against
Proslavery Religion: Abolitionism and the Northern Churches, 1830–1865* (Ithaca and
London: Cornell University Press, 1984), p. 31; Perry, *Radical Abolitionism*, pp. 121–2;

Proslavery ministers rested their case instead on a strict, literal interpretation of the Scriptures. "We are neither to question nor to doubt," James H. Thornwell explained, "but simply to interpret and believe." The *Southern Presbyterian* captured the essence and significance of this fundamental difference in 1861:

> The vital principle of all infidelity is that whatever claims to be the "written word," the *lex scripta* of God or man, must be subjected to the individual reason and the "moral sense," and if condemned by them, must be rejected and resisted. And this is the heart of the great current controversy, the authority of Divine and human law over man's reason and moral sense.

Clerics' doctrinaire insistence on placing the written law of God over individual judgment reflected and perhaps reinforced the South's strict constructionist view of the Constitution and their repudiation of the Northern "higher law" argument of the 1850s.[24]

The biblical justification of slavery and the critique of abolition as infidelity became closely identified with the defense of religious orthodoxy. Changing currents in European and American thought worked with rapidly intensifying sectional tensions to lead Southern clergymen to see an unmistakable connection between slavery and religious orthodoxy. A closer look at the intellectual context in which religious proslavery was framed sheds valuable light on the ideological origins of Southern separatism.

Challenges to the moral authority of the Bible were present in the larger intellectual currents flowing through antebellum America. The practice of biblical criticism, which began in Germany, appeared first among New England intellectuals in the early 1800s who had studied on the continent. Scholars like Andrews Norton of Harvard and Moses Stuart of Andover

ibid., p.143; McKivigan, *War Against Proslavery Religion*, p. 58; Robert William Fogel, *Without Consent or Contract: The Rise and Fall of American Slavery* (New York and London: W. W. Norton, 1989), p. 277. It should be noted that some prominent Northern ministers, such as Dartmouth president Nathan Lord and Vermont Bishop Henry Hopkins, accepted a literal interpretation of the Bible and actually contributed to the scriptural vindication of human bondage. McKivigan, *The War Against Proslavery Religion*, p. 30. See also Lloyd, *The Slavery Controversy*, pp. 168–9. The contribution of the Northern clergy to the proslavery argument is a central theme of Larry E. Tise, *Proslavery: A History of the Defense of Slavery in America, 1701–1840* (Athens and London: University of Georgia Press, 1987).

24. Paul Leslie Garber, "The Religious Thought of James Henley Thornwell," p. 78; *Central Presbyterian*, March 9, 1861. William W. Freehling also points out the ideological consonance between a literal interpretation of the Bible and a strict construction of the Constitution. "James Henley Thornwell's Mysterious Antislavery Moment," *Journal of Southern History* 57 (August 1991): 388.

Seminary maintained that human wisdom could capture the meaning of the Bible. Theodore Parker of Boston, a brilliant theologian and radical activist, even argued that the Bible should be approached with the same skepticism applied to any work of ancient history. Although Southern clergymen were aware of these traditions and even used Stuart's "grammatical" method of Biblical criticism, they remained firmly wedded to orthodoxy's apotheosis of the authenticity of the Scriptures.[25]

The growing claims of science also threatened a literal interpretation of the Bible, though the implicit conflicts between science and religion did not fully erupt in the antebellum era. Yet even within the South science showed its potential to cause problems for religion. Ethnology, the scientific study of racial differences, was enlisted in the proslavery argument to prove the innate inferiority of blacks. The ethnological belief in the plural origin of the races posed a direct challenge to the religious creed that all humans were descended from the same set of parents and did lead to divisions within proslavery ranks. Clergymen tried to distance themselves from racial justifications for black slavery. In 1849, Thomas Smyth of Charleston defended the unity of mankind in lectures before the Literary and Philosophical Society of Charleston. The Rev. John Bachman of Charleston openly challenged the views of such well-known ethnologists as Dr. Josiah Nott of Mobile.[26]

Although the portrayal of abolitionism as infidelity was common from the 1835 abolitionist postal campaign to the secession crisis, the more serious explanations of the theological and philosophical links between the two appeared most frequently during the 1850s. This can be explained in several ways. First, the decade witnessed an almost unrelenting intensification of political strife between the North and South, which undoubtedly made the defense of slavery and critique of abolition more pressing issues for the Southern clergy. In addition, the 1850s seemed to be a period of heightened intellectual ferment in the South. Natural sciences

25. Bruce Kuklick, *Churchmen and Philosophers: From Jonathan Edwards to John Dewey* (New Haven and London: Yale University Press, 1985), pp. 89–92; Holifield, *Gentlemen Theologians*, p. 98.
26. Thomas Erskine Clarke, "Thomas Smyth: Moderate of the Old South," Th.D. diss., Union Theological Seminary, 1970, pp. 168–70; Reginald Horseman, *Josiah Nott of Mobile: Southerner, Physician, and Racial Theorist* (Baton Rouge and London: Louisiana State University Press, 1987), pp. 113–15. For a brief discussion of the conflict between ethnology and religion, see Drew Gilpin Faust, ed., *The Ideology of Slavery: Proslavery Thought in the Antebellum South* (Baton Rouge and London: Louisiana State University Press, 1981), pp. 14–17. See also William Stanton, *The Leopard's Spot: Scientific Attitudes Toward Race in America, 1815–1859* (Chicago: University of Chicago Press, 1960).

were pressing their claims against religion while the nascent social sciences, in the hands of such men as Joseph LeConte and George Frederick Holmes, were being applied to legitimate an organic and hierarchical social order. Clergymen were aware of and participated in this discourse. In Columbia, South Carolina, for example, the Presbyterian divines James H. Thornwell and Benjamin M. Palmer joined LeConte in these early sociological investigations. Thornwell even solicited LeConte's essays for publication in the *Southern Presbyterian Review*. Finally, the publication of theological periodicals and the continued growth of colleges and seminaries in the 1850s provided Southern clergymen with an institutional basis for defending both sectional and religious orthodoxy. By the eve of the Civil War, the two had become mutually reinforcing.[27]

III

James Warley Miles, an Episcopalian minister from Charleston, wrote in 1861 that "it is much more forcible, and to the purpose, to affirm that the relations of the white and black races result from a Natural law, just as much as do the effects of the Law of gravitation." Along with the Bible, natural law was a major intellectual force for the justification of slavery. Here again, Southern clergymen drew upon a common American intellectual tradition for the sectional purpose of vindicating slavery. They articulated a conservative interpretation of natural law that repudiated the natural rights philosophy of the American Revolution. They championed the ideals of patriarchy and the family. In the hands of Southern clergymen, natural law not only countenanced but advocated slavery. An empirical demonstration of the naturalness of slavery provided supplemental strength to its scriptural defense.[28]

27. Theodore Dwight Bozeman, "Joseph LeConte: Organic Science and a 'Sociology for the South,'" *Journal of Southern History* 39 (November 1973): 572. Also valuable on the intellectual context of the South in the 1850s is Neal C. Gillespie, *The Collapse of Orthodoxy: The Intellectual Ordeal of George Frederick Holmes* (Charlottesville: University Press of Virginia, 1972).

28. James Warley Miles, *The Relation between the Races at the South* (Charleston, S.C.: Evans and Cogswell, 1861), p. 5. In his monumental study of slavery, David Brion Davis suggested that "justifications for slavery had long been interwoven with the justification for more widely accepted forms of dominion and subordination." *The Problem of Slavery in the Age of Revolution, 1770–1823* (Ithaca, N.Y.: Cornell University Press, 1975), p. 13. On natural law and the sectional conflict, see Benjamin F. Wright, Jr., *American Interpretations of Natural Law: A Study in the History of Political Thought* (Cambridge, Mass.: Harvard University Press, 1931), pp. 210–42.

The essence of the natural law argument was that some form of submission was perfectly natural in any social order. This line of reasoning began with an inquiry into the origins of society. Southern ministers argued that in the state of nature man was dependent on other men and was thus a social creature. "It is pure fiction," explained the *Southern Presbyterian Review,* "to assert that the state of nature ever was a state of individual independence. Mankind from the beginning never have existed otherwise than in society and under government." The Methodist *Quarterly Review* also refuted the Lockean notion of the origin of society, maintaining that "a state of disintegration and isolated self-government never in fact existed." Religious writers were trying to establish that man was by nature a social being, with society as his natural environment, a concept common among American moral philosophers. As Mark Hopkins of Williams College explained, man's social nature was inherent, "a condition of his being rather than the object of a specific desire."[29]

Inequality was another condition of nature that vindicated human bondage. Rejecting the emphasis on natural equality popularized during the American Revolution, Southern ministers insisted that God did not create all men equal. "The plain matter of fact," asserted the Rev. W. T. Hamilton of Mobile, "is, that there ever has been, and there must be, great inequality in the condition of men." The Methodist *Quarterly Review,* in a review of William A. Smith's *Lectures on the Philosophy and Practice of Slavery* (1856), agreed that inequality is "inseparable from existence." To Joseph R. Wilson of Georgia, inequality was "a fundamental law." The Southern religious precept of natural inequality was well summarized by a Baptist from Gillisonville, South Carolina: "Men are unequal in all respects – in power, in talents, in virtue, in wealth, in industry and in degree; and so long as the relations of parent and child, magistrate and subject, master and servant – so long in other words as Society shall endure – this inequality will continue." A conception of society as naturally hierarchical, ordered by a series of ranks and subordination, flowed from this assumption of human inequality. John B. Adger, a Presbyterian minister from Charleston, believed that "it is part of the divine arrangement to have ranks and orders in human society." Similarly, the *Southern Presbyterian Review* considered that "all those rights and all those various subordinations of personal conditions, which are necessary

29. *Southern Presbyterian Review* 2 (March 1849): 569; *Quarterly Review* 11 (April 1857): 250; Donald H. Meyer, *The Instructed Conscience: The Shaping of the American National Ethic* (Philadelphia: University of Pennsylvania Press, 1972), p. 111. Southern slaveholders tended similarly to view freedom in the context of society. See Eugene D. Genovese, *The Slaveholders' Dilemma: Freedom and Progress in Southern Conservative Thought, 1820–1860* (Columbia: University of South Carolina Press, 1991), p. 51.

to the perfection of society and to the full development of humanity, are strictly and perfectly natural."[30]

The final point in the Southern use of the natural law argument was the rejection of the Enlightenment notion of natural rights, a popular weapon of the abolitionists. In attacking this doctrine, ministers participated in the conservative onslaught on Jeffersonian liberalism. Southern churchmen believed that rights are not abstract and universal but conditional. The *Southern Presbyterian Review* explained that rights are not given to man for simply being man, but "to man in particular providential circumstances and relations." The same journal significantly used the familial metaphor to illustrate this concept of conditional rights: "The rights of a father are natural, but they belong only to fathers. Rights of property are natural, but they belong only to those who have property." William A. Smith, in his course on moral and intellectual philosophy at Randolph–Macon College, also linked rights with conditions. "If their conditions be different," noted one of his students, "their rights will be different. For different conditions give different advantages." This interpretation of natural rights precluded the idea that man inherently possessed abstract rights. "And he, who enters into society with the full privileges of manhood," argued a South Carolina Baptist, "never at the same time enters upon the possession of any abstract rights."[31]

The interpretation of natural rights as conditional provided the basis for refuting the abolitionists' use of the Biblical Golden Rule (Matthew 7:12). Even though critics of slavery acknowledged that Jesus never explicitly condemned slavery, they insisted that his injunction to "do unto others" was contrary in spirit to human bondage. Religious defenders of slavery argued that the Golden Rule did not enjoin Southerners to accept racial equality. "I only doubt its particular application to the question of slavery, as it exists among us," stated Samuel Dunwody of South Caro-

---

30. W. T. Hamilton, *The Duties of Masters and Slaves Respectively: Or Domestic Servitude Sanctioned by the Bible* (Mobile, Ala.: F. A. Brooks, 1845), p. 8; *Quarterly Review* 11 (April 1857): 248; Joseph R. Wilson, *Mutual Relation of Masters and Slaves as Taught in the Bible. A Discourse preached in the First Presbyterian Church, Augusta, Georgia, on Sabbath morning, January 6, 1861* (Augusta, Ga.: Steam Press of *Chronicle Sentinel*, 1861), p. 9; *Southern Baptist*, November 6, 1850; John B. Adger, *The Religious Instruction of the Colored Population. A Sermon preached by the Rev. John B. Adger, in the Second Presbyterian Church, Charleston, S.C. May 9th, 1847* (Charleston, S.C.: T. W. Haynes, 1847), p. 570; *Southern Presbyterian Review* 2 (March 1849): 570.

31. *Southern Presbyterian Review* 2 (March 1849): 572–3; "Lectures given by William A. Smith, Professor of Moral and Intellectual Philosophy at Randolph–Macon College in Virginia in 1854," Adolphus W. Mangum Papers, Southern Historical Collection, University of North Carolina Library, Chapel Hill, N. C.; *Southern Baptist*, November 6, 1850.

lina. To demonstrate the inapplicability of the Golden Rule to slavery, ministers invoked the notion that rights depend on condition. "All we can make of the precept," wrote one Georgian, "is, that it is our duty to do unto others as it would be *reasonable* for us to wish others to do unto us, were our situation reversed." The *Quarterly Review* also argued that by the Golden Rule, "we are not to understand as taught that whatever one man may lawfully desire in one condition of life, another may lawfully desire in another condition of life." Relying on the ideas of hierarchy, subordination, and conditional rights, the rebuttal of the Golden Rule argument thus tied together several strands of religious proslavery philosophy.[32]

The natural law defense of slavery embodied an organic and hierarchical view of society that permeated the ideology of the Southern clergy. At the heart of this world view was the theme of patriarchy. For proslavery clergymen, patriarchy was not only the underlying principle of slavery but also the basis for other social and civil relations. The Bible exalted the family as a fundamental human institution. As pervasive metaphors used to describe slavery, patriarchy and family coincided neatly with conservative social thought and religion.

Religious writings on slavery insisted that the relation between master and slave sanctioned in the Bible was based on patriarchy. "The true Scriptural idea of slavery," wrote a Presbyterian minister from Crawfordsville, Mississippi, "is that of a patriarchal relation." He explained that the master "is essentially the head of the household in all relations – the head of his wife – the head over his children – and the head over his servants." The widow of a small planter in Alabama recalled that slavery was regarded "in a patriarchal sense." If the relationship between master and slave was similar to that between a father and child, then the institution of slavery itself suggested a family. The *Central Presbyterian* of Richmond thus maintained that the "only true and Bible view of slavery is the family view." Thornwell agreed that slavery must be "predicated upon the idea of the family." The Baptist minister Richard Furman elaborated on this idea, explaining that for the master, slaves "become a part of his family (the whole, forming under him a little community) and the care of ordering it and of providing for its welfare, devolves on him."[33]

32. Dunwody, *A Sermon Upon the Subject of Slavery*, p. 21; [Mell], *Slavery*, p. 19; *Quarterly Review* 11 (January 1857): 41.
33. E. T. Baird, "The Religious Instruction of Our Colored Population," *Southern Presbyterian Review* 12 (July 1859): 348; Touchstone, "Planters and Slave Religion," p. 105; *Central Presbyterian*, May 3, 1856; James H. Thornwell, "Duties of Masters," *Southern Presbyterian Review* 8 (October 1854): 271; Furman, *Exposition*, p. 89. See also *Southern Baptist and General Intelligencer*, September 18, 1835, and [Mell], *Slavery*, p. 20.

Clergymen often extended the family metaphor to prescribe all social and civil relations, providing a significant ideological unity between family, slavery, and government. To enhance their justification of slavery on moral grounds, they continually promoted the family as a model for both slavery and society. "Kindred relations should be fostered," exhorted a New Orleans minister while discussing the relationship between master and slave, "for they give to society its strongest bonds." William A. Smith, according to one of his students, taught that domestic slavery was one element of civil government, "called domestic because it is part of the family government." Family, slavery, and civil society were linked further by their sanctification from God, which bestowed upon them the stamp of morality. In a sermon delivered at Augusta's First Presbyterian Church on the eve of Georgia's secession, Joseph R. Wilson argued that God "included slavery as an organizing element in that family order which lies at the very foundation of Church and State."[34]

This patriarchal ideal, coupled with the natural law tenets of dependence and inequality, necessitated some form of subjugation within a society. Accordingly, the natural law of submission became the defining characteristic of slavery. William A. Smith, in a well-known definition, explained that slavery embodied "the abstract principle of submission or subjugation to control by the will of another." Like all natural conditions, submission reflected the will of God. "The subjection," declared the *Southern Presbyterian Review*, "by God, of one man and one nation, to another man and another nation, is supposed throughout the Bible as an ordinary and recurring fact."[35]

Ministers often extended the idea of slavery to explain other forms of social relations, reflecting the essential unity of their social thought. Specifically, they argued that all governments incorporated the principle of subjection. A student of Smith's noted: "Without slavery there could be no government. The very idea is absurd. Government involves the idea of slavery. It restricts the wills of men in greater or less degrees and is to that

34. H. N. McTyeire, C. F. Sturgis, and A. T. Holmes, *Duties of Masters and Servants: Three Premium Essays* (Charleston, S.C.: Southern Baptist Publication Society, 1851), p. 31; "Lectures given by William A. Smith," Mangum Papers; Wilson, *Mutual Duties of Masters and Slaves*, p. 7. The close ideological affinity between familialism and proslavery is sensitively explored in Stephanie McCurry, "Defense of Their World: Gender, Class and the Yeomanry of the South Carolina Lowcountry, 1820–1860," Ph.D. diss., State University of New York at Binghamton, 1988, especially chaps. 3–5, and "The Two Faces of Republicanism: Gender and Proslavery Politics in Antebellum South Carolina," *Journal of American History* 78 (March 1992): 1245–64.
35. Harmon Smith, "William Capers and William A. Smith, Neglected Advocates of the Pro-Slavery Moral Argument," *Methodist History* 3 (October 1964): 25; *Southern Presbyterian Review* 2 (March 1849): 571.

extent slavery." The *Central Presbyterian* of Richmond therefore insisted that slavery was "essential to the existence of civilized society." Cementing the bonds between religion, slavery, and civil society, the *Southern Presbyterian Review* affirmed that the "principle of subjection to government is a conscientious submission to the will of God."[36]

The conservative view of social relations expressed by proslavery clerics both reflected and contributed toward paternalism, a central issue in the historical debate over the character of the Old South. Eugene D. Genovese, in a number of important works over the past few decades, argues essentially that the master–slave relationship was the determining factor in antebellum Southern civilization. What defined this relationship was paternalism, which exercised a powerful hegemonic function in Southern society and politics. In a series of articles with Elizabeth Fox-Genovese, Genovese has extended his analysis of paternalism and planter hegemony to explain the ideology of the South. To Southern Christians, these two historians argue, the ideal society was molded around the principles of patriarchy and subordination, by class and gender as well as by race. Proslavery sermons, the denominational press, and personal letters make evident that Southern clergymen shared these assumptions. The defense of slavery, patriarchy, inequality, and hierarchy by Southern clerics thus lends strong support to a paternalistic interpretation of the Old South.[37]

Yet in a social order with a "complex structure of diverse castes and classes," paternalism was not the only, and perhaps not the dominant world view. An alternative social vision, for example, of community self-sufficiency emerged among the nonslaveholding yeomanry who lived and farmed in small communities relatively isolated from a market economy. In addition, Jacksonianism in the South stressed a radical ethic of subsistence, liberty, and a fear of manipulation and dependence. The emphasis on inequality and hierarchy so prominent in the writings of Southern proslavery clergymen might have conflicted with these social visions.[38]

36. "Lectures given by William A. Smith," Mangum Papers; *Central Presbyterian,* January 28, 1860; *Southern Presbyterian Review* 2 (March 1849): 569.

37. Eugene D. Genovese and Elizabeth Fox-Genovese, "The Divine Sanction of Social Order: Religious Foundations of the Southern Slaveholders' World View," *Journal of the American Academy of Religion* 55 (Summer 1987): 220–1. See also Eugene D. Genovese and Elizabeth Fox-Genovese, "The Religious Ideals of Southern Slave Society," *Georgia Historical Quarterly* 70 (Spring 1986), and Jack P. Maddex, Jr., "'The Southern Apostacy' Revisited: The Significance of Proslavery Christianity," *Marxist Perspectives* 7 (Fall 1979): 137.

38. For good descriptions of the ideology of the yeomanry, see Steven Hahn, *The Roots of Southern Populism: Yeoman Farmers and the Transformation of the Georgia Upcountry, 1850–1890* (New York and Oxford: Oxford University Press, 1983), and John T. Schlot-

For several reasons, the conservative social views of proslavery ministers went unchallenged by Southern whites. First, the ideals of subordination and patriarchy were specifically tied to the defense of slavery and were probably more acceptable in this context. In addition, Southerners truly believed that black slavery could comfortably coexist with white republicanism. The views of clergymen concurred with the popular Southern precept that black slavery created equality among whites and generated a high spirit of liberty among them. There were further ideological affinities between proslavery Christianity and Southern white republicanism. In the lowcountry of South Carolina, for example, white male yeomen accepted inequality for slaves, women, and other dependents and embraced the organic social vision and particularistic view of social relations that were central to the religious defense of slavery.[39]

IV

Religious proslavery illustrates two themes central to explaining the relationship between religion and the growth of Southern separatism. First, the development and influence of proslavery Christianity involved a dynamic exchange between religious and political discourse. Second, the use of shared national values and ideas was essential in shaping the creation of a sectional proslavery ideology. Before demonstrating these themes, it is important to recognize how the religious defense of slavery changed over time.

The proslavery argument contained a dynamic set of ideas that were continually being recast over the course of the antebellum decades. The Southern defense of slavery became manifest in the early 1820s, ignited by

terbeck, "The 'Social Economy' of an Upper South Community: Orange and Greene Counties, Virginia, 1815–1860," in Orville Vernon Burton and Robert C. McMath, Jr., eds., *Class, Conflict and Consensus: Antebellum Southern Community Studies* (Westport, Conn.: Greenwood Press, 1982), pp. 3–29. On the political ideology of nonslaveholders, see J. Mills Thornton III, *Politics and Power in a Slave Society: Alabama, 1800–1860* (Baton Rouge: Louisiana State University Press, 1978).

39. The coexistence of slavery and republicanism, the Southern insistence that black slavery was necessary to white liberty, has been a complex riddle for historians to unravel. For the colonial and revolutionary eras, see especially Edmund S. Morgan, *American Slavery, American Freedom: The Ordeal of Colonial Virginia* (New York: W. W. Norton, 1975). For the antebellum period, see Robert E. Shalhope, "Thomas Jefferson's Republicanism and Antebellum Southern Thought," *Journal of Southern History* 42 (November 1976): 529–56. For an interesting if labored attempt to demonstrate the compatibility between slavery and republicanism, see Iveson L. Brookes, *A Defense of the South against the Reproaches and Incroachments of the North* (Hamburg, S.C.: Republican Office, 1850); McCurry, "Two Faces of Republicanism," especially p. 1258.

the Missouri controversy and the Denmark Vesey slave plot in South Carolina. The growth of the antislavery movement during the 1830s, with its postal campaign and petition drives to Congress, led to a more fully developed argument that slavery was a "positive good." During these two decades, slavery was justified primarily on scriptural and historical evidence and defended as a benevolent and paternalistic institution. Proslavery thought underwent important transformations in the 1840s. Slavery was now justified on the additional grounds of alleged black racial inferiority. By the 1850s, proslavery thought was moving toward an aggressive culmination. There was a movement in the lower South to reopen the African slave trade and expand the peculiar institution to Central and South America. Some proslavery advocates, notably George Fitzhugh and Henry Hughes, suggested seriously that slavery might become a model for all social relations, suitable for whites as well as blacks. In this context, there was a greater emphasis placed in the late antebellum era on the basic incompatibility between the slave society of the South and the free labor order of the North.[40]

The religious defense of slavery changed over time as well. It responded to some of these larger rhythms in the proslavery argument while simultaneously reflecting its own distinctive pattern of change. In the 1830s, Southern clerical works on slavery may be properly characterized as antiabolitionist. They were a response to the antislavery attack and therefore focused on the scriptural testimony that vindicated human bondage. The biblical defense of slavery remained a staple element in religious proslavery writings through the rest of the antebellum era.

Yet by the late 1840s and especially during the 1850s, religious proslavery arguments became increasingly strident. In 1856, for example, the *Central Presbyterian* of Richmond exalted slavery as "the most blessed and beautiful form of social government known; the only one that solves the problem, how rich and poor may dwell together; a beneficent patriarchate." Four years later, the paper reaffirmed that slavery was a "relation essential to the existence of civilized society." Some Southern clerics, especially in the lower South, argued aggressively for the perpetuation of slavery. "We are sure," heralded the *Texas Baptist* in 1861, "that God has given us the right to buy and own slaves as a perpetual inheritance, and to transmit them to our children." The *Christian Index* of Georgia supported the expansion of slavery to Mexico and Central America be-

40. A good survey of these changes is John M. McCardell, *The Idea of a Southern Nation: Southern Nationalists and Southern Nationalism, 1830–1860* (New York: W. W. Norton, 1979) pp. 49–91. On the 1850s, see especially Genovese and Fox-Genovese, "Divine Sanction of Social Order," p. 223, and Genovese and Fox-Genovese, "Religious Ideals of Southern Slave Society," p. 6.

cause "Providence designs the spreading out of African slavery into regions congenial and suitable to its prosperity." The Rev. E. W. Warren of Georgia expressed the extreme to which religious proslavery attitudes had come by 1861: "Both Christianity and Slavery are from Heaven; both are blessings to humanity; both are to be perpetuated to the end of time." This radicalization of religious proslavery views reflected the general direction of Southern thought in the 1850s.[41]

Proslavery Christianity both contributed to and borrowed from the political discourse on slavery. The biblical justification of human bondage was the most tangible contribution religion made to the Southern cause. It was at least mentioned in practically every piece of proslavery writing in the antebellum South. Thomas R. Dew of Virginia, in his important defense of slavery published in 1832, used the Scriptures to justify slavery. In his *Two Letters on Slavery in the United States* (1845), James Henry Hammond insisted that it was impossible to believe that slavery was "contrary to the will of God." The two major anthologies of proslavery writings in the Old South, *The Proslavery Argument* (1852) and *Cotton is King* (1860), contained substantial sections outlining the biblical justification of human bondage. Southern clergymen in return paid tribute to secular proslavery developments. A Baptist journal in Charleston reprinted a proslavery speech delivered before the citizens of Barnwell Village by Edmund Bellinger. The *Alabama Baptist* published Hammond's letters in 1845, claiming his scriptural argument on slavery was "utterly irresistible." Scientific racism – the ethnological justification for believing in black inferiority – was one secular argument generally absent in the writings of proslavery clerics. As explained earlier, the theory of the plural origins of the races advanced by ethnologists conflicted with the biblical account of creation. To protect the orthodoxy of the Scriptures, clergymen had to distance themselves from these kinds of arguments even as they accepted a racial defense of black enslavement.[42]

Locating the sources of clerical ideas on slavery and abolition also sheds valuable light on their significance. It is clear that proslavery clergymen drew upon nationally shared intellectual resources – the Bible and natural law – to create a distinctive sectional ideology. The "Americanness" of Southern religious proslavery beliefs is further suggested by the

---

41. *Central Presbyterian*, March 22, 1856; *Central Presbyterian*, January 28, 1860; *Texas Baptist*, January 3, 1861; *Christian Index*, February 27, 1861; *Christian Index*, February 13, 1861. See also Thrasher, *Slavery a Divine Institution*, p. 21, and for an early expression of these views, see [Mell], *Slavery*, p. 36.

42. McCardell, *Idea of a Southern Nation*, p. 54; Lloyd, *The Slavery Controversy*, p. 177; *Southern Baptist and General Intelligencer*, September 18, 1835; *Alabama Baptist*, July 19, 1845.

high number of Northern-born clergymen active in the proslavery movement. Theodore Clapp, for example, was a New Orleans minister born in Massachusetts and educated at Harvard. He wrote a lengthy justification of human bondage, published in 1835 as *Slavery*. Northerners brought to proslavery a conservative view of society and hierarchical assumptions inherited from New England Federalism in the early part of the nineteenth century. These ideas surfaced in proslavery thought in the writings of transplanted Northern clergymen. In addition, the conservative values of New England Federalists infiltrated the South through the voluntary associations and reform societies of the "Benevolent Empire." Lingering vestiges of New England Federalism served to reinforce conservative and organic thought already existing in the South. Secular proslavery thinkers, from Thomas R. Dew to Henry Hughes, had developed justifications for inequality and hierarchy in the social order. Politicians like John C. Calhoun and James Henry Hammond had helped overturn the natural rights philosophy of the American Revolution.[43]

If Northern influences shaped the ideological content and expression of religious proslavery, the structure and nature of antebellum Southern society provided perhaps its original foundation. As emphatically stated by Eugene D. Genovese and Elizabeth Fox-Genovese: "The distinctive religious character of antebellum southern society was directly related to slavery as a social system." The values of inequality and hierarchy that were the essence of religious proslavery were precisely those values forged in the paternalistic relations between master and slave and planter and yeoman. Religious proslavery clearly reflected and served the interests of the slaveholding class of the antebellum South. Not surprisingly, many proslavery ministers came from these ranks. James Smylie, for example, pastor of the Presbyterian Church in Port Gibson, Mississippi, wrote a religious defense of slavery in 1836. Smylie owned fifty-three slaves, making him the third largest slaveowner in Amite County, Mississippi. One historian has estimated that a little over 50 percent of the clergy in Beaufort, Columbia, and Spartanburg, South Carolina, owned slaves. These figures lend support to one historian's contention that "proslavery Christianity took form as a coherent ideological expression by conscientious ruling class Christians who experienced the master–slave relationship as normative." As both a product of the Southern social environment and

43. On Clapp, see Tise, *Proslavery*, p. 327. The significance of Northerners in the development of Southern proslavery is a central theme of Tise, *Proslavery*, especially chap. 6. On benevolent societies in the South, see John W. Kuykendall, *Southern Enterprize: The Work of National Evangelical Societies in the Antebellum South* (Westport, Conn.: Greenwood Press, 1982).

national ideological influences, proslavery Christianity exhibits the dual threads that composed the fabric of antebellum Southern separatism.[44]

V

The justification of slavery based on the Bible and natural law and the portrayal of abolitionism as infidelity were perhaps the most visible and influential contributions religion made to the cause of Southern separatism. Proslavery clergymen had forged a formidable alliance between religion, morality, and slavery that could withstand the onslaught of abolition. They had bestowed divine sanction on the South's peculiar institution. Having securely established the rectitude of human bondage, Southern clergymen ventured boldly forth to make the practice of Southern slaveholders conform to the moral law of God.

44. Genovese and Fox-Genovese, "Religious Ideals of Southern Slave Society," p. 2; Holifield, *Gentlemen Theologians,* pp. 11, 30, 221. In comparison, Otto H. Olsen estimates that 31 percent of white families owned slaves in the states that would form the Confederacy. "Historians and the Extent of Slave Ownership in the Southern United States," *Civil War History* 18 (June 1972): 111; Jack P. Maddex, Jr., " 'The Southern Apostacy' Revisited: The Significance of Proslavery Christianity," *Marxist Perspectives* 7 (Fall 1979): 137.

3

Slavery sanctified: The slaveholding ethic and the religious mission to the slaves

As a Presbyterian pastor, educator, and theologian, Robert Lewis Dabney of Virginia had little time to read newspapers. Yet the sectional crisis of 1850 seems to have kindled his political interests. In 1851, he wrote a series of articles on the slavery controversy for the Richmond *Enquirer*. Earlier that year, Dabney had penned a long letter to his brother in which he mused over the relations between North and South. "This question of *moral right*," Dabney insisted, "is at the bottom of the whole matter." Behind the Wilmot Proviso and the entire Northern effort to stop the spread of slavery in the territories was the simple and basic belief that slavery was wrong. To Dabney, this was a religious and ethical position that was most effectively met by the Bible. Because the Bible defended slavery, pressing the sectional controversy on the Word of God would push the abolitionists "to unveil their true infidel tendencies." They would be forced to array themselves against the Bible, which would alienate true believers in the North. The end result would be to compel the "whole Christianity of the North" to ally itself with the slaveholding South.

Dabney then added a long and significant caveat that laid bare one of the most basic assumptions of religious proslavery:

> But to enjoy the advantages of this Bible argument in our favor slaveholders will have to pay a price. And the price is this. They must be willing to recognize and grant in slaves those rights which are a part of our essential humanity, some of which are left without recognition or guarantee by law, and some infringed by law. These are the rights of immortal and domestic beings. If we take the ground that the power to neglect and infringe these interests is an essential and necessary part of the institution of slavery; then it cannot be defended.

As he made explicit in this passage, slavery could be defended only as a Christian institution.[1]

After they had established the rectitude of slavery, Southern clergymen proceeded to broaden and deepen its identification with religion and morality. They devised a slaveholding ethic to guide the conduct of masters toward their servants. They called for and were instrumental in establishing religious missions to bring the Gospel into the slave quarters. Along with the biblical defense of slavery, the slaveholding ethic and the religious mission to the slaves constituted a distinctive and coherent ideology aimed at sanctifying slavery, a conscious effort to make the South's peculiar institution conform to the moral laws of God.

The clerical effort to sanctify slavery illustrates several of the major factors that shaped the relationship between religion and the growth of Southern separatism. To become involved with slavery, ministers had to draw a crucial distinction between its civil and religious realms, again defining the boundaries between religion and sectional politics. Like the defense of slavery, the slaveholding ethic and religious mission to the slaves were also products of common American intellectual resources adapted to the sectional purpose of sanctifying slavery. Moral philosophy, a popular academic discipline designed for a systematic study of ethics, provided Southern clergymen with the framework and vocabulary for creating a Christian code of conduct for slaveholders. Evangelicalism, the dominant mode of religious expression in antebellum America, was a driving force behind the religious mission to the slaves. Finally, the sanctification of slavery shows how the characteristics and social role of Southern clergymen shaped their sectional ideology.

I

The sanctification of slavery necessitated Southern clergymen to define the proper boundaries between religion and politics. The essential outline of their position was first articulated during the abolitionist crisis of 1835. Southern ministers generally condemned clerical involvement in politics, except if a political issue was perceived as possessing any kind of *moral* significance. Then clergymen claimed that it fell within their realm and justified their attention. These guidelines were forged in the specific context of the slavery controversy and were thus reflected in the arguments used to gain access to the slaves.

Southern clergymen began with the assumption that slavery contained

1. Thomas C. Johnson, *The Life and Letters of Robert Lewis Dabney* (Richmond, Va.: The Presbyterian Committee of Publication, 1903), pp. 128–9.

two distinct but related realms, the civil and the religious. The Rev. E. T. Baird, a Presbyterian minister from Crawfordsville, Mississippi, viewed this dichotomy in terms of a partnership. He conceded that the state had jurisdiction over the physical well-being and civil rights of the slaves, "but those other duties, pertaining to the spiritual welfare of the servant" belonged to the church. What separated the civil and religious realms of slavery was the principle of morality. To Southern clergymen, slavery raised certain moral questions that called for their counsel. Indeed, the synonymy between religion and morality became the basis for distinguishing between the civil and religious aspects of slavery. The language of sermons, newspaper editorials, and even personal correspondence testifies to this emphasis placed on morality. In a report on the religious instruction of slaves, Presbyterians in the Synod of South Carolina and Georgia assured anxious planters "that we separate entirely [the slave's] *nmoral* and their *civil condition*." Richard Furman, a Baptist clergyman from Beaufort, South Carolina, began his proslavery address by stating that he was considering his subject "in a moral and religious point of view." In requesting a copy of James H. Thornwell's sermon on slavery, a student at Emory University emphasized to the Presbyterian divine that "it is not so essential that I should form any opinion with reference to any part of the question except the moral and religious." That morality was the defining element in the religious realm of slavery was reaffirmed by the Nashville *Christian Advocate* during the secession crisis: "But when emancipationists urge their scheme on moral grounds; when the assumed idea that slavery is a sin underlies their plans, it is time for Bible Christians to intervene in that extent, and help to withdraw from the controversy its moral and religious element."[2]

The suspicion ministers encountered during the abolitionist crisis of 1835 forced them to drive this wedge of morality between the civil and religious spheres even deeper and to disavow any involvement in the former. Clergymen heeded the lessons of 1835 and steered clear of politics when discussing slavery. "So far as the practice of Slavery is connected with the political institutions of the country," declared the Rev. Samuel

---

2. E. T. Baird, "The Religious Instruction of our Coloured Population," *Southern Presbyterian Review* 12 (July 1959): 319; *Report of the Committee to Whom Was Referred the Subject of the Religious Instruction of the Colored Population of the Synod of South Carolina and Georgia* (Charleston, S.C.: *Observer* Office Press, 1834), p. 25; Richard Furman, *Rev. Dr. Richard Furman's Exposition of the Views of the Baptists, Relative to the Coloured Population in the United States* (1822; reprint ed., Charleston, S.C.: A. E. Miller, 1833), p. 3; John Patillo to James H. Thornwell, November 9, 1852, James H. Thornwell Papers, South Caroliniana Library, University of South Carolina, Columbia; *Christian Advocate*, February 21, 1861.

Dunwody of South Carolina at the beginning of his proslavery sermon, "I have nothing to do." Denying any interest in the political aspect of slaveholding became an important measure when Southern clerics sought religious access to slaves. This attitude was evident in a warning given to missionaries by the Methodist South Carolina Conference in 1836: "We advise the brethren to go on in their work, without regard to political discussions of any kind. They have no time, and we trust, no inclination, for anything aside of their grand aim, the salvation of souls." Three years later, South Carolina Methodists reiterated their promise, while evangelizing slaves, not to meddle with "the delicate questions of political rights, of forms of civil and social organizations." Undoubtedly, Southern clergymen found this two-realm theory of slavery useful in gaining religious access to the slaves. It provided a convenient and convincing rationale to masters that clergymen would neither question the institution nor stir up discontent among the slaves.[3]

The moral dimension of slavery became the ideological imperative for developing a slaveholding ethic. To Southern clerics, the biblical vindication of human bondage was inextricably linked to the just and moral treatment of slaves. The religious defense of slavery, as Robert Lewis Dabney had said in 1851, was conditional upon the adherence to certain ethical standards. The Rev. E. T. Baird of Mississippi explained further: "The Scriptural argument for slavery, as an institution recognized by God, has no force the moment we deny these moral and religious duties; but, in so far as we recognize the Scriptural argument, it carries with it a tremendous power in enforcing on the conscience of the master these heavy and tremendous obligations for which he must render an account to God." Slavery became immoral only when the ethical guidelines for slaveholding were not met. The *Biblical Recorder and Southern Watchman* of North Carolina admitted that slaveholding, "like all other practices, is capable of abuses, and may easily be rendered sinful by the sinful usages connected or incorporated with it." In a sermon on the mutual duties of masters and slaves, Joseph R. Wilson of Augusta, Georgia, warned that slavery would be wrong "only when masters and servants misconceive and abuse their relationship to each other." A Virginian agreed that any sin associated with slavery "lies not in the relations, but in neglecting to perform the duties which the relation involves."[4]

3. Samuel Dunwody, *A Sermon upon the Subject of Slavery* (Columbia, S.C.: S. Weir, 1837), p. 3; *Minutes of the South Carolina Conference of the Methodist Episcopal Church, for the year 1836* (Charleston, S.C.: J. S. Burges, 1836), p. 21; *Minutes of the South Carolina Conference of the Methodist Episcopal Church, for the year 1839* (Charleston, S.C.: Burges & James, 1839), p. 14.

4. Baird, "The Religious Instruction of our Coloured Population," p. 347; *Biblical Recorder*

II

Although religion gave impetus to the slaveholding ethic, moral philosophy provided its main conceptual framework. Like the justification of human bondage by the Bible and natural law, the slaveholding ethic was a product of the sectionalization of a national intellectual resource. Southerners borrowed selectively but legitimately from the precepts of moral philosophy to construct an ideology that was explicitly sectional. In this way, the slaveholding ethic underscores the centrality of American thought in the creation of Southern distinctiveness. Moral philosophy was a nineteenth-century academic discipline designed to provide a systematic basis for the study of ethics, covering a wide range of subjects from mental philosophy (psychology) to political theory. Although many Northern moral philosophers, such as the influential Francis Wayland of Brown University, held antislavery views, the emphasis moral philosophy placed on rights, duties, and relations as categories of analysis made it highly useful to Southern clergymen concerned with the relationship between master and servant. What really made moral philosophy so attractive to Southern clergymen was its intimate link with religion. Strongly wedded to Protestantism, moral philosophers wanted to give a rational basis to God's moral law. Antebellum moral philosophy relied heavily on the assumptions and methods of Common Sense Realism, an intellectual legacy of the Scottish Enlightenment highly influential in America. Particularly important to moral philosophers was the notion of conscience, an innate moral sense that verified the rationality of moral judgments. By providing a discourse for philosophical debate that was firmly grounded in religion, moral philosophy and its Scottish Common Sense background were thus instrumental in articulating a slaveholding ethic.[5]

and *Southern Watchman*, October 17, 1840; Joseph R. Wilson, *Mutual Duties of Masters and Slaves as Taught in the Bible. A Discourse Preached in the First Presbyterian Church, Augusta, Georgia, on Sabbath Morning, January 6, 1861* (Augusta: Steam Press of Chronicle & Sentinel, 1861), p. 12; S. Taylor, *Relation of Master and Servant, as Exhibited in the New Testament* (Richmond, Va.: T. W. White, 1836), p. 11.

5. E. Brooks Holifield, *The Gentlemen Theologians: American Theology in Southern Culture, 1795–1860* (Durham, N.C.: Duke University Press, 1978), pp. 127–33. On the tradition of moral philosophy in nineteenth-century America, see Donald H. Meyer, *The Instructed Conscience: The Shaping of the American National Ethic* (Philadelphia: University of Pennsylvania Press, 1972); Daniel Walker Howe, *The Unitarian Conscience: Harvard Moral Philosophy* (Cambridge, Mass.: Harvard University Press, 1970); Wilson Smith, *Professors and Public Ethics: Northern Moral Philosophy Before the Civil War* (Ithaca, N.Y.: Published for the American Historical Association by Cornell University Press, 1956); Theodore Dwight Bozeman, *Protestants in an Age of Science: The Baconian Ideal and Antebellum American Religious Thought* (Chapel Hill: University of North

"The Christian Doctrine of Slavery," a sermon delivered in Charleston on May 26, 1850, by the renowned Presbyterian theologian James Henley Thornwell, clearly illustrates this intellectual influence. Conversant in theology, philosophy, and literature, Thornwell was one of the leading intellectuals of the Old South. George Bancroft considered him "the most learned of the learned." He was born in 1812 on a plantation in Marlborough District, South Carolina, the son of an overseer. Thornwell was educated at South Carolina College and studied theology briefly at Andover Seminary in New England. He was a leader in ecclesiastical affairs throughout his life, staunchly defending Presbyterian orthodoxy against liberal onslaughts. Thornwell was equally active and influential outside the church. He served as president of South Carolina College and for a short time edited the *Southern Quarterly Review*. Loyal to his native land, Thornwell was a resolute defender of slavery and became a Southern nationalist in 1861.[6]

Explicitly written as a defense of the religious instruction of slaves, Thornwell's Charleston sermon was in essence a philosophical vindication of slavery and a carefully reasoned demonstration of the Christian duties

Carolina Press, 1977). For a good introduction to the Scottish "science of man," see Gladys Bryson, *Man and Society: The Scottish Inquiry of the Eighteenth Century* (Princeton, N.J.: Princeton University Press, 1945). On Common Sense philosophy, see Selwyn A. Grave, *The Scottish Philosophy of Common Sense* (Oxford: Clarendon Press, 1960). Scottish thought has recently received a great deal of attention from intellectual historians. See for example J. David Hoeveler, *James McCosh and the Scottish Intellectual Tradition: From Glasgow to Princeton* (Princeton, N.J.: Princeton University Press, 1981); Richard B. Sher, *Church and University in the Scottish Enlightenment: The Moderate Literati of Edinburgh* (Princeton, N.J.: Princeton University Press, 1985); Istvan Hont and Michael Ignatieff, eds., *Wealth and Virtue: The Shaping of Political Economy in the Scottish Enlightenment* (Cambridge: Cambridge University Press, 1983); Nicholas T. Phillipson, "The Scottish Enlightenment," in *The Enlightenment in National Context,* eds. Roy Porter and Mikulas Teich (Cambridge: Cambridge University Press, 1981); and "Culture and Society in the Eighteenth Century Province: The Case of Edinburgh and the Scottish Enlightenment" in *The University in Society, Vol. 2,* ed. Lawrence Stone (Princeton, N.J.: Princeton University Press, 1974). On the influence of Scottish thought in America, consult Henry F. May, *The Enlightenment in America* (New York: Oxford University Press, 1976), and Douglas Sloan, *The Scottish Enlightenment and the American College Ideal* (New York: Columbia University Press, 1971).

6. Benjamin M. Palmer, *The Life and Letters of James Henley Thornwell, D.D., LL.D.* (Richmond, Va.: Whittet & Shepperson, 1875), p. 537. Palmer's biography, although dated, is still a valuable source on Thornwell's thought. See also James Oscar Farmer, Jr., *The Metaphysical Confederacy: James Henley Thornwell and the Synthesis of Southern Values* (Macon, Ga.: Mercer University Press, 1986). William W. Freehling offers another interpretation of Thornwell's views on slavery. "James Henley Thornwell's Mysterious Antislavery Moment," *Journal of Southern History* 57 (August 1991): 383–406.

of masters. Because Thornwell was a theologian heavily influenced by
Scottish thinkers and a Southerner eager to provide a solid philosophical
foundation for the religious defense of slavery, his address provides an
excellent means for observing the influence of moral philosophy and its
Scottish sources on the sanctification of slavery.[7]

The heart of Thornwell's sermon dealt with the question of the definition of slavery. In particular, Thornwell sought to refute the arguments of
antislavery intellectuals William Ellery Channing and William Whewell.
As pastor of the Federal Street Church in Boston, Channing was the
leading Unitarian clergyman of his era. His brief book *Slavery* (1835) gave
intellectual respectability to the growing abolitionist crusade. William
Whewell was an English moral philosopher who, according to the *Southern Presbyterian Review,* exerted widespread influence in New England.
Both Channing and Whewell defined slavery as the property of man in
man. "The very idea of a slave," Channing wrote, "is that he belongs to
another, that he is bound to live and labour for another, to be another's
instrument, and to make another's will his habitual law, however adverse
to his own." By divesting the slave of his humanity, Whewell explained,
human bondage was "contrary to the fundamental principles of morality.
It neglects the great primary distinction of persons and things – converting a person into a thing, an object merely passive, without any recognized attributes of human nature." As Thornwell understood the logic of
Channing and Whewell, slavery was thus wrong because it denied a man
his humanity and converted him into a chattel.[8]

Thornwell insisted that this argument was fundamentally false and proceeded to attack it. The core of his refutation of Channing and Whewell
was his belief that the slave, "in his moral, religious and intellectual nature," enjoyed "the same humanity in which we glory as the image of
God." Drawing upon the Scottish Common Sense exaltation of the conscience, Thornwell explained that what made the slave human was his
possession of a conscience – that is, his moral nature. Echoing Scottish
philosophers, he described the conscience as "*the moral and responsible
agency.*" As a "faculty and element of human nature," the conscience was

7. On the Scottish background to Thornwell's thought, see Mitchell Snay, "American
Thought and Southern Distinctiveness: The Southern Clergy and the Sanctification of
Slavery," *Civil War History* 35 (December 1989): 314–15.
8. Benjamin M. Palmer, *The Life and Letters of James Henley Thornwell, D.D., LL.D.*
(Richmond, Va.: Whittet & Shepperson, 1875), p. 345; William Sumner Jenkins, *Pro-
slavery Thought in the Old South* (Chapel Hill: University of North Carolina Press, 1935),
p. 228; James H. Thornwell, "The Christian Doctrine of Slavery," in *The Collected
Writings of James Henley Thornwell, D.D., LL.D.,* eds. John B. Adger and John L.
Girardeau (Richmond, Va.: Presbyterian Committee of Publication, 1873), pp. 408–9.

inviolate. It "can never be owned by another; it is not an article of barter or exchange." Thornwell reinforced this crucial point by comparing the conscience to a natural human organ, an analogical method of reasoning common among moral philosophers: "We do not even pretend that the organs of the body can be said strictly to belong to another. The limbs and members of my servant are not mine, but his."[9]

If a slave possessed a conscience, and if this conscience could not be taken away or owned by another, then slavery could not divest its victims of their humanity because a slave never ceased to be human. Channing and Whewell were thus wrong in their assertion that slavery was the property of man in man. Instead, Thornwell maintained, slavery consisted in the "obligation to labour for another, determined by the Providence of God, independently of the provisions of a contract." A master did not own a servant but, rather, the labor of a servant: "The right which the master has is a right, not to the *man,* but to his labour; the duty which the slave owes is the service which, in conformity with this right, the master exacts."[10]

Thornwell's recognition that the slave possessed an inviolate moral nature became the cornerstone of his slaveholding ethic. A logical corollary of the slave's humanity was that the institution of slavery became a set of relations between morally responsible beings. In developing this theme, Thornwell revealed his intellectual reliance upon moral philosophy. A dominant theme of Southern ethical thought was the category of relations, another intellectual heritage of Scottish philosophy. In his *Elements of Moral Philosophy* (1859), the Methodist R. H. Rivers of Alabama stated that it was the purpose of moral science "to exhibit man in his relations" to other men, to the law, and to God. Thornwell coupled these two essential ideas of moral philosophy, the notion of the conscience and the category of relations, in defining slavery: "It is a relation of man to man – a form of civil society of which persons are the only elements – and not a relation of man to things."[11]

The concept of relations provided by moral philosophy furnished a justification for the next stage in the development of the slaveholding ethic: the ideal of mutual responsibility between master and servant. Southern moral philosophy textbooks emphasized the notion that the duties and obligations of man were determined by his various relations

9. Thornwell, "Christian Doctrine of Slavery," p. 403; Holifield, *Gentlemen Theologians,* pp. 131–3; Thornwell, "Christian Doctrine of Slavery," pp. 412–13. On the use of analogy in moral philosophy, see Meyer, *Instructed Conscience,* p. 43.
10. Thornwell, "Christian Doctrine of Slavery," p. 414.
11. Holifield, *Gentlemen Theologians,* p. 146; Thornwell, "Christian Doctrine of Slavery," p. 410.

in society. They spoke of the duties of citizen and ruler and child and parent, for instance, rather than those of "man" as an abstraction. In advocating the principle of mutual responsibility between master and slave, Thornwell reflected these tenets of moral philosophy. He too believed that "the specific duties – the things actually required to be done – are as various as the circumstances in which men are placed." Like most moral philosophers, Thornwell linked rights with conditions. No proposition could be clearer, he argued, "than that the rights of man must be ultimately traced to his duties, and are nothing more than the obligations of his fellows to let him alone in the discharge of all the functions, and the enjoyment of all the blessings, of his lot."[12]

Thornwell's Christian doctrine of slavery united these notions of moral philosophy with the scriptural defense of human bondage. The Presbyterian divine argued that such concepts as the innate moral nature of the slave, the category of relations, and the linkage of duties with conditions were present in the apostolic sanction of slavery. Unlike Channing and Whewell, "the Apostles did not regard the personality of the slave as lost or swallowed up in the property of the master." Instead, he was considered a responsible, moral agent, "possessed of conscience, reason, and will." The relationship between master and servant was accordingly regarded by the apostle "as a social and political economy, in which relations subsisted betwixt moral, intelligent, responsible beings, involving reciprocal rights and reciprocal obligations." The idea that duties flowed from one's condition in a relation was also sanctioned by God. The Apostle Paul told slaves "that their services to their masters are duties which they owe to God – that a moral character attaches to their works, and that they are the subjects of praise or blame according to the principles upon which their obedience is rendered." The apostolic injunction applied to masters as well as servants. It was the responsibility of Christianity, Thornwell believed, "to enforce upon masters the necessity, the moral obligation, of rendering to their bondmen that which is just and equal." Thus a view of slavery that recognized the humanity of the slave and the moral responsibility incumbent on both master and servant "was clearly the aspect in which the Apostle contemplated the subject."[13]

Thornwell's sermon on slavery demonstrates how the major precepts of American moral philosophy and Scottish Common Sense Realism provided an ideological foundation for the slaveholding ethic. These ideas

---

12. Holifield, *Gentlemen Theologians,* pp. 146–7; Thornwell, "Christian Doctrine of Slavery," pp. 423–6.
13. Thornwell, "Christian Doctrine of Slavery," pp. 410, 411–12.

complemented and gave a rational basis to the evangelical impulse toward Christianizing slavery. Many Southern ministers who wrote on slavery echoed Thornwell's ideas, revealing the widespread influence of Scottish ethical thought. They portrayed slavery as a relationship between morally responsible beings. They argued that the just treatment of slaves was a natural moral law dictated by the conscience. "The duties a master owes to his servants," argued the Rev. H. N. McTyeire of New Orleans, "are as binding upon the conscience as those the servant owes to the master: neither can be neglected without sin." Here, the conscience was considered as God's moral law written in man's heart, reflecting again the harmony between moral philosophy and religion. The Rev. H. T. Holmes, a Baptist minister from Hayneville, Georgia, maintained that "the law of equity dwells in the heart, is regulated by circumstances, and determines according to its convictions of right and wrong." Holmes thus saw the just treatment of slaves as a natural law dictated by the conscience and if violated, punishable by God.[14]

The prominent influence of moral philosophy in the sanctification of slavery can be partially explained by the fact that many proslavery ministers also taught college in the antebellum South. Thornwell, for example, taught logic and belles lettres at South Carolina College and theology at the Presbyterian Theological Seminary in Columbia. Stephen Elliott, the bishop of the Protestant Episcopal Church in Georgia, was another strong defender of slavery. In the 1830s, Elliott was a professor of sacred literature at South Carolina College. He later helped found the University of the South at Sewannee. Even Charles Colcock Jones, the well-known founder of the Liberty County Association for the Religious Instruction of Negroes, was for some time professor of church history at Columbia Theological Seminary. The academic involvements of these proslavery ministers undoubtedly helped strengthen the links between the teaching of ethics and the sanctification of slavery, suggesting the importance of social role in explaining clerical ideology.[15]

14. H. N. McTyeire, C. F. Sturgis, and A. T. Holmes, *Duties of Masters and Servants: Three Premium Essays* (Charleston, S.C.: Southern Baptist Publication Society, 1851), pp. 8, 135. For another example of the influence of moral philosophy on the slaveholding ethic, see John B. Adger, *The Religious Instruction of the Colored Population. A Sermon Preached by the Rev. John B. Adger, in the Second Presbyterian Church, Charleston, S.C. May 9th, 1847* (Charleston, S.C.: T. W. Haynes, 1847), p. 6.

15. Samuel S. Hill, Jr., ed., *Encyclopedia of Religion in the South* (Macon, Ga.: Mercer University Press, 1984), pp. 780, 223-4, 336. For further information on Jones, see Donald G. Mathews, "Charles Colcock Jones and the Southern Evangelical Crusade to Form a Biracial Community," *Journal of Southern History* 40 (August 1975): 299-320, and Erskine Clark, *Wrestlin' Jacob: A Portrait of Religion in the Old South* (Atlanta: John Knox Press, 1979), pp. 1-81.

III

"But of all other duties that masters owe to their servants," declared the Rev. Samuel Dunwody of South Carolina, "there is none so important, as that of teaching them the genuine precepts of religion." The two-realm theory of slavery and the logic of the slaveholding ethic provided a basis for religious missions to the slaves. Throughout the antebellum era, Southern clergymen launched extensive efforts to bring the Gospel to enslaved blacks on the plantations and in the towns of the South. The impressive network of missions created by the clergy is vivid testimony to their deeply rooted desire to Christianize the peculiar institution. Their appeals to Southern slaveholders for religious missions offer further insight into the meaning of the sanctification of slavery.[16]

The axioms of both moral philosophy and evangelicalism led logically toward giving religious attention to the slaves. From the former, masters not only learned that certain duties accompanied their position but also that their servants were human beings possessed of a moral nature that deserved spiritual attention. Evangelicalism complemented these ideas with the belief that all men and women, bond as well as free, stood as equals before God. "For though they are slaves," explained the Baptist leader Richard Furman in 1822, "they are also men; and are with ourselves accountable creatures; having immortal souls, and being destined to future eternal award." The Mississippi Presbyterian E. T. Baird insisted that the "Savior Jesus who died for us, died for them." A New Orleans Baptist argued similarly that concerning God and eternity, "ser-

16. Dunwody, *A Sermon Upon the Subject of Slavery*, p. 26. The religious mission to the slave was an enigmatic movement that reveals the complexity and subtle ambivalences of slavery. As such, it has appropriately lured the interest of historians of religion, Southern society, and the black experience in America. The best monographic treatments of the subject include Erskine Clark, *Wrestlin' Jacob;* Milton Sernett, *Black Religion and American Evangelicalism: White Protestants, Plantation Missions, and the Flowering of Negro Christianity, 1787–1865* (Metuchen, N.J.: Scarecrow Press, 1975); Albert J. Raboteau, *Slave Religion: The Invisible Institution of the Old South* (New York: Oxford University Press, 1978). Donald G. Mathews, *Religion in the Old South* (Chicago: University of Chicago Press, 1977); Loveland, *Southern Evangelicals and the Social Order*; and Eugene D. Genovese, *Roll, Jordan, Roll: The World the Slaves Made* (New York: Pantheon Books, 1974) have perceptive treatments of the subject. Of the many articles, see Carlton Hayden, "Conversion and Control: Dilemma of Episcopalians in Providing for the Religious Instruction of Slaves, Charleston, South Carolina, 1845–1860," *Historical Magazine of the Protestant Episcopal Church* 36 (March 1967): 35–61; Timothy Reilly, "Slavery and the Southwestern Evangelist in New Orleans (1800–1861)," *Journal of Mississippi History* 41 (November 1979): 301–18; George C. Whately, "The Alabama Presbyterian and His Slave, 1830–1864," *Alabama Review* 13 (January 1960): 40–51.

vants stand upon a common platform with their master." At a meeting of
the Association for the Religious Instruction of the Negroes in Liberty
County, Georgia, both clergymen and laymen affirmed their belief in the
spiritual equality between master and slave: "There is a variety of nations,
there are different degrees of civilization, and different degrees of guilt,
but there is but one salvation." The evangelical precept that each person
had the potential for spiritual salvation proved a strong reminder to masters of their religious obligations to their servants.[17]

Echoes of moral philosophy and evangelicalism are distinctly audible in
clerical pleas for these missionary endeavors. "Among Christian people,"
declared the *Southern Presbyterian Review,* "there can be but one opinion
as to the *duty* of providing for the religious instruction of the slave. The
Gospel is God's message of salvation to the *bond* as well as the *free.*" The
Rev. H. N. McTyeire of New Orleans reminded each master that he had
souls as well as bodies under his care, so the "responsibility of eternal as
well as temporal interests rests upon his shoulders." A judicial decision
involving the payment of a minister for teaching slaves suggests that these
ideas infused secular discourse on slavery. "Though they are property,"
insisted the Supreme Court of Alabama, "they are intelligent beings, and
under moral accountability. The master, or whoever stands in his place, is
morally bound to furnish his dependent and subject class such moral and
religious instruction as is adapted to its political status." With the combined influence of moral philosophy and evangelicalism, Southern clerics
had primed the consciences of slaveowners for a missionary crusade to
bring the Gospel to the slaves.[18]

The first stirring of this impulse surfaced in the 1820s. Its sources were
varied and complex. Smoldering antislavery embers among Southern
evangelicals might have sparked the desire to squelch the worst abuses of
slavery. Nationally, the evangelical revivals of the Second Great Awakening had ignited an intense fervor to save souls. In the slaveholding
South, this sentiment would be channeled to the slaves, who were poor,

17. Furman, *Exposition of the Views of the Baptists,* p. 13; Baird, "The Religious Instruction
    of Our Colored Population," p. 352; *Duties of Masters and Servants,* p. 35; *Seventh
    Annual Report of the Association for the Religious Instruction of the Negroes in Liberty
    County, Georgia* (Savannah, Ga.: Thomas Purse, 1842), p. 15. For further evidence, see
    *Minutes of the South Carolina Conference of the Methodist Episcopal Church for the Year
    1832* (Charleston, S.C.: James S. Burges, 1832), p. 11, and *Southern Presbyterian Review*
    4 (July 1850): 111.
18. *Southern Presbyterian Review* 1 (September 1847): 142; "Duties of Masters and Ser-
    vants," p. 36; James B. Sellers, *Slavery in Alabama* (University: University of Alabama
    Press, 1950), p. 295. For a similar view of slavery in the Southern legal system, see Mark
    Tushnet, *The American Law of Slavery, 1810–1860* (Princeton, N.J.: Princeton Univer-
    sity Press, 1981).

oppressed, and destitute of religion. The Denmark Vesey slave conspiracy in Charleston in 1822 and Nat Turner's revolt in Virginia in 1831 were equally important in explaining the rise of the religious mission to the slaves. The association between slave religion and rebellion that emerged from these events probably alerted Southern slaveholders to the need for white control of Afro-American religion. Finally, the abolitionist assault on the morality of slavery in the 1830s wakened Southern clerics to the need to make Southern slavery moral and Christian. Fanny Kemble, who observed Georgia plantation life in the 1830s, believed that the "outcry which has been raised with three-fold force within the last few years against the whole system had induced its upholders and defenders to adopt . . . some appearance of religious instruction."[19]

The first denomination in the South to take up missionary work among the slaves were the Methodists. In 1829, William Capers of Charleston helped form the Methodist Missionary Society for the lowcountry of South Carolina. That same year, the missionary committee of the Mississippi Methodist Conference began to explore the feasibility of religious instruction to the slaves. In 1831, Alabama Methodists appointed 2 missionaries to "people of color" in Madison and Limestone counties. As a result of their missionary zeal, theological simplicity, and emotional appeal, the Methodists remained the leaders in spiritual endeavors among blacks. By the 1840s, eighty Methodist missionaries were serving the religious needs of more than 20,000 slaves. The report submitted by the Dayton mission to the Alabama Conference in 1855 illustrates the depth of Methodist involvement. Beginning with 10 active missionaries, they ended the year with 14. More than 1,700 slaves were reached by their preaching. Missionaries baptized 17 adults and 45 children and added 338 new members to the Methodist Church.[20]

The other major denominations in the South followed the Methodist lead. After they had formed a separate sectional church in 1845, Southern Baptists told their Board of Domestic Missions to "take all prudent measures for the religious instruction of the colored population." Presbyterians could point with pride to the indefatigable labors of the Rev.

19. Mathews, *Religion in the Old South*, p. 139; Loveland, *Southern Evangelicals and the Social Order*, pp. 221–2, 227; Donald B. Touchstone, "Planters and Slave Religion in the Deep South," Ph.D. diss., Tulane University, 1973, p. 37. See also Raboteau, *Slave Religion*, p. 161.

20. Loveland, *Southern Evangelicals and the Social Order*, p. 227; Marjorie Jordan, "Mississippi Methodists and the Division of the Church over Slavery," Ph.D. diss., University of Southern Mississippi, 1972, p. 192; Touchstone, "Planters and Slave Religion in the Deep South," p. 46; Sellers, *Slavery in Alabama*, p. 301; Loveland, *Southern Evangelicals and the Social Order*, p. 227; Sellers, *Slavery in Alabama*, p. 304.

Charles Colcock Jones of Liberty County, Georgia. From 1832 to 1847, Jones offered religious instruction to the slaves on the coastal plantations in his area. His missionary efforts were institutionalized in the Liberty County Association for the Religious Instruction of Negroes. Jones also published a catechism for slaves that became quite popular in the antebellum South. Although Episcopalians were less active than the other denominations, one tireless missionary, Bishop Nicholas Cobb of Alabama, baptized more than 1,500 blacks from 1845 to 1860.[21]

The mission to the slaves was perhaps most prominent in the plantation region of the lower South. Slaves received religious instruction in a variety of ways, from catechetical instruction for children to regular Sunday preaching for adults. Some estates had full-time preachers. Mississippi planter Greenwood Leflore employed a minister to preach to his nearly 400 slaves every Sunday. On a plantation near Natchez, Dr. William Mercer built a chapel and rectory for his slaves, paying a rector $1,200 a year for his services. Often, members of the planter class did the religious teaching. In 1835, the Liberty County Association recommended that masters devote the Sabbath or another night each week to the religious edification of their servants. At least some planter families heeded this advice. Dr. Martin W. Philips of Mississippi instructed his slaves for an hour each Sabbath evening. In 1857, Eliza B. Magruder, a plantation mistress near Washington, Mississippi, "commenced sunday school for the darkeys."[22]

Ministers argued that bringing the Gospel to the slave quarters would be beneficial in two ways. By making masters conscious of their obligations and inculcating obedience and passivity in slaves, the mission would

---

21. Loveland, *Southern Evangelicals and the Social Order*, p. 231; Clark, *Wrestlin' Jacob*, p. xii and pp. 3–81; Sellers, *Slavery in Alabama*, p. 319.

22. Loveland, *Southern Evangelicals and the Social Order*, pp. 234–5; Sydnor, *Slavery in Mississippi*, p. 57; Walter B. Posey, *Frontier Mission: A History of Religion West of the Appalachians to 1861* (Lexington: University of Kentucky Press, 1966), p. 200; *Second Annual Report of the Missionary to the Negroes in Liberty County, Georgia* (Charleston, S.C.: 1835), p. 6; Touchstone, "Planters and Slave Religion in the Deep South," pp. 130, 134. Of course, many ministers preached to slaves as part of their ministerial careers. Joseph Stratton, a Presbyterian minister from Mississippi, considered his experience "the most satisfactory of any that belong to my public ministrations." Stratton, *Memorial of a Quarter Century Pastorate. A Sermon Preached on the Sabbaths, Jan 3rd and 17th, 1869 in the Presbyterian Church, Natchez, Miss.* (Philadelphia: Lippincott, 1869), p. 36. For further examples, see also Simon P. Richardson, *The Light and Shadows of Itinerant Life: An Autobiography of Rev. Simon Peter Richardson, D.D. of the North Georgia Conference* (Nashville and Dallas: Publishing House of the Methodist Episcopal Church, South, 1901), p. 23, and John A. Broadus, *Memoir of James Petigru Boyce, D.D., LL.D., Late President of Southern Baptist Theological Seminary, Louisville, KY* (New York: Armstrong and Son, 1893), p. 91.

bolster the morality and safety of the peculiar institution. The humaniza-
tion of slavery would also rebuff abolitionist attacks, thereby strengthening the cause of the South.

Clergymen assured planters that religious instruction would improve
the functioning of the slave system. The *Central Presbyterian* of Richmond declared that "true religion makes slaves better servants, and better
contented with their condition: and consequently, if all were pious, the
system would last as long as the masters should wish." Presbyterians in
the Synod of South Carolina and Georgia argued similarly that religious
instruction would foster "a better understanding of the relation of master
and servant, and of their reciprocal duties." One satisfied planter attested
to the validity of this argument. "They are never injured by preaching,"
remarked Robert Collins of Macon County, Georgia, "but thousands
become wiser and better people, and more trustworthy servants, by their
attendance at church."[23]

Masters were specifically promised that religious instruction would foster obedience in their servants. William Mercer Green, an Episcopalian
minister from Mississippi, stressed that religion would bring a "blessed
change in their spiritual condition – which will make them orderly and
obedient upon principle and not from fear alone." A North Carolina
master substantiated Green's claim. "I find them [converted slaves] more
easily controlled, than any of my other thirty-seven working hands," he
wrote, " – and much more trustworthy." One planter from Georgia be-
queathed $200 for the religious instruction of slaves because he had ob-
served that with his own servants, the teaching "developed a stronger
sense to obey, as they feared to offend against the obligations of religion."
A former slave in North Carolina testified to this disciplinary function of
religious instruction. "The first commandment was to obey our masters,"
recalled Lunsford Lane, "and the second was like unto it."[24]

Finally, Southern clerics advocated the spiritual education of slaves on
the ground that it would safely channel their religious impulses. This
argument rested on the assumption that blacks inherently possessed a
strong, emotional religiosity. While discussing the racial characteristics of
slaves, the Rev. C. F. Sturgis, a Baptist clergyman from Greensborough,
Alabama, noted particularly "the religious element that so strongly distin-
guishes them." Because of the slave's "evident tendency to run into the

23. *Central Presbyterian*, March 22, 1856; *Report of the Committee*, p. 14; Touchstone,
"Planters and Slave Religion in the Deep South," p. 84.

24. Touchstone, "Planters and Slave Religion in the Deep South," p. 85; *Biblical Recorder*,
June 10, 1835; Ralph Flanders, *Plantation Slavery in Georgia* (Cos Cob, Conn.: John E.
Edwards, 1969), p. 180; John S. Bassett, *Slavery in the State of North Carolina* (Balti-
more, Md.: Johns Hopkins University Press, 1899), p. 50.

marvellous," Sturgis argued, "it is obviously an important part of the master's duty, to have this sentiment cultivated with care and assiduity." Black religious feeling could be controlled, agreed the *Southern Presbyterian Review*, by giving it a wise direction and turning it into safe and salutary channels. Ministers were suggesting that native slave religion was unsound, excessively emotional, and potentially volatile. They thus sought to replace black preachers with white missionaries. The *Southern Presbyterian Review* warned masters that black religious exhorters gave slaves "fanaticism for piety, excitement for devotion, and enthusiasm for faith." James H. Thornwell urged instead that white religion from missionaries "should be something more than the noisy, and often unintelligible harangues they hear from those of their own color. To leave them to such, would be to leave the blind to be led by the blind."[25]

Clerical anxiety over slave religion clearly exposes an ethnocentric approach to Afro-American culture. Yet it also suggests a basic distrust and fear of unrestrained emotionalism characteristic of nineteenth-century reformers. White religion was seen as an agent of social control, preserving order within the system of slavery by curbing unbridled emotions. "The tendency of religion," explained the Synod of South Carolina and Georgia while discussing religion and the slaves, "is to soften down and curb the passions of man, to make him more respectful of another's interests, and more solicitous of his favour." The controlling role of religion was echoed by the Association for the Religious Instruction of the Negroes in Liberty County: "They need instruction, not feeling; understanding not excitement: they are like a ship at sea without a helmsman, driven about by every wind and carried by the current until dashed on a rock." The desire to substitute white Christianity for black religion resembled the kind of paternal stewardship typical of benevolent reform in antebellum America, furnishing another instance of the symmetry between American and Southern values.[26]

By claiming that spiritual instruction would make better slaves, Southern clergymen were clearly appealing to the interests of slaveowners. To gain religious access to the slaves, ministers had to calm planters' fear that religion in the slave quarters would lead to unrest. Yet the desire to Chris-

25. *Duties of Masters and Servants*, pp. 100–1; *Southern Presbyterian Review* 1 (March 1847): 146; Thornwell, "Duties of Masters and Servants," p. 278.

26. *Report of the Committee*, p. 17; *Seventh Annual Report*, p. 20. Historians have recognized that anxiety over unbridled passions was a characteristic of antebellum reform. See especially Ronald Walters, "The Erotic South: Civilization and Sexuality in American Abolitionism," *American Quarterly* 25 (1973): 177–201. On the tradition of theocratic reform, see John R. Bodo, *The Protestant Clergy and Public Issues, 1812–1848* (Princeton, N.J.: Princeton University Press, 1954).

tianize slavery that was manifest in these appeals was sincere. It expressed a deeper attempt by proslavery clerics to prove the compatibility between slavery and Christianity.[27] Ministers accordingly tapped an emerging sectional consciousness in pleading for the religious instruction of slaves. Plantation missions, these clergymen urged, were an endeavor unique to the South. By ameliorating the harsher conditions of slavery, the mission movement would also provide an effective rebuke to abolitionist critics. In appealing to sectional pride for missionary support, clergymen deepened the identification between slavery, religion, and Southern separatism.

Churchmen argued that the spiritual welfare of slaves was a missionary field providentially destined for Southerners. "God has opened to us here in the South a wide door of usefulness," declared Mississippi Baptists. In 1835, the Association for the Religious Instruction of Negroes in Liberty County insisted that the slave population in the South created such a large field for missionary work that no concerned Christian "need leave it for any other part of the United States or the world for want of opportunities of doing good." John B. Adger, a Presbyterian minister from Charleston and active missionary among blacks in that city, saw other benefits flowing from these efforts: "Here is THE WORK, my brethren, which will raise up a SOUTHERN MINISTRY. This business of preaching the gospel to our poor is what will fill your recently endowed seminary with students."[28]

This call for a distinctive Southern missionary field, however, was more prescription than description. The neglect of plantations was a constant refrain in contemporary literature on the religious instruction of slaves. "There is not a sufficiently deep sense of this responsibility abroad in the community," complained the Rev. I. S. K. Axson of Georgia, "nor is the measure of personal duty in this enterprise fully met." A writer to the Presbyterian *Southern Religious Telegraph* of Richmond also lamented that "we are far behind in our duty." Clergymen were particularly pained at the hypocrisy of spending money and energy abroad while Southern slaves were being neglected at home. "In our zeal for the distant heathen," noted the Baptist *Biblical Recorder* of North Carolina, "we have forgotten those of our own household." A South Carolina Baptist wondered similarly "whether there is not room to fear that charity to be spurious,

---

27. A similar point is made in Mathews, *Religion in the Old South*, p. 178.

28. *Minutes of the Twenty Third Anniversary of the Chickasaw Baptist Association, Held with the Cherry Creek Church, Pontotoc Co., Miss. on the 13th, 14th, and 18th September, 1861* (Jackson: *Mississippi Baptist* Book and Job Office, 1861), p. 25; *Second Annual Report of the Missionary to the Negroes in Liberty County, GA, presented to the Association* (Charleston: *Observer* Office Press, 1835), p. 23; Adger, *Religious Instruction of the Colored Population*, p. 12.

which seeks to benefit those that are far away, while it leaves neglected objects of compassion around its home." To the Liberty County Association, missionary zeal that searched abroad while ignoring those in need at home was a philanthropy full of "infatuation and folly."[29]

The strongest sectional appeal to Southern masters was the argument that the religious instruction of slaves would furnish a resilient defense against abolitionism. In the 1830s, Northern critics of slavery focused primarily on the institution's inherent sinfulness and immorality. Clergymen answered the abolitionists by affirming that Southern slavery was indeed a moral institution and that missions to the slaves would provide tangible evidence of this fact. In this way, abolitionism made masters more sensitive about their duty to instruct slaves. An Alabama minister, for example, admitted that one of the principal reasons for discussing the spiritual duties of masters toward their servants was for "the sake of our beloved country, which is so frequently and so severely agitated, almost to dismemberment, by the question of the moral rectitude of domestic slavery." The religious instruction of the slaves became an important weapon in the proslavery arsenal.[30]

The mission to the slaves, clergymen contested further, would enhance the institution's morality by removing its worst abuses. "Our principle should be, *amelioration*," explained James H. Thornwell, " – the softening down of the harsher features in their condition, and the removal of all unnecessary evils." A South Carolina Baptist also saw the instruction of slaves as an "effort, humble though it is, to correct the evils" of slavery. If religion could curb the fervor and passion of slaves, it could also regulate the behavior of masters. "Surely none could thus affectionately seek the salvation of their souls," reasoned the Episcopalian Bishop William Meade of Virginia, "and at the same time be unjust, cruel, or severe in other respects."[31]

Summarizing this line of thinking, Southern clergymen insisted that making slavery more moral would destroy the basis of abolitionist criti-

---

29. I. S. K. Axson, *Individual Responsibility: An Address before the Association for the Religious Instruction of the Negroes, in Liberty County, Georgia; delivered at the Annual Meeting, January 31, 1843* (Savannah: Thomas Purse, 1843), p. 34; *Biblical Recorder*, April 12, 1837; idem, January 28, 1835; *Southern Baptist*, February 28, 1849; *Seventh Annual Report*, p. 17.

30. Raboteau, *Slave Religion*, p. 161; Touchstone, "Planters and Slave Religion in the Deep South," p. 37; *Duties of Masters and Servants*, p. 54.

31. Thornwell, "Duties of Masters and Servants," p. 272; *Southern Baptist*, February 28, 1849; William Meade, *Pastoral Letter of the Right Rev. William Meade, Assistant Bishop of Virginia, to the Ministers, Members and Friends of the Protestant Episcopal Church in the Diocese of Virginia, on the Duty of Affording Religious Instruction to Those in Bondage* (1834; reprint ed. Richmond: H. K. Ellyson, 1853), p. 20.

cism. "Let us, as one man, come up to this work," declared the Alabama Baptist State Convention in 1846, "and by united and persevering efforts wipe off at least, from our denomination, the opprobrium of the South." William Meade called upon Episcopalians in Virginia to join the missions to the slaves because "then can we with clean consciences bid those whom we call intruders from a distance, not to intermeddle with a duty delicate and difficult in the extreme and which none but ourselves are competent to reform." The *South Western Baptist* of Alabama also believed an important result of the religious instruction would be that "the mouths of the abolitionists would be hushed." In a fast day sermon before the General Assembly of South Carolina in 1850, the Rev. Whitefoord Smith paid tribute to the critical role the missions played in the fight against abolitionism. "Had the torrent of fanaticism, which now threatens to desolate the land," the Methodist minister recalled, "come upon us, and found us unprepared – had we no moral and religious barrier to interpose against this professed philanthropy – its progress had been irresistible." The religious mission to the slaves, Smith concluded, "has turned the attention of Christians to the more calm and correct appreciation of slavery."[32]

Ministering to the spiritual needs of enslaved blacks would thus help Christianize slavery and enhance the Southern cause. The religious mission to the slaves worked in still other ways to strengthen the bonds between religion and Southern distinctiveness. First, it helped cement ties among sectionally minded clerics, reflecting and reinforcing the underlying ideological unity between proslavery and religious missions. Liberty County, Georgia, provides an intriguing example of this kind of integration. This small coastal area of Georgia contained a surprisingly large and impressive list of ministers involved with slavery. The Midway Church was the pastorate of Charles Colcock Jones, perhaps the most active Southern clergyman in the mission movement. Co-pastor of the church from 1836 to 1853 was I. S. K. Axson, who delivered the annual address before the Association for the Religious Instruction of the Negroes in Liberty County in 1843. Patrick Hues Mell, minister of the Greensborough Baptist Church, wrote a proslavery tract published anonymously in 1844. Samuel J. Cassells contributed an article on the conscience for the *Southern Presbyterian Review* that served as an important demonstration of the infidelity of abolitionism. Fated to be the most conspicuous among Liberty County ministers for his involvement with slavery was the Methodist Bishop James Osgood Andrew. His inheritance

32. *Minutes of the Twenty-Second Anniversary of the Alabama Baptist State Convention* (n.p., 1846), p. 15; Meade, *Pastoral Letter*, p. 21; Sellers, *Slavery in Alabama*, p. 328; Whitefoord Smith, *God the Refuge of His People. A Sermon, Delivered before the General Assembly of South Carolina, on Friday, December 6, 1850* (Columbia: A. S. Johnson, 1850), p. 11.

of slaves through marriage precipitated the final breakup of the Methodist Church in 1844.[33]

Second, plantation missions brought clerics closer to the slaveholding order. Clergymen often sought the assistance of political leaders when launching missionary efforts to the slaves. In the case of South Carolina, this support was forthcoming. When William Capers and his fellow Methodists began thinking about providing religious instruction to slaves in the late 1820s, they received the blessings of Charles Cotesworth Pinckney, the wealthy South Carolina planter, and Edward R. Laurens. At a meeting for the religious instruction of slaves held in Charleston in 1845, the cream of lowcountry leadership was there to give their support: Daniel Huger, Robert Barnwell Rhett, Joel R. Poinsett, and J. Drayton Grimke. A little over a decade before, these politicians had been at odds over nullification.[34]

Yet in other important ways, the mission to the slaves thwarted religion's contribution to Southern separatism. For one thing, clerical relations with the planter class were not always so harmonious. Resistance to the religious instruction of the slaves was present throughout the antebellum period. Many Southerners feared that the shadows of abolitionism lurked behind these efforts. Jeremiah B. Jeter, pastor of the First Baptist Church in Richmond, recalled that the rise of the antislavery movement had produced "a most unpleasant counter-excitement at the South. All efforts for meliorating the condition of the slaves were opposed by many on the ground that they favored the designs of the abolitionists." When John B. Adger tried to establish religious missions to the slaves in Charleston in the 1840s, his efforts were hindered by the fears and distrust provoked by the Denmark Vesey conspiracy. Four concerned citizens of Cambridge, South Carolina, asked one Methodist missionary to the slaves to resign. As late as 1859, John L. Giradeau was criticized in the secular press for his work with a "nigger church." These examples suggest that the suspicion of their loyalty to Southern institutions continued to haunt the Southern clergy.[35]

33. The names of these ministers are listed in James Stacy, *A History of the Presbyterian Church in Georgia* (n.p., Elberton, Ga., 1912), p. 90.
34. William M. Wightman, *Life of William Capers, D.D., Including an Autobiography* (Nashville, Tenn.: Publishing House of the Methodist Episcopal Church, South, 1902), p. 81; "Address to the Holders of Slaves in South Carolina," in *Proceedings of the Meeting in Charleston, S.C., May 13–15, 1845 on the Religious Instruction of the Negroes* (Charleston: B. Jenkins, 1845), p. 15.
35. Jeremiah Bell Jeter, *The Recollections of a Long Life* (Richmond: Religious Herald Co., 1891), pp. 209–10; John B. Adger, *My Life and Times, 1810–1899* (Richmond: Presbyterian Committee of Publication, 1899), p. 55; Rosser H. Taylor, *Antebellum South Carolina: A Social History* (Originally published 1942. Reprint ed., New York: Da Capo Press, 1970), p. 163; Loveland, *Southern Evangelicals and the Social Order*, p. 254.

The religious mission to the slaves and the slaveholding ethic posed a more serious if more subtle threat to the formation of a separate sectional identity based on slavery. The ideology of sanctifying slavery contained within itself the means for weakening the peculiar institution. By publicly establishing rigorous moral standards for masters, the slaveholding ethic could become an invitation to judge and possibly condemn the practice of slavery. When adverses on Civil War battlefields led Southern clergymen to inquire into God's controversy with the Confederacy, abuses in the practice of slavery would rank high on the list of national sins. The sanctification of slavery posed another, potentially more explosive threat to the institution. Subtly but unmistakably, it acknowledged the slave as a moral and spiritual being in full possession of a conscience and a soul recognized by God. The admission of the slave's humanity could raise thorny problems for the justification of human bondage. The sanctification of slavery, then, reveals the powerful and unresolved tensions inevitable in bringing Christianity and slavery together, serving as a fitting example of an important countertheme to the role of religion in the growth of Southern separatism.[36]

The efforts to make slavery conform to the moral law of God implicitly suggested that the institution was falling short of its Christian ideals and hence needed to be reformed. Some ministers made this claim explicit by calling openly for the amelioration of the abuses of slavery, such as excessive labor, extreme punishments, and the lack of adequate food and clothing. They urged Southern Christians to support those laws that protected slaves from cruel punishments. To Southern clergymen, the most serious sins of slaveholding were the separation of families and the denial of religious worship to slaves. They looked to the coercive power of the state to correct these abuses and enforce a Christian system of slavery. In 1847, the Presbyterian Synod of South Carolina created a committee, with Thornwell as chair, to develop a petition to the South Carolina legislature arguing for the protection of families and the repeal of laws that banned slaves from reading. For a variety of reasons, clerical attempts at state-supported reforms of slavery were ineffective.[37]

36. See also the similar discussion in Mathews, *Religion in the Old South*, p. 179. On clerical jeremiads on slavery during the Civil War, see Drew Gilpin Faust, *The Creation of Southern Nationalism: Ideology and Identity in the Civil War South* (Baton Rouge and London: Louisiana State University Press, 1988), chaps. 2–4. There is a revealing letter on this theme from the Baptist minister James Petigru Boyce quoted in Broadus, *Memoir of James Petigru Boyce*, p. 185. For an earlier expression of this jeremiad thinking, see *Report of the Committee to whom was referred the subject of the Religious Instruction of the Colored Population of the Synod of South Carolina and Georgia, At its late session in Columbia, December 5th–9th, 1833* (Charleston: *Observer* Office Press, 1834), p. 13.

37. Loveland, *Southern Evangelicals and the Social Order*, pp. 209–10; Freehling, "James Henley Thornwell's Mysterious Antislavery Moment," p. 397; Bertram Wyatt-Brown,

Despite their genuine efforts to reform and sanctify slavery, the vast majority of Southern clergymen were steadfast in their fundamental commitment to the defense and preservation of slavery. In their minds, making the peculiar institution conform to the moral laws of God did not question the essential rectitude of the slaveholding relationship. In fact, the reformation of slavery fit neatly with the postmillennial thinking of antebellum Southern clergymen. They argued that the institution would evolve, improve, and persist as an essential component of millennial society.[38]

IV

Together, the biblical justification of human bondage, the portrayal of abolitionism as infidelity, the slaveholding ethic, and the religious mission to the slaves comprised a coherent ideology aimed at sanctifying slavery. This ideology was shaped by an interaction of several factors: the dialogue with Northern abolitionists, the defense of religious orthodoxy, and shared American values and ways of thinking. In important ways, however, the Christian doctrine of slavery was a product of the social and religious context of the Old South. Proslavery clerics tended to represent the elite of the Southern clergy, whose social roles and expectations generated pressures on them to become involved with slavery. In addition, these same clergymen were occupied in building an institutional infrastructure to support denominational growth in the South. The sectional

"Modernizing Southern Slavery: The Proslavery Argument Reinterpreted," in J. Morgan Kousser and James M. McPherson, eds., *Region, Race, and Reconstruction: Essays in Honor of C. Vann Woodward* (New York and Oxford: Oxford University Press, 1982), p. 35.

38. On this point, see especially Jack P. Maddex, Jr., "Proslavery Millennialism: Social Eschatology in Antebellum Southern Calvinism," *American Quarterly* 31 (Spring 1979): 46–62. Bertram Wyatt-Brown has also suggested that the ideas of evolution and improvement were important components of proslavery thought, in "Modernizing Southern Slavery," pp. 27–49. Some historians have suggested that clerical efforts to reform slavery masked antislavery sentiments, an interpretation I do not support. See for example Clarence Mohr, "Slaves and White Churches in Confederate Georgia," in John B. Boles, ed., *Masters & Slaves in the House of the Lord: Race and Religion in the American South, 1740–1870* (Lexington: University Press of Kentucky, 1988), pp. 153–72 and especially Freehling, "James Henley Thornwell's Mysterious Antislavery Moment." Their arguments come close to the "guilt thesis" on Southern slaveholders, which is explored in Gaines M. Foster, "Guilt Over Slavery: A Historiographical Analysis," *Journal of Southern History* 56 (November 1990): 665–94. Freehling's interpretation of Thornwell is challenged by Eugene D. Genovese in *The Slaveholders' Dilemma: Freedom and Progress in Southern Conservative Thought, 1820–1860* (Columbia: University of South Carolina Press, 1991), p. 60.

conflict over slavery sharply intensified this pursuit, helping make Southern religious institutions distinctly sectional ones.

The ministers who wrote sermons or journal articles on slavery shared common characteristics that placed them among the South's "Gentlemen Theologians." They tended to have pastorates in cities and towns and were active in denominational affairs, serving in church offices or as editors of religious newspapers. They were involved with education, as professors but often as presidents at academies, colleges, or seminaries. The characteristics and social roles of proslavery clerics go a long way in explaining their ideology.[39]

One of the most important features distinguishing the "Gentlemen Theologians" was their urban orientation, which reflected a crucial distinction among Southern clergymen. Even in 1860, the amateur Southern sociologist Daniel R. Hundley noted the contrast between the illiterate and dogmatic preachers of the yeomanry and the genteel pastors of the middle class. Ministers catering to the wealthier, better educated, and more refined congregations could almost always be found in the towns and cities of the Old South. There were many appealing things about an urban pastorate, not the least of which was money. Frederick Law Olmsted, designer of New York's Central Park and Yankee commentator on life in the Old South, estimated that the annual salary of a rural minister in South Carolina was between $150 and $200. In contrast, the Presbyterian Bethel Church in Walterboro paid its minister $1,000 in 1827. There were advantages besides financial ones. The urban mercantile and professional classes to whom the clergy catered aspired to gentility and refinement. As a result, most Southern cities and towns could boast of academies, libraries, literary clubs, and lyceums. Ministers in the towns and cities certainly had more opportunities to speak outside the church on such civic occasions as the Fourth of July. Perhaps most appealing to clergymen was the rise in status and influence denoted by an urban pastorate. On accepting an offer from the First Presbyterian Church of Columbia, Benjamin M. Palmer claimed he "could preach to a large resident audience of worthy and influential people..." Similarly, the Methodist minister Landon C. Garland found the "intelligent and refined" citizens of Tuscaloosa appealing.[40]

39. For a description of this group, see the fuller discussion in the Introduction and note 12.
40. Taylor, *Antebellum South Carolina*, p. 153; Loveland, *Southern Evangelicals and the Social Order*, pp. 50, 58; Stephanie McCurry, "Defense of Their World: Gender, Class and the Yeomanry of the South Carolina Lowcountry, 1820–1860," Ph.D. diss., State University of New York at Binghamton, 1988, p. 214; Holifield, *Gentlemen Theologians*, p. 10. Yet cities and towns had their disadvantages as well. The greater wealth could distract congregants from religion. Urban pastorates could also exact high expectations

Urban pastorates tended to reflect the denominational pattern and even class structure of Southern religion. Presbyterians and especially Episcopalians drew their heaviest support from the economic and social elites. It was the merchants, professional men, and government officials in the towns of North Carolina who supported the Episcopal Church. Most of Mobile's city elite attended an Episcopal church, a pattern duplicated in Montgomery, Savannah, and New Orleans. The Presbyterians also did well among the urban gentry and middle classes. In Mobile, for instance, the Government Street Presbyterian Church, founded in 1831, boasted a congregation with a most prestigious membership. The First Presbyterian Church in Columbia, South Carolina, similarly drew families of commanding position and influence.[41]

Thomas Smyth, pastor of the Second Presbyterian Church of Charleston, illustrates many of the characteristics of the urban clergyman. Smyth was as much theologian as pastor. Most of his emphasis was on the preparation of his sermons. He participated in the major doctrinal and ecclesiastical debates of the times, including the Oxford Controversy and debates over mission boards within the Presbyterian church. He was one of the editors of the prestigious *Southern Presbyterian Review*. Smyth was also active in Charleston's intellectual circles, often attending the informal gatherings in Russell's Bookstore with the likes of aspiring poets Paul Hamilton Hayne and Henry Timrod.[42]

The distinctive social features and ministerial roles of the "Gentlemen Theologians" that characterized proslavery clerics provided a larger framework in which their ideas and arguments were framed. Anxious about their status in society and seeking means of influence, the clergy saw

of gentility and standing that were often hard for clergymen to meet. Loveland, *Southern Evangelicals and the Social Order*, p. 48; Holifield, *Gentlemen Theologians*, pp. 8–11, 13–24; Guion Griffis Johnson, *Antebellum North Carolina: A Social History* (Chapel Hill: University of North Carolina Press, 1937), p. 167. For a good recent overview of urbanization in the antebellum South, see David R. Goldfield, *Cotton Fields and Skyscrapers: Southern City and Region, 1607–1980* (Baton Rouge and London: Louisiana State University Press, 1982), pp. 28–79. Important for understanding the town setting for the clergy is Holifield, *Gentlemen Theologians*, chap. 1.

41. Johnson, *Antebellum North Carolina*, p. 336; Harriet Amos, *Cotton City: Urban Development in Antebellum Mobile* (University: University of Alabama Press, 1985), p. 67, 107; McCurry, "In Defense of Their World," p. 214; Johnson, *Antebellum North Carolina*, p. 348. Class and denominational patterns were of course not so clearly drawn. Methodists and Baptists did have prestigious and influential churches in the cities.

42. Thomas Erskine Clarke, "Thomas Smyth: Moderate of the Old South," Th. D. diss., Union Theological Seminary, Richmond, 1970, pp. 15, 89–105; Ernest Trice Thompson, *Presbyterians in the South, Vol. 1: 1607–1861* (Richmond, Va.: John Knox Press, 1963), p. 453; Michael O'Brien and David Moltke-Hansen, eds., *Intellectual Life in Antebellum Charleston* (Knoxville: University of Tennessee Press, 1986), p. 177.

in the sanctification of slavery a means of achieving power and prestige. In addition, these clergymen shared a common social vision with the elites in the towns and cities that reinforced the structure and values of a slave-holding society. Again, the Rev. Thomas Smyth provides a useful illustration. His social philosophy, which rested on a corporate and organic view of society, neatly corresponded to the ideals of Charleston's upper class. His belief that government should conform to the natural order and his adherence to the Constitution as a bulwark against the forces of irrationalism and democracy were shared by Charleston lawyers. The common roles and aspirations of the "Gentlemen Theologians" was important to the ideology of proslavery clerics in still another way. They created a consensus around basic values that tended to unite clergymen of different denominations and regions of the South, helping to unify the South on the critical sectional issue of slavery.[43]

Another characteristic of the "Gentlemen Theologians" was their widespread involvement in building and maintaining religious institutions. They set up schools and academies, edited newspapers and journals, taught at colleges and seminaries, and supported the organizations and agencies of their denominations. The growth of religious institutions is very important in understanding the sectional ideology of Southern clergymen. At key points during the antebellum era, denominational needs converged with sectional interests. The growing separation between North and South over the issue of slavery spurred the denominational pursuit of institutional growth. It helped make Southern religious institutions peculiarly sectional ones.[44]

43. Tise, *Proslavery*, p. 178; Holifield, *Gentlemen Theologians*, p. 33; Kenneth S. Moore, "The Root of All Evil: The Southern Clergy and the Economic Mind of the Old South" (unpublished ms), p. 20; Clarke, "Thomas Smyth," pp. 54–57; Genovese and Fox-Genovese, "The Divine Sanction of Social Order," p. 228. Bertram Wyatt-Brown, "Proslavery and Antislavery Intellectuals: Class Concepts and Polemical Struggle," in Michael Fellman and Lewis Perry, eds., *Antislavery Reconsidered: New Perspectives on the Abolitionists* (Baton Rouge and London: Louisiana State University Press, 1979) offers a valuable discussion on how secular proslavery intellectuals sought class leadership. See also Drew Gilpin Faust, *The Sacred Circle: The Dilemma of the Intellectual in the Old South, 1830–1860* (Baltimore and London: Johns Hopkins University Press, 1977).

44. My inquiry along these lines originated by my reading of the sources. But my thinking has also been inspired by Stanley M. Elkins's writings about the role of institutions in the slavery controversy. See *Slavery: A Problem in American Institutional and Intellectual Life* (Chicago: University of Chicago Press, 1959), pp. 140–267. Although I do not necessarily agree with his argument about the anti-institutional orientation of the abolitionists, I do believe that Elkins captured an important link between institutions and ideology. Also relevant, though on the end of the Civil War era, is Eric L. McKittrick, *Andrew Johnson and Reconstruction* (Chicago: University of Chicago Press, 1960).

In a pluralistic and voluntary religious order, the importance of denom-
inationalism led to fierce competition for church adherents. One modern
scholar of Southern religion explained that denominations in the nineteenth century "sharpened their dissimilarities, assumed attitudes of extreme antagonism toward each other, and shunned cooperation among
themselves in order to reach a scattered folk." Indeed, sectarianism ran
rampant throughout the antebellum South. The rivalry between Baptists
and Methodists, evangelical churches that appealed to the masses of Southerners, was perhaps the most prevalent. The difference between infant
baptism and adult immersion was the major doctrinal conflict between
these two denominations. North Carolina Baptists and Methodists argued
the issue in 1832. A similar debate over modes of baptism raged for weeks
in the columns of the *South Western Baptist* of Alabama.[45]

Denominational competition was the key incentive for establishing religious institutions in the South. This was especially true for schools, colleges, and seminaries. "And if our Baptist principles are so dear to us,"
reasoned the *Christian Index* of Georgia, "shall we not rightly instruct
those whose duty it will be to hold, maintain, and transmit them, when we
are dead and gone?" In 1835, South Carolina Methodists called attention
to "the pains beginning to be taken by different denominations to bring
education back to sound principles. We may not, we cannot, linger behind all others." Another Methodist worried that those young men not
educated in their denominational colleges "have been lost to our cause."
When Presbyterian Oglethorpe College in Georgia was experiencing
financial difficulties, its founders appealed for support "in view of what
sister denominations are doing, and of the deep and lasting blot which a
failure in this enterprise would fix upon us." The sectarian rationale for
establishing educational colleges was well captured by F. A. P. Barnard of
the University of Mississippi in 1856: "They are regarded as important
instrumentalities, through which the peculiarities of doctrine which distin-
guish their founders are to be maintained, propagated, or defended."[46]

45. Walter B. Posey, *Religious Strife on the Southern Frontier* (Baton Rouge: Louisiana State
University Press, 1965), p. viii; Johnson, *Antebellum North Carolina*, p. 445; Minnie
Claire Boyd, *Alabama in the Fifties: A Social Study* (New York and London: Columbia
University Press, 1931), p. 168. For further evidence of interdenominational conflict, see
Elizabeth H. Hancock, ed., *Autobiography of John E. Massey* (New York and Washing-
ton: Neale Publishing, 1909), p. 25; Richardson, *Shadows of an Itinerant Life*, p. 28;
and Wightman, *Life of William Capers*, p. 255.

46. *Christian Index*, February 13, 1861; John M. McCardell, *The Idea of a Southern Nation:
Southern Nationalists and Southern Nationalism, 1830–1860* (New York: W. W. Norton,
1979), p. 180; Wightman, *Life of William Capers*, p. 357; McCardell, *Idea of a Southern
Nation*, p. 180; Sidney E. Mead, "The Rise of the Evangelical Conception of the Ministry
in America," in H. Richard Niebuhr and Daniel D. Williams, eds., *The Ministry in*

From 1830 to the mid-1840s, Baptists, Methodists, and Presbyterians created a variety of educational institutions throughout the South. In North Carolina, Baptists opened Wake Forest in 1834, and Presbyterians founded Davidson College three years later. Although North Carolina Methodists did not open a school until 1859, Methodists were active in other Southern states with the founding of Centenary College in Louisiana and Randolph–Macon in Virginia. Baptists countered with Mercer in Georgia and Richmond College in Virginia. With their traditional emphasis on an educated ministry, Presbyterians were often in the vanguard of the educational movement. In Milledgeville, Georgia, for instance, they established Midway Seminary in 1835. Other Presbyterian colleges included Oglethorpe in Georgia and Erskine in South Carolina. Each denomination also paid attention to the education of women. In Georgia, Methodists opened Georgia Female School in 1839, and Baptists began Southern Female College in LaGrange in 1843.[47]

The desire for denominational distinctiveness, then, furnished the major impetus for the formation of religious institutions. Each church believed its particular doctrines were the correct interpretation of the Gospel Truth. Each denomination also recognized the need for a better educated ministry, which remained a priority throughout the antebellum period. Yet merging with these distinctly sectarian motives for institution building were sectional considerations. During the 1820s and 1830s, Southern churchmen desired religious journals and schools that could match in quantity and quality those of the North. Heightening political tensions over slavery, especially in the late 1840s, increased the sectional incentive to build separate religious institutions. As denominational and sectional interests converged, the connection between religion and Southern distinctiveness deepened.[48]

The feeling that Southern religious institutions were inferior to Northern ones surfaced often in the private and public writings of the antebellum Southern clergy. As early as 1824, the Rev. John B. Adger recalled, "The ideal then prevailed with many in our Southern country, and especially in Charleston, that schools in the North were far superior to ours." John Holt Rice, minister, educator, and editor of *The Virginia Literary*

Historical Perspectives (New York: Harper, 1956), p. 243. For a similar if more hostile appraisal, see the quotation by Landon C. Garland in Boyd, *Alabama in the Fifties*, p. 139.

47. Johnson, *Antebellum North Carolina*, pp. 297–9; McCardell, *Idea of a Southern Nation*, p. 180; James C. Bonner, *Milledgeville: Georgia's Antebellum Capital* (Athens: University of Georgia Press, 1978), p. 99; McCardell, *Idea of a Southern Nation*, p. 180; Stacy, *History of the Presbyterian Church in Georgia*, p. 158.

48. Taylor, *Antebellum South Carolina*, p. 152.

and Evangelical Magazine, worked hard to build up Presbyterianism in
Virginia in the 1820s. His pleas for the church reveal an image of the
South as a religiously underdeveloped region, one dependent on and
hence inferior to the North. Holt commented, for example, on the "feeble-
ness of our Southern churches, and the reliance which we must place for
some years to come on our brethren to the North for assistance." As late
as 1857, another Presbyterian noted that the South "must, to Europe,
continue to appear inferior to the North in intellectual cultivation."[49]

Southern clergymen acknowledged that their region was too dependent
on outside sources for ideas and institutions. In advertising a Southern
journal of medicine and pharmacy, the *Carolina Baptist* lamented: "We
have been too long dependent upon other portions of our country, and
upon transatlantic countries, for every thing. It is time we awake out
of sleep." Discussing the building of schools in Alabama, the Baptist
Christian Index similarly objected to "such a state of dependence on the
North." The newly founded *Central Presbyterian* of Richmond worried in
1856 about the "preoccupation of the field by Northern newspapers."
Clerics in particular pointed out the hypocrisy of complaining about
Southern intellectual inferiority while lending their support to Northern
endeavors. "Our folly at the South," suggested the *Central Presbyterian,*
"is that we complain of the overwhelming growth of Northern influence,
and then turn around and build up the very agencies that are increasing
that influence, and neglect those at home that might antagonize them."
Images associated with slavery were ironically used to convey this fear of
intellectual dependency. Unless Southerners supported religious publications, Virginia Baptists warned, the South invites "the imposition of the
yoke and handcuff." The Presbyterian Robert Lewis Dabney similarly
alerted Virginians to the danger of sinking "into this state of intellectual
and spiritual vassalage to other communities."[50]

Behind the laments about Southern dependency on Northern literature
and institutions lay the ubiquitous anxiety over slavery. As early as 1835,
the *Southern Religious Telegraph* of Richmond warned that "a crisis in
our Southern churches is rapidly approaching. We have never supplied

49. Adger, *My Life and Times,* p. 56; William Maxwell, *A Memoir of John Holt Rice* (Phila-
    delphia: J. Whetham, 1835), p. 358; Samuel Tyler to James Henley Thornwell, July 13,
    1857, James Henley Thornwell Papers, South Caroliniana Library, Columbia.
50. *Carolina Baptist* (June 1846): 239; *Christian Index,* February 8, 1845; *Central Presbyte-
    rian,* January 5, 1856; *Central Presbyterian,* December 20, 1856; *Minutes of the Appomat-
    tox Baptist Association, Held in the Town of Farmville, August 6th and 7th, 1861* (Rich-
    mond, Va.: H. K. Ellyson, 1861), p. 9; Johnson, *The Life and Letters of Robert Lewis
    Dabney,* p. 133. See also *Watchman and Observer,* March 6, 1851, and *True Witness and
    Sentinel,* January 12, 1861.

our pulpits from our own resources, and differences of opinion among Christians, as to a certain species of property, seems to be raising a barrier between North and South." By the 1840s, clergymen noted with increasing frequency the insults Southern students were suffering at Northern schools because of slavery. The *Christian Index* of Georgia complained that divinity students were sent North to the best seminaries only "to be insulted at meals, and in prayers." A Presbyterian weekly in Richmond commented similarly on "the growing unwillingness of Southern parents to send their children North, on account of the antislavery sentiment which prevails there."[51]

Their sense of intellectual inferiority to and dependence upon the North prompted Southern clergymen to support separate sectional institutions. Only in this way would slavery be secure. The editors of the Methodist *Quarterly Review,* justifying their new publication in 1847, claimed that the South and North "differ both in circumstances and character, and interest, and always must be more or less diverse and unlike, in much that belongs to the stable history of people." They worried if "to what extent southern interests may be different from those of the north, will not the monopoly of American literature on the part of the north, by giving birth and character to public opinion and private conviction in the south, tend to the injury of southern interests?" During the secession crisis, the *Southern Presbyterian* confirmed that "if we are to preserve our own institutions, our own ideas, our own manners and customs, our own style and character of society, and our own *type* of Southern men and women, we must educate our own children."[52]

The establishment of seminaries to train ministers reveals how sectional pressures reinforced the denominational need for religious institutions in the South. The demand for educated ministers emerged from the intense competition between Baptists, Methodists, and Presbyterians for church members. With their emphasis upon an educated ministry, the Presbyterians had taken a lead in this movement, setting up Union Theological Seminary in Virginia in 1823 and Columbia Theological Seminary

---

51. *Southern Religious Telegraph,* January 9, 1835; *Christian Index,* February 8, 1845; *Watchman and Observer,* September 26, 1850.

52. *Quarterly Review* 1 (January 1847): 15; *Southern Presbyterian,* January 26, 1861. For further evidence, see *Carolina Baptist* (June 1846): 167, and *Alabama Baptist,* September 27, 1845. By driving home the need for separate sectional institutions, the denominational schisms of the 1840s became an impetus to institutional growth in the South. In the wake of the schisms, the Baptists established Baylor, Southwestern, Furman, and Bethel Colleges, and the Methodists founded Wofford College in South Carolina and Southern University. McCardell, *Idea of a Southern Nation,* p. 202.

in South Carolina in 1828. In the last two decades of the antebellum era, Baptists and Methodists recognized the need for a more educated ministry. The fact that the Baptists were encountering trained ministers from other denominations was a key motivation for founding a Southern Baptist theological seminary. Significantly, discussion for this seminary began in 1845, the year Southern Baptists formally split from their Northern brethren over slavery. Revealing this junction between denominational and sectional concerns, a correspondent to the *Religious Herald* of Richmond stated in March 1845 that "the South needs one Theological Seminary of high grade, equal to Andover, or Newton..." The Southern Baptist Theological Seminary was finally established in 1859 in Greenville, South Carolina. The next year, the *Baptist Messenger* of Tennessee defended the newly founded institution for timely sectional purposes: "Our young brethren, who may be called to the ministry, are now under no necessity of going to Northern theological schools, in order to receive the training required to fit them better for their work."[53]

The connection between sectionalism and the growth of religious institutions is strengthened by the fact that proslavery clerics were strongly represented among church leaders, college teachers, and editors of religious journals. The impressionistic evidence on this point is striking and revealing. Several personal examples, one from each of the major denominations, illustrate and confirm the links between religious institutions and sectionalism.

John B. Adger, a Presbyterian minister from South Carolina who had served as a missionary in Constantinople and Smyrna, was an influential leader in his denomination. He served as editor of the prestigious *Southern Presbyterian Review* and was engaged in the major ecclesiastical and doctrinal controversies of his church. Adger spent time as a missionary in the Middle East. He was also an educator – professor of church history at Columbia Theological Seminary. Adger was a native Southerner who became a slaveholder through his wife's inheritance in 1847. He immediately channeled his missionary efforts toward converting the slaves of Charleston, preaching a sermon on "The Religious Instruction of the Colored Population" before the Second Presbyterian Church. Four years later, Adger organized a separate black congregation, the Anson Street Chapel. His involvement with slavery inevitably led him, like many Southern clerics, to support a separate Southern nation. In December 1860, he

53. Broadus, *Memoir of James Petigru Boyce*, p. 87; Holifield, *Gentlemen Theologians*, p. 39; Broadus, *Memoir of James Petigru Boyce*, pp. 113–15; *Religious Herald*, May 1, 1845; *Baptist Messenger*, November 8, 1860.

wrote the defense of the Synod of South Carolina's endorsement of secession.[54]

William Capers, a Methodist minister from South Carolina, was especially active in denominational affairs. At different times, he edited both the *Wesleyan Journal* and the *Southern Christian Advocate*. He attended the Methodist General Conference in 1832 and was elected a bishop of the newly formed Methodist Episcopal Church, South, in 1846. Capers was also Professor of Moral and Intellectual Philosophy at South Carolina College. The Methodist divine smoothly integrated his support for slavery into this busy religious career. In 1829, Capers was appointed superintendent of home missions to the slaves in South Carolina, one of the earliest such missions in the antebellum South. In addition, he contributed to the proslavery argument, publishing a series of articles in the *Southern Christian Advocate* in 1838 attacking abolitionism and defending slavery.[55]

The Baptist clergyman James Petigru Boyce, another South Carolinian, furnishes a third confirmation for the connection between institutions and sectionalism. In 1848, Boyce became editor of the *Southern Baptist*. Like Adger and Capers, he was also an educator. He was a professor of theology at Furman, and when the Southern Baptist Theological Seminary opened in 1859, Boyce became president and treasurer of the school as well as a professor there. The Baptist minister was also involved with slavery. He ministered to the religious education of slaves on plantations. Boyce clearly supported the South's peculiar institution, although he opposed secession in 1860.[56]

The ministerial careers of Adger, Capers, and Boyce underscore the connection among the "Gentlemen Theologians," denominational institutions, and the ideology of slavery. The leading proslavery clerics, like James H. Thornwell, were usually prominent ministers in the Southern church. The most sophisticated critiques of abolitionism as infidelity, such as the articles by Samuel J. Cassels and S. W. Stanford, were most fully developed in theological journals like the *Southern Presbyterian Review* and the Methodist *Quarterly Review*. These journals catered to the genteel and educated pastors of the towns and cities of the South. The

54. Thompson, *Presbyterians in the South*, pp. 452, 453, 441, 558. See also the short biographical sketch in Samuel S. Hill, ed., *Encyclopedia of Religion in the South* (Macon, Ga.: Mercer University Press, 1984), p. 3. For his own account of his ministry and an informed history of Presbyterianism in the South, see Adger, *My Life and Times*.

55. Wightman, *Life of William Capers*, p. 249; Harmon Smith, "William Capers and William A. Smith, Neglected Advocates of the Pro-Slavery Moral Argument," *Methodist History* 3 (October 1964): 23; Wightman, *Life of William Capers*, pp. 291, 324–5, 352; Smith, "William Capers and William A. Smith," pp. 26–7.

56. Broadus, *Memoir of James Petigru Boyce*, pp. 60, 100; Hill, ed., *Encyclopedia of Religion in the South*, p. 113; Broadus, *Memoir of James Petigru Boyce*, pp. 91, 183–5.

intimate association between institutions and sectionalism might have worked in another way to promote Southern unity. The quest for denominational distinctiveness that fueled institutional growth was a centrifugal tendency in Southern society. It accentuated differences, at least among Southern Protestants. Yet sectionalism might have countered this inclination. When the defense of slavery and Southern institutions became an additional motive for establishing religious newspapers and schools, Baptists, Methodists, and Presbyterians now shared an identity peculiarly *Southern* as well as denominational.

V

Slavery was the cornerstone of antebellum Southern distinctiveness. As the Virginia jurist Abel P. Upshur noted, it was "the great distinguishing characteristic of the Southern states." To the New Orleans minister Benjamin M. Palmer, it had "fashioned our modes of life, and determined all our habits of thought and feeling, and moulded the very type of civilization." Through the biblical vindication of human bondage, the slaveholding ethic, and the religious mission to the slaves, Southern clergymen had placed slavery on a firm foundation of religion and morality. This was of priceless value in assuring Southerners that their peculiar institution had divine blessings, which provided them with a powerful rebuttal to their Northern critics. When the sectional controversy crept into the national churches in the 1840s and drifted inexorably toward secession and war, the sanctification of slavery would remain a staple of Southern separatism.[57]

57. Upshur is quoted in McCardell, *Idea of a Southern Nation*, pp. 57–8; *Fast Day Sermons: or the Pulpit on the State of the Country* (New York: Rudd & Carlton, 1861), pp. 64–5.

PART THREE

Religion and separatism

4

Harbingers of disunion: The denominational schisms

The moral debate over slavery eventually seeped into the institutional foundations of American Protestantism, fracturing the major national denominations into separate sectional churches. Slavery played a crucial if indirect role in the division of the Presbyterian church into Old and New School factions in 1837–8. In 1844, a conflict over slavery prompted Southern Methodists to sever their ties with their Northern brethren and form the Methodist Episcopal Church, South. Baptists in the slave states withdrew from their national denominational organizations a year later. Like the Methodists, they too established a separate sectional church. Southern Protestants realized that these disruptions of ecclesiastical harmony posed a clear threat to political unity. "Let the three great religious denominations," warned an Alabama Baptist in 1845, "the Presbyterian, the Methodist and the Baptist, declare off from union of effort to do good, North and South, and our glorious union of States will be greatly weakened, if not sundered entirely." Apprehension was also evident among politicians. "If our religious men cannot live together in peace," noted the Great Compromiser Henry Clay, "what can be expected of us politicians, very few of whom profess to be governed by the great principles of love?" These fears were realized a little more than a decade later as the secession crisis reenacted the scenario of religious schism on the political stage. The denominational splits of the 1830s and 1840s had truly been, in the words of Tennessee Methodist William A. Booth, a "harbinger of disunion."[1]

The obvious parallels between these religious divisions and secession has justifiably attracted the attention of scholars seeking to explain the origins of Southern nationalism and the coming of the Civil War. Almost every major historian of the antebellum sectional controversy has ac-

1. *Alabama Baptist*, December 6, 1845; C. C. Goen, *Broken Churches, Broken Nation: Denominational Schisms and the Coming of the Civil War* (Macon, Ga.: Mercer University Press, 1985), p. 106; William Booth, *The Writings of William A. Booth, M.D. during the Controversy upon Slavery* (Somerville, Tenn.: Reeves and Yancey, 1845), p. 6.

knowledged the important role that the denominational schisms played in the hardening of sectional attitudes. Their political implications were clearly set forth by Charles Sydnor in *The Development of Southern Sectionalism, 1819–1848:*

> The division of the churches was something more than an ecclesiastical event. The churches were among the great cohesive forces in America, serving along with the Whig and Democratic parties, business organizations, and other institutions to reinforce the Federal government in the maintenance of the American union. The snapping of any one of these bonds under the stress of sectional tension inevitably increased the strain upon the others. The churches were the first to break; and when they did, tension upon the other national organizations was brought nearer to the danger point.

During the past few decades, historians have continued to explore the connections between the denominational schisms and the coming of the Civil War. In a recent monograph, C. C. Goen has persuasively demonstrated how the divisions of the major denominations anticipated, precipitated, and shaped the political crisis of the 1850s.[2]

For the most part, however, historians have seemed content merely to note the obvious similarities between the denominational schisms and secession. They assume that religious separatism exerted some kind of causal influence on political separatism but fail to explain precisely how this influence worked. The relationship between religious division and political and cultural separatism was more complex and multifaceted. Therefore, in seeking to clarify and demonstrate the impact of the denominational schisms on Southern sectionalism, we must frame our inquiry carefully.

The relationship between religious and political separatism can be ascertained in several ways. First, the denominational splits must be examined in the political context of their time. While conflicts over slavery were rending the churches, Southern politicians were becoming increasingly

---

2. Charles S. Sydnor, *The Development of Southern Sectionalism, 1819–1848* (Baton Rouge: Louisiana State University Press, 1934), pp. 299–300; Goen, *Broken Churches, Broken Nation*, pp. 6, 109. The religious historian William Warren Sweet argues similarly that "the snapping of ecclesiastical cords binding North and South together had a powerful influence in bringing about the final breach between the sections...." *Methodism in American History* (New York: Methodist Book Concern, 1933), p. 277. John M. McCardell, *The Idea of a Southern Nation: Southern Nationalists and Southern Nationalism, 1830–1860* (New York: W. W. Norton, 1979), pp. 183–200 and H. Shelton Smith, *In His Image, But ... Racism in Southern Religion, 1790–1910* (Durham, N.C.: Duke University Press, 1972), chap. 2, deal most explicitly with the influence of the denominational schisms on the development of Southern sectionalism.

consumed with the slavery extension issue. While the Methodists debated
division in the spring of 1844, the Southern political press was filled with
agitation over the annexation of Texas. The introduction of the Wilmot
Proviso two years later, barring slavery from territories acquired during
the Mexican War, raised similar issues about the equality of the slaveholding South in a union with the North. Considering the similarity in
which the issue of slavery was framed in the denominational schisms and
the controversy over the extension of slavery, it would not be surprising if
clergymen and politicians borrowed from each other's experience. Second, if close correlations between the rhetoric and arguments used by
Southern clergymen during their schisms and during secession could be
established, it would provide strong evidence that the religious divisions
did indeed shape the political thought and behavior of the clergy.[3]

The schisms that occurred within the Presbyterian, Methodist, and
Baptist denominations are excellent places to continue our exploration
of the relationship between religion and sectionalism in the antebellum
South. They demonstrate the centrality of slavery in the sectional thinking
of Southern clergymen. They show once again the reciprocal relationship
between religious and political discourse. The denominational schisms tie
together various strands of Southern clerical thinking on the sectional
conflict by showing how distinctive views of slavery, abolitionism, and the
relationship between religion and politics were fused in justifying separation from Northern Protestants. They look forward as well, anticipating
and in many ways prefiguring secession.

I

The Presbyterian schism of 1837–8 had several peculiar characteristics
that distinguished it from the Methodist and Baptist splits. First, slavery

3. The attempt to establish a causal connection between the denominational schisms and
Southern sectionalism does risk what one historian has termed the "Civil War synthesis," a bias caused by looking first at the Civil War and then viewing the events of the
previous decades solely as factors leading up to the war. Although they were aware that
there were political implications to their schisms, Southern Presbyterians, Methodists,
and Baptists did not act with a future of secession in mind. Yet historical hindsight – in
this case the knowledge that the Civil War did happen – can be a useful tool of analysis
when handled with care and discrimination. It enables us to search out the sources and
tendencies within the denominational schisms that can help explain the intensification of
sectional animosities and the coming of the Civil War. Joel H. Silbey, "The Civil War
Synthesis in American Political History," in Stanley N. Katz and Stanley I. Kutler,
eds., New Perspectives on the American Past: Vol. 1, 1607–1877 (Boston: Little, Brown,
1969), p. 280.

was neither the sole nor the primary issue of division. Disagreements over theology, ecclesiastical law, and church policy sundered Presbyterians into Old School and New School factions. Second, there was an intrasectional dimension to this schism. In the North as well as in the South, the church divided along doctrinal lines. The fact that the Presbyterian schism pitted Southerners of different doctrinal schools against one another was the most significant feature shaping its influence on Southern political separatism. Old and New Schoolmen in the South rehearsed arguments in the 1830s that would become center stage during the antebellum sectional controversy.

The schism in the Presbyterian church resulted from disagreements over theology, Presbyterian constitutional law, and ecclesiastical policy that had been brewing for years. To facilitate the spread of evangelicalism in the West, Presbyterians and Congregationalists in New England agreed to interdenominational cooperation in the Plan of Union in 1801. In the early decades of the nineteenth century, the emergence and spread of liberal Calvinism and a debate over the use of voluntary missionary societies led to the creation of two distinct parties in the Presbyterian church, the Old and New School. Old School leaders defended Presbyterian orthodoxy against the liberal New Haven Theology of New School ministers, objected to the participation of Congregationalists in Presbyterian courts, and opposed the use of interdenominational voluntary societies in benevolent enterprises. Old School leaders sought to remove New School heresies from the church but were frustrated because the New School had always commanded a majority in the Presbyterian General Assembly. By 1837, the Old School party had garnered enough strength to dominate the General Assembly, which abrogated the Plan of Union of 1801 and exscinded the four synods in Ohio and New York, where New School influence was strong. The General Assembly of 1838 completed this purge of New School Presbyterians, who proceeded to form an independent General Assembly. The New School body, with approximately 1,200 churches and 100,000 members, constituted slightly less than half of American Presbyterians.[4]

The South played a critical role in the Presbyterian schism, adding a sectional dimension to a theological and doctrinal division. The Old School party in the North consisted essentially of Philadelphia Presbyterians opposed to New School doctrine, a moderate group of Presbyterians

4. For the best narrative and analysis of the schism, see Ernest Trice Thompson, *Presbyterians in the South, Vol. 1: 1607–1861* (Richmond: John Knox Press, 1963), pp. 336–413; George M. Marsden, *The Evangelical Mind and the New School Presbyterian Experience: A Case Study of Thought and Theology in Nineteenth Century America* (New Haven, Conn.: Yale University Press, 1970), pp. 65–6.

associated with Princeton and the Synod of New York. Because Southern support could assure a victory of the Old School forces, orthodox Presbyterians seized on the slavery issue as a means of courting this crucial Southern support. In 1836, Old School Northerners gave Southerners a tacit understanding that they would oppose any General Assembly action on slavery, promising the South the silence on slavery it desired. Consequently, at the General Assembly of 1837, Southern delegates voted 50 to 9 to abrogate the Plan of Union. The alliance between Old School Presbyterians in the North and South was primarily a concert of like-minded theological conservatives. The connection between the liberal Calvinism of the New School and abolitionism, however, served to strengthen the Southern union with the Old School.[5]

At the same time, the South itself was divided between Old School and New School factions. During the summer and early autumn of 1837, Southern Presbyterians extensively debated the actions of the General Assembly and chose allegiance to one of the contending parties. Most Southerners cast their lot with the Old School, for reasons just explained. They counted the leading ministers and newspapers among their spokesmen. Such influential Southern Presbyterians as Thomas Smyth of Charleston, James H. Thornwell, Benjamin Gildersleeve, editor of the Charleston *Observer,* and George A. Baxter of Virginia supported the acts of the 1837 General Assembly. In the summer of 1837, the Rev. William S. Plumer, pastor of the First Presbyterian Church in Richmond, began the *Watchman of the South* to support the Old School. Meanwhile, a minority of New Schoolmen existed in the South. New School synods were formed in Virginia and Kentucky, whereas the established Synod of Tennessee voted to go with the New School. There was a small but vocal New School minority in Mississippi. All together, six New School synods were formed in the South, five in the border states and one in Mississippi. The voice for these scattered Presbyterians in the South was the *Southern Religious Telegraph* in Richmond, edited by Amasa Converse, a transplanted Northerner who disapproved of the exscinding actions of the 1837 General Assembly.[6]

5. The position of the South is clarified in Elwyn A. Smith, "The Role of the South in the Presbyterian Schism of 1837–38," *Church History* 29 (March 1960): 44–63, and in C. Bruce Staiger, "Abolitionism and the Presbyterian Schism of 1837–1838," *Mississippi Valley Historical Review* 36 (December 1949): 391–414. The figures on voting are from Marsden, *The Evangelical Mind and the New School Presbyterian Experience,* p. 98.

6. Thompson, *Presbyterians in the South,* pp. 399–411. Much of the evidence for New School views must thus rest on the *Southern Religious Telegraph.* The most obvious explanation for the fact that most of the New School synods were in the upper South is the relatively weak place of slavery there. The evidence on this point, however, is not conclusive. Thompson, *Presbyterians in the South,* p. 411.

The simultaneous existence of both Old School and New School factions in the antebellum South is important in understanding the influence of the Presbyterian schism on Southern sectionalism and secession. In the course of a polemical struggle to justify their actions, each group advanced specific interpretations of the causes, events, and meaning of the Presbyterian schism. These explanations paid particular attention to slavery and the needs of a peculiarly Southern church. In different ways, both arguments had significant political implications.

Southern Old School Presbyterians maintained that their opposition to New School theology was the primary reason for denominational schism. This theology was essentially an effort to liberalize Calvinism and make it more conducive to revivalism by enlarging the freedom of man and redefining the idea of sin. New School Presbyterians drew upon the New Divinity of Samuel Hopkins but more directly on the New Haven Theology of Nathaniel William Taylor. Departing from the tenets of orthodox Calvinism and adopting the Hopkinsian notion that sin consisted in the act of sinning itself, Taylor maintained that man was free to choose and hence sin was voluntary. In Taylor's view, man could be a sinner without being created sinful by God. New School theology, drawing heavily on Taylor, achieved a liberal version of Calvinism, one useful to revivalists, by stressing the ability of man to aid in his salvation.[7]

Southern Old Schoolmen directed their critique of New School theology on this exaltation of human ability. "This is a metaphysical dogma of the New England philosophy," explained the *Southern Christian Herald* of South Carolina, "maintaining that the *will* only is active and alone capable of depravity." Old Schoolmen in the South saw in New School theology an attack on God's absolute sovereignty and authority. To the Charleston *Observer,* New School theology showed "a want of confidence in Him, who is the King of Zion." For both these reasons, the *Southern Christian Herald* concluded that New School theology had "departed altogether from the Gospel platform."[8]

The Southern Old School critique of New School theology merged into a broader assault on modern tendencies in thought that undermined Calvinist orthodoxy. This significant shift in emphasis rested on the assumption that New School doctrines evolved from an unsound philosophical

7. For good introductions to New School theology, see Marsden, *The Evangelical Mind and the New School Presbyterian Experience,* pp. 9–60, and Sidney E. Mead, *Nathaniel William Taylor, 1786–1858: A Connecticut Liberal* (Chicago: University of Chicago Press, 1942), pp. 96–131, 195–204. Also relevant is H. Shelton Smith, *Changing Conceptions of Original Sin: American Theology since 1750* (New York: Scribner's, 1955).

8. *Southern Christian Herald,* February 3, 1836; Charleston *Observer,* August 19, 1837; *Southern Christian Herald,* June 3, 1836.

foundation. "Error in religion," explained the *Southern Christian Herald*, "is usually the result of some false maxim in morals or philosophy." Old School leaders often associated New School thought with contemporary European and American philosophical movements considered dangerous to orthodoxy. "It is surely time," warned the *Southern Christian Herald*, "for Southern Presbyterians to awake out of sleep." German rationalism and Boston Unitarianism were the particular targets of the South Carolina paper. As part of their rhetorical strategy against the New School, Southerners significantly drew a connection between this unsound philosophy and contemporary religious and social turmoil. James H. Thornwell succinctly articulated what he considered the dangerous political implications of the New Haven theology: "The very same spirit of rationalism, which has made the prophets and apostles succumb to philosophy and impulse in relation to the doctrine of salvation, lies at the foundation of modern speculation in relation to the rights of man." The Southern Old School inclination to generalize and broaden the attack on New School theology provided the basis for fusing the doctrinal and sectional rationales for denominational division.[9]

The Southern Presbyterian critique of abolitionism flowed directly from the Old School opposition to New School theology. The first step of Old School leaders in the South was to narrow their attack on heterodox doctrine to New England, thus sectionalizing heresy and preparing the stage for an identification of New School thought and abolitionism. In New England, the Charleston *Observer* pointed out, "most of the errors in doctrine and practice, the present subjects of complaint – have been most rife." The source of the conflict raging in the Presbyterian Church, according to a correspondent to the *Southern Christian Herald*, "seemed to be in New England." The Rev. William Hill of Virginia accused Northerners in general of an "extravagant rage for innovation, or an indiscreet zeal for orthodoxy."[10]

This analysis of New School theology provided the basis for the Old School attack on abolitionism, discrediting both the religious and political movement simultaneously. Both were seen as variations of the same

9. *Southern Christian Herald*, February 10, 1836; Charleston *Observer*, September 2, 1837; *Southern Christian Herald*, March 10, 1837; *Southern Religious Telegraph*, August 12, 1836; quoted in Staiger, "Abolitionism and the Presbyterian Schism," p. 394.
10. Charleston *Observer*, June 10, 1837; *Southern Christian Herald*, September 10, 1836; William Henry Foote, *Sketches of Virginia, Historical and Biographical*, 2nd ed. (Philadelphia: Lippincott, 1856), p. 459. It should be noted that New Schoolmen in the South were also defenders of slavery. Frederick A. Ross of Huntsville, Alabama, for instance, wrote the proslavery tract *Slavery Ordained of God* (1857); see Thompson, *Presbyterians in the South*, pp. 542–3.

theme. "Our opinion," explained the *Southern Christian Herald*, "is that the same traits of mind that lead to error in religion, lead to fanaticism in other matters." Like New School theology, abolitionism was subversive of religion because it was unscriptural. "And is it the Gospel which they preach," asked the Charleston *Observer*, "when their energies are devoted to the uprooting of our Civil Institutions?" The abolitionist claim that slavery is sinful, according to a Virginia paper, was "a novelty, which its abettors will look in vain for in the Bible." Southern Old Schoolmen made their strongest case against the New School when they explicitly linked the spread of abolitionism with departures from Presbyterian orthodoxy. Describing areas of New School strength in the North, the Charleston *Observer* reflected: "For there Anti-Presbyterianism, and Perfectionism, and ecclesiastical radicalism, and a host of errors in doctrine and practice, have grown up side by side with the spirit of abolitionism scattering far and wide their poisonous fruits." The complicity between abolitionism and New Schoolism was finally cemented when this dangerous duo was linked in a conspiracy to destroy the Presbyterian Church. "Here then a revolution has been attempted at two points;" a Richmond paper admonished, "an attempt to change our creed, and to pour a flood of abolition into the bosom of the Presbyterian church." Perhaps the threat was best expressed by the Charleston *Observer* when it stated that "the peculiar tenets of fanaticism, and the abolition of slavery have been welded together, and together have marched, till by their joint action they have nearly completed the destruction of the Christian intercourse which once obtained between the North and South." By playing up the sectional issue and keeping a steady assault on doctrinal heterodoxy at the same time, the intentional linkage between abolitionism and New School thought was a persuasive tool in convincing Southern Presbyterians of the dangers of the New School and the safety of Southern interests with the Old School.[11]

With these views, it was easy for Southern Old School Presbyterians to justify schism as an act of religious purification. The argument that the actions of the General Assembly of 1837 constituted a necessary purification of the Presbyterian church was the central theme in the responses of the Southern synods and presbyteries siding with the Old School.

11. *Southern Christian Herald*, March 23, 1836; Charleston *Observer*, September 2, 1837; *Southern Religious Telegraph*, December 2, 1837; Charleston *Observer*, July 8, 1837; *Watchman of the South*, September 14, 1837; Charleston *Observer*, September 26, 1837. For further Southern Presbyterian hostility to abolitionism, see the comments by John Witherspoon of South Carolina in Lyman Beecher, *The Autobiography of Lyman Beecher*, ed. Barbara M. Cross, 2 vols. (Cambridge, Mass.: Harvard University Press, 1961), vol. II, p. 322.

Grounded in the critique of New School theology, the purification argument often began by establishing the subversive, poisonous nature of the heterodox New School elements to be purged. The Plan of Union of 1801 between Presbyterians and Connecticut Congregationalists, through which many New School ministers gained influence in the church, was considered by the Bethel Presbytery in South Carolina as "manifestly subversive of the fundamental principles of Presbyterian Government." The voluntary societies for mission work rejected by the General Assembly, according to the South Carolinians, "have been perverted from the great ends of Christian benevolence." The churches formed under the Plan of Union and exscinded by the General Assembly were also offspring of subversion. The Flint Presbytery in Georgia referred to them as an "injurious Foreign influence," and the Amite Presbytery in Louisiana argued that "many of the members are well understood to inculcate Doctrines at variance with the Standards of the Presbyterian Church, and highly prejudicial to its peace and prosperity." In revealing language, the Charleston *Observer* described the removal of the four synods as an "excision of an excrescence upon the body, the removal of which leaves it in its full and fair and symmetrical proportions." The Tombeckee Presbytery in Mississippi resolved that "the peace of our beloved Church has been much disturbed, and, as we believe, her purity endangered."[12]

The religious subversion that the New School represented cut so deep into the fundamental structure of Presbyterianism that it was no longer considered an organic and unified church. The underlying assumption was that the New School elements introduced through Congregationalism were never part of the Presbyterian Church. Schism was therefore justified because a prior unity had never existed. "Long did we endeavor to conceal from our view," admitted the Harmony Presbytery in South Carolina, "that in doctrine and government we were not one; but the delusion could not be maintained." Similarly, the Charleston *Observer* asked, "why attempt to constrain a union where it does not exist?" Old Schoolmen strengthened their argument from the Scriptures, which enjoined separation from those who were deemed to have abandoned the standards of the church. As explained by the Harmony Presbytery, "God does not require us to be confederate with error. Charity itself has its limits: and while a pure piety and a generous benevolence consort with

---

12. "The Records of the Presbytery of Bethel, 1824–1839," p. 247; "The Records of the Flint Presbytery, Vol. 1"; Charleston *Observer*, July 15, 1837; "Records of the Tombeckee Presbytery, 1825–1838," p. 155. All records are located at the Historical Foundation of the Presbyterian and Reformed Churches, Inc., Montreat, N.C. (hereafter cited as Montreat).

toleration, conscience and that which we owe to society require that we preserve a separation between ourselves and heresy – the most malignant of all error."[13]

The justification of the schism as purification resounded throughout the South, testifying to the power of its appeal. Most Southern presbyteries and synods that approved the actions of the General Assembly termed the schism a purification rather than division of the church. "We are strongly attached," proclaimed the Tuscaloosa Presbytery in Alabama, "to the standards of our Church in their commonly received meaning and are determined to be first *pure* than peaceable." The Synod of North Carolina declared the acts of the General Assembly "important to the preservation of our Ecclesiastical order, doctrine, & discipline." To the Concord Presbytery in that synod, the acts were "in accordance with the will of God; and that His blessing will rest on all lawful efforts to purify his own Church." Mississippi Presbyterians believed that the excision of the New School synods was "indispensably necessary not only to maintain the peace and purity of the Church, but that the dignity and honour of religion may be promoted."[14]

The reaction of the small New School party in the South was also shaped by the particular configuration of the Presbyterian schism. Southern New Schoolmen found themselves in a difficult situation, for they were the minority party purged from their denomination. In addition, New School Southerners bore the burden of their theology linked with abolitionism. Thus, whereas Old School Southerners focused on theology and doctrine, New School leaders in the South concentrated their response on the ecclesiastical and constitutional aspects of the struggle. In their struggle with the Old School, New Schoolmen adopted republican principles in defending their rights as a minority, drew significant sectional implications from their ecclesiastical conflicts, and demonstrated to all Southerners some powerful ideological defenses against Northern aggression.

The strongest and most widespread argument made against the Old School was that their actions at the General Assembly of 1837 constituted a tyrannical abuse of majority power. The Charleston Union Presbytery,

13. "Records of the Harmony Presbytery, 1830–1848," Montreat; Charleston *Observer,* July 22, 1837; Edmund A. Moore, "Robert J. Breckinridge and the Slavery Aspect of the Presbyterian Schism of 1837," *Church History* 4 (December 1935): 291; "Records of the Harmony Presbytery, 1825–1838," Montreat, p. 155.

14. "Records of the Tuscaloosa Presbytery constituted February 1835," Montreat, p. 65; quoted in William Warren Sweet, *Religion on the American Fronier, Vol. 2: The Presbyterians, 1783–1840* (New York: Harper, 1936), p. 859; "Records of the Presbytery of Concord, Vol. 4, 1836–1846," Montreat, p. 58; "Records of the Tombeckee Presbytery, 1825–1838," Montreat, p. 155.

for example, declared the acts of the Assembly "Unconstitutional, Unjust and Oppressive." The Holston Presbytery in East Tennessee thought them "contrary to the Constitution of the Presbyterian Church, and an arbitrary assumption of power." Alabama Presbyterians considered the exscinding acts "a judicial act of the utmost severity." New Schoolmen saw the ecclesiastical conflict in terms of the classic republican struggle between power and liberty. "They strike at the RIGHTS AND LIBERTIES of ministers and people throughout the whole church," protested the *Southern Religious Telegraph*. In Mississippi, New School Presbyterians warned that the General Assembly's actions "will end in ecclesiastical despotism and in 'driving the plowshare of ruin through the bosoms' of our ecclesiastical rights." New Schoolmen invoked appeals to an earlier defense of religious liberty in American history. "Ratify the doings of the Assembly," a Virginian wrote, "and in vain was it that our pilgrim fathers left their fatherland and came here, that they might enjoy the blessings of religious and civil freedom."[15]

Depicting Old School actions as tyrannical had potent sectional implications. By explicitly suggesting that the actions of the General Assembly set a dangerous precedent for tyranny of the majority, New Schoolmen contributed to the growing Southern concern that minority rights (i.e., slavery) could not be safely protected under a written constitution. Although this argument expressed a genuine concern for Southern rights, it undoubtedly functioned as a conscious appeal to Southern political fears in behalf of the New School's religious cause. To Southerners who sided with the New School, the political lessons of the Presbyterian schism were painfully clear. "The arbitrary and high handed act of the late General Assembly," wrote a correspondent to the *Southern Religious Telegraph*, "is fraught with the most disastrous consequences to both church and state." Specifically, the Presbyterian schism revealed to New School Southerners the precariousness of constitutional guarantees. As the *Southern Religious Telegraph* noted: "The politician cannot look at those proceedings without concern. For, in those proceedings, the important question is involved, whether men can be governed by written constitutions?"[16]

15. *Southern Religious Telegraph*, November 17, 1837; Sweet, *Religion on the American Frontier*, p. 863; *Southern Religious Telegraph*, June 30, 1837; Sweet, *Religion on the American Frontier*, p. 864; Thompson, *Presbyterians in the South*, p. 399; "Records of the Presbytery of North Alabama, 1825–1844," Montreat, p. 225; *Southern Religious Telegraph*, October 27, 1837. Ernest Trice Thompson discovered the same phenomenon, arguing that New School opposition was based "overwhelmingly on opposition to what seemed like usurpations of constitutional authority." *Presbyterians in the South*, p. 412.
16. *Southern Religious Telegraph*, July 14, 1837; ibid., October 6, 1837.

The threat to slavery through the constitutional abuse of minority rights was the logical culmination of New School thought. Raising the danger to slavery served to demonstrate that the New School provided the soundest guarantee of Southern rights. In a letter to a Richmond paper, a South Carolinian assured his New School brethren that "your cause is the cause of the South – THE WHOLE SOUTH." He proceeded to explain:

> And when this the Constitution is trampled under foot, in Church or State, or its well-defined and limited powers are lost in the 'general welfare' as defined by an interested majority of the General Assembly, or Congress, our peculiar institutions, dear as life are *annihilated*.

The *Southern Religious Telegraph* echoed the South Carolinian's concerns. "The south is waking up to examine this subject – and many are beginning to see that the exercise of the powers assumed by the majority in the last Assembly will leave Southern rights and interests at the mercy of any future majority that may choose to sacrifice them to what they consider the general good." When constitutional safeguards disappear, the editor wondered, "*where* will our Southern churches look for defense against the power of that despotic weapon, which the majority of the late Assembly have taught the Abolitionists to wield with tremendous effect?" In raising anxiety over slavery during a conflict not ostensibly concerned with the peculiar institution, the arguments of New School Southern Presbyterians resembled those of the nullification leaders.[17]

The political implications of New School Presbyterianism in the South can be further gleaned by looking at the Charleston Union Presbytery. This denominational body consisted of churches in Charleston and the lowcountry of South Carolina and Georgia, about a half dozen or more of which were of Congregational extraction. This presbytery denounced the reforming acts of the General Assembly in the fall of 1837. Although in 1838 they did not firmly commit to either body claiming to be the General Assembly, the Charleston Union Presbytery in essence sided with the New School. During complicated maneuverings over the next few years, the minority of the presbytery – which professed its allegiance to the Old School – managed to be recognized by the Synod of South Carolina and Georgia as the true presbytery. The majority of the former Charleston Union Presbytery continued as an independent body. They even began their own journal, the *Southern Christian Sentinel*, edited by

---

17. *Southern Religious Telegraph*, August 4, 1837, and October 27, 1837. For another example of Southern New School hostility to abolitionism, see *Southern Religious Telegraph*, April 21, 1837. In his study of the denominational schisms, H. Shelton Smith noted that the New School supporters were more defensive of slavery and Southern rights. *In His Image, But ...*, p. 44.

Thomas Magruder, to challenge the Old School's Charleston *Observer*.[18]

In their reaction to the Presbyterian schism, members of the Charleston Union Presbytery voiced the standard arguments of the New School minority in the South. They declared in 1837, for instance, that the reforming acts of the General Assembly were "unconstitutional, null and oppressive." William C. Dana, a member of the presbytery, argued similarly that the Assembly possessed "absolute and uncontrolled legislation and executive as well as judicial power, not only making it supreme over the churches, but also placing it above even the constitution." In 1839, the *Southern Christian Sentinel* complained that the Assembly "possesses absolute supremacy over the constitution and disposes at pleasure the civil, as well as ecclesiastical rights of all the church in its connection." As late as 1841, this paper still insisted that the acts of the General Assembly were passed "in open violation of the Constitution."[19]

Like their New School brethren in the South, the Charleston Union Presbytery recognized the sectional implications of their ecclesiastical arguments. A commissioner from the presbytery to the General Assembly of 1838 worried that further connection to the Old School would be done "with the rod of abolitionists held over their head." A concern for slavery seemed uppermost in the minds of the Charleston Union Presbytery. The *Southern Christian Herald* republished Richard Fuller's letters on slavery. The paper's editor, Thomas Magruder, even suggested that a separate Southern church would be a safeguard to abolitionism: "Southern Presbyterians must act together. They must write in supporting Theological seminaries; in sustaining their own feeble churches; and in enlisting in defense of truth the powerful influence of the Press..." The commitment of the Charleston Union Presbytery to slavery and Southern rights was apparently strong enough to merit the support of the Charleston *Mercury*, which printed their letters but denied this right to the other local Presbyterians in the controversy, such as Thomas Smyth.[20]

The Charleston Union Presbytery expressed perhaps the most extreme form of sectionalism found among Southern Presbyterians during the schism. The unique intensity of their response can be partially explained by several peculiar features of the presbytery. It was located primarily in

---

18. Thompson, *Presbyterians in the South*, pp. 401–3.

19. Ibid.; *Southern Christian Sentinel* (May 1841): 1.

20. Thompson, *Presbyterians in the South*, pp. 402–3; *Southern Christian Sentinel* (May 1841): 16–20, 25; Thomas Erskine Clarke, "Thomas Smyth: Moderate of the Old South," Th.D. diss., Union Theological Seminary, Richmond, 1970, pp. 119–25. For similar calls by other New School Presbyterians in the South for a separate Southern church, see *Southern Religious Telegraph*, November 3, 1837, and the comments of "Rusticus" in *Southern Religious Telegraph*, December 8, 1837.

the South Carolina lowcountry, an area that had already shown its penchant for radicalism during the nullification crisis. Another distinctive feature of the Charleston Union Presbytery was the strong New England influence on its religious personnel and institutions. About a half dozen or more churches in the area were of Congregational background and had drifted into association with the Presbyterian church. Some of its ministers were of New England descent. Elipha White of John's Island was a graduate of Brown University and Andover Theological Seminary. The Vermont native Erastus Hopkins was minister at Beech Island. The recently recognized connection between clergymen of New England Federalist backgrounds and proslavery views seems evident in the Charleston Union Presbytery. William C. Dana, for example, was a Northern-born Congregationalist who became a proslavery clergyman in the South.[21]

Because of its intrasectional dimension, the Presbyterian schism of 1837–38 worked on several levels to influence an emerging Southern sectionalism. The Old School majority in the South was instrumental in forging a linkage between abolitionism and New England theology, sectionalizing heresy and deepening the ideological conflict over slavery. They also presented a model of division that valued purity over unity, a precedent that would shape the thinking of Southern clergymen during the secession crisis. Southern New School Presbyterians, on the other hand, tried to show that the exercise of majority tyranny over minority rights could be turned against the slaveholding South. In their own ways, then, each party in the Presbyterian split contributed to Southern separatism.

The existence of these two factions serves as an important reminder that the Southern clergy was not a monolithic whole. Yet it also demonstrates how the sectional conflict thrust a certain unity upon the clergy. By the late 1830s, slavery and abolition were issues that *had* to be addressed by Southern clergymen, regardless of doctrinal orientation.

II

The conflict that split the Methodist Church in 1844 differed significantly from the Presbyterian schism. First, Methodists were more numerous than the Presbyterians. They were the largest denomination in the South

---

21. Clarke, "Thomas Smyth: Moderate of the Old South," pp. 118–25; Larry E. Tise, *Proslavery: The Defense of Slavery in America, 1701–1840* (Athens and London: University of Georgia Press, 1987), p. 364.

in 1850, comprising 37.4 percent of the churches in the eleven states that would become the Confederacy, plus Kentucky and Maryland. They outnumbered all other denominations in North Carolina, South Carolina, Florida, Mississippi, Louisiana, Texas, Arkansas, and Tennessee. A cataclysmic rupture in the Methodist Church would simply touch more Southerners. Second, the Methodist schism was more directly sectional. Slavery was explicitly and exclusively the cause of division. Unlike the Presbyterians, a separate sectional church – the Methodist Episcopal Church, South – was formed as a result of the split. Finally, the theological controversies so central to the Presbyterians were absent in the Methodist split. Here, political and constitutional issues were primary. Yet like the Presbyterian schism, the division of the Methodist Church was significantly shaped by ecclesiastical factors.[22]

American Methodists had a highly structured ecclesiastical organization that gave a distinctive configuration to the controversy over slavery. The church consisted of a hierarchy of ministerial conferences and church officers. The General Conference, a representative body of ministers that met every four years, was at the top of the hierarchy, followed by the local conference, the circuit, and then the congregation. The debate over slavery raised jurisdictional conflicts between these various ecclesiastical bodies. Since 1836, abolitionist petitions had been rejected by local bishops and presiding elders. Antislavery Methodists argued that this local censorship struck at the power of the General Conference. Southerners, believing that the church had no jurisdiction over slavery, contended that the General Conference should support the actions of local censoring officials. The Southern argument advocating the power of the local conferences was victorious when this issue emerged at the General Conference of 1840. The Church held that the presiding officers could freely control the activities of the local conference and hence could block abolitionist petitions.[23]

The other major factor shaping the Methodist schism was a series of compromises between antislavery and Southern Methodists codified in the *Discipline,* the authoritative rule book for American Methodism. When the Methodist Episcopal Church was established in America in 1784, the first General Conference issued a strong statement condemning slavery. Every slaveholding member had to free his slaves except in those states where manumission was prohibited. By the early nineteenth century, however, the entrenchment of slavery in the South and the rapid

22. For statistics on Southern Methodists, see McCardell, *Idea of a Southern Nation,* p. 350, and Goen, *Broken Churches, Broken Nation,* pp. 51–54.
23. Sweet, *Methodism in American History,* p. 240; McCardell, *Idea of a Southern Nation,* p. 193; Smith, *In His Image, But . . . ,* p. 105.

growth of Methodism forced the General Conference to ease its rigorous antislavery position. In 1808, the General Conference gave the local annual conferences the power to "form their own regulations relative to buying and selling slaves." In 1824, the sections in the *Discipline* on slavery were changed for the last time before the schism. Civil laws were to take priority over church law regarding slavery, and slaveholders were prohibited from holding church offices where slavery was outlawed. A commitment to these compromises, reflected in a strict constructionist view of the *Discipline*, would become an important point in the Southern Methodist position in 1844.[24]

The Methodist schism began with the emergence of abolitionism in New England in the early 1830s. The close connection between evangelical Protestantism and abolition naturally drew Northern Methodists into the antislavery movement. La Roy Sunderland, the Methodist minister at Andover, Massachusetts, helped organize the American Anti-Slavery Society in 1833. Perhaps the man most responsible for the growth of abolitionism within Northern Methodism was Orange Scott. Born to a poor Vermont family, Scott was converted to Christianity at a Methodist camp meeting. He became an ordained minister in 1826 and a vociferous abolitionist by 1834, opposing slavery for its "unjust assumption over the rights of man." Scott was instrumental in opening the columns of the *Zion's Herald* in Boston to a discussion of slavery and thereby thrusting the issue upon church leaders. Antislavery Methodism grew quickly. By 1835, antislavery societies had been formed in both the New England and New Hampshire Conferences. Methodist ministers held antislavery conventions and began to publish their own papers, such as the *Wesleyan Journal* of Maine and *Zion's Watchman* in New York. Under the leadership of Scott, Methodist abolitionists eventually seceded from the Church to form their own Wesleyan Methodist Connection of America in 1843.[25]

The issue of slavery came to a crisis at the General Conference of 1844. Methodist leaders in the North, fearful of losing more members to the Wesleyans, took a stronger stance against slavery. The debate in 1844 centered on the case of Bishop James Osgood Andrew of Georgia. Although Andrew did not own slaves when he was elected to the episcopacy, he inherited slaves through marriage and in 1844 was a slaveholder. On June 1, 1844, the General Conference voted 110 to 69 in favor of a motion that asked Bishop Andrew to desist from exercising his office

24. Norwood, *Schism in the Methodist Episcopal Church*, p. 13; Mathews, *Slavery and Methodism*, p. 32; McCardell, *Idea of a Southern Nation*, p. 193.
25. See Sweet, *Methodism in American History*, pp. 236–9, and Mathews, *Slavery and Methodism*, pp. 120–4.

so long as he owned slaves. The minority was almost entirely Southern. Outraged at this affront to Andrew and to slavery, the Southern delegates withdrew from the General Conference, and in May 1845 met in Louis- ville to establish the Methodist Episcopal Church, South.[26]

During the year between the General Conference of 1844 and the gathering in Louisville, Methodists across the South met in local con- ferences and circuits to endorse and justify their separation from their Northern brethren. The explanations of Southern Methodists centered around constitutional interpretations of Methodist church structure and doctrine forged during the conflict with the abolitionists. These explana- tions are the key to understanding the influence of the Methodist schism on the growth of Southern sectionalism, for they reveal how constitu- tional discourse lent shape and potency to the slavery controversy.[27]

Southern Methodists insisted that the interference with slavery by the General Conference violated the compromise upon which Northern and Southern Methodists had cooperated. They considered this argument "their principal ground of complaint and remonstrance." In a lengthy protest against the actions of the General Conference, Henry Bidleman Bascom of Kentucky attempted to demonstrate

> ... that the legislation of the Church on slavery, especially since 1800, originated in concession and compromise, call it by what name you will, the South have always relied on it as a solemn compact, based upon the good faith of the parties, and regard the violation of it, by the late General Conference, as inconsistent with fidelity to the obli- gations of a grave public engagement.

Recognizing the obvious parallel to the compromises on slavery forged by politicians, Bascom emphasized that "... the same specific reasons, calling for a compromise adjustment in our political, require it in our ecclesiastical relations, North and South." A similar argument in the po- litical realm – that the North had violated the compromise on slavery

26. Sweet, *Methodism in American History*, pp. 241–2; Smith, *In His Image, But...*, p. 107– 8. Thirteen Northerners joined with the Southern delegates. For narratives of the Gen- eral Conference vote, see Mathews, *Slavery and Methodism*, pp. 258–64; Smith, *In His Image, But...*, pp. 108–10; and Norwood, *Schism in the Methodist Episcopal Church*, pp. 58–81; Smith, *In His Image, But...*, p. 109.
27. Between July 4, 1844, and March 1, 1845, the Richmond *Christian Advocate* printed at least sixty-seven records of resolutions passed at these meetings; see Norwood, *Schism in the Methodist Episcopal Church*, pp. 87–8. For a representative example of these resolu- tions, see the report of a meeting in Concord, N.C., in the *Southern Christian Advocate*, July 5, 1844.

which had kept the Union together – would become a staple of secessionist thought.[28]

Southern Methodists next claimed that the General Conference's suspension of Bishop Andrew constituted a tyrannical abuse of power. Methodists in Spartanburg, South Carolina, declared the actions of the General Conference "unconstitutional, tyrannical, and oppressive," and their brethren in Charleston thought them "unconstitutional, injurious, and cannot be tolerated." To Methodists meeting in Covington, Louisiana, the decision on Andrew represented "the manifestation of this reckless spirit of usurpation of authority and assumption of power." Henry Bidleman Bascom argued that the claim of "unlimited, arbitrary power" by the General Conference was "offensive to the genius of our government..."[29]

The Southern interpretation of unconstitutionality rested upon two arguments, the first revolving around the issue of the relationship between the General Conference and a bishop. Northern Methodists argued that the bishop was an officer of the General Conference and could therefore be called before that body to account for his behavior. Southern Methodists to the contrary insisted that the episcopacy and the General Conference were coordinate bodies, equal in authority, so that the bishop was not a subject of the General Conference. In the perspective of Southerners, then, the General Conference, by suspending a bishop, had exceeded the boundaries of its authority. Second, they maintained that Bishop Andrew had held his slaves in full accordance with the *Discipline,* which gave primacy to state laws in regard to emancipation. Hence, it was illegal to condemn him for owning slaves in Georgia.[30]

These two arguments, which filled the writings of Southern Methodists after the schism, were grounded in the particular structure and doctrines of the denomination. Yet the constitutional thinking of Southern Methodists clearly reflected contemporary political discourse. They saw the obvious parallels between their experience and the position of the slaveholding Southern minority. Methodists borrowed concepts and language from the political sphere and adapted them to their own ecclesiastical conflict. They conceived of their struggle with Northern Methodists, for

28. Smith, *In His Image, But ...*, p. 111; Whitefoord Smith, *The Discipline of the Methodist E. Church, South, in Regard to Slavery* (n.p., 1849), p. 2; Henry B. Bascom, *Methodism and Slavery: with other Matters in Controversy between the North and the South; being a review of the Manifesto of the Majority in reply to the Protest of the Minority, of the late General Conference of the Methodist E. Church, in the Case of Bishop Andrew* (Frankfort, Ky.: Hodges, Todd & Pruett, 1845), pp. 8–9, 36.

29. *Southern Christian Advocate,* August 30, 1844; June 21, 1844; August 9, 1844; Bascom, *Methodism and Slavery,* p. 153.

30. Mathews, *Slavery and Methodism,* p. 249; Smith, *In His Image, But ...*, p. 109. See also *Southern Christian Advocate,* August 2, 1844.

example, in Calhounite terms as a conflict between a slaveholding minority and a majority hostile to slavery. Throughout the General Conference of 1844, Southern Methodists became increasingly aware of their minority status. Henry B. Bascom worried that Northern ascendancy was "distinctly visible, as the power of control has been in fact with Northern Conferences, and the South truly is a minority." This recognition of their status led Southerners to argue that the Andrew case represented an abuse of minority rights by a majority hostile to the South. The Methodist church in Georgetown, South Carolina, spoke of "the wrongs inflicted by a tyrannical majority." Methodists of Twiggs and Wilkinson counties in Georgia considered the recent actions of the General Conference as an "illegal and unconstitutional mandate of a reckless majority." Southern delegates protesting the Andrew decision cited "the lawless imprudence and unrestrained discretion of a prejudiced and avowedly interested majority."[31]

The final argument of Southern Methodists combined concepts peculiar to Methodism with an understanding of slavery common to Southern clergymen – the insistence that the abolitionists had violated a sacred tenet of Methodism by injecting slavery, a political issue, into the life of the church. According to Southern Methodists, the General Conference's actions on slavery violated the *Discipline,* which placed civil laws over church regulations regarding slavery. The *Southern Christian Advocate,* on these grounds, attacked the decision of the Baltimore Conference to expel Francis Harding for his refusal to manumit his slaves. Not only was Harding complying with the laws of the state, the *Southern Christian Advocate* argued, but he was adhering to the *Discipline,* which "teaches that subordination to the civil powers is the duty both of ministers and members." The Methodist Episcopal church in Savannah also emphasized that the actions of the General Conference were "antagonistic to the civil laws of the land, and in violation of that unalterable article of the Methodist Faith, which requires subjection to the civil authorities of these United States."[32]

The Southern Methodist aversion to slavery agitation in the church also drew upon the peculiar religious conception of slavery forged during the

31. Bascom, *Methodism and Slavery,* p. 24; *Southern Christian Advocate,* July 26, 1844, and August 30, 1844; "Resolution of the delegates of the slaveholding states," Eugene R. Hendrix Papers, William R. Perkins Library, Duke University, Durham, N.C. For further evidence, see the resolutions of the Cokesbury Circuit, South Carolina Conference in *Southern Christian Advocate,* July 26, 1844.

32. *Southern Christian Advocate,* May 31, 1844. The other case of the General Conference of 1844 involved Bishop Harding. Smith, *In His Image, But ...,* p. 108; *Southern Christian Advocate,* June 28, 1844.

sectional strife of the 1830s. That is, the issue of slavery had both a religious and a civil dimension. The question of the existence of slavery, fomented by the abolitionists under the garb of morality and religion, was a civil concern that was outside the domain of the church. In 1844, Southern Methodists closely followed this understanding of the slavery issue. Methodists in Georgia's Columbia Circuit, for example, regarded slavery "as a civil institution with which the Church has nothing to do..." In Mississippi, the Cole's Creek Circuit agreed that the peculiar institution was "extraneous to the Church." Southern Methodists therefore protested any ecclesiastical action on slavery because it was outside the domain of the church. The Methodist church in Eutaw, South Carolina, declared it "exceedingly unwise and improper for any ecclesiastical association to interfere with the civil institutions of the country." The actions of the General Conference, argued the church in Talbotton, Georgia, were "an assumption by that body, of jurisdiction over a question belonging to civil, and not ecclesiastical government." Methodists meeting in Mobile feared that the recent actions of the General Conference had "exposed the Church to the imputation of interfering with the civil institutions of the country."[33]

For these reasons, Northern agitation over slavery through the General Conference was portrayed as a dangerous departure from the principles of Methodism. To members of Damascus Church in the Chesterfield Circuit of South Carolina, the actions of the General Conference were "an entire subversion" of the conservative principles that had held the denomination together. Meeting in Lafayette County, Alabama, Methodists resolved "that any act of an ecclesiastical judicature, bringing the church into a position antagonistical to the state, is arrogant and revolutionary, and fit only to be repudiated and denounced by all good Christians." The Centre Circuit of South Carolina agreed that the actions of the General Conference on slavery were an "innovation" upon the principle of separation of church and state, and "hence revolutionary and disorganizing in its tendency." The Richmond *Christian Advocate* portrayed New England antislavery Methodists as "seeking extraneous objects by novel and pernicious means." The rhetoric used to depict antislavery agitation in the church reflects the strong Southern conviction that by expelling slaveholders unjustly, Northern Methodists had subverted the doctrinal integrity of the denomination. "The *Discipline* had been contemptuously

33. *Southern Christian Advocate*, August 9, 1844; Marjorie Jordan, "Mississippi Methodists and the Division of the Church over Slavery," Ph.D. diss., University of Southern Mississippi, 1972, p. 238; *Southern Christian Advocate*, September 13, 1844, August 2, 1844, and July 12, 1844. See also the resolutions of the Methodist church in Woodville, Alabama, in *Southern Christian Advocate*, August 30, 1844.

disregarded and trodden under foot," George Scarburgh explained to Methodists in Accomac County, Virginia. "The very point of our quarrel with our Northern neighbors," agreed the *Southern Christian Advocate,* "is, that *they* have departed from the provisions of that discipline, both in its letter and in the interpretation given to it by former acts and solemn resolutions of the highest court of appeals in the Church."[34]

The representation of Northern antislavery actions as subversive provided the basis for the Southern Methodist justification of schism. If the North had departed from the doctrinal standards of the denomination, then Southern separation was necessary to preserve true Methodism. "The South never thought of a separate organization," explained Henry B. Bascom, "until it became necessary to preserve Methodism as it was before the innovations of the last General Conference." The South Carolina Conference assured its members that a division of the church "cannot touch a vital principle of either doctrine or polity." In their reactions to the schism, Methodists throughout the South maintained that the new Southern church had acted on behalf of the true principles of Methodism. At a meeting in New Orleans, Methodists stated that they were "fully convinced that the South occupies a position in perfect keeping with the discipline of the Church..." George Scarburgh persuaded his brethren in Virginia that in separating from the North, "we sustain the Methodist Episcopal Church as it was." The Methodist church in Eutaw, South Carolina, affirmed this widespread belief in the integrity and continuity of the new sectional domination: "We declare our firm and undying attachment to her pure principles, and honour and love her doctrines and usages."[35]

In arguing that separation was necessary to preserve doctrinal purity, Southern Methodists were motivated by important tactical considerations. They hoped that the border conferences in Virginia and Tennessee would cast their lot with the Southern branch of the church. They also anticipated a legal fight to claim their share of the financial resources of the old Methodist church. The Rev. William Parks of Georgia worried that Northern Methodists would quickly label Southerners as "seceders" to claim the Church's property for themselves. For these reasons,

34. *Southern Christian Advocate,* June 28, 1844, September 13, 1844, and September 20, 1844; Richmond *Christian Advocate,* February 29, 1844; George Baxter Scarburgh, *Address to the People of Accomac* (n.p., n.d.), p. 27; *Southern Christian Advocate,* July 12, 1844.

35. Bascom, *Methodism and Slavery,* p. 115; *Minutes of the South Carolina Conference of the Methodist Episcopal Church for the Year 1844* (Charleston, S.C.: Office of the *Southern Christian Advocate,* 1845), p. 15; *Southern Christian Advocate,* July 26, 1844; Scarburgh, *Address to the People,* p. 27; *Southern Christian Advocate,* September 13, 1844.

Southern Methodists required a rhetorical strategy that could construe Northern actions as departures from Methodism, minimize the radical appearance of Southern separation, and portray their new denomination as the true Methodist church. Henry B. Bascom thus explained that "those who ... have represented the South as aiming at the disruption of the Church, and a separation from it, either do not understand the subject themselves, or are resolved that others shall not." George Scarburgh of Virginia insisted similarly that there was "no 'schism,' no 'secession,' but an actual division of the Church, according to a *Constitutional* plan, deliberately formed and as deliberately authorized by an immense majority of the General Conference." The *Southern Christian Advocate* strongly rebuffed the critics of the South: "Schismatics – seceders – from what, pray? – From the doctrines of Methodism found in her standards? They are no where on this continent so clung to as in the South." The Southern decision to adopt the *Discipline* of the Methodist Church with only minor verbal changes can be explained within this strategic context. Southern Methodists feared that "any change made in the Discipline of the Church, South, might be interpreted into a departure from Methodism." This strategy apparently paid off. Seeking its share of church property through an equitable distribution of the Book Concerns property, Southern Methodists brought suit in the *Methodist Church Property Case*. The case eventually came before the United States Supreme Court, which in 1854 ordered a pro rata division of the Book Concerns properties, in effect declaring the Methodist schism legal and valid.[36]

III

In its basic outline, the Baptist schism of 1845 closely resembled the split in the Methodist Church. In each case, the denomination divided along clear sectional lines because of a conflict over slavery. Also, separate sectional churches were formed from each schism. Yet the Baptists had a much looser church organization than did the Methodists, and the Southern Baptist response to the schism reflected this different ecclesiastical context. The structural differences between the two churches are impor-

36. Franklin N. Parker, ed., *A Diary-Letter Written from the Methodist General Conference of 1844 by the Rev. W. J. Parks* (Atlanta: Emory University Library, 1944), p. 7; Bascom, *Methodism and Slavery*, p. 103; Scarburgh, *Address to the People*, p. 29; *Southern Christian Advocate*, July 12, 1844; Norwood, *Schism in the Methodist Episcopal Church*, p. 99; "The Discipline of the Methodist Episcopal Church, South, in Regard to Slavery," Whitefoord Smith Papers, South Caroliniana Library, University of South Carolina, Columbia; Sweet, *Methodism in American History*, pp. 265–7.

tant, for they make the similarities in the experience of religious separation all the more striking and significant.

Like the Methodists, the Baptists had grown rapidly from a dissenting
sect during the late eighteenth century to a denomination in the early
nineteenth century. They were the second largest church in the antebellum South. With 34.6 percent of the churchgoing population in 1850, the
Baptists were only slightly smaller than the Methodists. They were the
biggest denomination in both Alabama and Georgia. Baptists in America
were loosely organized, lacking the rigid hierarchical structure of the
Methodists. Each Baptist congregation was an autonomous body. The
desire for some kind of church structure led to formation of state conventions, though often over strong local opposition. Northern and Southern
Baptists were united in the Baptist Triennial Convention, composed of the
Foreign Mission Board (1814) and the American Baptist Home Missionary Society (1832). The controversy over slavery revolved around these
missionary groups. In 1840, abolitionists formed the American Baptist
Anti-slavery Society and three years later established the American Baptist Free Mission Society, which excluded slaveholders. Northern conservatives, anxious to maintain ecclesiastical unity with abolitionists and
the South, sought compromise. In 1840, the Board of Foreign Missions
agreed that slavery fell outside their constitutional functions. A year later,
the Home Mission Society similarly announced its neutrality on this
troublesome issue.[37]

Northern Baptists – especially in New England – had been growing
increasingly antislavery during the 1830s. The Maine Baptist Association declared in 1836 that slavery was "the most abominable" of all the
systems of iniquity that had cursed the world. Like their Methodist
brethren, Baptist abolitionists gradually succeeded in convincing Northern conservatives that slavery had no place in the church. In 1844, Georgia Baptists requested that James Reeve, a slaveholder, be appointed a
missionary to the Indians. The Home Missionary Society rejected Reeve's
application because of his complicity with slavery. Shortly thereafter, the
Baptist State Convention of Alabama demanded from the Foreign Mission meeting in Boston "the distinct, explicit avowal that slaveholders are
eligible and entitled equally with non-slaveholders to all the privileges and
immunities of their several unions." The board replied that they could
"never be a party to any arrangement which would imply approbation of
slavery." Smarting from this insult, Southern Baptists gathered in Au-

---

37. McCardell, *Idea of a Southern Nation*, pp. 188, 350; Mary B. Putnam, *The Baptists
    and Slavery, 1840–1845* (Ann Arbor, Mich.: George Wohr, Publisher, 1913), pp. 21, 30;
    Smith, *In His Image, But . . .*, pp. 119–20.

gusta, Georgia, in May 1845, withdrew from the Triennial Convention's Boards, and created the Southern Baptist Convention.[38]

The Baptist and Methodist schisms shared important similarities. It was Northern abolitionists who first injected moral questions about slavery into the church. To suppress abolitionist agitation, Southerners relied upon both certain compromises with Northern conservatives and specific interpretations of church government and doctrine. Southern Baptists and Methodists eventually left their national churches because of what they considered an unwarranted abuse of power by ecclesiastical bodies. It should not be surprising then that the responses of Southern Baptists to their schism would echo those of Southern Methodists. Yet at the same time, the Baptist understanding and justification of separation reflected the distinctive doctrines and structure of their denomination.

The most common argument of Southern Baptists during and after the schism was the contention that by legislating on slavery – by refusing to appoint slaveholders as missionaries – the mission boards had transcended the boundaries of their authority. The action of the boards, declared the Incorporated Baptist Church of Charleston, represented "an assumption of power expressly denied to them, by the very body under which they hold their authority." The *Alabama Baptist* asserted similarly that the American Baptist Home Mission Board "... greatly transcended their legitimate authority in adopting such an interpretation." This argument rested upon a particular interpretation of the powers possessed by the mission boards and their relationship to the rest of the denomination. Southerners maintained that the boards were simply agents of the Triennial Convention whose functions were limited to missionary endeavors. The *Christian Index* of Georgia suggested that the Triennial Convention was merely "a large Missionary Society, composed of the delegates of local societies – having nothing, absolutely nothing to do with ecclesiastical or religious matters." Ultimate sovereignty resided instead in each individual church. As an Alabama Baptist explained, "as these Societies and Boards are mere handmaids of the churches, I would have them by no means transcend the limits of their legitimate bounds of operation. The churches exist independent of and above all." The *Alabama Baptist* maintained "there is no such thing as *the Baptist Church*." The journal believed that each church was "republican, all authority being invested in the people."[39]

38. McCardell, *Idea of a Southern Nation*, p. 183; Walter B. Posey, *Frontier Mission: A History of Religion West of the Appalachians to 1861* (Lexington: University of Kentucky Press, 1966), p. 367; Putnam, *Baptists and Slavery*, pp. 53–5; Smith, *In His Image, But....* pp. 126–7.
39. *Christian Index*, April 25, 1845; *Alabama Baptist*, October 24, 1844; *Minutes of the North Carolina Baptist State Convention, held in Raleigh, October 17–25, 1845* (Raleigh:

On the basis of these interpretations of ecclesiastical order, Southern Baptists labeled the deeds of the mission boards as unconstitutional. The Bethel Baptist Church in Sumter District, South Carolina, denounced the "non-constitutional and unscriptural conduct of many of our Northern brethren." A Baptist church in Chambers County, Alabama, argued that Northern actions regarding slavery "abrogated the constitution by which we were bound together as one in Foreign and Domestic Missions." Revealingly, the inaugural address of the Southern Baptist Convention explained that division occurred "not because we reside at the South but because they have adopted an unconstitutional and unscriptural principal to govern their future course." The rhetoric of unconstitutionality, a constant refrain in the writings of Southern Baptists, is almost identical to the language used by Southern Methodists. This consonance can be partially explained by the close parallels between the causes and nature of the schisms.[40]

The Southern Baptist justification of schism parallels other arguments used by Methodists. Schism was explained as a restoration of denominational integrity, and the new Southern churches were depicted as safe depositories of denominational principles. Baptists too contended that the North had violated ecclesiastical doctrine, which made separation imperative. "Great scriptural principles had been trampled under foot," declared the Baptist Foreign Mission Society of Virginia, "by those to whom we had confided our Missionary operations. To vindicate these principles as well as our own rights, the convention was summoned." The Savannah River Baptist Association of South Carolina explained that although they had separated from their brethren in the North, they had not departed "from our principles or Christ's cause." Underscoring the preservative nature of the schism served to ameliorate the radical appearance of the Southern separation and to bolster the religious integrity of the new Southern Baptist Convention. As the *Biblical Recorder* of North Carolina explained: "For the preservation of the authority of Divine Truth we have separated – not that we love our Northern brethren less, but that we love principles and its Divine Author more – not that we are disorganizers, but conservatives." In their inaugural address to Baptists around the world, the Southern Baptist Convention stressed that its principles were "conservative." The doctrinal continuity between the Triennial Convention and the new sectional denomination vindicated the position of Southern

Recorder Office, 1846), p. 37; *Christian Index*, April 11, 1845; *Alabama Baptist*, April 26, 1845, June 7, 1845. See also *Journal of the Proceedings of the Baptist State Convention, in Alabama, at its Twentieth Anniversary, at Marion, Perry County: Commencing on Saturday, November 16th, 1844* (n.p., 1844), p. 8.

40. *Biblical Recorder*, July 26, 1845; *Alabama Baptist*, June 10, 1845; Putnam, *Baptists and Slavery*, p. 61.

Baptists. "By adopting the old constitution, with only a change in names and Board," explained the *Christian Index* of Georgia, "it will be rendered manifest to all future ages, that the action of the Boston Board was the *true* and *only* cause of our separation."[41]

IV

Contemporary Southerners recognized that the religious divisions would have political consequences. Running through the Southern responses to the Presbyterian, Methodist, and Baptist schisms were predictions on the impact that the sundering of national denominational ties would have on the civil relations between North and South. The prognostications of clergymen, laymen, and politicians were ambiguous, confused, and conflicting. Some feared that the schisms would indeed be "harbingers of disunion," foreshadowing a rupture in the political sphere. Others argued that the denominational divisions would actually temper and restrain sectional passions. Contemporary analysis of the political implications of the denominational schisms merits our close attention, for it brought to the surface deeply held assumptions on religion and politics that were shaping the sectional thought of Southern clergymen.

The Southern political press closely noted the Baptist and Methodist schisms in 1844 and 1845, often reprinting the proceedings of ecclesiastical meetings. The Democratic Milledgeville *Federal Union* considered the schisms in the Methodist and Baptist churches a subject "of great importance." To the Charleston *Mercury,* the Methodist split was "one of the momentous events of these days," and the *Mississippi Free Trader* of Natchez, another Democratic sheet, also noted its significance. Although the Frankfort *Commonwealth* considered the schisms "purely a Church' question," they nonetheless acknowledged that "one political aspect connects with it, and that is the supposed effect of tendency of such division upon the National Union." The Savannah *Republican* insisted that the Baptist schism was "intimately connected with our Southern institutions, and perhaps may have a remote bearing on the ultimate political relations of the Northern and Southern portions of the Union." The denomina-

41. *Proceedings of the Twenty-Second Annual Meeting of the Baptist General Association of Virginia assembled at Lynchburg, Virginia, May 31st, 1845* (n.p., n.d.), p. 27; *Minutes of the Savannah River Baptist Association, at its Forty-Fourth Anniversary, held with the Beech Branch Church, S. C. November 22, 23, 24, 25, and 26, 1845* (Savannah: Office of P. G. Thomas, 1845); *Biblical Recorder,* July 12, 1845; *Proceedings of the Southern Baptist Convention, Held in Augusta, Georgia* (Richmond, Va.: H. K. Ellyson, 1845), p. 19; *Christian Index,* April 4, 1845.

tional schisms, especially those in the Baptist and Methodist churches in the 1840s, seemed to receive more attention in the Democratic press, although they were also noted in some Whig newspapers. The *Georgia Messenger*, for instance, considered the division in the Methodist church the "most alarming symptom of a sectional disaffection."[42]

Most Southern politicians believed that the severance of religious ties was an obvious and ominous threat to political unity. The Democratic and strongly states' rights Richmond *Enquirer* feared the "most injurious consequences" from the schisms. The *Southern Recorder*, a Whig paper from Milledgeville, Georgia, saw in the denominational splits a "weakening of the bonds of our Union." To the radical Charleston *Mercury*, the Methodist schism marked "an epoch – the *first dissolution* of *the Union*." The Whig-oriented Charleston *Courier* insisted that the religious divisions struck "the first blow at our political union, by compelling severance of religious union, between worshippers of the same creed." Politicians seemed to fear that separate sectional churches would worsen relations between the North and South. "The jealousies of rival religious institutions," explained the Richmond *Enquirer*, "may create embittered feelings and, in the end, destroy the highest incentives to the love of the Union." The Charleston *Mercury* agreed: "With religions arrayed against and scowling at each other on opposite sides of the line – not only with that peaceful influence lost, but with all its mighty power thrown into the scale of discord, how long will the political union of the North and South continue?"[43]

Some religious leaders believed similarly that a disruption of ecclesiastical harmony would threaten political unity and possibly lead toward disunion. "Let the three great religious denominations," wrote a Baptist from Alabama, "the Presbyterian, the Methodist, and the Baptist, de-

42. Milledgeville *Federal Union*, May 27, 1845; Charleston *Mercury*, June 14, 1844; *Mississippi Free Trader*, May 29, 1844; Frankfort *Commonwealth* quoted in Charleston *Mercury*, June 3, 1845; Savannah *Republican*, May 7, 1845; *Georgia Messenger*, May 30, 1844. For another example in the Whig Press, see the Milledgeville *Southern Recorder* for June 18 and June 25, 1844.
43. Richmond *Enquirer*, May 27, 1845; Milledgeville *Southern Recorder*, May 20, 1845; Charleston *Mercury*, June 20, 1844; Charleston *Courier*, June 2, 1845; Richmond *Enquirer*, May 6, 1845; Charleston *Mercury*, June 14, 1844. See also Richmond *Compiler* quoted in Raleigh *Standard*, May 15, 1844, and *United States Gazette* quoted in Charleston *Mercury*, May 28, 1845. The reaction of the Charleston *Mercury* to the religious schisms was colored by the radical political views of the newspaper. There was renewed talk about secession in South Carolina in 1844. Because the *Mercury* had been advocating this course since the early 1840s, it tended to exaggerate the impact of the schisms and applaud any movement toward disunion. I am indebted to Michael F. Holt for suggesting this interpretation of the editorials from the *Mercury*.

clare off from union of effort to do good, North and South, and our glorious union of States will be greatly weakened, if not sundered entirely." William B. Johnson, a Baptist clergyman from South Carolina, agreed that a division of so large a group of Christians as the Baptists "cannot fail to exert a powerful influence on the condition of these States, in relation to the perpetuation of their Union." The *Religious Herald* of Richmond reasoned that slavery was the only issue "which threatens this union; and if religious bodies must divide upon it, how can we expect political bodies to bear the excitement." The danger to the nation posed by the Methodist split was aptly summarized by the Tennessee Methodist William C. Booth: "It has, in truth, been already hailed as the harbinger of disunion."[44]

The contention that the denominational schisms foreshadowed political disunion rested on the assumption that religious unity provided an important moral bond that held the political union together. A disruption of moral unity would dangerously weaken the whole political system. "We have always considered the moral ties, which bind the two together," stated the Baptist *Christian Index* of Georgia, "much stronger than the political. Let each of the great leading denominations of christians be severed, and alienation in other respects must ensue." The role of religion in preserving political stability was explained by the *Alabama Baptist:*

> See the ponderous rock imbedded in the top of yon high Mountain; while at the base are deposited all our hopes and interest, no danger threatens until the instant you move that rock from its foundation. By whatever course may be adopted, there is a great moral influence to be exerted, for weal or for woe, upon the destiny of republics.

The assumption that political unity was to a great extent conditional on religious harmony led some Southerners to wonder how a political union could survive if a religious one failed. A writer to the Charleston *Mercury* suggested that Northerners "know how little is to be expected from any other *Union*, if the union of Christians fail." The South Carolina Baptist Convention questioned similarly: "If *we*, who profess to have but one Lord, one faith, one baptism, one God and Father, cannot remain united in the cause of benevolent effort, how can they be expected to perpetuate their union on mere political principles?"[45]

44. *Alabama Baptist,* December 6, 1845; William B. Johnson 1844 ms, William Johnson Papers, Furman University; *Religious Herald,* May 8, 1845; Booth, *Writings of William A. Booth, M.D. during the Controversy upon Slavery,* p. 6.
45. *Christian Index,* March 14, 1845; *Alabama Baptist,* April 5, 1845; Charleston *Mercury,* May 9, 1845; *Minutes of the State Convention of the Baptist Denomination in South Carolina, at its Twenty-Fourth anniversary, held at Darlington Baptist Church* (n.p., n.d.), p. 7.

In contrast, some politicians and religious leaders argued that ecclesiastical division would dampen sectional strife and thus preserve the Union. The Georgia *Messenger,* a Whig paper from Macon, did not believe "that any injury is to result from the secession, either to the cause of religion, or when looked upon in a political aspect." Similarly, the Charleston *Courier* referred to the schisms as "decidedly conservative." This journal explained that controversies were settled "in deliberation and peace, which might otherwise have occurred in passion and tempest, to the ruin of social order and disruption of political bonds, as well as the ... destruction of religious ties." Similar arguments were found among churchmen. In a public appeal to South Carolina Baptists, John B. Miller maintained that "we do trust & devoutly pray & Hope that the ties of our government and Union may not be weakened, but strengthened and perpetuated while time shall last." The *Southern Christian Advocate* of Charleston contended similarly that "the safety of the country is to a much greater extent bound up with a division of the church, than a continued union."[46]

The belief that the denominational schisms would preserve rather than endanger the Union rested primarily on two arguments. First, separation between Northern and Southern Christians would stifle the abolitionists by taking away a powerful and visible forum. "The question of slavery," reasoned the Georgia *Messenger,* "which, with the greatest difficulty, has been kept smothered in those large promiscuous assemblies which periodically hold their meetings to legislate for the government of their churches, is a most prolific source of discord and contention." William Winans, a Methodist minister from Mississippi, argued that a division of the church would "put a stop to the agitation of the slavery question on religious grounds." The layman J. E. Evans of Savannah explained that the Methodist General Conference "was a common centre from which the whole church and country was thrilled with excitement every four years," and that separation "will destroy these causes of excited feeling." Southern Baptists concurred with their Methodist brethren: "Sever all the ecclesiastical cords which bind us to the Northern people, and they will have but little pretext to interfere with the subject, and *no* opportunity to reach us with their abolitionist agitation." The *Christian Index* of Georgia maintained similarly that separation from the "professedly religious fanatics at the North" would "lessen their opportunities of getting up an excitement on the subject of slavery."[47]

46. *Georgia Messenger,* May 22, 1845; Charleston *Courier,* June 2, 1845; Address [1845?] to "The Southern Convention of the Baptists," Miller–Furman–Dabbs Papers, South Caroliniana Library, Columbia; *Southern Christian Advocate,* November 22, 1844.
47. *Georgia Messenger,* May 22, 1845; Charleston *Mercury,* May 15, 1845; *Southern Chris-*

Southern Protestants argued also that the resistance they displayed by seceding from their denominations would serve as an example to thwart antislavery aggression. "The division of the Methodist Church," proclaimed the *Southern Christian Advocate,* "will demonstrate this fact to the country, that southern forbearance has its limits, and that a vigorous and united resistance will be made at all costs, to the spread of pseudo-religious phrenzy called abolitionism." As a group of Methodists from Alabama explained, "Northern politicians, seeing that Southern Christians prefer a division to compromising principles, will be led to pause and weigh the consequences before they push matters to extremes." In general, Southern politicians applauded the resolve demonstrated by the denominations and held up the church as a model of Southern resistance. Langdon Cheves of South Carolina, a former congressman who would represent the Palmetto state at the Nashville convention of 1850, thought the action of Southern Methodists worthy of imitation, and the *Georgia Messenger* looked upon them as "champions of Southern Institutions." This adulation of the church was perhaps best expressed by the Charleston *Mercury:* "Thank God! it is the church which heralds the way to redemption and safety."[48]

The existence of conflicting assessments of the political impact of the denominational schisms can be explained by viewing them as polemical. Southern Methodists, for instance, needed support in the border states and faced a legal battle to claim their share of the financial resources of the Methodist Church. Requiring a rhetorical strategy that minimized the revolutionary appearance of their actions, the Methodists generally denied the separatist tendencies of their schism. This is one possible explanation why the Methodists more than the Baptists downplayed the fear of disunion. In the political sphere, politicians eager to agitate the slavery issue for partisan purposes understandably magnified the political threat of the schisms. The Democratic and more pro-Southern papers, such as the *Mercury* and the *Enquirer,* tended to give more space and attention to the schisms.

The arguments Southern Protestants put forth regarding the political implications of their separation from the North reveal deeply held assumptions about the relationship between politics and religion. Lurking just beneath the surface of both the secular and religious writings of

tian Advocate, October 4, 1844; *A Calm Appeal to Southern Baptists in Advocacy of Separation from the North* (n.p., n.d.), p. 11; *Christian Index,* June 6, 1845. For a contrary opinion, see the Richmond *Compiler* quoted in the Raleigh *Standard,* May 15, 1844.

48. *Southern Christian Advocate,* November 22, 1844, and September 6, 1844; Booth, *Writings of William A. Booth,* p. 34; Georgia *Messenger,* June 13, 1844; Charleston *Mercury,* June 4, 1845.

Southerners in the 1840s was the perception that religion and politics occupied distinct – and in some ways incompatible – spheres. Religion seemed to be assigned the higher virtues of order, charity, and forbearance, whereas politics was an arena of strife and contention. "If we compare the course of these peaceful and private Christians," explained the Charleston *Mercury,* "with the course of the politicians of the South, how superior in Christian duty – how far above our Government has the church towered in manliness, dignity and patriotism." A writer to the Charleston *Courier* wrote similarly that "none other than Christian men could have been carried through such a crisis, with so much temper, so much judgment, order and wisdom." There was simply far more faith placed in religion. The Milledgeville *Southern Recorder* argued that the moral unity of religion was essential "to counteract the effect of divided and discrepant feelings in other ways." These comments help explain why the denominational schisms appeared to be so ominous in church and state alike. Religious divisions over slavery were a sign that the slavery controversy might eventually move beyond the reach of the political system.[49]

V

In the mid-1840s, then, religious and political leaders in the South saw an obvious connection between the denominational divisions over slavery and the growing political controversy pitting North against South. For the historian, the central problem of interpretation is to determine what significance the denominational splits had on the development of Southern sectionalism. A direct line of influence from the religious schisms to Southern politics is difficult to demonstrate. The language of religious schisms and the political discourse of the 1840s does, however, strongly suggest that religious and political leaders shared a common framework for understanding the sectional conflict over slavery. It is easier to establish the impact of the denominational schisms on the sectional thought of Southern clergymen. Parallels can be drawn between the clerical understanding of religious separation in the 1830s and 1840s and their conception of secession in 1860–1. In addition, the heightened sectional awareness that surfaced among Southern clergymen after the schisms provides additional evidence for the influence of the denominational divisions.

49. Charleston *Mercury,* June 4, 1845; Charleston *Courier,* May 12, 1845; *Southern Recorder,* May 20, 1845.

The impact of the denominational schisms on Southern sectionalism was shaped largely by the political context of the 1840s. The sectional crises of this decade firmly and irrevocably fixed the politics of slavery on the South. Beginning in earnest in 1843, Whig President John Tyler made the annexation of Texas the primary focus of his administration. As a proslavery, states' rights Virginian hoping to be elected in 1844, Tyler anticipated that his efforts would be popular among Southerners eager for additional slave territory. He was joined by John C. Calhoun, who saw in annexation a means of achieving his dream of a political party uniting the proslavery South. Texas consumed the election of 1844. Democratic hopeful Martin Van Buren alienated his Southern support by opposing annexation. Whig candidate Henry Clay, misreading Southern opinion, also opposed it. Southern Democrats threw their support behind James K. Polk of Tennessee. Polk defeated Clay in the presidential election, and annexation became a reality in December 1844.

The slavery controversy took on additional intensity with the introduction of the Wilmot Proviso in 1846, which banned slavery from any territories acquired as a result of the Mexican War. The proviso created the explosive issue of slavery in the territories, crumbling party lines in Congress and replacing them with sectional loyalties. During the 1848 election, Southern Whigs and Democrats were portraying themselves as the best friends of slavery. Regular Democrats soon fell in line with the Calhounites. By 1850, the South was firmly committed to the politics of slavery. The discourse of Southern politicians, fashioned in the political furnace of the 1840s, provides a promising place to look for the influence of religious divisions over slavery.[50]

The language of constitutionalism filled the writings of Southern politicians and editors. The annexation of Texas did raise the issue of the

---

50. In examining the responses of Southern politicians to both the annexation and territorial issues, the important party divisions between Democrats and Whigs must be kept in mind. In general, Southern Democrats were more enthusiastic about annexation than Whigs, who tended to defuse it as a political ploy of President Tyler. For political reasons, the Whigs wanted to keep slavery out of politics. See William J. Cooper, Jr., *The South and the Politics of Slavery, 1828–1856* (Baton Rouge and London: Louisiana State University Press, 1978), chaps. 6 and 7. The most recent and thorough account of Southern politics in the 1840s is William W. Freehling, *The Road to Disunion, Vol. I: Secessionists at Bay, 1776–1854* (New York: Oxford University Press, 1990), Part VI. See also William R. Brock, *Parties and Political Conscience: American Dilemmas, 1840–1850* (Millwood, N.Y.: KTO Press, 1979); Chaplain W. Morrison, *Democratic Politics and Sectionalism: The Wilmot Proviso Controversy* (Chapel Hill: University of North Carolina Press, 1967); Norman A. Graebner, "1848: Southern Politics at the Crossroads," *The Historian* 25 (November 1962): 14–35; and Eric Foner, "The Wilmot Proviso Revisited," *Journal of American History* LVI (September 1969): 262–79.

constitutional authority of treaty making, although it was a minor theme in the political press. Constitutional discourse was far more prevalent in the Southern reaction to the Wilmot Proviso. The Southern position was essentially that of Calhoun's, who argued that the territories belonged to all the states in common and that therefore Congress had no right to legislate against slaveholders in these areas. Calhoun's views were incorporated into resolutions by the Virginia legislature that became known as the "Platform of the South" and that were subsequently adopted by Alabama and Texas. Citizens meeting in the Chesterfield District of South Carolina in 1847 declared the Wilmot Proviso "a direct attempt at invasion of the constitutional and natural rights of the slaveholding citizens of our Republic." To the Democratic Republicans of Norfolk, Virginia, it was "in direct conflict with the spirit of the Federal Constitution." Politicians in the South, like the churchmen, insisted that the best protection of their particular interests lay in constitutional guarantees. "The whole South must see," explained the Democratic *Federal Union* of Georgia, "that her only security is in a rigid adherence to the letter of the national compact. She is in the minority and is destined there to remain. If the constitution will not protect her, nothing can."[51]

Constitutional discourse was also common in the writings of Southern Protestants of different denominations to characterize and conceptualize ecclesiastical conflict. Southern Baptists and Methodists, for example, described the actions of Northern-dominated church bodies as "unconstitutional." The Methodists and the small group of New School Presbyterians in the South portrayed their ecclesiastical conflict as a constitutional struggle between majority power and minority rights. The Baptists emphasized the sovereignty and independence of the local church. In their ecclesiastical struggles, Southern Protestants freely borrowed constitutional discourse from the political sphere to strengthen constitutional arguments developed within a particular denominational context. The process of denominational schism, in turn, gave added depth and meaning to political discourse. The ecclesiastical conflict between majority tyranny and minority rights strengthened the inclination to view sectional politics in these terms.

Honor and equality were other themes that emerged in both the religious and political discourse of the 1840s. The Wilmot Proviso in particular was portrayed as an assault on Southern honor and equality. "We

51. Jesse T. Carpenter, *The South as a Conscious Minority, 1789–1861: A Study in Political Thought* (New York: New York University Press, 1930), pp. 147–8; Cooper, *South and the Politics of Slavery*, p. 253; Richmond *Enquirer*, February 27, 1847; Charleston *Mercury*, November 9, 1847; Milledgeville *Federal Union*, June 29, 1847. See also the resolutions of a meeting in Charleston printed in the Charleston *Mercury*, March 10, 1847.

have heretofore denounced it as a national libel on our character and institutions," insisted the radical Charleston *Mercury:* "It is a proclamation to the world that we of the South are not deemed worthy of communion and equality." Citizens meeting in the Georgetown District, South Carolina, regarded the Wilmot Proviso as "designed to stamp with political inferiority one entire section of the Confederacy." The Henrico Democratic Association in Virginia similarly considered an antiannexation resolution passed in New York as "in the last degree intolerant and proscriptive towards the slaveholding States." Southerners claimed that the Wilmot Proviso would cut them off "from an equal participation of the benefits of any annexation." The fear, of course, was that prohibition of slavery in the territories would further increase the minority status of the slaveholding South. "If the principle here maintained shall be carried into effect," reasoned the Milledgeville *Federal Union,* "the South is proscribed, her equality with other sections of the Republic destroyed, and the letter and spirit of the constitution utterly set at nought."[52]

Similar language can be found in the justifications Southern Baptists and Methodists put forth during their denominational schisms. Citizens in Russell County, Alabama, for instance, argued that the action of the Methodist General Conference regarding slavery "involves both insult and outrage to the people of an entire section of the Union." The Beech Island Church in South Carolina spoke also of the "the revilings and odium" cast upon Baptists in the South by their Northern brethren. Southern Baptists claimed that abolitionists in their church had roused the entire North to "systematic attempts to deprive us of our rights in the General Societies, and to affix a stigma upon us . . ." In the 1840s, the issue in church and state was the same: An antislavery majority was depriving Southern slaveholders of their rights and equalities in a union with the North.[53]

52. Charleston *Mercury,* February 24, 1847, and November 12, 1847; Richmond *Enquirer,* May 3, 1844, and May 10, 1844; Milledgeville *Federal Union,* March 2, 1847. See also a report of the meeting of citizens in Clarke County in Richmond *Enquirer,* May 28, 1844. For a good summary of the Southern response to the Wilmot Proviso, see Cooper, *South and the Politics of Slavery,* pp. 238–44. For valuable discussions of Southern honor and the sectional conflict, see Bertram Wyatt-Brown, *Southern Honor: Ethics and Behavior in the Old South* (New York: Oxford University Press, 1982); Edward L. Ayers, *Vengeance and Justice: Crime and Punishment in the 19th-Century American South* (New York: Oxford University Press, 1984); and Kenneth Greenberg, *Masters and Statesmen: The Political Culture of American Slavery* (Baltimore and London: Johns Hopkins University Press, 1985).

53. *Southern Christian Advocate,* July 12, 1844; *Christian Index,* April 25, 1845; [A Southern Baptist], *A Calm Appeal to Southern Baptists, in Advocacy of Separation from the North in all the Works of Christian Benevolence* (n.p., n.d.), p. 10.

The schisms in the Baptist and Methodist churches were thus played out against the backdrop of Texas and the Wilmot Proviso. While the two major denominations in the nation were dividing over the issue of slavery in 1844 and 1845, the South was embroiled in the heated debate over the annexation of Texas and the presidential election of 1844. Accounts of the Methodist General Conference were placed beside reports from pro-Texas meetings held across the South. Considering the timing of events, it would be surprising if Southern perceptions of the denominational schisms were *not* in some ways conditioned by the intensification of sectional politics. Southerners who read either or both secular and religious journals could not have helped but notice the parallels between church and state. In each realm, the slaveholding South was being insulted and threatened by an aggressive antislavery power in the North. After the 1840s, Southerners had learned from both religion and politics to see the dangers of Northern aggression and the necessity of protecting slavery and Southern rights.

The denominational schisms influenced the growth of Southern separatism in yet another way. In their experience with separating from their Northern brethren, Southern churchmen articulated ideas of union and division that would help facilitate secession in 1860–1. One such legacy was the conception of a union that was conditional on peace and harmony. For religious and political Southerners in the 1840s, separation was preferable to a union that produced conflict and strife. "Highly as we estimate the importance of religious union to cement and strengthen the bonds of our political union," explained the Charleston *Courier*, "we have long regarded union without harmony as a prolific and bitter foundation of discord and ultimate disunion, perhaps in wrath and desolation." An Alabamian believed that the religious schisms "will teach us that no union can be of long duration, unless the several members of that union, in their conduct toward each other, adhere to the principles of justice." To the Methodist *Southern Christian Advocate,* a union "inflamed by sectional jealousies and affording an arena for endless strife" was only a "nominal union."[54]

It was the meaning of separation, however, that became the most important ideological legacy to secession of the denominational schisms. Southern Baptists and Methodists portrayed their schisms as conservative acts necessary to preserve the doctrinal and institutional integrity of the church. For Old School Presbyterians in the South, religious schism was an imperative purification of heterodoxy from the true church.

---

54. Charleston *Courier*, June 2, 1844; *Southern Christian Advocate*, September 20, 1844; and November 22, 1844.

Taken together, these depictions point to a fundamental conception of separation as a restorative act aimed at purging subversive elements and preserving original principles and institutions. This paradigm of separation provided the framework in which Southern clergymen thought about political separation from the North. It was this kind of mind set that encouraged Southerners to see their enemies as the true seceders, who had departed from established principles. This interpretation of religious schism anticipated the core of the secessionist argument that disunion was a conservative movement aimed at preserving the constitutional integrity of the original Union.[55]

The argument for secession from the Union set forth by Southern clergymen of all denominations closely followed the pattern used to justify religious schism: Northern subversion destroyed the institutions and principles binding the sections, these violations necessitated separation, and the new Southern nation embodied and thus preserved the integrity of the former union. In 1850, the Baptist minister Iveson L. Brookes warned that the North was "bent on overleaping every constitutional barrier" to sacrifice Southern interests. The Rev. William H. Barnwell, in a fast day sermon delivered before the South Carolina legislature that year, significantly labeled the federal government a "Usurper" for threatening Southern rights. Just as antislavery churchmen had annulled ecclesiastical agreements and subverted constitutions by expelling slaveholders, Northern politicians had similarly destroyed the Union. On the eve of the Civil War, the Rev. Daniel I. Dreher of Concord, North Carolina, argued that "these violations of the original compact, annulled the agreement" binding together the sections. "Whenever any contracting party fails to comply with the articles of agreement," he explained in justifying secession, "the contract becomes null and void, and the contracting parties absolved from their obligations to the agreement." James H. Thornwell contended similarly that Southern secession was motivated by the "profound conviction that the Constitution, in its relation to slavery, has been virtually repealed." In these ways, Northern politicians, like their region's clergymen, were really responsible for the dissolution of the nation.[56]

55. The Southern religious logic of secession is more fully explored in Chapter 5.
56. Iveson L. Brookes, *A Defense of the South Against the Reproaches of and Incroachments of the North: In which Slavery is shown to be an Institution of God intended to form the basis of the best social state and the only safeguard to the permanence of a Republican Government* (Hamburg, S. C.: Republican Office, 1850), p. 6; William H. Barnwell, *Views upon the present Crisis. A Discourse, delivered in St. Peter's Church, Charleston, on the 6th of December, 1850, the Day of Fasting, Humiliation and Prayer, appointed by the Legislature of South Carolina* (Charleston: E. C. Councell, 1850), p. 7; Daniel I. Dreher, *A Sermon Delivered by Rev. Daniel I. Dreher, pastor of St. James Church, Concord, N. C.,*

The belief that the Southern Baptist Convention and the Methodist Episcopal Church, South, retained the doctrinal integrity of the denomination from which they separated was similar to the idea that the Confederacy preserved the constitutional integrity of the former Union. The Rev. W. T. Leacock assured his New Orleans audience that "we will administer among ourselves the Constitution which our Fathers have left us." On the Confederate fast day of June 13, 1861, a Mobile minister argued that "the land of the slave is the last refuge on this continent... of rational, constitutional liberty." The Southern Baptist Convention, in announcing their support of the Confederacy in 1861, well expressed the interpretation of secession as a conservative act of preservation: "[T]he Southern States have practically asserted the right of seceding from a Union so degenerated from that established by the Constitution, and they have formed for themselves a government based upon the principles of the original compact – adopting a charter which secures to each state its sovereign rights and privileges."[57]

With the impending dissolution of the Union, the denominational schisms acquired a new and powerful relevance. Southern churchmen recognized the contribution they had made and urged the rest of the South to heed the lesson learned in the 1840s. The schisms, looking back from 1861, prefigured secession. They had indeed become "harbingers of disunion." In 1860, the Savannah River Baptist Association of South Carolina argued that "the sectional feeling which lately split in twain the bonds that united us with the North in Christian communion, was a sure indication that those who could not live together as a church, would scarcely continue in Political Union." Similarly, the *Texas Baptist* feared the ascendancy of an antislavery faction "because its power in producing divisions has been tested and fully proven by the separations it has caused between Northern and Southern Christians of the same denomination." Southern Methodists, insisted the Nashville *Christian Advocate,* had "diagnosed the reigning fanaticism in all its stages of emancipationism, free-soilism, conservative abolitionism, conditional abolitionism, and

June 13, 1861. Day of Humiliation and Prayer, as per Appointment of the President of the Confederate States of America (Salisbury, N.C.: *Watchman* Office, 1861), p. 8; Benjamin M. Palmer, *The Life and Letters of James Henley Thornwell, D.D., LL.D.* (Richmond, Va.: Whittet & Shepperson, 1875), p. 595.

57. Quoted in Palmer, *Rights of the South*, p. 16; H. N. Pierce, *Sermons Preached in St. John's Church, Mobile, on the 13th of June, 1861, the National Fast appointed by His Excellency Jefferson Davis, President of the Confederate States of America* (Mobile, Ala.: Farrow & Dennett, Book and Job Printers, 1861), p. 6; *Proceedings of the Southern Baptist Convention at its Eighth Biennial Session, Held in the First Baptist Church, Savannah, GA, May 10th, 11th, 12th, and 13th, 1861* (Richmond, Va.: MacFarlane and Fergusson, 1861), p. 62.

ultra-abolitionism." Before the rest of the South understood the dangers of abolitionism, Methodists "had experienced how that power would be used which, in its own nature, was grasping, overbearing, and touched with malignity."[58]

Besides prefiguring secession, the schisms served as an inspiration to the new Confederacy, providing a precedent of courage and rectitude in separating from the North. Southern Protestants harkened back to the 1830s and 1840s with pride. "The history of Southern Methodism has been known and read to little purpose," argued a New Orleans Methodist in 1861, "if, at this late date, our position has to be defined. You politicians are ungrateful and exacting. We cut short the quarrel in 1844." The Alabama Baptist State Convention believed that "the unparalleled unanimity and moral strength now exhibited by our beloved land, is due, under God, in no small degree to the labors of Southern Christians – preachers, and Missionaries, and private members – who have not been hampered nor directed by Northern Boards." Perhaps the inspirational influence of the denominational schisms was best articulated by the *Central Presbyterian* of Richmond shortly after Abraham Lincoln had been elected president:

> Is it to be wondered at then that the people of the South are not all prepared tamely to submit to the issues of the day? The Southern Presbyterians did not do it – the Southern Methodists did not do it – the Southern Baptists did not do it. And as they are *of* the people, and *with* the people, it is passing strange that their example given years ago, has not been read with greater profit – an example which serves to show that the same cause which has produced sectional disruptions in ecclesiastical brotherhoods, may also rend asunder the brotherhood of states.

By the time of secession, the denominational schisms had become a legacy to which all Southerners could look for guidance and strength. It was their final and fitting bestowal to the emergence of Southern nationalism.[59]

---

58. *Minutes of the Savannah River Baptist Association*, p. 3; *Texas Baptist*, January 3, 1861; *Christian Advocate*, April 11, 1861.

59. *Christian Advocate*, January 3, 1861; *Minutes of the Thirty-Ninth Annual Session of the Ala. Baptist State Convention. Held at Marion, Nov. 8th, 9th, 10th, 11th, 12th, 1861* (Tuskegee, Ala.: Office of *South Western Baptist*, 1861), p. 20; *Central Presbyterian*, November 17, 1860. See also the statement by "A Baptist Resident" in *Texas Baptist*, November 29, 1860.

5

The religious logic of secession

"We regard the election of Lincoln," wrote the Rev. Moses Drury Hoge of Richmond, "as the greatest calamity that ever befell this Union." To the *Mississippi Baptist,* it was "the culmination of a series of aggressive acts which have been perpetuated against the South by the same party for years past." The triumph of Abraham Lincoln in the presidential contest of 1860 made the fear of a Northern antislavery majority a reality. The victory of the Republican Party – with its undisguised threat to envelop the slave South with a cordon of free states – triggered the final transformation from Southern sectionalism to Southern nationalism. The Charleston Baptist Association stated that the North and the South were now "utterly at variance," and the Savannah River Baptist Association, also of South Carolina, acknowledged that Lincoln's election had "made us a distinct and separate people." Words turned quickly into political action. On December 20, 1860, South Carolina became the first slave state to secede from the Union. By February 1861, six more states from the lower South had joined the Palmetto State in secession, and together they formed the new Confederate nation. The bombardment of Ft. Sumter on April 12, immediately followed by Lincoln's call for 70,000 troops to crush the rebellion, prompted four more slave states from the upper South to secede and enlist in the Confederacy. The sectional conflict over slavery that had begun decades before had finally erupted into war.[1]

The Southern clergy and churches played a visible and influential role during the secession crisis. Clergymen spoke openly and enthusiastically on behalf of disunion. Through fast day sermons and the columns of religious newspapers, they provided Southerners with reasoned and scripturally documented rationales for separation from the Union. Denominational groups across the South officially endorsed secession and conferred

1. Ernest Trice Thompson, *Presbyterians in the South, Vol. 1: 1607–1861* (Richmond, Va.: John Knox Press, 1963), p. 553; *Mississippi Baptist,* November 15, 1860; H. Harrison Daniel, "Southern Protestantism and Secession," *The Historian* 29 (May 1967): 394. For the best short survey of Lincoln's election and the secession crisis, see David M. Potter, *The Impending Crisis, 1848–1861* (New York: Harper & Row, 1976), chaps. 16–20.

their blessings on the new Southern nation. An official of the new Confederate government paid tribute to the key contribution of religion. "This revolution," acknowledged Thomas R. R. Cobb in the *Southern Presbyterian,* "has been accomplished mainly by the Churches."[2]

The prominent role of Southern religion in the secession crisis culminated three decades of religious contributions to the development of sectional distinctiveness. Southern clerical justifications of secession wove together various themes pursued throughout this study: the defense of slavery and the critique of abolitionism, models of separation from the denominational schisms, and the proper relationship between religion and politics. Moreover, the religious response to secession continued the debate with Northern abolitionists over the morality of slavery but broadened the discussion into a larger dialogue over the relative merits of free and slave societies. Finally, Southern clergymen once again drew upon shared American discourse to fashion a distinctly Southern ideology. In the hands of sectionally minded ministers, the Bible and evangelicalism became the tools for dissolving the Union.

I

Shortly after Abraham Lincoln was elected president, the slave states of the lower South held special conventions to consider the question of secession. Secessionist leaders such as Robert Barnwell Rhett of South Carolina and William Lowndes Yancey of Alabama, capitalizing on the frenzied reaction to Lincoln's election, sought to convert the Southern people to the necessity of immediate withdrawal from the Union. They organized mass public meetings and created voluntary military units to arouse sectional passions. It was in this atmosphere that the church joined the vanguard of the movement converting Southern sentiment toward secession. Denominational groups and newspapers gave their official endorsement of disunion, and clergymen spoke eagerly on its behalf. Although the church did not initiate calls for secession, it was quick to enlist in the disunionist crusade. Historians since have commented on the contribution of the clergy during the secession crisis. David Potter noted that "clergymen from the pulpit were almost as vocal as politicians from the stump in warning of the danger to the South, exhorting the people to declare their independence, and keeping emotions at a high pitch." These

---

2. *Southern Presbyterian,* April 20, 1861. See also William B. McCash, *Thomas R. R. Cobb (1823–1862): The Making of a Southern Nationalist* (Macon, Ga.: Mercer University Press, 1983), p. 89.

comments suggest a clerical influence on politics unusual for their position and numbers.[3]

Clergymen from various denominations throughout the lower South spoke out in support of secession. "Several preachers have been drawn out to express themselves by deliverances," a Mississippi Methodist noted in February 1861. The Methodist minister George G. Smith, "wild with the war fever," made speeches, wrote "fiery poems," and "talked war all the time." An Episcopalian minister from Aiken, South Carolina, delivered a speech on behalf of secession in December 1860 and noted similar addresses by three Baptist preachers in his vicinity. On the eve of Florida's secession convention, the rector of St. John's Church in Tallahassee preached a sermon supporting immediate secession. Thomas W. Caskey, pastor of the Christian church in Jackson, accompanied the attorney general of Mississippi as he traveled the state urging secession. Ministerial support for secession did provide history with at least one amusing anecdote. A prominent member of a Presbyterian church told his pastor that he would quit the church if the pastor did not pray for the Union. Unmoved by this threat, the pastor replied that "our Church does not believe in praying for the dead!"[4]

Clergymen also served in the state conventions called throughout the lower South in the early winter of 1860–1 to consider secession. South Carolina's secession convention, for example, included several ministers committed to Southern nationalism. The Presbyterian preacher David Pressley Robinson received 505 of the 536 votes cast in the Lancaster District for delegates to the convention. James C. Furman, a prominent Baptist minister and educator, represented the Greenville District. John Gill Landrum, another Baptist preacher, served as a delegate from Spartanburg. During the Civil War, Landrum became chaplain of the 13th

3. David Potter, *The Impending Crisis,* p. 501. Avery O. Craven remarked that secession was notable "for the unusual part played by the clergy." *The Growth of Southern Nationalism, 1848–1861* (Baton Rouge: Louisiana State University Press, 1953), p. 374. For additional confirmation of the contribution of the Southern clergy to secession, see James W. Silver, *Confederate Morale and Church Propaganda* (New York: W. W. Norton, 1967), p. 24; William H. Barney, *The Secessionist Impulse: Alabama and Mississippi in 1860* (Princeton, N.J.: Princeton University Press, 1974), p. 223; Percy Lee Rainwater, *Mississippi: Storm Center of Secession, 1856–1861* (Originally published 1938. Reprint ed., New York: Da Capo Press, 1969), p. 173; and Dorothy Dodd, "The Secession Movement in Florida, 1850–1860. Part II," *Florida Historical Quarterly* 12 (October 1933): 57.

4. *Christian Advocate,* February 7, 1861; George G. Smith Diary, Southern Historical Collection, University of North Carolina, Chapel Hill, p. 65; John Hamilton Cornish Diary, December 21, 1860, Southern Historical Collection, University of North Carolina, Chapel Hill, N.C.; Dodd, "Secession Movement in Florida," p. 60; Silver, *Confederate Morale and Church Propaganda,* p. 17; *Southern Presbyterian,* March 2, 1861.

Regiment of South Carolina volunteers. The Presbyterian clergyman Thomas R. English, who had previously served as a delegate to the Southern Rights Convention of 1852, represented the Sumter District in the South Carolina secession convention. Clergymen were present in the conventions of other lower South states. In Georgia, five ministers served as delegates, and four clergymen could be found at Alabama's secession convention. Because Southern Protestants generally frowned upon ministers running for elected office, participation in secession conventions was perhaps the boldest step for clergymen to take. It suggests the extent to which the clergy saw in the crisis of the Union the kinds of vital moral and religious issues that would justify their entry into the political realm.[5]

Denominational groups across the lower South often advocated separation from the Union before their respective states seceded. Only a few days after Lincoln's election, the Alabama Baptist State Convention, "in defense of the sovereignty and independence of Alabama," proclaimed "her right, as a sovereignty, to withdraw from the Union." A month before Georgia seceded, the Methodist Conference in the state voted 87 to 9 in favor of secession. Even the small Baptist Church of Christ in Bethesda, Mississippi, endorsed the call of Gov. John J. Pettus for an extra session of the legislature to consider withdrawing from the Union. The Savannah River Baptist Association of South Carolina declared that "it is our duty as Christian gentlemen and patriots, to sustain our beloved state at all hazards in the maintenance of her sovereignty, and in the protection of her constitutional rights and liberty." Baptists in Florida also gave their "hearty approbation" to the militant defense of Southern rights. The South Carolina Methodist Conference felt "bound by honor and duty, to move in harmony with the South in resisting Northern domination."[6]

Influential denominational newspapers in the South joined ecclesiastical organizations in supporting secession. Again, these religious papers often advocated disunion before their states seceded. "The separation of

5. John A. May and Joan R. Faunt, *South Carolina Secedes* (Columbia: University of South Carolina Press, 1960), pp. 141–2, 172, 203; Ralph A. Wooster, *The Secession Conventions of the South* (Princeton, N.J.: Princeton University Press, 1962), pp. 53, 61, 94; Anne C. Loveland, *Southern Evangelicals and the Social Order, 1800–1860* (Baton Rouge: Louisiana State University Press, 1980), p. 113.

6. *Minutes of the Thirty-Eighth Annual Session of the Alabama Baptist State Convention, Held at Tuskegee, November 9–13, 1860* (Tuskegee, Ala.: Office of the South Western Baptist, 1860), p. 11; Richmond *Enquirer*, December 18, 1860; Barney, *The Secessionist Impulse*, p. 224; John Lee Eighmy, *Churches in Cultural Captivity: A History of the Social Attitudes of Southern Baptists* (Knoxville: University of Tennessee Press, 1972), p. 23; Dodd, "Secession Movement in Florida," p. 61; *Southern Methodist Intelligencer*, January 2, 1861.

these States from the Federal Union is a political necessity," the *Mississippi Baptist* declared on January 3, 1861, "and must be effected at any cost, regardless of consequences." The *Southern Episcopalian* of Charleston similarly considered secession as "the only position that Southern freemen or Southern Christians can consistently occupy." The *Southern Presbyterian* of South Carolina urged secession only days after Lincoln was elected. By the end of the month, the *South Western Baptist* of Alabama also declared its support for disunion.[7]

The role of the Southern clergy in the secession crisis was strong enough to capture the attention of Northern churchmen. "Almost without exception," the *Western Christian Advocate* of Cincinnati observed, "they are unconditional secessionists." The Northern clergy portrayed their Southern brethren as radicals who were inflaming the sectional crisis. Remarking on prosecession sermons delivered on Thanksgiving Day, another Methodist weekly remarked that the Southern pulpit was "fairly embarked on the sea of politics." The Baptist *Christian Watchman and Reflector* of Boston noted that "there enters into secession a feeling largely of religious fanaticism." Northern clergymen feared that religious intervention in political controversy would inflame the sectional crisis beyond the point of compromise. "When the pulpit urges treason expressly in order that injustice and inhumanity may flourish," worried the Unitarian *Christian Register*, "what is to be expected of politicians?" In February 1861, the *Western Christian Advocate* stated that Southern Methodist ministers "are at this moment the strongest obstacle in the way of preserving the Union of these States." This portrayal of the Southern clergy in the Northern religious press serves to confirm that their role in the secession crisis was indeed notable for its visibility and influence. Although these depictions were an accurate picture of the secessionist South, they also served the polemical purpose of showing that Southern ministers were irresponsibly dragging religion into the political fray. In this way, the Northern clergy contributed to the belief in an irrepressible conflict, arousing the same kind of political passions they were condemning in their Southern brethren.[8]

One of the most notable characteristics of the involvement of Southern clergymen in the secession crisis was the unity and consensus that existed within their ranks. With a few exceptions to be discussed in the next chapter, the overwhelming majority of clergymen in the lower South sup-

7. *Mississippi Baptist*, January 3, 1861; *Southern Episcopalian* (December 1860): 498; Daniel, "Southern Protestantism and Secession," pp. 394, 399.
8. *Western Christian Advocate*, March 27, 1861; *Pittsburgh Christian Advocate*, November 27, 1860; *Christian Watchman and Reflector*, January 17, 1861; *Christian Register*, January 5, 1861; *Western Christian Advocate*, February 27, 1861.

ported the Southern drive for independent nationhood. There were no clearly discernible differences in this support among the major denominations. This unanimity in the Southern church is all the more striking considering the deep and significant divisions that existed in the South over the timing and methods of secession. Why these internal divisions were not reflected in the ranks of the clergy can be explained by the peculiar way the clergy approached the question of secession. With the experience of the abolitionist crisis of 1835, the denominational schisms and decades of defending slavery from the pulpit, Southern clergymen had become accustomed to view sectional politics in religious terms. They focused on issues of principle and eschewed the more practical questions of policy. Along with all Southerners, ministers saw in secession a larger conflict of principles between a free-labor North and the slave South. But the debates between immediate secessionists and cooperationists involved precisely the kinds of issues clergymen saw as "political" and hence outside their realm. As the *Central Presbyterian* of Richmond acknowledged in late November 1860, "it is not for us to discuss the propriety or policy of secession now." A deeper look into the way Southern clergymen conceptualized the religious significance of secession will help explain both the depth and unity of their commitment to Southern nationalism on the eve of the Civil War.[9]

II

The relationship between religion and politics – the proper role of the minister in political controversy – was at the forefront of clerical thought and behavior during the winter of 1860–1. Most Southern ministers began their sermons on the sectional crisis by justifying their discussion of politics from the pulpit. These brief explanations reveal that clerical participation in the secession movement continued previous patterns of involvement in sectional politics. The justifications offered for pulpit politics during the secession crisis were essentially the same ones put forth during the abolitionist postal campaign of 1835. Discussing the issues behind secession was not a radical departure for Southern clergymen.

The Southern clerical conception of the relationship between religion and politics can best be clarified by examining in close detail how one Southern minister justified his discussion of secession from the pulpit. On December 9, 1860, the Presbyterian R. K. Porter delivered a sermon on "Christian Duty in the Present Crisis" to his congregation in

9. *Central Presbyterian*, November 24, 1860.

Waynesboro, Georgia. Like other Southern ministers at the time, Porter began his sermon by justifying a political discussion from the pulpit. Informing his congregation that he spoke to them as God's "minister and your pastor," Porter established at the outset that his remarks on the political crisis would come from the special province of religion. He began his rationale by denouncing the general principle of clerical participation in politics. He stated that a clergyman was both a citizen and minister of God. As a citizen, Porter explained, it was his right and duty to hold political opinions, but "as a minister of Christ, and by that higher obligation," he had abstained from voicing those opinions. The differentiation between these two roles was important, for it helped establish the religious significance of secession. Having condemned pulpit politics in principle, Porter turned next to its practice in the North. In an attack on the abolitionists' moral and religious challenge to slavery, Porter denounced the "sad and unhallowed example" of ministers who dragged politics into the pulpit. They "have dishonored the very temple of God, and contributed so largely to bring about the melancholy condition in which our country...is now placed." By bringing religion into politics, Porter implied, Northern ministers threatened both the integrity of religion and the stability of the Union.[10]

How could Porter condemn Northern ministers for mixing religion and politics while he was launching his own religious discussion of the sectional crisis? The answer lies in how the Georgia minister understood the issue of secession and how he defined politics. Essentially, Porter raised secession beyond the confines of a partisan conflict or question of policy to an event of profound religious significance: "Deeper and broader than all the temporary questions of party, far more powerful and sweeping than any measure of passing policy, are those principles which, before God, I believe to be in issue." Although Porter did not define precisely what those principles were, he did state that secession involved "the tremendous question of giving up or maintaining the great principles of eternal justice, righteousness and truth." In the process of exalting the significance of secession, Porter implicitly defined two distinct types of politics: one that dealt with immediate questions of policy and one that embodied higher, more timeless questions of morality. "It is not mere policy," the Georgia Presbyterian concluded, "but fundamental and vital principle, that is in the great questions now up for adjudication." Viewing secession as a political issue of high moral significance enabled Porter to

10. R. K. Porter, *Christian Duty in the Present Crisis: The Substance of a sermon delivered in the Presbyterian church in Waynesboro', Georgia ... December 9, 1860* (Savannah, Ga.: Steam Press of J. M. Cooper & Company, 1860), p. 5.

circumvent the traditional objections to pulpit politics and allowed him to speak on secession.[11]

Porter's understanding of secession, the linchpin of his argument, rested on a definition of politics that was widely accepted among Southern clergymen. When politics referred to immediate, pragmatic questions of policy, it was deemed unworthy of Christian consideration. As the Episcopalian minister Thomas Atkinson explained to a Wilmington, North Carolina, congregation, "what is the best kind of government, and which is the most rightful and expedient institution, are matters as to which it [the pulpit] is profoundly silent." If a political issue was perceived as possessing any kind of moral significance, however, Southern clergymen claimed that it fell within their jurisdiction and justified their attention. "The teaching of the Bible seems to be," explained the Presbyterian *True Witness and Sentinel* of New Orleans, "that where no important religious principles are endangered in political affairs, the ministry is bound by their relations to God to stand aloof from the disputes which may arise." The Rev. James A. Lyon of Columbus, Mississippi, further clarified this conceptualization of the problem of religion and politics. Political questions, he argued, "I leave to the politician, except when politics cross the line into the domain of Christian morals, and invade the territories of religion: then I will discuss so called politics, since it thereby becomes a question of morals, and a legitimate subject for the pulpit." Morality was thus the main criterion for determining religious involvement in politics. "We hold that political morality lies as properly within the range of pulpit discussion," asserted a Mississippi Methodist, "as morality between man and man." William C. Dana, a Presbyterian clergyman from South Carolina, concurred that in the church, "only the moral and religious relations of our political positions can properly come under review." This conception of the relationship between religion and politics guided Southern clergymen during the secession crisis. Thomas Atkinson, for example, told his audience that he would speak "not of the political causes which have brought on our present calamitous condition, but of the religious and moral causes of that condition."[12]

11. Porter, *Christian Duty in the Present Crisis*, pp. 5-6.
12. Thomas Atkinson, *On the Causes of our National Troubles, A Sermon delivered in St. James Church, Wilmington, N. C. on Friday, the 4th of January, 1861* (Wilmington, N.C.: *Herald* Book and Job Office, 1861), p. 6; *True Witness and Sentinel*, March 30, 1861; James A. Lyon, *Christianity and the Civil Laws: A Lecture on Christianity and the Civil Laws by Rev. James A. Lyon, D.D., of Columbus, Mississippi* (Columbus: *Mississippi Democrat* Print, 1859), p. 11; Loveland, *Southern Evangelicals and the Social Order*, p. 115; William C. Dana, *A Sermon delivered in the Central Presbyterian Church, Charleston, SC, November 21st, 1860, being the Day appointed by State Authority for Fast-*

The other central assumption in Porter's argument was that secession involved moral and religious principles that elevated it as an issue beyond partisanship and policy. As such, the question of secession summoned clerical guidance. This view was also widespread among Southern clergymen. The *Southern Episcopalian* of Charleston acknowledged that although the religious press had not usually meddled in politics, this practice could not "continue to be so when the very existence of the Union is so seriously menaced." Drawing upon the imagery of a ship at sea commonly used to portray the Union, one Southern minister reasoned that "as an impressed seaman cannot innocently withhold his service in a storm, if this were needed to save a ship from floundering, so the clergyman...may be impelled by duty to country to exert himself in the dark hour of revolution." The *Central Presbyterian* of Richmond agreed that "there are times when none can be silent without betraying a criminal indifference to the principles in controversy." Samuel B. Wilson, a professor at Union Theological Seminary in Virginia, thought that the clergy, "as well as politicians, may properly express their views, and use their influence, to avert evil, and secure the right and the good." Even the Southern political press considered the crisis grave enough to sanction politics from the pulpit. "Generally speaking, we have no fancy for political sermons," the Raleigh *Register and North Carolina Gazette* editorialized during the secession crisis, "but at a crisis like the present, when civil and fratricidal war threatens to deluge the country with blood, it is very meet and right, aye the bounden duty of God's minister of peace to come forward with words of wisdom, warning and charity." The traditional barrier to discussing politics from the pulpit was thus overcome by investing the sectional crisis with religious and moral significance.[13]

III

During the winter of 1860–1, Southern clergymen provided the South with a religious interpretation of the crisis of the Union. Southern clergy-

ing, Humiliation, and Prayer (Charleston: Steam Power Presses of Evans and Cogswell, 1860), p. 6; Atkinson, *On the Causes of our National Troubles*, p. 6. It may be significant that both Lyon and Atkinson were Unionists at this point in the secession crisis. Those clergymen who opposed sectional extremism were more likely to be careful about mixing religion and politics, a pattern that was repeated in the writings of the Northern clergy.

13. *Southern Episcopalian*, December 1860, p. 491; James Preston Fugitt, *Our Country and Slavery. A Friendly Word to the Rev. Francis L. Hawks, D.D., LL.D. and other Northern Clergymen* (Baltimore: Joseph Robinson, 1861), p. 3; *Central Presbyterian*, December 15, 1860; *North Carolina Presbyterian*, December 1, 1860; Raleigh *Register and North Carolina Gazette*, December 5, 1860.

men brought to this problem of state a deeply ingrained way of thinking about history, the rise and fall of nations, the meaning and destiny of America, and the relationship between religion and politics. This world view – the lenses through which clergymen examined the dissolution of the Union – encompassed elements of philosophy, theology, rhetoric, and logic. It combined patterns of ideas and expression from seventeenth-century Puritanism, eighteenth-century republicanism, American civil religion, and evangelical Protestantism. As such, the paradigm Southern clergymen brought to bear on the problem of disunion was distinctly American. How Southern clergymen used shared modes of thought to justify secession is central to understanding the religious contribution to Southern nationalism.

The perspective through which Southern clergymen viewed political affairs was inextricably related to the ritual of the fast day, occasions when extraordinary secular or natural events were interpreted as signs of divine rewards or punishments and as a summons to spiritual and moral rebirth. Such occurrences as cholera epidemics or deaths of public leaders, for example, would prompt a call for a fast day. Through this tradition, Southerners, along with other Americans, had become accustomed to collective self-examination and reformation during times of crisis. It is not surprising, then, that Americans turned to fasting and prayer during the winter of 1860–1. Along with his other abortive attempts to save the Union, President James Buchanan proclaimed a national fast day for January 4, 1861.[14]

In response to the secession crisis, religious and political leaders in the South also called for fast days. The initiative was often taken by individual states. Gov. Joseph E. Brown of Georgia, for instance, declared November 28, 1860, as a day of fasting, humiliation, and prayer for his state. South Carolina's fast day was November 21, 1860. The new Confederacy continued the tradition of fast days. Jefferson Davis declared June 13, 1861, as the first official Confederate fast day. Denominational

14. Kenneth M. Stampp, *And the War Came: The North and the Secession Crisis, 1860–1861* (Baton Rouge: Louisiana State University Press, 1950), p. 61. On the origins of the fast day in colonial New England, see A. W. Plumstead, ed., *The Wall and the Garden: The Massachusetts Election Sermons, 1670–1775* (Minneapolis: University of Minnesota Press, 1968); Babette Levy, *Preaching in the First Half of New England History* (Hartford, Conn.: American Society of Church History, 1945); William D. Love, *The Fast and Thanksgiving Days of New England* (Boston and New York: Houghton Mifflin, 1895); Harry P. Kerr, "Politics and Religion in Colonial Fast and Thanksgiving Sermons, 1763–1783," *Quarterly Journal of Speech* 46 (December 1960): 372–82; and Richard P. Gildrie, "The Ceremonial Puritan: Days of Humiliation and Thanksgiving," *New England Historical and Genealogical Register* 136 (January 1982): 3–16.

groups throughout the South followed Davis's lead in calling Southerners to fasting and prayer. The Baptist State Convention of Georgia, imploring "that God would deliver us from the power of our enemies and restore peace to our country," declared fast days for June 1 and 2, 1861. The Yalobusha Baptist Association of Mississippi resolved later in 1861 that "in view of the present condition of our country, our churches be requested to observe a day of fasting, humiliation and prayer, once in three months for our Confederacy." Significantly, leading secessionist papers applauded these calls for fast days, reinforcing the religious step into the political arena. "If ever there was a time in the history of this country," suggested the Richmond *Enquirer,* "when a whole people should bow before Him who rules among nations as among men, and with humble confessions implore His guidance and protection; if ever there was a time which solemnly called upon the people of this land to ask deliverance from the evils that beset us on every side . . . now is the time." The Charleston *Mercury* agreed that "a Christian people, struggling in a good cause, should invoke providence for its success."[15]

Fast days in the South during secession and the early months of war were marked by earnestness and solemnity. Business was usually suspended for the day. According to one secular newspaper, people in Columbus, Georgia, "seemed more impressed with the solemn character of the occasion than on any former day of the like kind we have ever witnessed." Fasting itself was taken seriously if not always quite literally. "I kept the fast faithfully, not eating anything from Sun Rise to Sunset but a cracker and cup of coffee," wrote one Southern Protestant after the national fast day. A Virginia planter, although not as committed, nonetheless promised that day "to try to keep it in part." As community rituals, fast days inspired interdenominational cooperation and unity. On the Confederate fast day of June 13, 1861, citizens in Fayetteville, North Carolina, heard sermons by Baptist, Methodist, Presbyterian, and Episcopalian clergymen. At least five ministers participated in services that day in Columbia, South Carolina. Describing the national fast day in his diary, a Virginia planter remarked: "All denominations united & all

15. *Central Presbyterian,* December 1, 1860; John H. Cornish Diary, November 21, 1860, Southern Historical Collection, University of North Carolina, Chapel Hill; Jefferson Davis called for nine fast days during the life of the Confederacy. Silver, *Confederate Morale and Church Propaganda,* p. 64; *Christian Index,* May 29, 1861; *Minutes of the Twenty-Fifth Annual Meeting of the Yalobusha Baptist Association, Held with the Providence Church, Carroll Co., Miss., Sept. 20th, 21st, and 22nd, 1861* (Grenada, Miss.: *Southern Rural Gentleman* Job Office, 1861), p. 4; Richmond *Enquirer,* December 18, 1860; Charleston *Mercury,* November 21, 1860.

seemed solemn." The seriousness displayed on fast days testifies to the centrality of religion in Southern society on the eve of the Civil War.[16]

Fast days were also observed in the North, particularly the fast day called by President James Buchanan for January 4, 1861. In cities and towns throughout the North, business was suspended and offices closed. Clergymen of the same denomination would often meet in one designated church for sermons and prayer meetings. The observance of the fast day in Chicago seems typical of other Northern cities. The Chicago *Tribune* noted that "a very large number of our citizens turned aside from their usual avocations for a portion of the day at least, and assembled in their several places of worship, where the exercises, under the influence of the alarming aspects of the times, were of an impressive and interesting character." The Rev. W. N. Patton of Chicago's First Congregational Church gave a sermon on the crisis of the Union. Methodists met at the Clark Street Methodist Episcopal Church, and Chicago's Episcopalians gathered at Trinity Church on Madison Street. At noon, there was even a Union Prayer Meeting at the YMCA. The Chicago *Tribune,* a Republican newspaper supporting Lincoln, seemed pleased that the meetings evinced "much of the Union saving spirit but of a nature of saving to reform and check the growth of evil, rather than to buy present quiet by a concession of right and justice."[17]

Buchanan's call for a national fast day was apparently more widely observed in the North than the South. This discrepancy can primarily be explained by the fact that the states of the lower South were on their way out of the Union by then and would have been less likely to heed a call from a national official. The Virginia secessionist Edmund Ruffin, for example, was in Tallahassee on January 4 awaiting the opening of the Florida secession convention. He declined to attend church that day, explaining that Buchanan's call for a national fast was "a rebuke & censure of the seceding states, & of their cause, & of the very action which this Convention is assembled to consummate." Like Ruffin, Francis Rutledge, Episcopal bishop of Florida and a South Carolinian by birth, also decided

16. Raleigh *Register and North Carolina Gazette,* January 9, 1861, and January 12, 1861; Columbus (Ga.) *Inquirer* quoted in *Christian Advocate,* June 27, 1861; Mathew P. Andrews to Anna Robinson, January 6, 1861, Charles W. Andrews Papers, William R. Perkins Library, Duke University, Durham, N.C.; William C. Adams Diary, January 4, 1861, William R. Perkins Library, Duke University, Durham, N.C.; *Biblical Recorder,* June 19, 1861; Charles Vedder Diary, June 13, 1861, South Caroliniana Library, University of South Carolina, Columbia; William C. Adams Diary, January 4, 1861, William R. Perkins Library, Duke University, Durham.

17. Chicago *Tribune,* January 5, 1861. For observances in other Northern cities, see the Boston *Daily Advertiser,* January 5, 1861; *Daily Evening Bulletin* (Philadelphia), January 5, 1861; and New York *Daily Tribune,* January 5, 1861.

not to observe the national fast, explaining that he had already seceded with his native state. In general, the more radical secessionists were inclined to ignore the national fast day. Both the Richmond *Enquirer* and Charleston *Mercury,* strongly secessionist papers, did not mention the observance of this fast. In contrast, the Richmond *Daily Whig,* Unionist in sentiment, suspended publication on January 5 and hoped that "our citizens generally will suspend business today, and duly observe the occasion in accordance with the President's recommendation." The *Weekly Vicksburg Whig,* another Unionist paper, similarly noted the fast day and even reprinted a fast day sermon.[18]

The fast day ritual provided the medium through which the religious perspective on politics was applied to the crisis of the Union – the fast day sermon. The form and style of the fast day sermon shaped its message. Although these addresses do not adhere to a uniform and rigid style, they do constitute an oratorical genre that generally followed a prescribed pattern of rhetoric and structure. As such, they invite a particular rhetorical analysis. As the art of persuasive discourse, rhetoric imposes structure and meaning on the world, giving form to problems and thereby implicitly suggesting solutions. As a dialogue between speaker and audience, rhetoric involves a conscious choice of vocabulary and symbols that have a peculiar resonance in the common culture. The important thing in these sermons, then, are the words and concepts chosen to explain the meaning of events, language that would quickly hit home in a time of deep crisis. Moreover, speech had a special importance in the Old South where the orator was assigned a prominent role in society. Also, the persuasive and powerful role of religion in the South gave distinctive significance to pulpit oratory. For all these reasons, Southern fast day sermons provide the most revealing insight into clerical perceptions of the sectional crisis.[19]

18. Dodd, "Secession Movement in Florida," p. 60; Richmond *Daily Whig,* January 4, 1861; *Weekly Vicksburg Whig,* January 5, 1861. See also the Raleigh *Register,* January 9, 1861, another Unionist paper that noted the fast day. One exception to this pattern was the Natchez *Daily Courier,* which reported the fast day, reprinted a sermon, and seemed to support secession. See the issue for January 4, 1861. For the Charleston *Mercury* and the Richmond *Enquirer,* see issues for January 4 and 5, 1861. It should be noted, however, that the *Enquirer* did not heed the call for the January 4 fast day; Richmond *Enquirer,* December 18, 1860. Close to half of the Northern fast day sermons read for this study were from this day, whereas fewer than 15 percent of the Southern fast day sermons were delivered on January 4.

19. To understand the conceptual framework behind the religious logic of secession, I have examined a sample of fast day sermons, both political and nonpolitical, delivered in the South from 1830 to 1860. An interesting explication of a similar genre can be found in Drew Gilpin Faust, "The Rhetoric and Ritual of Agriculture in Antebellum South Carolina," *Journal of Southern History* 45 (November 1979): 541–68.

The Southern religious logic of secession was a thorough and carefully reasoned justification for disunion, a vision of the sectional crisis seen through the eyes of the clerical perspective on politics. At the heart of this logic, and accordingly at the center of the Southern fast day sermon, were the themes of withdrawal and separation. These themes were conveyed in terms central to the religious sensibility of Southern Protestants. With their rhetorical and ideological tools, Southern ministers explained secession as the logical end of a pattern of events that led inexorably to a purifying act of separation from a sinful and decaying nation. In religious terms, secession became an act of withdrawal of the righteous from the ungodly, an idea deeply rooted in Protestant thought. To give their logic additional force and meaning, Southern clergymen frequently resorted to the familiar language of evangelicalism. They used certain aspects of the individual conversion experience to clarify the process of Southern separation from the North. The application of evangelicalism to the defense of secession was natural and effective in a culture steeped in evangelical Protestantism. By applying to the public sphere the evangelical standards universally accepted in the private sphere, ministers gave secession a power and immediacy that brought it closer to the hearts and minds of Southerners.[20]

The Southern clerical perspective on politics rested upon certain basic premises about the role of God in human affairs and the nature of history. Southern ministers shared with all antebellum Protestants the deeply held belief that all human and natural affairs were designed and controlled by God. They were trained to detect in any unusual natural or human event the hidden hand of providence. Special occurrences should thus be examined to ascertain, if possible, the intentions of God. "Extraordinary providences," the Rev. Thomas Smyth of Charleston explained, "are instructive warnings, of great importance in God's government of the world, and to be very solemnly considered." A Louisiana Methodist agreed that "His government extends to the concerns of nations." The Rev. H. M. Painter succinctly described the providential interpretation of human affairs when

20. Donald G. Mathews states that evangelicalism was "the single most influential strain of religious activity in the South during the formative years before 1860"; *Religion in the Old South* (Chicago: University of Chicago Press, 1977), p. xiv. For further studies of evangelicalism in the antebellum South, see especially Donald G. Mathews, "Religion in the Old South: Speculations on Methodology," *South Atlantic Quarterly* 73 (Winter 1974): 34–53; Dickson D. Bruce, Jr., "Religion, Society and Culture in the Old South: A Comparative View," *American Quarterly* 26 (October 1974): 399–416; Dickson D. Bruce, Jr., *And They All Sang Hallelujah: Plain Folk Camp Meeting Religion, 1800–1845* (Knoxville: University of Tennessee Press, 1974); John B. Boles, *The Great Revival, 1787–1805: The Origins of the Southern Evangelical Mind* (Lexington: University Press of Kentucky, 1972).

he told the First Presbyterian church in Boonville, Missouri, that "events speak to us in a language."[21]

Unusual events most often came in the form of adversity, and the message almost always assigned to adversity was divine judgment. This interpretation of the source of adversity strongly resembled, and undoubtedly drew upon, the Puritan tradition of covenantal theology. Seventeenth-century Puritans maintained that the settlers of New England had entered into a unique and mutual covenant with God. The idea that God and the American people were bound by this special relationship persisted into the nineteenth century and surfaced in the writings of Southern clergymen during the secession movement. They explained the sectional crisis within this context, suggesting that the impending dissolution of the Union was a form of divine chastisement. "Surely, God has a controversy with us," James H. Thornwell insisted in an 1860 fast day sermon. "That God is judging us for our national sins and transgressions, I firmly believe," declared an Episcopal minister from Mobile. In his fast day sermon, Jeremiah B. Jeter, pastor of the First Baptist Church of Richmond, argued similarly that national sins "have provoked God's displeasure, and brought on us his judgments."[22]

The call for collective humiliation and prayer, explicit in the ritual of the fast day, flowed directly from the providential interpretation of adversity. If the sectional crisis was a divine judgment for national sins, then a collective repentance was necessary to avert further chastisement. "The idea of fasting, implies some evil or sin," the Baptist minister J. M. Stillwell of Georgia explained. The Southern Baptist Convention formally declared a day of fasting and prayer in 1861 to "avert any calamities

21. Thomas Smyth, *The Battle of Fort Sumter: Its Mastery and Miracle: God's Mastery and Mercy. A Discourse preached on the Day of National Fasting, Thanksgiving and Prayer, in the First Presbyterian Church, Charleston, S.C. June 13, 1861* (Columbia, S.C.: *Southern Guardian* Steam Power Press, 1861), p. 9; Reynolds Trippett, *A Fast Day Discourse by Rev. Reynolds Trippett, of the M. E. Church, South. Preached in the Court House Square, Richmond, La., Thursday, June 13th, 1861* (Vicksburg, Miss.: *Whig* Power Press Job Office, 1861), p. 6; H. M. Painter, *The Duty of the Southern Patriot and Christian in the Present Crisis. A Sermon preached in the First Presbyterian Church, Boonville, Mo. on Friday, January 4th, 1861, being the Day of the National Fast* (Boonville, Mo.: Caldwell & Stahl, 1861), p. 25.

22. *Fast Day Sermons: or The Pulpit on the State of the Country* (New York: Rudd & Carlton, 1861), p. 28; H. N. Pierce, *Sermon Preached in St. John's Church, Mobile, on the 13th of June, 1861, the National Fast appointed by His Excellency Jefferson Davis, President of the Confederate States of America* (Mobile, Ala.: Farrow & Dennett, Book and Job Printers, 1861), p. 7; Jeremiah B. Jeter Diary, p. 144, Jeremiah B. Jeter Papers, Virginia Baptist Historical Society, University of Richmond, Richmond, Va. See also *Christian Index*, January 30, 1861, and the fast day sermon by S. Henderson reprinted in the *South Western Baptist*, June 13, 1861.

due to sins as a people." On the Confederate fast day, the Rev. Simeon
Colton, a Presbyterian preacher in North Carolina, wrote in his diary that
there were "abundant causes for fasting, for the judgments of God are
upon us and doubtless for our sins." In evangelical terms, the call to
national humiliation was similar to summoning the individual to seek
divine guidance as the first step toward conversion. "As the individual, in
coming to God, must believe that He is, and that He is the rewarder of
them that diligently search Him," James H. Thornwell suggested, "so
the State must be impressed with a profound sense of His all-pervading
providence, and of its responsibility to Him, as the moral Ruler of the
world."[23]

A collective humiliation before God contained within itself the future
promise of divine forgiveness and deliverance. Southern clergymen, reflecting again a major tenet of American civil religion, believed that a
nation determined its relationship to God by its own morality. According to the covenantal theology of the seventeenth century, New England
Puritans had received God's favor and protection by being a righteous
and religious people. When the Elect Nation strayed from this path, it
broke its contract with God, invoking His punishment. God rewarded
righteousness, and He punished a sinful people. Many Southern fast day
sermons opened with the biblical text from Proverbs 14:34: "Righteousness exalteth a nation, but sin is a reproach to any people." Providential
logic thus dictated that God would answer the prayers of a repentant
nation. As a Presbyterian minister from Charleston explained, "it is for us
by penitence, by confession of our sins, by humble protestation before
God, to seek, that his just anger may be turned away; and that his Almighty arm may be stretched out for our protection." Simeon Colton of
North Carolina noted that God "has commenced the work of chastisement, but out of chastisement, good may come." In a fast day sermon
delivered in June 1861, a Baptist clergyman from Tuskegee, Alabama,
explained that humiliation would bring ultimate security from God: "And
as we profess to be a Christian people, it becomes a duty stern as the law
of God and the direst necessity can make it, to recognize his hands in these
events, deprecate his wrath, confess our sins and the sins of our people,
and implore his protecting power."[24]

23. *Christian Index*, May 29, 1861; *Proceedings of the Southern Baptist Convention at its
    Eighth Biennial Session, Held in the First Baptist Church, Savannah, GA, May 10th,
    11th, 12th and 13th, 1861* (Richmond, Va.: MacFarlane and Fergusson, 1861), p. 64;
    Simeon Colton Diary, June 13, 1861, Southern Historical Collection, University of
    North Carolina Library, Chapel Hill; *Fast Day Sermons*, p. 14.
24. Dana, *Sermon delivered in the Central Presbyterian Church*, p. 10; Simeon Colton Diary,
    January 27, 1861, Southern Historical Collection, University of North Carolina Library,
    Chapel Hill; *South Western Baptist*, June 13, 1861.

The providential interpretation of adversity was closely related to the Southern clerical view of history. To Southern ministers, history rested on the premise that the fate of nations was determined by God. Because God directed the course of nations, history became a screen on which His will was revealed. Thus, extraordinary events in the course of a nation's history were considered providentially ordained. The Rev. J. E. Carnes of Galveston, Texas, interpreted the secession crisis with these assumptions: "The God of the Bible is the Lord of nations, and every crisis in their history is but a revelation of His Providence." History, however, was more than a chronicle displaying the hidden hand of Providence. It exhibited a cyclical pattern that gave human experience uniformity and unity, binding the past and present. This conception mirrored the cyclical view of history characteristic of eighteenth-century republicanism. In a fast day sermon of 1860, a Georgia minister reminded his Savannah church that "the past repeats itself." The Rev. J. R. Kendrick of Charleston elaborated more fully: "The successive ages, in their histories, are much like concentric circles, ever increasing in numbers, ever expanding, but ever preserving a fixed resemblance to each other."[25]

Specifically, history repeated itself in the sense that the history of nations exhibited a common cycle of birth, growth, and death. According to the Rev. H. M. Painter of Missouri, nations "rise and flourish for their appointed period and then decline and perish." Fast day sermons commonly described a pattern of national prosperity followed by internal decay and ultimate ruin. "All have run one cycle, as regular as if it were fated," noted the Presbyterian Robert L. Dabney of Virginia, "first the hardy virtues, then greatness and prosperity as their reward; then arrogance, luxury and other vices; and then decline and ultimate ruin."[26]

Southern clergymen described in some detail the process by which a nation declined from prosperity. The universal belief was that a nation destroyed itself through sin and corruption. This idea not only reflected the assumption that sin provoked divine chastisement but drew upon a central tenet of republicanism – that virtue was necessary for the survival

25. J. E. Carnes, *Address, on the Duty of the Slave States in the Present Crisis, delivered in Galveston, December 12th, 1860* (Galveston: *News* Book and Job Office, 1860), p. 3; George H. Clark, *The Union, A Sermon, delivered in St. John's Church, Savannah, on Fast Day, November 28, 1860* (Savannah, Ga.: Geo. N. Nichols, Printer, 1860), p. 10; J. R. Kendrick, *Lessons from an Ancient Fast. A Discourse delivered in the Citadel Square Church, Charleston, S.C. on the occasion of the General Fast, Thursday, June 13, 1861* (Charleston, S.C.: Steam Power Press of Evans & Cogswell, 1861), p. 5.
26. Painter, *Duty of the Southern Patriot and Christian*, p. 23; *Central Presbyterian*, July 20, 1861.

of a state. "Wherever a nation has perished," the Rev. A. M. Randolph of Fredricksburg, Virginia, pointed out, "it has been the weight of its falsehood, and secret corruption, which has dragged it down to ruin." Augustine Verot, the Catholic Bishop of Florida, used the disintegration of the Roman Republic to demonstrate how a nation dissolved through corruption. This lesson of history was succinctly captured by an Alabama clergyman on the Confederate fast day. "Read the annals of other nations," the Rev. J. C. Mitchell urged, "and see what destroyed them. It was not foreign force, but internal evil. Nations die suicide." History thus taught Southern clergymen that a nation could destroy itself through corruption and decay. Their belief in the providential direction of human affairs conditioned them to see in adversity the judgment of God. It was not surprising, then, when clergymen faced the impending dissolution of the Union in 1860–1 that they sought to understand how their sins had brought down the wrath of Jehovah. They turned inward to discover how America had destroyed itself.[27]

The Southern clerical explanation of secession accordingly moved to an inquiry into the sins that had provoked divine chastisement in the form of the sectional crisis. The sins cataloged in Southern fast day sermons were national ones, implicating both North and South. They were the kinds of transgressions clergymen had been complaining about for decades. The breaking of the Sabbath was perhaps the sin most often cited in the litany. "We profess to be a Christian people," protested the Rev. J. C. Mitchell of Alabama, "and yet the Christian Sabbath is utterly disregarded by many of our people, and even by some in high places." Profanity joined Sabbath breaking at the top of the list of national sins. In a typical jeremiad on national transgressions, the Rev. H. M. Painter of Missouri began his litany of sins with that of ingratitude: "What have we rendered to the Lord for this profession of benefits for all his kindness shown?" He too decried the disregard of the Sabbath and intemperance, adding finally that iniquity "of every kind abounds, and vice in every form displays its hideous front." In their inventory of sins, Southern fast day sermons rarely included anything with a direct bearing on sectional politics. This would seem to fit the general predilection of ministers to diagnose the

27. A. M. Randolph, *Address on the Day of Fasting and Prayer appointed by the President of the Confederate States, June 13, 1861. Delivered in St. George's Church, Fredricksburg, VA* (Fredricksburg: *Recorder* Job Office, 1861), p. 9; Augustine Verot, *A Tract for the Times. Slavery and Abolitionism, being the Substance of a Sermon, Preached in the Church of St. Augustine, Florida, on the 4th Day of January, 1861, Day of Public Humiliation, Fasting and Prayer* (St. Augustine? 1861?), p. 2; J. C. Mitchell, *A Sermon delivered in the Government Street Church, on the National Fast Appointed by Jefferson Davis, President of these Confederate States, June 13, 1861* (Mobile, Ala.: Farrow & Dennett, 1861), p. 22.

religious and moral ills of the nation without mentioning specific political issues.[28]

Southern ministers focused particularly on the dangers of material prosperity. "Who can fail to see that, as a nation," a Virginia Presbyterian pointed out, "we are characterized by a devotion to mammon, perhaps not exceeded, if equalled, by any people on earth?" The *Christian Index* of Georgia agreed that "we have been drifting towards materialism." This concern reflected the clerical belief in the cyclical pattern of the life of nations. Prosperity signaled God's blessings to His chosen nation, but it opened the way to temptation, corruption, and eventual decline. "We have been tried by prosperity as no nation ever was tried before," the Rev. Thomas Atkinson explained to his audience in Wilmington, North Carolina, "and we have yielded to temptation as completely and unresistingly as any people ever did." To Charles C. Pinckney of Charleston, America was "the last recorded example of a people spoiled by prosperity and overthrown by pride." This preoccupation with the decaying nature of material prosperity suggests how Southern clergymen applied their vision of history to the crisis of the Union, placing America in the continuum of the rise and fall of nations. At the same time, it reflected an understandable response to the expansion and modernization of the Southern economy during the 1850s.[29]

The confession of sins set the stage for the central act of the Southern fast day sermon – the explanation and justification of separation from the Union. Relying on the principle that nations decline through internal dissolution, Southern clergymen argued that the North, and the Union it

28. Mitchell, *A Sermon*, p. 22; Painter, *Duty of the Southern Patriot and Christian*, pp. 19, 20–3. For further jeremiads on profanity and Sabbath breaking, see C. H. Read, *National Fast. A Discourse delivered on the Day of Fasting, Humiliation and Prayer, appointed by the President of the United States, January 4, 1861* (Richmond, Va.: West & Johnson, 1861), p. 13, and Andrew H. H. Boyd, *Thanksgiving Sermon, delivered in Winchester, VA on Thursday, 29th November, 1860* (Winchester: Office of the *Winchester Virginian*, 1860), p. 18.

29. Boyd, *Thanksgiving Sermon*, p. 10; *Christian Index*, July 24, 1861; Thomas Atkinson, *Christian Duty in the Present Time of Trouble. A Sermon Preached at St. James Church, Wilmington, N. C. on the Fifth Sunday after Easter, 1861* (Wilmington, N.C.: Fulton & Price, 1861), p. 8; Charles C. Pinckney, *Nebuchadnezzar's Fault and Fall: A Sermon, preached at Grace Church, Charleston, S.C. on the 17th of February, 1861* (Charleston: A. J. Burke, 1861), p. 10; Drew Gilpin Faust, *The Creation of Confederate Nationalism: Ideology and Identity in the Civil War South* (Baton Rouge and London: Louisiana State University Press, 1988), pp. 43–4. The lamentation over materialism had been a concern of the Southern clergy throughout the antebellum era and remained a central preoccupation during the Confederacy. See Kenneth Moore Stardup, "The Root of All Evil: The Southern Clergy and the Economic Mind of the Old South," Ph.D. diss., Louisiana State University, 1983, and Faust, *Creation of Confederate Nationalism*, chap. 3.

now dominated, had become corrupted and decayed. Only a dramatic break from this diseased body could save the South from ruin. For Southern Protestants, this interpretation of secession probably brought to mind the stage of "conviction" in the individual conversion process, the point at which the tension between the sinner's worldly life and religion could no longer be borne. With the moment of conversion, separation from the former life of sin was complete and the tension of conviction was resolved. The analogy between the individual sinner and the South, however, was not exactly this precise. Rather, the South was like the godly man who walks away from evil company to avoid temptation and ruin. The Rev. William O. Prentiss of Charleston illustrates this metaphorical concept as it applied to secession:

> St. Paul, in his first epistle to Timothy, farseeing, as I believe, this day, has warned us to withdraw ourselves from men who disturbed the relations existing between masters and servants, because they are unholy persons, men of corrupt minds, destitute of the truth, identifying gain with godliness.

The use of religious and particularly evangelical metaphors to explain secession implied that separating from the Union was as much a religious obligation as withdrawing from sin.[30]

The effectiveness of the religious and evangelical metaphors rested in large part on presenting the differences between the North and South as a conflict between Good and Evil. To this end, Southern clergymen frequently portrayed the North as a decadent and sinful society. Prentiss, for example, suggested that the Northern social order was "corrupted in its very root and principle." Andrew H. H. Boyd, a Presbyterian minister from Winchester, Virginia, pointed out the infidelity rampant in the North, lamenting that "streams of moral desolation are flowing through some portions of the country." The North was commonly portrayed as a society destroying itself, engaged in a kind of sectional suicide. "God must intend a scourge for them in this contest," a North Carolina preacher explained on the Confederate fast day, "and for that purpose, permits the North to rush madly on to her own destruction."[31]

30. Bruce, *And They All Sang Hallelujah*, pp. 66–7; William O. Prentiss, *A Sermon Preached at St. Peter's Church, Charleston by the Rev. William O. Prentiss, on Wednesday, November 21, 1860, being a Day of Public Fasting, Humiliation, and Prayer* (Charleston, S.C.: Evans & Cogswell, 1860), p. 8.

31. Prentiss, *Sermon Preached at St. Peter's Church*, p. 15; Boyd, *Thanksgiving Sermon*, p. 12; Daniel I. Dreher, *A Sermon Delivered by Rev. Daniel I. Dreher, pastor of St. James Church, Concord, N.C., June 13, 1861. Day of Humiliation and Prayer, as per Appointment of the President of the Confederate States of America* (Salisbury, N.C.: *Watchman* Office, 1861), p. 13.

In particular, Northern domination of the federal government had subverted the political union that bound the sections together. James H. Thornwell urged his listeners on South Carolina's fast day to "consider the manner in which the organs of Government have been perverted from their real design, and changed in their essential character." In December 1860, the *North Carolina Presbyterian* suggested that the North had "broken faith" with the South. The Southern Baptist Convention, in endorsing secession, argued that a revolution is justified when "any government is perverted from its proper design..." Like the federal government, the deeply venerated Union of the Founding Fathers had lost its original integrity. Benjamin M. Palmer mourned that the "Union of our forefathers" was gone. The Southern Baptist Convention considered the American nation "a Union so degenerated from that established by the Constitution." Southern churchmen were implying that the North had perverted the integrity of constitutional, republican government, a common theme in the writings of Southern secessionists.[32]

The logic presented in Southern fast day sermons led inexorably toward secession. If the North was sinful and degenerate, the obvious course was to purify the South and rescue it from ruin by seceding from the Union. "We cannot coalesce with men," the Rev. William O. Prentiss explained on the eve of South Carolina's secession, "whose society will eventually corrupt our own, and bring down upon us the awful doom which awaits them." On the Confederate fast day, St. John's Church in Mobile was told that the South "cannot give up this fair land to degradation and infamy; we cannot permit our churches, our schools...our temples of justice, to be swept into one common ruin..."[33]

Southern clergymen often employed the vivid and powerful imagery of disease and death to underscore the necessity of secession. Northern degeneracy was portrayed as a contagious disease that could destroy healthy organisms attached to it. An Alabama Baptist explained: "Sin, like that loathsome disease, the leprosy to which it is often compared, though it attacks the least member of the body, soon spreads itself throughout the whole." Comparing the body politic to the human body, he reasoned that "when a distemper seizes it, and spreads through all its members, there must be an entire change in its habits, or destruction is inevitable." Secession thus became a necessary amputation to save a healthy and living

32. *Fast Day Sermons*, p. 38; *North Carolina Presbyterian*, December 1, 1860; *Proceedings of the Southern Baptist Convention*, p. 62; Benjamin M. Palmer, *The Rights of the South Defended in the Pulpits: by B. M. Palmer, D. D. and W. T. Leacock, D.D.* (Mobile, Ala.: J. Y. Thompson, 1860), p. 13; *Proceedings of the Southern Baptist Convention*, p. 62.
33. Prentiss, *Sermon Preached at St. Peter's*, p. 17; H. N. Pierce, *Sermons Preached in St. John's Church*, p. 12.

South from a diseased and dying North. "Have we not done well," the *Southern Presbyterian* asked in March 1861, "to cut the bonds that bound us to such a body of death?" On the national fast day, the Rev. Thomas Atkinson assured his Wilmington, North Carolina, audience that nowhere in the natural order will God "permit a decaying body, out of which the life and spirit are gone, a mere carcase, to taint the atmosphere, to spread disease and death around it, but He will cause it to be removed, and He has provided instruments for the work ... to tear in pieces, and take out of the way, any such dead and corrupting body."[34]

The creation of a separate Southern nation was the final step in the religious logic of secession. Like the saved sinner, the South experienced a new birth with secession, breaking its former connection with sin and beginning a new life as an independent nation. The comparison between secession and the evangelical new birth is suggested by the language of fast day sermons, as the new Southern nation was often likened to a newborn child. Proclaiming that the South was "commencing a new mode of political existence," an Alabama clergyman noted that "we are in our infancy as a nation." The Rev. J. R. Kendrick of Charleston also referred to the new Southern nation as "just born." To his listeners in Fredericksburg, Virginia, the Rev. A. M. Randolph explained that the purpose of the fast day was to "bring our new born nation to the temple of Jehovah, to baptize it today with our Christian faith, to consecrate it to Christ and his cause ..."[35]

According to the tenets of evangelicalism, a conversion experience was followed by a commitment to a life of Christian holiness. Conforming to this pattern, Southern ministers expressed the hope that the new Southern nation would become an exemplary Christian republic. The birth of the Confederacy demanded a spiritual reawakening. "What shall the moral character of our nation be?" the Nashville *Christian Advocate* pondered in June 1861. Expressing the vision of the clergy, this Methodist weekly hoped that "these Southern States would compare themselves, not with other States, but with God's law, and set out with a high standard of national morality." Indeed, the demand for a strong religious foundation to the new Southern nation became a recurrent theme in Confederate religious writings. "Our laws should rest upon the eternal principles of

---

34. *South Western Baptist*, June 13, 1861; *Southern Presbyterian*, March 9, 1861; Atkinson, *On the Causes of Our National Troubles*, p. 6.

35. Mitchell, *Sermon in Government Street Church*, p. 15; William C. Butler, *Sermon Preached in St. John's Church, Richmond, Virginia, on the Sunday after the Battle at Manassas, July 21, 1861* (Richmond, Va.: Chas. H. Wynne, 1861), p. 19; Kendrick, *Lessons from an Ancient Fast*, p. 8; Randolph, *Address on the Day of Fasting and Prayer*, p. 16.

right and wrong which the Scriptures reveal," a Charleston minister urged, "our national, social life, be regulated by the rules of truth and justice, which God has therein given us." The *Southern Presbyterian* warned similarly that political independence "will be but a poor prize if it be won at the sacrifices of our Christian character and our religious interests." With a national commitment to holiness, the conversion of the South was complete. The justification of secession and the establishment of the Confederacy portrayed in evangelical terms was succinctly summed up by the Rev. T. L. DeVeaux as he stood before his congregation at Good Hope Church in rural Alabama on a spring day in 1861. "She will arise from her position," DeVeaux proclaimed, "cleansed from these sins, and clothed in the strength of God manfully vindicate the right, and rescue it from the hands of destroyers."[36]

This conception of Confederate religious nationalism was a natural result of the efforts of Southern ministers to invest sectional politics with religious significance. Since the 1830s, the clergy had carved out a religious sphere within the institution and issue of slavery. They had invested secession with moral significance, transforming it into an issue that invited religious involvement. From a religious interpretation of secession, the goal to Christianize the new Southern nation was logical and appropriate. The call for a purified, Christian Southern nation might be seen as a subtle but determined attempt at a theocratic revolution. Resembling the efforts of such New England divines as Timothy Dwight and Lyman Beecher at the turn of the nineteenth century, Southern ministers sought to secure their new nation by infusing the people with religion, committing them to morality and righteousness, and offering them their leadership. "It would be a glorious sight," the *Southern Presbyterian* suggested, "to see this Southern Confederacy of ours stepping forth amid the nations of the world animated with a Christian spirit, guided by Christian principles, administered by Christian men, and adhering faithfully to Christian precepts."[37]

36. *Christian Advocate*, June 27, 1861; Pinckney, *Nebuchadnezzar's Fault and Fall*, p. 12; *Southern Presbyterian*, January 12, 1861; Rev. T. L. DeVeaux, *A Fast Day Sermon, preached in the Good Hope Church, Lowndes County, Alabama, Thursday, June 13th, 1861* (Wytheville: D. A. St. Clair, 1861), p. 10.

37. Elwyn A. Smith, "The Voluntary Establishment of Religion," in Elywn A. Smith, ed., *The Religion of the Republic* (Philadelphia: Fortress Press, 1971), p. 155; *Southern Presbyterian*, February 23, 1861. The best explanations of this transformation are James F. MacLear, "'The True American Union' of Church and State: The Reconstruction of the Theocratic Tradition," *Church History* 28 (March 1959): 41–62, and Perry Miller, "From the Covenant to the Revival," in *Nature's Nation* (Cambridge, Mass.: Harvard University Press, 1967), pp. 90–120. See also O. S. Barten, *A Sermon Preached in St. James Church, Warrenton, VA., on Fast Day June 13, 1861 by the Rector* (Richmond,

Southern clergymen approached secession from a predominantly religious perspective. The Bible and evangelicalism provided the primary determinants for their analysis of the crisis of the Union. Yet as they had done in the 1830s and 1840s, Southern clerics during the secession crisis borrowed arguments from politicians. Secessionists maintained, for example, that the Constitution was a compact of the states. In their view, political power resided in the sovereignty of the states, a view that legitimated independent state secession. That these views found their way into fast day sermons and denominational newspapers provides another example of the interplay between religious and political discourse.[38]

Southern ministers closely followed their politicians' constitutional defense of states' rights. When the Southern Baptist Convention supported secession at their annual meeting in 1861, they maintained that the Union consisted of equal sovereign states. James H. Thornwell argued similarly that "the ultimate ground of the authority of federal legislation is the consent of the confederating States." It was a false conception of the Constitution, stated the Rev. Daniel Dreher of Concord, North Carolina, to view it as "a law consolidating the several States into an inseparable Union." Rather, he explained, "it is only a mutual compact or covenant, and each State an integral member, having separate laws for its internal regulation." An adherence to the states' rights philosophy became the foundation for a constitutional defense of secession. "The right of a state to secede is an undoubted right," reasoned the *Universalist Herald* of Montgomery. "They are each sovereign and independent. They came into the Union separately, and have a right to go out so." The *Central Presbyterian* of Richmond believed that the states reserved the right of resuming the trusts they had confided in the federal government.[39]

On the basis of their belief in states' rights, Southern clergymen insisted that the North had perverted true constitutional government. The Rev. J. R. Kendrick of Charleston argued that "the attempt to hold sovereign States together against their will, and coerce them into union by a war of

Va.: *Enquirer* Book and Job Press, 1861), p. 7. For a good analysis of the clergy in the creation of Confederate nationalism, see Faust, *Creation of Confederate Nationalism*, chap. 3.

38. J. L. M. Curry, *Perils and Duty of the South. Substance of a Speech delivered by Jabez L. M. Curry in Talledega, Alabama, November 26, 1860* (Washington, D.C.: L. Towers, 1860), p. 1; James B. Owens, *The Right, Causes and Necessity for Secession. Argument of the Hon. James B. Owens, Delegate to the State Convention of Florida on the Secession Resolutions* (Appalachicola, Fla.: 1861), pp. 11–4. For the constitutional defense of secession, see Jesse T. Carpenter, *The South as a Conscious Minority, 1789–1861: A Study in Political Thought* (New York: New York University Press, 1930), pp. 171–220.

39. *Proceedings of the Southern Baptist Convention*, p. 62; *Fast Day Sermons*, p. 30; Dreher, p. 11; *Universalist Herald*, March 1, 1861; *Central Presbyterian*, December 15, 1860.

invasion, is utterly opposed to the genius of our institutions and to all the traditions and maxims in which we have been educated touching a people's right to self-government." The Southern clergy saw in the Northern domination of the federal government a consolidating tendency that would lead to despotism and tyranny. In January 1861, for instance, the *Texas Baptist* maintained that Northern Republicans were "anti-republican in politics because they sought to engraft into the Constitution of these United States, these federal powers by which the National Government might become the oppressive tyrant of a minority of the States, without their consent." Thomas Smyth of Charleston spoke similarly that "the soul of the Northern confederacy was consolidated despotism – the many headed monster of a blind, heartless and unprincipled majority." If the Confederate cause failed, warned the Rev. Daniel Dreher of North Carolina, "a military despotism [would] take the place of popular government the most wretched of all governments." In stating that the North had perverted the true meaning of the Constitution, Southern ministers echoed previous arguments made during the denominational schisms that it was the North that had departed from national standards.[40]

IV

A close explication of one specific text allows us to see the secessionist argument in its original form as it unfolded in one mind and one place. *Slavery a Divine Trust: Duty of the South to Preserve and Perpetuate It*, a sermon delivered on Thanksgiving Day, 1860, by the Presbyterian minister Benjamin M. Palmer of New Orleans, is perhaps the best text for this purpose. By all contemporary accounts, Palmer's address had a powerful influence in converting Southern sentiments to secession. It illustrates as well as any other text the religious understanding of the sectional conflict.

Benjamin Morgan Palmer was one of the most prominent Presbyterian clergymen in the antebellum South. He was a classic representative of the "Gentlemen Theologians." Born in Charleston in 1818, he was educated at Walterboro Academy in South Carolina. Palmer's Southronism may ironically have begun at Amherst College in Massachusetts. He and his fellow Southerners were drawn closer together by taunts from other students about South Carolina's defiance in the nullification crisis. Palmer

---

40. Kendrick, *Lessons from an Ancient Fast*, p. 14; *Texas Baptist*, January 3, 1861; Smyth, *Battle of Ft. Sumter*, p. 20; Dreher, *A Sermon*, p. 6. See also Stephen Elliott, *The Silver Trumpets of the Sanctuary. A Sermon preached to the Pulaski Guards in Christ Church, Savannah, on the Second Sunday after Trinity* (Savannah, Ga.: Steam Press of John M. Cooper, 1861), p. 8.

graduated from the University of Georgia in 1838 and entered Columbia Theological Seminary in South Carolina the next year. After a brief stay in Savannah, he returned to Columbia, where he became pastor of the First Presbyterian Church. He taught for a short time at the Presbyterian Seminary and in 1856 accepted a call from the First Presbyterian Church in New Orleans. When the first General Assembly of the Presbyterian Church in the Confederate States of America convened in 1861, Palmer was elected moderator.[41]

Palmer's New Orleans pulpit befitted his personal prominence. Fronting Lafayette Square from the south, the First Presbyterian Church was one of the most imposing buildings in the Crescent City and a magnificent example of Gothic architecture in America. In its membership and clientele, it reflected the cosmopolitan nature of antebellum New Orleans. Because more than half its members came from the mercantile and professional elite, it was often considered "one of the most respectable congregations in the city." It drew members formerly belonging to churches in such cities as Boston, New York, and St. Louis. Because of Palmer's oratorical reputation, his overflow audiences often included non-Protestants as well as visitors from across the country. On Thanksgiving Day, 1860, the crowd that packed into the auditorium of the First Presbyterian Church to listen to Palmer discuss the impending crisis of the Union numbered close to 2,000.[42]

Significantly, Palmer began his sermon by establishing a religious niche in the political realm. Reflecting the providential interpretation of human affairs, he first explained that the Thanksgiving Day proclamation by the governor of Louisiana "recognizes the existence of a personal God, whose will shapes the destiny of nations, and that sentiment of religion in man which points to Him as the needle to the pole." For many of the previous Thanksgiving observances, the dominant feeling was gratitude. At the present, however, America was in "the most fearful and perilous crisis which has occurred in our history as a nation." It was this crisis that

41. This brief portrait was pieced together from Wayne C. Eubank, "Benjamin Morgan Palmer's Thanksgiving Sermon, 1860," in J. Jeffrey Auer, ed., *Antislavery and Disunion, 1858–1861: Studies in the Rhetoric of Compromise and Conflict* (New York and Evanston: Harper & Row, 1963), pp. 291–5, and Samuel S. Hill, ed., *Encyclopedia of Southern Religion* (Macon, Ga.: Mercer University Press, 1984), p. 577. On his education at Amherst, see Thomas Cary Johnson, *The Life and Letters of Benjamin Morgan Palmer* (Richmond, Va.: Presbyterian Committee on Publication, 1906), pp. 47–9. For further information on Palmer, consult Dorolyn J. Hickey, "Benjamin Morgan Palmer: Churchman of the Old South," Ph.D. diss., Duke University, 1962, and Timothy F. Reilly, "Benjamin M. Palmer: Secessionist Become Nationalist," *Louisiana History* 18 (Summer 1977): 287–301.

42. Eubank, "Benjamin Morgan Palmer's Thanksgiving Sermon," p. 291, 296–7.

justified Palmer's excursion into pulpit politics. His explanation echoed the thinking of most antebellum Southern clergymen. "The party questions which have hitherto divided the political world," Palmer explained, "have seemed to me to involve no issue sufficiently momentous to warrant my turning aside, even for a moment, from my chosen calling." But Lincoln's election had brought "one issue before us" which had created a crisis that called forth the guidance of the clergy: "At a juncture so solemn as the present, with the destiny of a great people waiting upon the decision of an hour, it is not lawful to be still."[43]

That issue was slavery. Palmer recognized and emphasized its religious dimension. Implicitly recalling the significance of the abolitionist postal campaign of 1835, Palmer insisted that the question of slavery "was, in its origin, a question of morals and religion." It was debated in the church before it became an issue in the state. With recent memory of the denominational schisms, Palmer reminded his audience that slavery had "riven asunder the two largest religious communions in the land." Very simply, slavery was at the center of the crisis of the Union: "[T]he right determination of this primary question will go far toward fixing the attitude we must assume in the coming struggle."[44]

After having established the centrality of slavery, Palmer moved toward the central thesis of his sermon. The South, according to the New Orleans minister, had a providential trust *"to conserve and to perpetuate the institution of slavery as now existing."* In defending this point, Palmer essentially portrayed the sectional crisis as an irrepressible conflict. The South was defined by slavery: "It has fashioned our modes of life, and determined all our habits of thought and feeling, and moulded the very type of our civilization." The North, however, was "working out the social problem under conditions peculiar to themselves." And the prospect was not hopeful. Palmer painted the North as a society plagued by overpopulation and class struggle between labor and capital. This depiction of the North echoes the writings of George Fitzhugh and other Southern theorists in the 1850s, who had pushed the proslavery argument to a broader attack on free-labor civilization. In a brief discussion of the nature of slavery, Palmer reflected the paternalism and patriarchy underlying the clerical sanctification of slavery. He stressed the mutual relations between masters and slaves. Echoing his clerical brethren and secular proslavery theorists, Palmer claimed that his servant "stands to me in the relation of a child."[45]

As Southern clergymen had been doing since the 1830s, Palmer added

---

43. *Fast Day Sermons*, pp. 57–61.
44. *Fast Day Sermons*, p. 61.
45. *Fast Day Sermons*, pp. 64–6.

to his defense of slavery a critique of abolitionism. Both were religious issues: "in this great struggle, *we defend the cause of God and religion*." To Palmer, abolitionism was "undeniably atheistic." Associating it with the French Revolution, he argued that abolition struck at God by striking at all subordination and law. It threatened the "obsolete idea that Providence must govern man, and not that man should control Providence." Palmer essentially transformed the political sectional conflict over slavery into a greater struggle:

> To the South the highest position is assigned, of defending, before all nations, the cause of all religion and of all truth. In this trust, we are resisting the power which wars against constitutions, and laws and compacts, against Sabbaths and sanctuaries, against the family, the State and the church; which blasphemously invades the prerogatives of God, and rebukes the Most High for the errors of his administration, which, if it cannot snatch the reins of empire from his grasp, will lay the universe in ruins at his feet.[46]

Palmer moved next toward the more immediate issues facing the South. Reflecting a major theme of Southern fast day sermons, Palmer sought to convince his audience that it was the North that had perverted American ideals and institutions. The Constitution had been "converted into an engine of oppression." In a brief and relatively vague history of the sectional controversy up to Lincoln's election, Palmer squarely placed the blame on the North. He anticipated the possible objections of those who would urge conciliation and caution. Mirroring the conspiratorial thinking that pervaded the discourse of sectional controversy, Palmer warned: "The elevation of their candidate is far from being the consummation of their aims; it is only the beginning of that consummation; and, if all history be not a lie, there will be cohesion enough till the end of the beginning is reached, and the dreadful banquet of slaughter and ruin shall glut the appetite." As the Presbyterian divine feared, "[T]he decree has gone forth that the institution of Southern slavery shall be constrained within assigned limits."[47]

The ultimate question for Palmer was whether the South should secede to protect its providential trust of slavery. He affirmed the calling of state conventions to consider secession and urged "measures for framing a new and homogeneous confederacy." Compromise seemed out of the question: "I fear the antagonism is too great, and the conscience of both parties too deeply implicated to allow such a composition of the strife."

46. *Fast Day Sermons*, pp. 68–70. See also the similar statement by James H. Thornwell quoted in Wilbur Cash, *The Mind of the South* (New York: Knopf, 1941), p. 80.
47. *Fast Day Sermons*, pp. 72–6.

The time was indeed "sublime," for the South would make a decision that would affect generations. He closed by affirming that he was "impelled to deepen the sentiment of resistance in the Southern mind, and to strengthen the current now flowing toward a union of the South in defence of her chartered rights."[48]

After the sermon, one listener recalled, the audience was "in solemn silence, no man speaking to his neighbor, the great congregation of serious and thoughtful men and women dispersed; but afterwards the drums beat and the bugles sounded; for New Orleans was shouting secession." Contemporaries agreed that Palmer's sermon exerted a powerful influence in enlisting support for secession. The Southern political press rang with praise for the sermon. The New Orleans *Daily Delta* published the sermon on December 2, claiming "...a more cogent, exhaustive, logical and impressive production of not greater length we have never met with coming either from pulpit or rostrum." The paper distributed more than 30,000 copies of Palmer's address. The *Tri-Weekly Southern Guardian* of Columbia, South Carolina, claimed the sermon "rose to the full height of great questions which now fill the public mind, and have so quickened the general conscience." The sermon was reprinted in full in the Jackson *Weekly Mississippian* and the Augusta *Southern Field and Fireside*. Far away in Virginia, one Southerner remarked that Palmer's address had created "a very great sensation in the South," and another later recalled that Palmer had done more than "any other non-combatant in the South to promote rebellion." When Union General Benjamin F. Butler occupied New Orleans in April 1862, he put a price on Benjamin M. Palmer's head. This perhaps was a most fitting testimony to the contribution of this fire-eating Presbyterian.[49]

Several factors help explain why *Slavery a Divine Trust* was so influential in the South during the winter of 1860. Palmer's reputation as an orator, Presbyterian leader, and theologian undoubtedly added to the weight of his words. Most important, however, his analysis of the sec-

---

48. *Fast Day Sermons,* pp. 76–80.
49. Eubank, "Benjamin Morgan Palmer's Thanksgiving Day Sermon," pp. 304–6; Arthur Lee Brent to unidentified friend in New York, February 2, 1861, John G. Webb Papers, Virginia Historical Society, Richmond; Thompson, *Presbyterians in the South,* p. 538; Eubank, "Benjamin Morgan Palmer's Thanksgiving Day Sermon," p. 309. One historian has argued that Palmer's sermon "unquestionably exerted a profound influence" on the course of Louisiana toward secession; Willie M. Caskey, *Secession and Restoration of Louisiana* (Baton Rouge: Louisiana State University Press, 1938), pp. 19–20. For one instance of politicians listening to Palmer, see the editorial in the New Orleans *Bee* for December 5, 1860 in Dwight L. Dumond, ed., *Southern Editorials on Secession* (Gloucester, Mass.: Peter Smith, 1964; originally published 1931, American Historical Association), pp. 305–6.

tional crisis must have had a special appeal to Southerners at that moment
in time. By presenting an irrepressible conflict between two distinctive
civilizations, Palmer provided a clear and persuasive call to action in a
time of confusion and uncertainty. His linking the cause of orthodox
religion to the destiny of the South reinforced the belief that slavery was
a divinely ordained institution, assuring Southerners that their perilous
course into secession and perhaps war would be sanctioned by God.

Benjamin M. Palmer's Thanksgiving Day sermon neatly sums up the
religious logic of secession. It reflects the major corpus of Southern fast
day sermons in his use of the evangelical metaphor and the language of
disease. ⸀ conveniently ties together the several strands of Southern clerical thinking on the sectional conflict – slavery, abolitionism, the legacy of
the denominational schisms and the relationship between religion and
politics. It establishes the centrality of slavery in the sectional thought of
Southern clergymen. Most important, Palmer's address is vivid testimony
to the intimate bonds between religion and the cause of the South that had
been forged during three decades of sectional strife. Not surprisingly,
this association would remain foremost in the minds of Southern clergymen as they turned to creating a new Southern identity as a Confederate
nation.[50]

50. *Fast Day Sermons*, pp. 59, 62, 71. Most Southern fast day sermons did include defenses
of slavery and attacks on abolitionism. But because I covered this material in Chapters
2 and 3, I have tended to deemphasize it here in constructing the Southern religious logic
of secession.

6

Religion and the formation
of a Southern national ideology

The departure of eleven slave states from the Union and the birth of the Confederacy marked the final transformation from Southern sectionalism to Southern nationalism. To those Southern clergymen who chose to defend disunion from the pulpit, the issue of nationalism became inescapable. The secession crisis had forced Southern clerics to diagnose the crisis of the Union and to justify severance from the Union in religious terms. Alongside these themes was the conscious attempt by the clergy to create a new national identity. It became one of the main purposes behind the fast day sermons and political editorials in denominational newspapers. This emerging national self-consciousness serves as an appropriate conclusion to the study of the relationship between religion and the development of Southern separatism. It provides another angle from which to view the ways in which clergymen wove religion into a distinctive Southern identity.[1]

The creation of Southern religious nationalism can best be appreciated through a direct comparison between the writings of Northern and Southern clergymen. A comparative strategy has several advantages. It is the most practical and reliable way to determine what is distinctly "Southern" in the writings of Southern ministers. It is also invaluable in understanding the origins of Southern religious nationalism during the winter and spring of 1860–1. The North was essential to the creation of a Southern national identity. It functioned as a negative reference point by which

1. Historians are beginning to recognize the ways in which nationalism is an intentional, self-conscious creation. See especially Drew Gilpin Faust, *The Creation of Confederate Nationalism: Ideology and Identity in the Civil War South* (Baton Rouge and London: Louisiana State University Press, 1988), pp. 4–7. A similar approach is taken in Carl N. Degler, *One Among Many: The Civil War in Comparative Perspective* (Gettysburg, Pa.: Gettysburg College, 1990), especially pp. 11–13. On the tensions between religion and nationalism, see James O. Farmer, Jr., "Southern Presbyterians and Southern Nationalism: A Study in Ambivalence," *Georgia Historical Quarterly* 75 (Summer 1991): 275–94.

Southern clergymen could demonstrate their region's allegiance to American values and institutions by explaining how the North had departed from and subverted this common tradition.[2]

When examined for points of comparison and contrast, the writings of Northern clergymen can yield great insight into the nature of Southern religious nationalism. By their similarity of discourse, the writings demonstrate the harmony between Southern separatism and national values. By their differences in emphasis, degree, and direction, they demonstrate the distinctive qualities of Southern religious nationalism. A comparative perspective, then, provides the best key to unlocking the sectional ideology that made secession and war possible.

I

Northern and Southern clergymen during the secession crisis shared the same rhetorical world. The similarity in discourse is indeed striking. Both groups of clergy used the same language and set of assumptions to explain and interpret the sectional controversy between North and South. They held in common an almost identical conception of the relationship between religion and politics. They both believed in a providential direction of the affairs of nations. Each made recourse to the imagery of American nationalism to lend divine sanction to their cause. This rhetorical unity between North and South ironically shaped the expression of Southern religious nationalism.

The way Northern ministers conceptualized the relationship between religion and politics closely paralleled the ideas of the Southern clergy.

2. For comparative purposes, I have examined fifty-two sermons and ten denominational newspapers. Seven of these sermons were antislavery sermons written primarily during the 1830s, and fourteen were delivered around the time of the Kansas–Nebraska controversy. The remaining thirty-one were written during the secession crisis. In terms of regional distribution, six sermons were from New York and Massachusetts, four were from Pennsylvania, three from New Hampshire, two each from Iowa, Maine, Michigan, and Wisconsin, and one sermon each from Connecticut, New Jersey, Ohio, and Rhode Island. I also attempted to cover the main denominations, although the majority were Congregationalist and Presbyterian. I am confident that these sources constitute a substantial and reliable sample of Northern clerical thought on the sectional crisis. The most recent and complete study of the Northern clergy and the Civil War is the fine book by James H. Moorhead, *American Apocalypse: Yankee Protestants and the Civil War, 1860–1869* (New Haven, Conn.: Yale University Press, 1978). See also Chester A. Dunham, *The Attitude of the Northern Clergy towards the South, 1860–1865* (Toledo: Gray Company, 1942), and Lewis G. Vander Velde, *The Presbyterian Churches and the Federal Union, 1861–1869* Harvard Historical Studies, vol. 33 (Cambridge, Mass.: Harvard University Press, 1932).

Northern clerics denied any interest in politics when it meant issues of party or policy but claimed that a political question became a legitimate topic for pulpit discourse if it possessed any kind of moral dimension. In a fast day sermon delivered on April 28, 1861, the Rev. Alonzo Quint of Massachusetts explained "that from the railing themes of partisan warfare, from political strife, I have never drawn materials for sermons, though at times my silence has been irksome to some." Quint nonetheless recognized in the extraordinary times "the call to a patriot minister." It was not time for silence, he argued, "when the great principles have taken the guise of war, in which the fate of our country is to be settled for years." John O. Fiske, pastor of the Winter Street Church in Bath, Maine, also shunned "party politics" and confined himself to "a few general principles and statements." The general understanding that guided the Northern clergy during the secession crisis was clearly summarized by the New York *Christian Advocate and Journal*:

> Ministers of the Gospel, as such (and the same rule applies to editors of religious newspapers,) should deal with political affairs only in their obviously moral and religious relations. In ordinary political contests about men and measures of administration, it is usually not expedient that the pulpit or, the religious press should take any part. Not so, however, when the interests of morals and religion are involved with political questions. Then the voice of the Church should be heard, calmly and sternly defending the right in the name of God, and carrying the authority of conscience into the strifes of party.[3]

This statement reflects thinking almost identical to that of Southern clergymen.

Like their brethren in the South, Northern clerics entered the political arena on the specific grounds that religion was intimately connected with the question of slavery. The Rev. Anthony Schyler, pastor of Christ Church in Oswego, New York, maintained that slavery had become such an absorbing political issue because "there was and there is a religious question about it." That question, Schyler concluded, "is as clearly and

3. Alonzo H. Quint, *The Christian Patriot's Present Duty. A Sermon addressed to the Mather Church and Society, Jamaica Plain, Mass., April 28, 1861* (Boston, Mass.: Hollis & Gunn, 1861), p. 5; John O. Fiske, *A Sermon on the Present National Troubles, delivered in the Winter Street Church, January 4, 1861, The Day of the National Fast.* (Bath, Me.: Daily Times Office, 1861), p. 3; *Christian Advocate and Journal*, March 14, 1861. See also B. R. Allen, *"The Constitution and the Union:" A Sermon preached in the First Congregational Church in Marblehead, on the Occasion of the National Fast, January 4th, 1861* (Boston, Mass.: J. H. Eastburn's Press, 1861), p. 4, and Heman Humphrey, *Our Nation, A Discourse delivered at Pittsfield, Mass., January 4, 1861, on the Day of the National Fast* (Pittsfield: Henry Chickering, 1861), p. 5.

entirely within the sphere of the Pulpit, as any question can be." The New Jersey minister William R. Gordon told his audience at a Dutch Reformed church that slavery "involves a mighty moral question covering the whole moral law." A New York minister agreed: "The fatal error of our legislation for forty years has been that of treating Slavery as a mere political institution to be calculated, instead of a moral wrong to be repudiated from our public policy." Although clergymen North and South agreed that there was a religious dimension to the slavery controversy, there was a significant difference between them. Southern clerics insisted that the existence of slavery itself was a civil and political question. For Northern antislavery ministers, the existence of slavery was a religious issue precisely because the holding of slaves was sinful.[4]

Besides sharing similar views on religion and politics, clerics both North and South adhered to a providential interpretation of history. Northern clergymen expressed the widely accepted belief among antebellum American Protestants that God directed and controlled the course of human history. The *Christian Advocate and Journal* of New York said simply: "God is in history." Another Methodist journal, the *Pittsburgh Christian Advocate,* agreed that "a calm and thoughtful survey of history, deciphered by the teachings of revealed religion, will show Him to be the disposer of human events – planting nations and plucking them up, exalting the humble and abasing the proud." History not only showed the hand of providence but also displayed cyclical patterns that made the present understandable by reference to the past. "History becomes pertinent and almost personal to present times," a New York minister explained on the national fast day, "because two of the principal factors of history, the depravity of man, and the righteous Providence of God, remain unchanged." Beginning his sermon with allusions to biblical history, the Rev. C. D. Helmer of Milwaukee confirmed the canon of the cyclical interpretation of history: "So exactly are the experiences of nations repeated in the course of ages."[5]

A providential interpretation of history could explain the sectional conflict that had torn asunder North and South. Because God directed hu-

4. Anthony Schyler, *Slaveholding as a Religious Question. A Sermon preached in Christ Church, Oswego, on the Evening of February 3, 1861* (n.p., n.d.), p. 4; William R. Gordon, *The Peril of our Ship of State: A Sermon on the Day of Fasting and Prayer, January 4th, 1861* (New York: John A. Gray, 1861), p. 12; Joseph P. Thompson, *The President's Fast: A Discourse upon Our National Crimes and Follies, preached in the Broadway Tabernacle Church, January 4, 1861* (New York: Thomas Holman, 1861), p. 20. See also Fiske, *Sermon on the Present National Troubles,* p. 4.

5. *Christian Advocate and Journal,* March 21, 1861; *Pittsburgh Christian Advocate,* April 23, 1861; Thompson, *The President's Fast,* p. 5; C. D. Helmer, *Two Sermons. I. Signs of Our National Atheism, II. The War Begun* (Milwaukee, Wis.: Terry & Cleaver, 1861), p. 19.

man affairs, adversity was seen as a sign of divine disfavor. As a Pennsylvania minister explained on the national fast day, "the Lord, who is God, visits individuals and nations with His just judgments for their sins." Heman Humphrey, speaking to his congregation in Pittsfield, Massachusetts, agreed that whatever "the secondary causes may be by which guilty nations are punished and destroyed, . . . His avenging hand is in it." The political strife that was threatening the Union was thus depicted as a punishment for sins. "Our present disturbances," suggested the *Christian Watchman and Reflector,* "may be Divine judgments for our sins." An Iowa minister maintained similarly that "the sins of the people and of the Government are in some way the cause of the calamities that are." In a fast day sermon delivered before Trinity Church in Claremont, New Hampshire, the Rev. Carlton Chase said that for the sins of the people, "God in his judgment has left us to this state of distraction." Northern clergymen listed a litany of sins that had brought the nation to the brink of disunion, including materialism, the spirit of party, forgetfulness of God, and "lusty avarice."[6]

But adversity contained within itself the seeds of redemption. An afflicted nation had only to recognize the sin that had brought on God's disfavor and to repent in order to renew His blessings. "The life of nations, as of individuals," explained the *Christian Watchman and Reflector,* "has its appointed trials, and its seasons of deep affliction, to lead them to humiliation, to repentance, to trust in the living God." The Congregational minister E. S. Atwood told his listeners in Grantville, Massachusetts, that sins against God "have brought us to this strait, and returning forth and allegiance will bring us out." The *Buffalo Christian Advocate* neatly summarized this logic of providential thought:

> Underlying all political and threatening agitations is an evil, a sin upon which heaven frowns. The cause whatever it is, of the present disturbance of the country must be looked after, repented of, and eradicated; then may we hope that Providence will smile and not frown.[7]

6. T. P. Bucher, *Union Fast Day Sermon, delivered in the United Presbyterian Church, Gettysburg, PA., Friday, January 4, A.D. 1861* (Gettysburg: H. C. Neinstedt, 1861), p. 5; Humphrey, *Our Nation,* p. 13; *Christian Watchman and Reflector,* March 14, 1861; Thacher, *A Sermon,* p. 8; Carlton Chase, *A Discourse, delivered in Trinity Church, Claremont, January 4, 1861, being the day appointed by the President of the United States, for General Fasting and Prayer on Account of the Distracted State of the Country* (Claremont, N.H.: George G. and Lemuel N. Ide, 1861), p. 7.

7. *Watchman and Reflector,* April 11, 1861; E. S. Atwood, *The Purse, the Knapsack, and the Sword. A Sermon delivered in the Congregational Church, Grantville, Mass., on Sunday, April 28, 1861* (Boston, Mass.: Bazin & Chandler, 1861), p. 19; quoted in *Christian Advocate,* January 3, 1861.

Trained to think in providential terms, preaching to an audience steeped in Protestantism, and eager to decode the religious significance of public events, Northern and Southern clergymen interpreted the sectional conflict in similar if predictable terms. It was also natural for clergymen North and South to turn to American civil religion as they fashioned a new national identity. The recourse to the symbol of America as God's Redeemer Nation and the image of the United States as the New Israel, two central components of this tradition, was another important similarity in the writings of Northern and Southern clerics.

The image of the United States as Redeemer Nation was part of the tradition of civil millennialism, a weaving of secular and religious motifs into a belief that America had a unique role in bringing the Kingdom of God to this world. Civil millennialism originated in the Puritan fascination with apocalyptic literature and the millennium. New England Puritans believed that they had been singled out by God to hasten the millennium on earth. During the American Revolution, religious eschatology fused with political republicanism as America's millennial hopes became synonymous with liberty and a morally virtuous republic. Civil millennialism persisted into the nineteenth century, when the belief that the American republic had a divine role in human history sanctified a maturing American nationalism. Although it often lacked explicit apocalyptic references, the idea that America had a peculiar destiny ordained by God became commonplace among American Protestants.[8]

Southern clergymen fully embraced the concept of Redeemer Nation. During the decades before secession, they joined the national chorus in proclaiming that the United States had a unique destiny and mighty responsibilities to fulfill. James H. Thornwell asserted in 1850 that Americans stood "in the momentous capacity of the federal representatives of the human race." Another Presbyterian minister, the Rev. George Bell of Greensboro, Alabama, portrayed America as "a nation which God's own hand hath planted, and on which he has, therefore, peculiar and special claims." In a Thanksgiving Day address delivered before citizens of Oxford, Mississippi, in 1856, university president Frederick A. P.

8. An accessible introduction to millennialism is James West Davidson, *The Logic of Millennial Thought: Eighteenth-Century New England* (New Haven, Conn.: Yale University Press, 1977), pp. 3–36. On the millennial motif in America, see Ernest Lee Tuveson, *Redeemer Nation: The Idea of America's Millennial Role* (Chicago: University of Chicago Press, 1968); Nathan O. Hatch, *The Sacred Cause of Liberty: Republican Thought and the Millennium in Revolutionary New England* (New Haven, Conn.: Yale University Press, 1977); John F. Berens, *Providence and Patriotism in Early America, 1640–1815* (Charlottesville: University Press of Virginia, 1978); Moorhead, *American Apocalypse*, pp. 1–23.

Barnard proclaimed that "in raising up this union, God has designed it as an instrument for the accomplishment of a great purpose – a purpose no less than the political regeneration of the whole human race." The Redeemer Nation theme was embellished with historical parallels by a Presbyterian minister in 1847. "God has a great design for this Continent," proclaimed the Rev. William Anderson Scott of New Orleans, "and for our generation. As the Jews of old – as the Apostles – as the Reformers – as our fathers of 1776 – so are we, as a race, and as a nation, a peculiar people and called to a high and glorious destiny."[9]

To Southern clergymen, the timing of America's entrance into the world presaged its peculiar destiny. The *Central Presbyterian* of Richmond stated in 1856 that God "kept this continent veiled from the view and knowledge of mankind until, in the procession of ages, the auspicious Era came, when the curtain was raised, disclosing the magnificent spectacle of a new world thrown open for the reception of a race ordained and trained by heaven to be worthy of the heritage." The Rev. Robert J. Breckinridge underscored the significance of America's arrival on the scene of history when he told the Presbyterian General Assembly in 1855 that "the earth never witnessed before, and can never witness again, such a people, upon such a theatre, passing through such a development." The language in these comments suggests a portrayal of human history as a providentially written drama in which America was ordained to play a leading role.[10]

The Redeemer Nation theme was also a staple in the writings of Northern clergymen during the secession crisis. "We cannot repress the conviction that God has great purposes to accomplish through the means of this nation," declared the *Congregationalist* of Boston. To a Methodist journal in Cincinnati, God had a "glorious mission for the American

9. J. P. Thomas, ed., *The Carolina Tribute to Calhoun* (Columbia, S.C.: Richard L. Bryan, 1857), p. 109; George Bell, *A Sermon, delivered in the Presbyterian Church, in Greensboro, Ala., on Sabbath, December 22, 1851.* (Tuscaloosa, Ala.: M. D. J. Slade, 1851), p. 12; Frederick A. P. Barnard, *Gratitude Due for National Blessings: A Discourse, delivered at Oxford, Mississippi, on Thanksgiving Day, November 20, 1856* (Memphis, Tenn.: Bulletin Company, 1857), p. 24; William Anderson Scott, *Progress of Civil Liberty, A Thanksgiving Discourse: Pronounced in the Presbyterian Church, on Lafayette Square, New Orleans, on Thursday, 9th December, 1847, Being Thanksgiving.* (New Orleans: Printed at the Office of *The Daily Delta*, 1848), p. 20.

10. *Central Presbyterian*, June 21, 1856; Robert J. Breckinridge, *Fidelity in our Lot. The Substance of a Discourse preached by the Appointment of the General Assembly of the Presbyterian Church, at their Annual Meeting in the City of Nashville, Tennessee, in May, 1855* (Philadelphia: Board of Missions, 1855), p. 16. Mason Lowance has characterized Puritan history in a similar way, in *The Language of Canaan: Metaphor and Symbol in New England from the Puritans to the Transcendentalists* (Cambridge, Mass., and London: Harvard University Press, 1980), p. vii.

people." Specifically, America was to be God's vehicle for the coming of the millennium on earth and the redemption of mankind. In a fast day sermon entitled *American Patriotism,* the Rev. Charles Wadsworth of Philadelphia described America as "a Divine instrumentality for the furtherance of the gospel, and the final conversion of the world!" He told his audience in the Arch Street Church in Philadelphia that "God hath raised us up, and rendered us mighty, that we may work out the world's political and evangelical redemption." Heman Humphrey, Congregational minister and former president of Amherst College, also claimed that God had "given us so much work in prospect for bringing on the millennium." A Marblehead, Massachusetts, minister agreed with Wadsworth and Humphrey that America was created "to light the nations to liberty and peace."[11]

The analogy between the United States and biblical Israel was another popular vehicle for expressing the fervent religious nationalism of the antebellum era. The symbol of America as the New Israel originated in the Puritan practice of typology, essentially an allegorical reading of the Old Testament. Typology rested on the belief that figures and events of the Old Testament foreshadowed or prefigured those in the New Testament. Such Old Testament figures as Moses, Nehemiah, and Joshua, for example, were seen as precursors or types of the Messiah. Departing from the strict correlation between the Old and New Testaments, New England Puritans used the typological approach to draw a comparison between biblical Israel and the Puritan commonwealth. The exile of the Jews from the wilderness, for instance, was considered as a type of the Puritan flight from England. By the nineteenth century, a typological reading of Old Testament history had suffused American thought and expression. Antebellum Americans both North and South made frequent recourse to biblical history on public occasions. In a fast day sermon delivered in 1837, for example, a Massachusetts clergyman reminded his audience that "we, as a people, are in circumstances not dissimilar to those of the Jews." A Presbyterian minister from Greensboro, Alabama, concurred in 1851 that the conditions of biblical Israel and the United States were "strikingly similar and analogous."[12]

11. *Congregationalist,* January 11, 1861; *Western Christian Advocate,* February 6, 1861; Charles Wadsworth, *American Patriotism. A Sermon preached in the Arch Street Church, Sabbath Morning, April 28th, 1861* (Philadelphia: J. W. Bradley, 1861), p. 14; Humphrey, *Our Nation,* p. 36; Allen, *"The Constitution and the Union",* p. 34.

12. Mark A. Noll, "The Image of the United States as a Biblical Nation, 1776–1865," in Nathan O. Hatch and Mark A. Noll, eds., *The Bible in America: Essays in Cultural History* (New York: Oxford University Press, 1982), pp. 41–6; John Mitchell, *A Sermon preached before the First Church and the Edwards Church, Northampton, on the Late*

Inclined to interpret extraordinary public events in providential terms, both Northern and Southern clergymen turned naturally to biblical history for guidance and justification during the secession crisis. The Bible was not really a determinant source of their political arguments but, rather, a storehouse for types to support their convictions. Discussing contemporary politics in Biblical terms was also an acceptable means of access to the realm of sectional politics.[13]

Northern clergymen used Old Testament history to illuminate the sectional conflict. This analogical reading of Biblical history is illustrated in *The American Vine*, a fast day sermon preached before Christ Church in Philadelphia by the Rev. Benjamin Dorr. "God graciously planted his people," Dorr began, "as a choice vine, in the promised land, and He largely multiplied and prospered them there." The Israelites became ungrateful for God's blessings and laxed into "irredeemable ruin." In the prosperity and downfall of Israel, Dorr told his audience, "we have an illustration of the momentous truth, 'Righteousness exalteth a nation; but sin is a reproach.'" The message to contemporary America was clear: "Look back over all the past in our history, our rapid increase, our multi-

Fast, September 1, 1837 (Northampton: W. A. Hawley, 1837), p. 3; Bell, *Sermon, delivered in the Presbyterian Church*, p. 7. For good introductions to the practice of typology, see Sacvan Bercovitch, "Typology in Puritan New England: The Williams-Cotton Controversy Reassessed," *American Quarterly* 19 (Summer 1967): 166–91, and Mason Lowance, "Typology and the New England Way: Cotton Mather and the Exegesis of Biblical Types," *Early American Literature* 4, no. 1 (1969): 15–37. On typology and American nationalism, see Ursula Brumm, *American Thought and Religious Typology*, John Hoaglund, trans. (New Brunswick, N.J.: Rutgers University Press, 1970) and Ruth Bloch, *Visionary Republic: Millennial Themes in American Thought, 1756–1800* (Cambridge: Cambridge University Press, 1985). For the use of the biblical analogy in the writings of Southern clergymen, see William M. Green, *Funeral Discourse, on the Death of Rev. Stephen Patterson, Late Rector of Christ's Church, Vicksburg, Miss. delivered in that Church, December 4, 1853* (Vicksburg: *Whig* Book and Job Office, 1854), p. 4; Whitefoord Smith, *An Oration delivered before the Euphradian and Clariosophic Societies of the South Carolina College, on the 6th December, 1848* (Columbia, S.C.: John G. Bowman, 1849), p. 10, and William Bacon Stevens, *The Providence of God, in the Settlement and Protection of Georgia. A Sermon preached in Athens, on the 13th February 1845, the Day set apart by Executive Proclamation for Prayer and Thanksgiving.* (Athens, Ga.: *Whig* Office, 1845), p. 6. For a similar use among Northern clergymen, see Augustus B. Reed, *Historical Sermon delivered at Ware First Parish, on Thanksgiving Day, Dec. 2nd, 1830* (n.p., 1889), p. 4; George C. Ingersoll, *A Sermon Preached on Fast Day, before the First Congregational Society, in Burlington, Vermont* (Burlington: Printed by Stillman Fletcher, 1843), p. 3; Jared P. Waterbury, *Influence of Religion on National Prosperity. A Sermon, delivered in Portsmouth, N.H. April 1, 1830, Being the Annual Fast* (Portsmouth: Published by John W. Shepard, 1830), p. 8.

13. This use fits the general pattern of how the Bible was seen in antebellum America. See Noll, "The Image of the United States as a Biblical Nation, 1776–1865," pp. 41–6.

plied blessings, our numerous deliverances, and our ungrateful returns for all God's mercies and tell me if the Psalmist does not describe these as truly and clearly, as if he intended the description for us alone?" The story of the prosperity and decline of biblical Israel, told in the republican lexicon of the rise and fall of nations, was helpful in explaining the crisis of the Union. The Rev. Heman Humphrey introduced biblical history as a "beacon to warn the proudest nations to beware how they abuse their privileges, till wrath comes upon them to the uttermost." Humphrey urged his listeners in Pittsfield, Massachusetts, to "glance at his dealings with us as a nation, and see if he has not done even more for us, than he did for the tribes of Israel." Humphrey concluded that God had even dealt better with the United States than with his "ancient covenant people."[14]

Although it began as a tale of prosperity followed by ruin, the lesson of biblical history was ultimately one of hope and redemption. If a nation repented its sins and corrected its ways, God would restore His blessings. "Sometimes," explained a Congregationalist minister from New Hampshire, "nations have been upon the brink of ruin, disasters thick and fearful have fallen upon them, the cause of truth and equity almost crushed out, and yet at that very hour that seemed to be the harbinger only of a graceful grave, we have seen some wonderful interposition of God arresting the tide of triumphant vice." God had, after all, delivered the Israelites from bondage in Egypt. The Rev. T. P. Bucher of Gettysburg assured his listeners that if America, "like Nineveh of old, clothes itself in the sackcloth of repentance, we need have no fear but that God will remove our affliction, and bid peace and happiness smile upon our borders." A Maine minister also used biblical history as an example of the efficacy of prayer. Those Northern clergymen who drew upon the analogy between ancient Israel and the United States adapted Old Testament history to support their political inclination toward moderation. In general, these clergymen were urging repentance as a means of averting a sectional war.[15]

The appeal to Old Testament history and the analogy between biblical Israel and the United States was far more prevalent in the writings of the Southern clergy during the secession crisis. Drawing freely and widely on

14. Benjamin Dorr, *The American Vine. A Sermon Preached in Christ Church, Philadelphia, Friday, January 4, 1861, on occasion of the National Fast* (Philadelphia: Collins, Printer, 1861), pp. 8–11; Humphrey, *Our Nation*, pp. 8–9.

15. C. E. Lord, *Sermons on the Country's Crisis, delivered in Mount Vernon, N. H., April 28, 1861, by C. E. Lord, pastor of the Congregational Church* (Milford, N. H.: Boutwell's Newspaper, Book and Job Office, 1861), p. 6; Bucher, *Union Fast Day Sermon*, p. 24; Fiske, *A Sermon on the Present National Troubles*, p. 14.

the narrative of Old Testament history, Southern ministers used the lessons of biblical history primarily to establish and defend the legitimacy of secession. Because the New Israel motif had given such a powerful appeal to American nationalism, clergymen sought to sanctify their own nascent nationalism by comparing the experiences of biblical Israel directly to those of the South. "I preached on Thanksgiving Day," recalled the Rev. William S. Plumer of Richmond, "on the parallel between Jewish National History & that of our country in 7 particulars." In a fast day sermon delivered in Tuskegee, Alabama, a Baptist preacher directed his congregation to "detect in this passage of Jewish history many solemn lessons for prayerful meditation." A brief look at the various ways in which Biblical history was used to explain and justify Southern actions provides important insight into the formation of a Southern national identity.[16]

To clergymen intent on establishing the importance of the fast day ritual, the history of biblical Israel demonstrated the value of prayer and fasting. "Let us remember," urged the Catholic cleric Augustine Verot of Florida, "how the Jews, under Esther, having recourse to penance and prayer, were saved miraculously from their enemies, who themselves fell into the pit they had dug for their unoffending brethren." A Presbyterian clergyman from Missouri explained that when Nineveh was threatened with destruction, a fast was proclaimed and the city was saved. To Southern clergymen, God rewarded those nations that came to Him in prayer. "The result of this arrangement," suggested the Rev. J. C. Mitchell of Mobile, "was that when Moses held up his hands in prayer, Israel prevailed and when he let down his hands from prayer, Amalek prevailed."[17]

16. William S. Plumer to his brother, December 1, 1860, William S. Plumer Papers, William R. Perkins Library, Duke University, Durham, N.C.; *South Western Baptist*, June 13, 1861.

17. Augustine Verot, *A Tract for the Times. Slavery and Abolitionism, being the Substance of a Sermon, Preached in the Church of St. Augustine, Florida, on the 4th Day of January, 1861, Day of Public Humiliation, Fasting, and Prayer* (St. Augustine? 1861?), p. 14; H. M. Painter, *The Duty of the Southern Patriot and Christian in the Present Crisis. A Sermon preached in the First Presbyterian Church, Boonville, Mo. on Friday, January 4th, 1861, being the Day of the National Fast* (Boonville: Caldwell & Stahl, 1861), p. 3; J. C. Mitchell, *A Sermon delivered in the Government Street Church, on the National Fast Appointed by Jefferson Davis, President of these Confederate States, June 13, 1861* (Mobile, Ala.: Farrow & Dennett, 1861), p. 11. For additional evidence, see also J. R. Kendrick, *Lessons from an Ancient Fast. A Discourse delivered in the Citadel Square Church, Charleston, S. C. on the occasion of the General Fast, Thursday, June 13, 1861* (Charleston: Steam Power Press of Evans & Cogswell, 1861), p. 7, and C. H. Read, *National Fast. A Discourse delivered on the Day of Fasting, Humiliation, and Prayer, appointed by the President of the United States, January 4, 1861* (Richmond, Va.: West & Johnson, 1861), p. 11.

More important, the history of the Jews showed that Israel and the South shared similar experiences of secession. Biblical history thus offered a precedent and powerful rationale for separating from the Union. The story of the dissolution of the Hebrew tribes (I Kings 12:23-4) was the biblical passage most often cited to justify secession. Around 922 B.C., Israel divided between the followers of Rehoboam, the son of Solomon, and Jeroboam, who separated with the Northern tribes. A national division along sectional lines of North and South understandably captured the imagination of Southern Protestants. On the Confederate fast day, Emma Holmes of Charleston heard "a most admirable sermon . . . showing an exact parallel between the separation of the Israelites from the Jewish Nation under Rehoboam's oppressive rule and our secession." To a Presbyterian from Summerville, Georgia, the story of Jeroboam's break from Rehoboam "should be carefully studied by every patriot." It was used in *The Scriptural Grounds for Secession from the Union,* a sermon delivered by the Rev. Lucius Cuthbert, Jr., in Aiken, South Carolina, on December 16, 1860, four days before the Palmetto State passed an ordinance of secession. Cuthbert told his congregation that "when Rehoboam placed heavy burthens upon his people, God sent Jeroboam to head the secession of the ten tribes." To justify disunion, he drew upon the assumptions of the cyclical nature of history and the providential direction to national affairs. Assuring his listeners that God is "the same yesterday, to-day, and forever," Cuthbert declared that "God's immutable justice will warrant us at this time in throwing off the Northern yoke, which has become intolerable." By vindicating the right of secession through the Scriptures, Cuthbert underscored the relevance of biblical history and deepened the identification between biblical Israel and the South.[18]

In accord with the interpretation of secession as an act consistent with American political values, Southern clergymen claimed that the South was the true heir to the American tradition of civil religion. They took these two central expressions of this tradition, the idea of America as God's Redeemer Nation and the image of the United States as the New Israel, and reshaped them to apply exclusively to the South. Through this process of sectionalization, symbols of American religious nationalism

18. John F. Marszalek, ed., *The Diary of Miss Emma Holmes, 1861–1865* (Baton Rouge: Louisiana State University Press, 1979), p. 57; *Southern Presbyterian,* January 5, 1861; Lucius Cuthbert, *The Scriptural Grounds for Secession from the Union. A Sermon, delivered by Rev. Lucius Cuthbert, Jr., at Aiken, S. C. Dec. 16. 1860* (Charleston: Welch, Harris & Co., 1861), p. 7; A valuable guide for understanding the history of ancient Israel is Bernhard W. Anderson, *Understanding the Old Testament,* 3rd ed. (Englewood Cliffs, N.J.: Prentice-Hall, 1975).

were transformed into sectional ones. The South had become the Redeemer Nation and the New Israel.[19]

With secession and the outbreak of the Civil War, Southern clergymen
boldly proclaimed that the Confederacy had replaced the United States as
God's chosen nation. A Methodist minister from Petersburg, Virginia,
assured soldiers bound for battle that God "has chosen us as His peculiar
people, made us the repository of His will and the light of the world."
The *Central Presbyterian* was equally confident that God "has already
given us many reasons for believing that He has favor toward us." The
Rev. O. S. Barten provided an impassioned expression of the idea of
the Confederacy as Redeemer Nation in a fast day sermon preached in
Warrenton, Virginia, on June 13, 1861: "In the gradual unrolling of the
mighty scroll, on which God has written the story of our future, as fold
after fold is spread before the nation, may there stand, emblazoned in
letters of living light, but this one testimony: 'They are my people, and I
am their God!'"[20]

The Southern vision of Redeemer Nation bore an important resemblance to the similar image of American nationalism in the antebellum
era, testifying to the close affinity Southerners felt toward American ideals
and values. Confederate religious nationalism reflected the messianic and
utopian strains prominent in the concept of the United States as Redeemer Nation. Like the former Union, the South, blessed with God's
favor, was destined for unparalleled greatness. "He has placed us in the
front rank of the most marked epochs of the world's history," boasted a
Richmond clergyman after Manassas. The Rev. Alexander Gregg of Austin, Texas, predicted that "we will occupy . . . a yet loftier position among
the nations of the earth." Methodists in Yorkville, South Carolina, were
assured that God was "leading the South along the pathway to the highest
culmination of Christian civilization."[21]

19. I have borrowed the general idea of sectionalization from Robert E. May, *The Southern
    Dream of a Caribbean Empire, 1854–1861* (Baton Rouge: Louisiana State University
    Press, 1973), chap. 2.
20. R. N. Sledd, *A Sermon, delivered in the Market Street M. E. Church, Petersburg, VA.,
    before the Confederate Cadets, on the Occasion of their Departure for the Seat of War,
    Sunday, September 22, 1861* (Petersburg: A. F. Crutchfield & Co., 1861), p. 20; *Central
    Presbyterian*, July 20, 1861; O. S. Barten, *A Sermon Preached in St. James Church,
    Warrenton, VA, on Fast Day June 13, 1861 by the Rector* (Richmond: Enquirer Book and
    Job Press, 1861), p. 13.
21. William C. Butler, *Sermon: Preached in St. John's Church, Richmond, Virginia, on the
    Sunday after the Battle at Manassas, July 21, 1861* (Richmond: Chas. H. Wynne, 1861),
    p. 19; Alexander Gregg, *The Duties Growing out of It, and the Benefits to be Expected,
    from the Present War. A Sermon, preached in St. David's Church, Austin, on Sunday, July
    7th, 1861* (Austin, Tex.: Office of the *State Gazette*, 1861), p. 12; John T. Wightman, *The

Confederate religious nationalism also followed its American roots in integrating political ideals into the concept of Redeemer Nation. According to Southern ministers, God's chosen nation would advance republican institutions as well as Christianity. The fusion of political and religious missions embodied in the image of Redeemer Nation was clearly expressed by the *Texas Christian Advocate* in May 1861: "The eye of history is upon us, because the hope of rational government is central to our cause. Such a cause we knew was destined to triumph somewhere at some time. We are devoutly thankful that the present day and the Southern people have been chosen as the witness and instrument of the triumph." Similarly, a Baptist clergyman from Tuskegee, Alabama, believed that the "stand we now make for constitutional liberty will decide, under God, the fate of unborn millions." The South, instead of the United States, was now ordained to play the leading role in human history.[22]

As they had done with the image of Redeemer Nation, Southern clergymen sectionalized the analogy between biblical Israel and the United States. The Rev. T. S. Winn of Alabama stated explicitly that the position of the Israelites "bears a marked similarity to that of the people of these Confederate States." He assured his listeners that the Jews "were fighting for their rights, their liberties and their religion." Because the South and biblical Israel were chosen nations of God, the history of the Jews foreshadowed the fate of the South. According to the *Christian Index* of Georgia, biblical history demonstrated that "when war becomes necessary in the defense of a nation's right and honor or safety, the God of battles sanctions resistive measures." This important lesson was underscored by the Rev. Stephen Elliott as he preached to Georgia soldiers bound for battle: "If defensive war was right then, it is right now, and surely it must have been right when God himself commanded the battle shout to be sounded from his own sanctuary, and promised that he himself would take part in it, and save his people from their enemies." If the South was indeed the New Israel, then the history of the Jews strongly indicated that the Southern cause was a righteous one and would merit the protection of God.[23]

Southern clergymen were especially fond of drawing analogies between

Glory of God, the Defense of the South. A Discourse delivered in the Methodist Episcopal Church, South, Yorkville, S. C., July 28, 1861, the Day of National Thanksgiving for the Victory at Manassas (Portland, Me.: B. Thurston & Co., 1871), p. 10.

22. Quoted in *Christian Advocate*, May 9, 1861; *South Western Baptist*, June 13, 1861.
23. T. S. Winn, *The Great Victory at Manassas Junction, God the Arbiter of Battles. A Thanksgiving Sermon, preached in the Presbyterian Church, at Concord, Greene County, Alabama, on the 28th day of July, 1861* (Tuscaloosa: J. F. Warren, 1861), p. 3; *Christian Index*, January 16, 1861; Stephen Elliott, *The Silver Trumpets of the Sanctuary. A Sermon preached to the Pulaski Guards in Christ Church, Savannah, on the Second Sunday after Trinity* (Savannah: Steam Press of John M. Cooper, 1861), p. 5.

the South's military victories and those of the ancient Israelites. With God's help, they argued, a smaller but more righteous force could prevail against larger numbers. The Rev. J. H. Elliott of Charleston, in a sermon entitled *The Bloodless Victory,* compared the fall of Ft. Sumter to the expedition of Israel against Midian: "[W]e confess the hand of God seems as plainly in it as in the conquest of the Midianites." The military history of biblical Israel seemed especially prophetic after Confederate armies turned back Northern forces at the First Battle of Manassas on July 21, 1861. The Rev. William C. Butler, pastor of St. John's Church in Richmond, related the battle to events in Isaiah 37:26–7. Stephen Elliott of Georgia, in a fast day sermon delivered on July 28, compared the Southern victory to the deliverance of Moses from Egypt: "It was the crowning token of his love – the most wonderful of all the manifestations of his divine presence with us." An Alabama clergyman even saw in the battle at Bull Run a struggle reminiscent of David's fight with Goliath.[24]

Southern clergymen accordingly associated the North with the enemies of Israel. In a Thanksgiving sermon to celebrate the Confederate victory at Manassas, the Rev. T. S. Winn compared the North with the Philistines, who "had neither truth nor justice on their side. The God of the Bible was not their God." Moreover, the war aims of the North resembled the objectives of the Philistines, who "seemed bent on the political and commercial subjugation of the Jews." The *Southern Episcopalian* of Charleston also compared the enemies of the Jews and those of the South, arguing that the North was "burning with a desire of spoil and subjugation, similar to that which the Egyptians deployed against Israel."[25]

Although a precise measurement is elusive, it seems clear that Southern clergymen chose to identify more closely with the New Israel motif than did Northern ministers. There was only one sermon in my sample of Northern fast day sermons that drew an explicit connection between the North and God's New Israel.[26] The more widespread use of the Old

24. J. H. Elliott, *Bloodless Victory. A Sermon preached in St. Michael's Church, Charleston, S. C. on Occasion of the taking of Ft. Sumter* (Charleston: A. E. Miller, 1861), pp. 3–4; Butler, *Sermon,* p. 6; Elliott, *God's Presence with our Army at Manassas! A Sermon, preached in Christ Church, Savannah, on Sunday, July 28th, being the Day Recommended by the Congress of the Confederate States, to be observed as a Day of Thanksgiving, in commemoration of the Victory of Manassas Junction, on Sunday, the 21st of July, 1861.* (Savannah: W. Thorne Williams, 1861), pp. 5–6; Winn, *Great Victory at Manassas Junction,* p. 4.

25. Winn, *Great Victory at Manassas Junction,* pp. 1–2; *Southern Episcopalian,* August 1861, p. 262.

26. See Homer M. Dunning, *Providential Design of the Slavery Agitation. A Sermon preached to the Congregational Church in Gloversville on the National Fast Day, January 4th, 1861* (Gloversville, N.Y.: A. Pierson, 1861), pp. 4–5.

Testament analogy among Southern clergymen may be more easily explained than its absence in the North. The use of traditional American symbols by the Southern clergy served to legitimize the revolutionary act of secession and the creation of a new nation. Southerners' familiarity with the analogy probably eased the difficult transition from American to Confederate nationalism. In addition, the identification between the Confederacy and biblical Israel suggests that the South saw itself and depicted itself as a more religious society than the North. Considering the ways in which Southern clergymen had sanctified slavery and portrayed abolitionism as infidelity throughout the antebellum era, this self-characterization was a logical culmination of the religious movement toward separate nationhood. Finally, clergymen identified with biblical Israel most often as a small nation surrounded by hostile enemies aiming at their destruction. This parallel was undoubtedly helpful in preparing the Southern people for the coming of war.

Along with the tenets of American civil religion, clergymen both North and South laid claims to the heritage of the American Revolution. To a generation still steeped in the legacy of 1776, establishing historical continuity to the Revolution lent profound legitimacy and sanctification to contemporary political positions. Not surprisingly, both Northern and Southern clergymen in 1860–1 sought to link their cause to that of the American patriots.

The idea that secession and the formation of a separate Southern nation represented a continuation of the struggle of 1776 was a central contention of Southern nationalists. "The tea has been thrown overboard," proclaimed the radical Charleston *Mercury* after Lincoln's election. "The revolution of 1860 has been initiated." Southern clergymen reflected and contributed to the belief that the South was the legitimate heir of the American revolutionary tradition. "If the reproach of our fathers so exactly corresponds to our reproach," reasoned the Baptist *Religious Herald* of Richmond, "have we not a strong presumption that our cause corresponds no less to the cause of our fathers?" When the Charleston Baptist Association endorsed secession at their meeting in November 1860, they cited the stand of their association in 1776. What united the revolutionaries of 1776 with the secessionists of 1860–1 was their legitimate drive for independence. "The same principles," declared a Presbyterian minister from Charleston, "that impelled our great ancestors, in their day of trial, to shake off (not without sundering many pleasant ties of early recollection) a foreign and hostile government, now dictate the same cause to their sons." The *Central Presbyterian* similarly characterized secession as "our second great conflict for independence." If the American revolutionaries in seeking independence were branded rebels, concluded the

Rev. J. C. Mitchell of Mobile, Alabama, "then we of these Confederate States are rebels."[27]

Northern ministers insisted that their cause represented the true legacy of the American Revolution. "In 1776, we fought for the *establishment* of a free government," a minister told Michigan soldiers bound for the battlefield; "we are now struggling for the *maintenance* of a free government." He even associated King George III of England with "King Davis." The Rev. Joseph Duryea of Troy, New York, believed that Northerners "owe it to the men who fought and died, who framed the charter of our rights and gave it their high sanction and loving submission, to preserve this Union entire." The connection between the struggles of 1776 and 1861 was evident to a Boston clergyman as he spoke of the attack by Baltimorians on soldiers of the 6th Massachusetts Regiment en route to Washington on April 19, 1861. "A special divine ordination and no chance," suggested the Rev. C. A. Bartol, "fixed the date of the now forever doubly illustrious nineteenth of April, for blood, from the very same locality of the first engagement of the revolution [the Battle of Concord], to be shed at the beginning of a far greater struggle." To refute the Southern claim to the Revolutionary heritage, Northern ministers argued that the South had really subverted the true spirit of 1776. The Rev. Samuel T. Spear, pastor of the South Presbyterian Church of Brooklyn, maintained that Southern secessionists "have deserted the platform and principles of the Revolutionary fathers, and demanded that the whole country should follow them in this apostasy." The *Christian Watchman and Reflector* agreed that the South was "determined to revolutionize the government, amend the Constitution, and subvert the principles of the Fathers of the Republic."[28]

27. Faust, *Creation of Confederate Nationalism*, p. 14; James M. McPherson, *Ordeal by Fire: The Civil War and Reconstruction* (New York: Knopf, 1982), p. 129; *Religious Herald*, May 23, 1861; *Minutes of the One Hundred and Ninth Session of the Charleston Baptist Association, held with the High Hills Baptist Church, November 17–19, 1860* (Charleston: A. J. Burke, 1860), p. 4; William C. Dana, *A Sermon delivered in the Central Presbyterian Church, Charleston, S. C., November 21st, 1860, being the Day appointed by State Authority for Fasting, Humiliation, and Prayer* (Charleston: Steam Power Presses of Evans and Cogswell, 1860), p. 7; *Central Presbyterian*, December 21, 1861; Mitchell, *A Sermon*, p. 6. For additional analogies drawn between secession and the American Revolution, see *Southern Episcopalian*, January 1861, p. 543, and *Christian Index*, May 1, 1861.

28. Horace C. Hovey, *Freedom's Banner. A Sermon preached to the Coldwater Light Artillery, and the Coldwater Zouave Cadets, April 28th 1861* (Coldwater, Mich.: *Republican* Print, 1861), p. 2; Joseph T. Duryea, *Loyalty to Our Government: A Divine Command and a Christian Duty. A Sermon delivered in the Sixth-St. Presbyterian Church, Troy, Sabbath Morning, April 28th, 1861* (Troy, N.Y.: A. W. Scribner & Company, 1861), p. 28; C. A. Bartol, *The Duty of the Time. A Discourse Preached in the West Church Sunday Morning, April 28, 1861.* (Boston, Mass.: Walker, Wise, 1861), p. 9; Samuel T. Spear, *Two Sermons*

The writings of Northern and Southern clergymen during the secession crisis exhibit important similarities. Both groups of clerics shared a similar understanding of the relationship between religion and politics. They held common assumptions about a providential direction of human affairs and the cyclical nature of history. They both appealed to the tradition of American civil religion and the heritage of 1776. Northern and Southern clergymen, simply, understood the sectional conflict in essentially the same terms.

That such a close correspondence in ideas and expression existed should not be surprising. Clergymen both North and South shared a common vocabulary and world view not only as ministers but as American citizens as well. What these similarities point to is a contest between Northern and Southern ministers over the discourse of American nationalism. In a fundamental sense, the antebellum sectional controversy was a war of words. Each side essentially sought political legitimacy through the appropriation of language. The debate over slavery involved a competition over the rights of interpreting the Constitution, the meaning of republicanism, the Bible, and civil religion. This contest over language was made possible and even encouraged by the ambivalent and incomplete nature of American nationalism in the decades between the Revolution and the Civil War. The Union was based on a loose consensus on principles embodied in the constitutional settlement of 1787. The sectional controversy over slavery forced Americans to define those principles with greater precision, which led to conflict and eventually disunion. Religion clearly reflected and undoubtedly contributed to this ambiguity. Like the concept of Union, the Bible and civil religion held contradictory tendencies that could nourish contrasting separate sectional ideologies while simultaneously uniting Northerners and Southerners under a common umbrella of beliefs.[29]

---

for the Times. Obedience to the Civil Authority; and Constitutional Government Against Treason. (New York: Nathan Lane, 1861), p. 8; *Christian Watchman and Reflector,* February 14, 1861.

29. John M. McCardell, *The Idea of a Southern Nation: Southern Nationalists and Southern Nationalism, 1830–1860* (New York: W. W. Norton, 1979), p. 336. On the pervasive doubts in the quest for an American national identity, see especially Fred Somkin, *Unquiet Eagle: Memory and Desire in the Idea of American Freedom, 1815–1860* (Ithaca, N.Y.: Cornell University Press, 1967), and Paul C. Nagel, *This Sacred Trust: American Nationality, 1798–1898* (New York: Oxford University Press, 1972). In interpreting this contest over discourse, it is useful to keep in mind David Potter's admonition about the hidden ideological meaning in the use of nationalism. Potter warns that nationalism can be used in a valuative way to approve what one considers a legitimate assertion of collective autonomy. Because the North was successful in the Civil War and could therefore claim the rights of interpretation, antebellum American nationalism has become

II

A comparative approach can also provide insight into the issue of Southern unity during the secession crisis. In terms of class structure and politics, the South was a diverse and often disunified region during the antebellum era. Yet in 1860–1, Southerners were able to momentarily unite behind secession, although the social and political conflicts remained close to the surface. One way to assess Southern unity is to compare the degrees of unity and diversity within the ranks of the Southern and Northern clergy. In the South, the presence of Unionist clergymen speaks clearly to diversity. A closer look into clerical Unionism, however, reveals an underlying consensus on fundamental values with secessionist clergymen. By comparison, the writings of Northern ministers disclose a wider variety of views on slavery and the role of religion in sectional politics. This diversity serves by contrast to underscore the essential unity of the Southern clergy on the eve of the Civil War.

Despite the eventual course to disunion and Civil War, the South during the winter of 1860–1 was deeply divided over the question of secession. The basic contest in the lower South was between immediate secessionists, who favored separate state action, and cooperationists, who preferred concerted action by a number of slave states. Cooperationist strength was considerable in the deep South. Except in South Carolina, where secessionist feeling ran unusually high, cooperationist voting may have been as high as 40 percent. The struggles in Georgia and Louisiana were particularly close. In addition, there was the more basic division between secessionists and Unionists, those Southerners who believed that the slave states should stay in the Union. Unionism was particularly strong in the states of the upper South. Virginia and North Carolina, for example, voted against secession in the winter of 1860–1 until Lincoln's call for troops in April drove them into the Confederacy. In each state, there were also significant divisions based on class, region, political affiliation, and other factors. As one historian has accurately concluded, the seces-

synonymous with the North and its cause. Southern claims to the language of American nationalism are by contrast often seen as spurious and illegitimate. This Whiggish view of the sectional conflict should not blind us to the Southern contention that *they* were the true Americans, preserving the Constitution and acting as legitimate heirs of the Revolutionary heritage. In other words, their claim to a separate national identity based on common American values should not be considered as deviant. See David Potter,"The Historian's Use of Nationalism and Vice Versa" in *The South and the Sectional Conflict* (Baton Rouge: Louisiana State University Press, 1968). Potter's essay might profitably be read in conjunction with Herbert Butterfield, *The Whig Interpretation of History*, 1st American ed. (New York: Scribner's, 1951).

sionist South was more "a mosaic than a monolith, a cacophony than a consensus."[30]

For the most part, the divisions that plagued the South during the secession crisis were not reflected in the Southern clergy. The majority of ministers and denominational groups supported secession in 1860–1. Yet there were Southern ministers who were Unionists and denominational groups and journals that opposed secession. A few Unionist clergy could be found in the lower South. James Petigru Boyce, for example, president of the Baptist Theological Seminary, ran on the Unionist ticket in the Greenville District for election to the South Carolina secession convention. He was overwhelmingly defeated. The fate of clergymen who opposed secession could be worse. The Presbyterian clergyman John Aughey fled from his churches in Attala and Choctaw counties in Mississippi. The Rev. James Phelan of Macon, Mississippi, was forced to resign his pulpit for his Unionist views and was then killed.[31]

Religious Unionism was far more prevalent in the states of the upper South, where denominations and ministers tended to reflect the political moderation of their respective states. In North Carolina, for example, the denominational journals opposed secession. The Methodist *North Carolina Christian Advocate* feared the consequences of a dissolution of the Union, and the *North Carolina Presbyterian* was similarly apprehensive of secession. The Baptist paper in the state, the *Biblical Recorder*, even wanted the Baptist journal in Alabama to withdraw its endorsement of secession. More Unionist clergymen could be found in the upper South. The Rev. Andrew H. H. Boyd of Winchester, Virginia, preached his 1860 Thanksgiving Day sermon on "Benefits We Enjoy as a Nation." A Baptist minister from western North Carolina was elected to the state convention in 1861 as an opponent of secession. James H. Otey, the first Episcopal bishop of Tennessee, was a Unionist throughout the 1850s and believed secession would place a "seal of ruin" upon both North and South.[32]

30. David M. Potter, *The Impending Crisis, 1848–1861* (New York: Harper & Row, 1976), pp. 494–6; McPherson, *Ordeal by Fire: The Civil War and Reconstruction*, pp. 127–8; Avery O. Craven, *The Growth of Southern Nationalism, 1848–1861* (Baton Rouge: Louisiana State University Press, 1953), pp. 384–5; James T. Moore, "Secession and the States: A Review Essay," *Virginia Magazine of History and Biography* 94 (January 1986): 76. For the most recent work on Unionism in the upper South, see Daniel W. Crofts, *Reluctant Confederates: Upper South Unionists in the Secession Crisis* (Chapel Hill and London: University of North Carolina Press, 1989).

31. Lillian A. Kibler, "Unionist Sentiment in South Carolina in 1860," *Journal of Southern History* 4 (May 1938): 361; John K. Bettersworth, "Mississippi Unionism: The Case of the Rev. James A. Lyon," *Journal of Mississippi History* 1 (January 1939): 38.

32. W. Harrison Daniel, "Southern Protestantism and Secession," *The Historian* 29 (May 1967): 397, 398; James W. Silver, *Confederate Morale and Church Propaganda* (New

Robert Lewis Dabney, an influential Presbyterian minister and educator from Virginia, illustrates the conflicting loyalties between section and nation and between church and state that characterized religious Unionism. Born in Louisa County, Virginia, in 1820, Dabney was educated at Hampden-Sydney College and the University of Virginia. He received his ministerial training at Union Theological Seminary and then served as missionary pastor for a church in the Shenandoah Valley. He joined the faculty of Union in 1853, where he taught church history, polity, and theology. Despite his opposition to disunion during the winter of 1860–1, Dabney identified deeply with the South. He accepted Virginia's secession when Lincoln called for troops to crush the rebellion and became a chaplain in the Confederate army. He even served on the staff of Stonewall Jackson. After the Civil War, Dabney's disillusionment with the outcome of the Civil War led him to promote the emigration of Southerners to Australia and Brazil.[33]

Dabney's devotion to the Union and his aversion to secession were strongly influenced by religion and his perspective as a clergyman. The peacemaking and mediating role of Christianity was the central theme in a fast day sermon Dabney delivered on November 1, 1860, entitled *The Christian's Best Motive for Patriotism*. Addressing his students in the College Church in Hampden-Sydney, Dabney argued that political convulsions were "most unfavorable to spiritual prosperity." It was the responsibility of the church, he continued, to save the country from the ruin of civil war: "[I]ts guilt will be second only to that of the apostate Church which betrayed the Savior of the world." Reflecting an aversion to the political strife that first surfaced among South Carolina clergymen during the nullification controversy, Dabney blamed the present crisis on politicians, "the reckless and incapable men." He urged his listeners to obey "the law of God rather than the unrighteous behests of party." Concluding in the mode of a typical jeremiad, Dabney explained that prayer and humiliation for both collective and individual sins would save the nation.[34]

York: W. W. Norton, 1967), p. 21; Daniel, "Southern Protestantism and Secession," p. 401; Willie Grier Todd, "North Carolina Baptists and Slavery," *North Carolina Historical Review* 24 (April 1947): 156; Samuel S. Hill, ed., *Encyclopedia of Religion in the South* (Macon, Ga.: Mercer University Press, 1984), p. 572.

33. Hill, *Encyclopedia of Religion in the South*, pp. 191–2.
34. Robert L. Dabney, *The Christian's Best Motive for Patriotism. A Sermon: preached in the College Church, Hampden Sidney, VA. on the 1st November, 1860* (Richmond: Chas. H. Wynne, 1860), p. 4, 8; Thomas Cary Johnson, *The Life and Letters of Robert Lewis Dabney* (1903; reprint ed., Edinburgh and Carlisle: The *Banner of Truth* Trust, 1977), p. 213; Dabney, *The Christian's Best Motive for Patriotism*, pp. 8–14.

Throughout the winter of 1861, Dabney continued to oppose secession. He called South Carolina "the little impudent vixen" for seceding and accused the Palmetto State as being "as great a pest as the Abolitionists." In January 1861, he prepared "A Pacific Appeal to Christians," which was signed by clergymen of several denominations and university professors. Unlike Southerners in the deep South, Dabney did not consider Lincoln's election a "proper *casus belli*, least of all for immediate separate secession, which could never be the right way under any circumstances." His opposition to secession was based on many of the reasons that influenced other Unionists, such as love of a transcendent Union and fear of the ravages of civil war. Dabney was perhaps influenced by his important ties with Presbyterians in the North. In 1860, he was both invited to the pulpit of the Fifth Avenue Presbyterian Church in New York and proffered a teaching post at Princeton Seminary, offers that he refused. Eventually, Dabney's devotion to his nation and denomination came into conflict with his loyalty to the South. He remained a defender of Southern rights and argued against the right of federal coercion. With Lincoln's call for troops, Dabney became a secessionist.[35]

A fast day sermon delivered on January 4, 1861, by the Rev. James A. Lyon, pastor of the First Presbyterian Church in Columbus, Mississippi, shows the ideological consensus between secessionist and Unionist clergymen. Lyon began by stressing the importance of the nation's call to a fast. It was "the most solemn day in the memory of our present generation." Similar to many Southern ministers during the secession crisis, Lyon then turned to biblical history for "a few examples of the efficacy of humiliation, fasting and prayer in averting threatened calamities, brought upon by a people in their own wickedness." Like his fellow Presbyterian Palmer who supported secession, Lyon carefully drew the boundaries between religion and politics: "We have not met together to-day to discuss politics nor to deliberate on the best plan to reconstruct a government." The next part of his sermon was devoted to a glorification of America's blessings. Lyon presented the United States essentially as God's Redeemer Nation, "a great and united country that promised to give light, and law, and liberty, and christianity to the whole earth!" Her history, physical geography, and nature of government all promised great glory for the young republic.[36]

With a call for repentance and salvation at the heart of his sermon, Lyon accepted the major premises underlying both Northern and South-

35. Johnson, *Life and Letters of Robert Lewis Dabney*, pp. 198–210; 222–3.
36. Lyon's sermon was printed in the *True Witness and Sentinel*, January 26, 1861. All quotations are taken from this text.

ern fast day sermons: "God is a merciful God and a kind Father; he does not willingly afflict his people. Nothing, therefore, but our sins – our aggravated sins – has brought us under his frown, and caused him to put on the aspect of wrath." His litany of sins was similar to other clergymen: ingratitude, infidelity, disregard for the law, and neglect of the Bible and religion. In a sectional attack on the North, Lyon did suggest that infidelity had "given birth to a monstrous brood of heresies in the shape of spiritualism, mormonism, woman's rightism, universalism, unitarianism, higher-lawism, abolitionism and atheism, which have been the fruitful source of disturbance in both Church and State, and now threatens to involve the country in ruin." He also lamented *"a perverted pulpit"* filled with political preaching. Befitting a Unionist sermon, Lyon pointed out that these sins were not confined to one section. Rather, the "whole nation is guilty before God."

Significantly, Lyon devoted special attention to the particularly Southern sins associated with the peculiar institution. He first made clear his firm belief that slavery was "a Bible institution and consistent with the highest type of piety and godliness." As to "African slavery," Lyon maintained with similar confidence that "the proper condition of the Negro in this country is that of servitude." Yet the rectitude of human bondage did not necessarily legitimate its practice: "Slavery does by no possible construction *sanction the violation of the moral law of God.*" Lyon pointed out that Southern laws left the marital and parental relations of slaves unprotected. He called for reforms to make slavery "the patriarchal institution recognized by the Bible." Lyon closed his sermon with a lament against the neglect of self-government and an attack on politicians.

Lyon's fast day sermon demonstrates how the same religious imagery and assumptions used to formulate the clerical logic of secession could be used to fashion its counterpart. Lyon clearly presented his argument in a form not dissimilar to Benjamin M. Palmer's Thanksgiving Day defense of secession. His underlying belief in the providential direction of human affairs was shared by all Southern clergymen. The analogy drawn between the United States and biblical Israel, widespread in the sermons of secessionist clergy, was also prominent in Lyon's discourse.

A similar example of the underlying unity between secessionist and Unionist clerical thought can be found in the biblical story of the dissolution of the Hebrew tribes discussed earlier in this chapter. On January 14, 1860, the *Central Presbyterian* of Richmond ran an editorial on the crisis of the Union based on the biblical analogy between the dissolution of the Jewish tribes and the sectional conflict. This piece was essentially a reading of this episode in Old Testament history through the lenses of the antebellum sectional controversy. The paper suggested that the dissolution of the Hebrew tribes "came, not as a sudden and abrupt schism, but, as the inevitable result of these chafing and loosening causes, that had been acting for years." Like the abolitionized North, the Northern tribes "began to suffer the natural consequence of their abandonment of the true worship and faith of Jehovah." Jeroboam's religious reforms were interpreted as idol worship. The Southern tribes, on the other hand, were "where the religion of the fathers, unpolluted by the isms of Jeroboam, and the priests of Baal, was still maintained." In the North, the kingdom of Israel fell, but the Southern section prospered "as long as they were true to God." Yet dissolution led to war with heavy losses on both sides. Each section eventually ended in national ruin. The Presbyterian weekly pointed out the lesson to be learned from Biblical history: "[I]f God allowed his own chosen people to divide, to plunge into Civil War, and waste each other in mutual injuries, and corrupt each other in mutual sins, until both perished as distinct nationalities, he may do so to us, if we copy their example." The *Central Presbyterian* thus accepted the dissolution of the Hebrew tribes as a model of secession but used it to express their fear of disunion.[37]

The presence of Unionist clergy in the South of 1860–1 serves as a reminder that the antebellum South was not a single cohesive unit drifting uniformly toward secession. Clerical Unionism also provides an excellent illustration of the ways in which religion could be used to thwart the formation of Southern separatism. Yet underlying the differences between Unionist and secessionist arguments were important areas of consensus. Southern clergymen of both persuasions approached sectional politics from the same conceptual and rhetorical framework. They both accepted slavery as a positive good and recognized the need to safeguard the South's rights as a slaveholding society. The unity of the Southern clergy becomes more striking when compared with the views of their Northern counterparts. The writings of Northern clergymen reveal a more substantial division between an antislavery and conservative approach to the sectional controversy. This difference of opinion originated with the rise of an abolitionist clergy in the 1830s. By the 1850s, it reflected a more basic divergence in Northern thought between radical individualism and institutionalism.[38]

As we have seen, Southern and Northern ministers shared an almost identical understanding of the relationship between religion and politics.

37. *Central Presbyterian*, January 14, 1860.
38. See Chapter 1 for a discussion of the antislavery clergy in the 1830s. George M. Fredrickson, *The Inner Civil War: Northern Intellectuals and the Crisis of the Union* (New York: Harper & Row, 1965), chap. 1–3, remains a most valuable discussion on Northern thought in the 1850s.

They agreed that the clergy should steer clear of political involvement except when a moral or religious issue was involved. Yet there were two other conceptions of the relationship between religion and sectional politics that were peculiar to the writings of Northern clergymen. Each represented an extreme position on the role the clergy and the religious press should take in the sectional controversy over slavery.

Some Northern ministers strenuously objected to the participation of the Northern church in the agitation over slavery. "The religious press has rushed into the melee," protested the *Presbyterian* of Philadelphia a few days before the firing on Ft. Sumter, "and taking its tone from sectional surroundings, has chimed in with the politics which prevailed in its neighborhood." The journal maintained that the church was a "community chosen out of the world" and expressed its "honest conviction that the Church question was separable from that of the State." In Iowa, the Rev. Joseph Trapnell argued similarly that the nation "must get rid of the moral and religious element with which a spurious Christianity, and a bastard Philanthropy, have complicated and embarrassed the question of American slavery." T. P. Bucher, a Pennsylvania minister, claimed that "preachers of politics as well as of the gospel" were spreading the party spirit into the church.[39]

At the other extreme, some Northern clerics during the secession crisis actually encouraged the participation of religion in the slavery controversy. These ministers forcefully contended that politics often demanded religious attention. The Rev. Homer M. Dunning of Gloversville, New York, considered the application of religion to politics "God's work and not man's; it is a thing to be welcomed and rejoiced over." According to a clergyman in Coldwater, Michigan, when a political discussion had religious bearings, a minister would be "guilty if he does not make the world feel to the utmost whatever power God has given him." A vindication of pulpit politics was presented in a Thanksgiving Day sermon delivered at the Church of the Puritans in New York in 1860. "As it is proved that all our institutions are based on a religious and Biblical public sentiment," explained the Rev. Theodore F. White, "and as the clergy are the anointed teachers of the word of God, *they are the authors of that public sentiment, they are its trainers,* and ... *they are responsible for it.*" The blessing placed on religious participation in politics rested on the belief that slavery was a moral issue that commanded the attention of men of God. "We believe that God has constituted the Church of Christ the great

39. *Presbyterian*, April 13, 1861; Joseph Trapnell, *A Word from the West. Our duty as American Citizens, in this, our Country's imminent Peril. A discourse delivered in St. John's Church, Keokuk, Iowa, on Friday January 4th, 1861* (Keokuk: Rees & Delaplaine, 1861), p. 14; Bucher, *Union Fast Day Sermon,* p. 14.

depository of moral influence," stated the *Congregationalist* of Boston, "hence that the well defined sentiment and position of the Church of our land with reference to slaveholding is imperiously demanded." The Unitarian *Christian Register,* also of Boston, agreed that slavery was a "legitimate subject for the comments of the pulpit." In February 1861, the *Christian Advocate and Journal* went so far as to say that it was "the quack, not the scientific physician, who forbids the clergymen to approach the patient because he is in danger. That is the very time when his moral condition should be considered, and when such consideration has a soothing and saving effect." This willingness to blur the boundaries between God's world and Caesar's is in itself an important difference from Southern clergymen, who never expressed this kind of enthusiasm for pulpit politics.[40]

These two approaches to the role of the clergy in sectional politics were closely associated with a particular view on slavery. Those clergymen who insisted on keeping religion out of sectional politics were usually conservative on the slavery issue. In their sermons, both Joseph Trapnell and T. P. Bucher, for example, accepted the existence of slavery. Throughout the secession crisis, the *Presbyterian* maintained a conciliatory and moderate stance toward the South. On the other hand, those Northern ministers who welcomed religious involvement in politics tended to be more radical on antislavery. Homer M. Dunning supported the abolitionists. The Thanksgiving Day sermon of Theodore White included an expression of free soil ideology and a willingness to sacrifice the Union if it included slaveholders.

The crucial difference among Northern clergymen concerned slavery. A majority of Northern ministers were antislavery and portrayed the war as an irrepressible conflict between slavery and freedom. A significant minority, however, defended the South's right to hold slaves, urged moderation and conciliation with the South, and blamed the abolitionists for inflaming sectional tensions. Recognizing these conflicting views of Northern clergymen points out by contrast the relative unity of the Southern clergy on the all-important issue of slavery.

40. Dunning, *Providential Design of the Slavery Agitation,* p. 17; Horace C. Hovey, *The National Fast. A Sermon, preached at Coldwater, Mich., January 4, 1861* (Coldwater: *Republican* Print, 1861), pp. 3–4; Theodore F. White, *The "Godly Heritage." A Sermon, delivered on Thanksgiving Day, November 29, 1860, in the Church of the Puritans, New York* (New York: Thomas Holman, 1860), p. 20; *Congregationalist,* February 22, 1861; *Christian Register,* March 30, 1861; *Christian Advocate and Journal,* February 7, 1861. See also Cyrus W. Wallace, *A Sermon on the Duty of Ministers to Oppose the Extension of American Slavery, preached in Manchester, N. H., Fast Day, April 3, 1857* (Manchester: Fisk & Gage, 1857), pp. 26–7.

Considering the strong religious underpinnings of abolitionism, it is not surprising that most Northern clergymen were opposed to slavery. Continuing to draw upon the original meaning of immediatism, ministers and church members described slavery as a sin. The Church Antislavery Society in Westboro, Massachusetts, for instance, affirmed in 1861 that "the underlying principle of Christian abolitionism is that slaveholding, according to its well understood meaning, is a sin in itself – a wrong and a crime – and ought, therefore, like very other sin, to be desisted from at once." Joseph P. Thompson of New York explained that "every principle and precept of Christianity touching the mutual relations of men is diametrically opposed to American Slavery as defined by its own laws."[41]

Antislavery ministers drew upon the free soil argument of the Republican party. They painted slavery as a predatory monster that would spread insidiously into the virgin lands of the West. In 1859, the *Northwestern Christian Advocate* of Chicago believed "that at no time in our history was American slavery more powerful or more intolerant, and that this moment, plans for expansion of a most startling character, are maturing." A Massachusetts clergyman agreed in April 1861 that slavery had, "in the course of natural events, spread far and broadly." Unless abolished, warned Horace C. Hovey of Coldwater, Michigan, "slavery will ultimately extend over the whole Union, and the entire country will be as unhappily situated as a portion of it now is." One Congregational minister from Maine depicted the spread of slavery in language familiar to readers of the Bible and John Milton. "The serpent our Fathers admitted to their bosom is warmed," explained the Rev. J. K. Mason, "and grown into a most vigorous life. Its fangs have often *inoculated* our body politic with their poison; but now, they are raised, and extended, for a final, and fatal strike, into our very heart."[42]

The antislavery arguments found in the writings of Northern clergymen in the late 1850s and during the secession crisis were essentially the same moral and religious ones that had formed the core of the abolitionist persuasion since the 1830s. Their widespread appearance in Northern reli-

41. Quoted in the *Congregationalist*, April 5, 1861; Thompson, *The President's Fast*, p. 23. See also *Christian Watchman and Reflector*, March 7, 1861. For further evidence of antislavery among Northern churchmen, see Wallace, *A Sermon on the Duty of Ministers to Oppose the Extension of American Slavery*, pp. 5–6; Thompson, *The President's Fast*, p. 21; and *Christian Advocate and Journal*, March 7, 1861.

42. *Northwestern Christian Advocate*, June 8, 1859; Alonzo H. Quint, *The Christian's Patriot's Present Duty. A Sermon addressed to the Mather Church and Society, Jamaica Plain, Mass., April 28, 1861* (Boston: Hollis & Gunn, 1861), p. 17; Hovey, *The National Fast*, p. 11; J. K. Mason, *The Sword. A Sermon preached at Hampden, Me.* (Bangor: Samuel S. Smith, 1861), p. 12. For an expression of the fear of a slave power empire extending into the Caribbean, see the *Western Christian Advocate*, January 16, 1861.

gious discourse during the secession crisis was clearly appropriate to the situation. Limiting themselves to the moral arguments against slavery and avoiding questions of policy probably suited the inclination of both ministers and the public to separate the civil and religious spheres. Moral arguments against slavery might also suggest that clergymen saw themselves as molders of the moral conscience of the North, seeking to ensure that the Republican majority remained loyal to its antislavery imperative. Finally, the repetition of familiar antislavery arguments hints that there were people still in need of conversion, a possibility confirmed by the existence of a small but significant faction of Northern clergymen who were content to let slavery exist in the South.

During the secession crisis, Northern ministers sympathetic to the South and slavery limited their proslavery statements to the argument that the Bible did not condemn slavery. "God has never authoritatively forbidden it," asserted the Rev. Charles Wadsworth of Philadelphia. To B. R. Allen of Marblehead, the Scriptures "plainly and unequivocally teach that slave-holding is not, in itself, irrespective of all the circumstances attending it, a crime." An Iowa clergyman agreed that the Bible recognized slavery "as an existing social and domestic institution, and it prescribes rules for the becoming discharge of the relative duties of master and slave."[43]

These defenses of slavery invariably included attacks on the abolitionists. To Northern proslavery clergymen, the agitation of the slavery issue was largely responsible for the political crisis threatening the nation. "They infused the poison into the veins of the social organism," accused the Rev. B. R. Allen, "and left it to work out its fruits in the heart and the brain." A New Hampshire minister insisted similarly that the abolitionists "have committed a grievous error in letting loose the war spirit, the spirit of harassment and contumely, in order to make their views of slavery more keenly felt." To Joseph Trapnell of Iowa, the abolitionists were "the active agents in goading on and provoking, if possible, a fatal severance of the Union." Echoing the views of the Southern clergy, Northern proslavery clergymen also linked abolitionism with religious infidelity. "The leading abolitionists among us, whose efforts have contributed so largely to give vitality to the modern anti-slavery enterprise," argued the Rev. John O. Fiske of Maine, "are undisguised infidels, who oppose and attack the Bible and Christianity persistently, because they see

43. Charles Wadsworth, *Our Own Sins. A Sermon Preached in the Arch Street Church, on the Day of Humiliation and Prayer, appointed by the President of the United States, Friday, January 4th, 1861* (Philadelphia: King & Baird, 1861), p. 10; Allen, *"The Constitution and the Union,"* p. 16; Trapnell, *A Word from the West,* p. 9. See also Schuyler, *Slaveholding as a Religious Question,* p. 9.

the Bible does not justify their notions of the inherent wrong of slavery under all circumstances." John C. Lord, pastor of the Central Presbyterian Church in Buffalo, also detected "infidel tendencies" in abolitionism. Criticisms of the abolitionists and the biblical defense of slavery were usually parts of the same sermons that urged a conservative and conciliatory approach to the secession crisis. The close similarities in discourse between proslavery Northern ministers and the Southern clergy indicates a conservative clerical tradition in mid-nineteenth century America that cut across regional lines.[44]

Although it is difficult to measure with precision, roughly one fourth of the Northern fast day sermons read for this study could be considered proslavery. Their existence confirms that the North was indeed split on the slavery issue even as late as the winter of 1860–1. The division among the Northern clergy was closely related to the confused state of Northern public opinion during the secession crisis. The lame-duck Buchanan administration was essentially paralyzed and the policy of Abraham Lincoln and the Republicans remained uncertain. The diversity of views found in the writings of the Northern clergy highlights by contrast the unanimity on slavery and the relationship between religion and politics that existed among Southern clergymen. This consensus will become key to understanding the role Southern religion played in the coming of the Civil War.[45]

---

44. Allen, *"The Constitution and the Union,"* p. 20; Chase, *A Discourse,* p. 13; Trapnell, *Word from the West,* p. 9; Fiske, *Sermon on the Present National Troubles,* p. 8; John C. Lord, *Causes and Remedies of the Present Convulsions: A Discourse* (Buffalo, N.Y.: Joseph Warren & Co., 1861), p. 9.

45. An insightful discussion of the North during the secession crisis can be found in Potter, *Impending Crisis,* pp. 514–55.

CONCLUSION

Religion, the origins of Southern nationalism, and the coming of the Civil War

The men who helped inaugurate Jefferson Davis as the first president of the Confederacy in February 1861 personified the different ways Southerners came to secession. First and foremost were the politicians. Those who assembled in Montgomergy represented the various political paths that converged on the road to disunion. William L. Yancey, who had introduced Davis to a welcoming throng the night before, was a radical fire-eater as was the South Carolinian Robert Barnwell Rhett, who escorted the new Confederate president up the steps of the capitol. Davis himself, though not as radical as Yancey or Rhett, was a staunch defender of Southern rights. Two Georgians represented a more moderate and halting approach to disunion. Howell Cobb, who administered the oath of office to Davis, was a late convert to Southern nationalism. A supporter of the Union party in the early 1850s, Cobb had but recently joined the Georgia secessionists. Alexander Stephens, the first and only vice-president of the Confederacy, was a former Whig who only a few months before had opposed separate state secession.

The Rev. Basil Manly represented another course that led down the road to disunion. His presence and prayer at the inauguration of Jefferson Davis symbolically recognized the role that religion played in preparing Southerners for separate nationhood. Beginning in the early 1830s, religious discourse and institutions strengthened the sectionalization of Southern culture and politics. Religion invested the sectional controversy over slavery with moral and religious significance, reinforced important elements in Southern political culture, and fostered a sense of separate sectional identity among Southerners.

The inauguration of Jefferson Davis crowned the antebellum drive toward Southern nationalism. By placing the clergy at the birth of the Confederacy, it points to the larger historical issues raised in this book: the role of Southern religion in the origins of Southern nationalism and the coming of the Civil War. At first glance, the essentially political nature of the antebellum sectional controversy discourages such an inquiry. Explanations about why the war happened have traditionally focused on politics. The major sectional incidents of the prewar period were political and constitutional in nature. Secession itself was a political event, triggered by a string of events that eventually led to the disintegration of the second American party system. Yet despite this political tenor, several themes in Civil War historiography may now be profitably addressed on the basis of what we have learned about religion and sectionalism in the antebellum South. By summarizing the most important ways in which religion contributed to the growth of Southern distinctiveness and placing these themes in their historiographical context, this conclusion offers a modest contribution to explaining the coming of the Civil War.[1]

I

The relationship between religious and political discourse was one way in which religion shaped the development of antebellum Southern separatism. Often, as with the biblical defense of slavery, this interaction worked simply as a borrowing of language and ideas from religion to politics. At

1. Traditionally, explanations on the coming of the Civil War have focused on politics. "The outbreak of a shooting war between North and South in April, 1861," historian Michael F. Holt has recently affirmed, "can be explained only by accounting for the chain of specific political events that precipitated it." See *Political Parties and American Political Development from the Age of Jackson to the Age of Lincoln* (Baton Rouge and London: Louisiana State University Press, 1992), p. 11. The major historical works on the Civil War have tended to be political narratives. The most noteworthy examples are Allan Nevins, *The Ordeal of the Union*, 2 vols. and *The Emergence of Lincoln*, 2 vols. (New York: Scribner's, 1947–1950), and David M. Potter, *The Impending Crisis, 1848–1861* (New York: Harper & Row, 1976). Unfortunately, there is no recent analysis of Civil War historiography summarizing the work of the past two decades. Thomas J. Pressly, *Historians Interpret Their Civil War* (Princeton, N.J.: Princeton University Press, 1954), and Eric Foner, "The Causes of the Civil War: Recent Interpretations and New Directions," *Civil War History* 20 (September 1974): 197–214, must therefore remain the most useful introductions to this subject. Bruce Levine, *Half Slave and Half Free: The Roots of the Civil War* (New York: Hill & Wang, 1992), which attempts to integrate social and political history, provides the most recent survey on the coming of the Civil War.

other times, such as the denominational schisms, religious and political discourse converged and became mutually reinforcing. In two particular cases, this confluence of religious and political discourse strengthened preexisting elements in Southern political culture that were crucial in leading the South down the road to disunion.

The coming of the Civil War was in a fundamental sense a constitutional crisis. As historian Arthur Bestor suggested, the Constitution played a configurative role in the sectional controversy, providing the "narrow channel" through which all aspects of the slavery debate flowed. During the 1840s, the simultaneous appearance of the Methodist and Baptist schisms with the annexation of Texas and the Wilmot Proviso reinforced the constitutionalism in Southern political discourse. While politicians insisted that Congress had no right to legislate against slaveholders in the territories, Southern churchmen claimed that the exclusionary actions of Northern dominated church bodies were unconstitutional. During the secession crisis, clergymen again contributed to Southern constitutionalism by defending states' rights in their religious vindications of secession. Religion then reinforced the Southern habit of thinking about the sectional controversy over slavery in constitutional terms, which gave it a configuration capable of disrupting the Union.[2]

The concept of honor was another central element in Southern political culture that has been used recently to explain secession. With its emphasis on a personal sense of worth and visible signs of respect from others, the code of honor gave Northern attacks on slavery and slaveholders a peculiarly intense emotional charge that demanded immediate vindication from Southerners. The well-known caning of Massachusetts Senator Charles Sumner by the South Carolinian Preston Brooks in 1856 is perhaps the clearest illustration of how honor inflamed sectional passions. Although they are often seen as separate and distinct ethical systems, religion reinforced the importance of honor, especially during the sectional politics of the 1840s. The controversies over the annexation of Texas and the Wilmot Proviso were seen by Southerners as attacks on their honor and equality. Barring slaveholders from the new territories was particulary insulting, for it implied moral inferiority. Similarly, Southern Baptists and Methodists claimed that by banning slaveholders, national denominations were depriving Southern Christians of their honor

2. Arthur Bestor, "The Civil War as a Constitutional Crisis," *American Historical Review* 69 (January 1964), especially pp. 329 and 352. The complexities and ambiguities inherent in Southern political thought are explored further in Bestor, "State Sovereignty and Slavery: A Reinterpretation of Proslavery Constitutional Doctrine, 1846–1860," *Journal of the Illinois State Historical Society* 54 (1961): 117–180.

and equality. By employing the rhetoric of honor, religion fortified a distinctive element in Southern society and politics.[3]

II

The variety of political persuasions represented at the inauguration of Jefferson Davis hints at the diversity and division that characterized the Old South. Historians have become increasingly aware of the extent to which the antebellum South was a dynamic and diverse society in which "change was omnipresent, varieties abounded, visions multiplied." Coupled with the recognition that the question of internal unity was paramount in the minds of Southern secessionists, this recent emphasis on Southern diversity poses perhaps the most pressing problem in interpreting secession. If there was not *a* single monolithic South committed to disunion, what made secession possible and successful? What centripetal forces helped achieve a working unity in 1861? Historians have suggested compelling answers to these questions: the obvious racial fears of slave rebellion, the widespread commitment to white supremacy, and the belief that containing slavery would ultimately doom the institution.[4]

I suggest that religion served as one of these unifying forces. It helped forge a moral consensus around slavery, a consensus capable of encompassing differing political views and uniting a diverse and disharmonious

3. For links between the culture of honor and the sectional conflict, see Bertram Wyatt-Brown, "Honor and Secession" in *Yankee Saints and Southern Sinners* (Baton Rouge and London: Louisiana State University Press, 1985), and Kenneth S. Greenberg, *Masters and Statesmen: The Political Culture of American Slavery* (Baltimore and London: Johns Hopkins University Press, 1985), especially chap. 7. Bertram Wyatt-Brown has suggested the compatibility between the value systems of honor and evangelicalism during the crisis of the Union. See "God and Honor in the Old South," *Southern Review* 25 (Spring 1989), p. 295. This consonance is also stressed in Edward R. Crowther, "Holy Honor: Sacred and Secular in the Old South," *Journal of Southern History* 58 (November 1992): 619–36.

4. William W. Freehling, *The Road to Disunion, Vol. 1: Secessionists at Bay, 1776–1854* (New York: Oxford University Press, 1990), p. vii. For other works that stress internal division, see the important essay by Freehling, "The Editorial Revolution, Virginia, and the Coming of the Civil War," *Civil War History* 16 (March 1969): 64–72, and Michael P. Johnson, *Towards a Patriarchal Republic: The Secession of Georgia* (Baton Rouge: Louisiana State University Press, 1977). For recent statements about Southern disunity, see Eric H. Walther, *The Fire-Eaters* (Baton Rouge and London: Louisiana State University Press, 1992), p. 5, and Bruce Levine, *Half Slave and Half Free*, pp. 15, 234–5. A good summary of the diversity of secession within the South is James Tice Moore, "Secession and the States: A Review Essay,"*Virginia Magazine of History and Biography* 94 (January 1986): 60–76.

South behind the banner of disunion. Religion contributed to this moral consensus primarily through the "spiritualization" of the sectional controversy over slavery. In several ways explored in this study, Southern clergymen invested the sectional conflict with religious meaning. They sanctified slavery through a scriptural justification of human bondage, a slaveholding ethic to guide the conduct of Christian masters, and efforts to bring the Gospel to the slaves. By translating secession into an evangelical language meaningful to Southern Christians, the ritual of the fast day sermon transformed the crisis of the Union into a larger struggle between the forces of orthodoxy and infidelity. The ways in which the spiritualization of the sectional controversy created a moral consensus around slavery provides additional insight into our understanding of the coming of the Civil War.[5]

The sanctification of slavery was perhaps the most important element in this moral consensus. The biblical justification of human bondage, pervasive in the religious and secular discourse of the antebellum South, served as one of the common denominators on which Southerners of differing political perspectives could agree. It could legitimately unite radical secessionists and Unionists on a shared platform. A meeting for the religious instruction of slaves held in Charleston in 1845 reveals the consensual potential of religious proslavery. At this meeting, former opponents during the nullification controversy submerged their political differences for this common cause. The radical nullifier and Southern nationalist Robert Barnwell Rhett was joined by former Unionists Daniel Huger and Joel R. Poinsett. Indeed, the scriptural defense of slavery might well have functioned as a sectional counterpoint to the free soil ideology of the Republican party, which could unite radical abolitionists with moderate Northerners who opposed the extension of slavery but believed in the racial inferiority of blacks.[6]

As the keystone of the religious contribution to a Southern moral consensus, the sanctification of slavery affirms the centrality of slavery in explaining the coming of the Civil War. Throughout the antebellum era, slavery remained at the center of Southern clerical thought on the sectional controversy. It was precisely their belief that slavery involved moral and religious issues that justified their entrance into the arena of sectional politics in 1835. The denominational schisms were in essence a division

5. My hypothesis about a moral consensus does not negate the previously discussed ways in which religion served as a counterforce to the development of separatism. As I suggested in the Introduction, the fact that religion could simultaneously encourage and inhibit sectionalism underscores the underlying ambiguities of the complex Civil War era.

6. See Eric Foner, *Free Soil, Free Labor, Free Men: The Ideology of the Republican Party before the Civil War* (New York: Oxford University Press, 1970), especially chap. 9.

between Northern and Southern churchmen over the morality of slavery. Slavery was also at the base of the religious logic of secession, which rested on the assumptions that human bondage was sanctioned by God and that abolitionism was infidelity. The manner in which Southern clergymen invested sectional politics with religious significance lends support to those secessionists and later historians who placed slavery at the heart of their explanations of why the Union dissolved.[7]

Besides the sanctification of slavery, religion worked in another way to create a moral consensus. By validating a hierarchical and organic vision of society and a particularistic and egalitarian approach to social relations, religious proslavery could incorporate the world views of both planters and yeomen. Two recent studies of South Carolina suggest the unifying power of evangelical religion. In her investigation of the formation of the planter class in upcountry South Carolina, Rachel Klein has shown how the hierarchical vision of religion provided the basis for a proslavery Christianity that was accepted by both wealthy planters and yeomen evangelical communities. This point is reinforced by Stephanie McCurry in her study of the South Carolina lowcountry: "[R]eligion and politics shared a discourse that effectively broached the divide between high and low culture and articulated the southern rights position in terms that appealed to both the yeoman majority and the planter elite." These works then demonstrate how religion could draw together in ideological wholeness the social visions of different and often conflicting classes.[8]

The moral consensus that the Southern clergy helped to create emphasizes the crucial role of ideology in the coming of the Civil War. Historians during the past few decades have paid a great deal of attention to sectional ideologies, those world views or belief systems that allowed both Northerners and Southerners to see the other as a mortal peril to their existence. Whereas Northerners came to believe that the extension of slavery threatened a social order based on free soil, free labor, and free men,

7. The centrality of slavery in explaining the Civil War has a long history beginning with John Ford Rhodes in the nineteenth century. For more current statements, see William Cooper, *The South and the Politics of Slavery, 1828–1856* (Baton Rouge and London: Louisiana State University Press, 1978), and most recently Levine, *Half Slave and Half Free,* pp. 227–9.

8. Rachel N. Klein, *Unification of a Slave State: The Rise of the Planter Class in the South Carolina Upcountry, 1760–1808* (Chapel Hill and London: Published for the Institute of Early American History and Culture, Williamsburg, Va., by the University of North Carolina Press, 1990), chap. 9; Stephanie McCurry, "Defense of Their World: Gender, Class and the Yeomanry of the South Carolina Lowcountry, 1820–1860," Ph.D. diss., State University of New York at Binghamton, 1988, p. 413.

Southern slaveholders saw their peculiar institution menaced by a hostile and aggressive North bent on stopping the spread of slavery. As soon as these ideologies entered and came to dominate American politics during the 1840s, historian Eric Foner has argued, the Civil War was inevitable. They injected basic values and moral judgments into a party system the very existence of which was predicated on compromise. Once this happened, the two major national parties lost their ability to reconcile domestic conflict and to serve as bonds of national unity. By creating and sustaining a moral dimension to sectional politics, religion played a key role in infusing sectional ideologies into the political process. Indeed, the spiritualization of the sectional controversy helped bring about secession by enhancing the notion of an "irrepressible conflict," the idea that the North and South were different civilizations with incompatible labor systems, institutions, and values. Most often associated with a speech given in 1858 by William H. Seward, the Republican Senator from New York, this idea had widespread support in both sections immediately before the Civil War.[9]

Despite its contribution to the formation of Southern nationalism and the eventual dissolution of the Union, the moral consensus about slavery was severely strained during the Civil War. For one thing, the hierarchical religious vision that bonded planter and yeoman in a common world view was obviously not strong enough to prevent the open class conflict so evident in the Confederate South. In addition, the Civil War exposed more fully the latent threats to slavery hidden in the Christian doctrine of slavery. As previously discussed, the slaveholding ethic established rigorous moral standards for masters that could easily become an invitation to judge and perhaps condemn the practice of slavery. Confederate clergymen increasingly discussed what they saw as the disparity between the ideals of Christian slaveholders and the actual practice of slavery

9. Eric Foner, "Politics, Ideology, and the Origins of the American Civil War," in *Politics and Ideology in the Age of the Civil War* (New York: Oxford University Press, 1980). The major work on ideology and the sectional conflict in the North is Foner, *Free Soil, Free Labor, Free Men*. There is not a comparable single work that articulates a coherent Southern ideology, a point reinforced by the argument of William W. Freehling in *The Road to Disunion*. Southern sectional thought can, however, be pieced together from a number of studies by Eugene Genovese, Kenneth Greenberg, J. Mills Thornton III, and Bertram Wyatt-Brown. Stanley M. Elkins makes a persuasive case for ideology in *Slavery: A Problem in American Institutional and Intellectual Life*, 3rd ed. rev. (Chicago: University of Chicago Press, 1976), pp. 223–66. For evidence of the "Irrepressible Conflict" thesis in both sections on the eve of the Civil War, see James M. McPherson, "Antebellum Southern Exceptionalism: A New Look at an Old Question," *Civil War History* 29 (September 1983), pp. 232–4.

itself, dissolving one of the ideological bonds that held the Confederate South together.[10]

III

Religion played an important role in the shaping of antebellum Southern separatism. It reinforced important elements in Southern political culture, invested sectional politics with a charged religious significance, and contributed to a moral consensus that made secession possible. It helped convince Southerners that slavery and Southern civilization were best protected in a separate Southern nation. In tandem with a variety of other social, political, economic, and ideological factors, religion helped lead the South toward secession and the Civil War.[11]

10. Richard E. Beringer, Herman Hattaway, Archer Jones, and William N. Still, Jr., *Elements of Confederate Defeat: Nationalism, War Aims, and Religion* (Athens and London: University of Georgia Press, 1988), p. 163, and Clarence L. Mohr, "Slaves and White Churches in Confederate Georgia," in John B. Boles, ed., *Masters and Slaves in the House of the Lord: Race and Religion in the American South, 1740–1870* (Lexington: University Press of Kentucky, 1988), p. 162. I do not go as far as the authors of *Elements of Confederate Defeat* in joining the "guilt thesis," the argument that slaveholders held ambivalent feelings about holding slaves. For a succinct discussion of this debate, see Beringer et al., *Elements of Confederate Defeat*, pp. 60–165. My own interpretation is closer to that of Drew Gilpin Faust, *The Creation of Confederate Nationalism: Ideology and Identity in the Civil War South* (Baton Rouge and London: Louisiana State University Press, 1988), especially p. 80.

11. Arthur Bestor provides a useful reminder that the Civil War resulted from the interaction of several factors and that the fundamental problem in historical explanation remains "to discover the pattern of their interaction with one another." See "The Civil War as a Constitutional Crisis," pp. 330–1.

Bibliography

Primary sources

Manuscripts

Alabama Department of Archives and History. Montgomery, Alabama.
    William H. Mitchell Papers
Historical Commission of the Southern Baptist Convention. Nashville, Tennessee.
    William Carey Crane Papers
Historical Foundation of the Presbyterian and Reformed Churches, Inc. Montreat, North Carolina.
    James Henley Thornwell Papers
Historical Society of Pennsylvania. Philadelphia, Pennsylvania.
    Simon Gratz Collection
Manuscript Division, Tennessee State Library and Archives. Nashville, Tennessee.
    Jesse Cox Diary
    Jeremiah Walker Cullom Diary
    Bradley Kimbrough Diary
Presbyterian Historical Society. Philadelphia, Pennsylvania.
    John Witherspoon Letters
South Caroliniana Library. University of South Carolina. Columbia, South Carolina.
    Iveson Lewis Brookes Papers
    Zelotus L. Holmes Papers
    Miller–Furman–Dabbs Papers
    Whitefoord Smith Papers
    James Henley Thornwell Papers
    Charles Vedder Diary
    William M. Wightman Papers

Southern Historical Collection. University of North Carolina Library. Chapel Hill, North Carolina.
    Samuel Agnew Diary
    Anderson–Thornwell Papers
    Jesse Bernard Diary
    Overton Bernard Diary
    Iveson Lewis Brookes Papers
    Simeon Colton Diary
    John Hamilton Cornish Papers
    Joseph Benson Cottrell Diary
    William P. Hill Diary
    Mitchell King Diary
    Drury Lacy Papers
    Henry Champlin Lay Papers
    Mangum Family Papers
    John S. Martin Papers
    James Hervey Otey Papers
    John Paris Papers
    Daniel A. Penick Papers
    Green W. Penn Papers
    Leonidas Polk Papers
    George G. Smith Papers
    James K. Stringfield Papers
Special Collections. Furman University Library. Greenville, South Carolina.
    James Clement Furman Papers
    William Bullein Johnson Papers
    Basil Manly, Jr., Papers
    McIver Family Papers
Union Theological Seminary Library. Richmond, Virginia.

Moses Drury Hoge Papers
Benjamin M. Smith Diary
University Archives. University of
South Carolina. Columbia, South
Carolina.
South Carolina College Euphradian
Society Minutes, 1823–1833
Virginia Baptist Historical Society.
University of Richmond.
Richmond, Virginia.
Jeremiah B. Jeter Diary
Virginia Historical Society. Richmond,
Virginia.
Edward Baptist Diary
Mary W. Holladay Commonplace
Book
William Huntington Diary
John T. Mason Commonplace Book

J. C. Rutherfoord Diary
Andrew Talcott Diary
Carolina Thornton Diary
John G. Webb Papers
William R. Perkins Library. Duke
University. Durham, North
Carolina.
William C. Adams Diary
Charles W. Andrews Papers
Iveson Lewis Brookes Papers
Eugene Russell Hendrix Papers
John F. Mallett Journal
Hector McNeill Papers
James Warley Miles Papers
William Swan Plumer Papers
James H. Saye Papers
Whitefoord Smith Papers
James M. Young Papers

Southern religious newspapers and periodicals

BAPTIST
Alabama Baptist
Arkansas Baptist
Baptist Messenger
Biblical Recorder
Carolina Baptist
Christian Index
Louisiana Baptist
Mississippi Baptist
North Carolina Baptist Interpreter
Primitive Baptist
Religious Herald
Southern Baptist
*Southern Baptist and General
   Intelligencer*
Southern Baptist Messenger
Southern Watchman
Southwestern Religious Luminary
Texas Baptist

METHODIST
*Quarterly Review of the Methodist
   Episcopal Church, South*

Nashville *Christian Advocate*
Richmond *Christian Advocate*
Southern *Christian Advocate*
Southern *Methodist Itinerant*
Virginia Conference Sentinel

PRESBYTERIAN
Calvinistic Magazine
Central Presbyterian
Charleston *Observer*
North Carolina Presbyterian
Southern Christian Sentinel
Southern Presbyterian
Southern Presbyterian Review
Southern Religious Telegraph
True Witness and Sentinel
Watchman and Observer

NONSECTARIAN AND OTHER
DENOMINATIONS
Southern Dial
Southern Episcopalian
Universalist Herald

Northern religious newspapers and periodicals

Boston *Recorder*
Christian Advocate and Journal (New York)
Christian Register (Boston)
Christian Watchman & Reflector (Boston)
Congregationalist (Boston)
Northwestern Christian Advocate (Chicago)

Pittsburgh *Christian Advocate*
Presbyterian (New York and Philadelphia)
Western Christian Advocate (Cincinnati)
Zion's Herald and Wesleyan Journal (Boston)

Southern secular newspapers

Augusta *Chronicle and Sentinel*
Camden (South Carolina) *Journal*
Charleston *Courier*
Charleston *Mercury*
Charleston *States' Rights and Free Trade Evening Post*
Columbia *Hive*
Edgefield (South Carolina) *Advertiser*
Greensborough *Patriot*
Hillsborough *Recorder*
Macon *Georgia Telegraph*
Macon *Telegraph*
Milledgeville *Federal Union*
Milledgeville *Georgia Journal*
Milledgeville *Southern Recorder*

Mobile *Daily Commercial Register and Patriot*
Natchez *Mississippi Free Trader and Natchez Gazette*
New Orleans *Daily Picayune*
Raleigh *Register and North Carolina Gazette*
Raleigh *Star and North Carolina Gazette*
Richmond *Enquirer*
Richmond *Whig*
Spartanburg (South Carolina) *Spartan*
Vicksburg *Whig*
Woodville (Mississippi) *Republican*

Denominational records

BAPTIST

"Abbott's Creek Baptist Church. Church Minute Book. Vol. 1, 1832–1881." Baptist Historical Collection, Wake Forest University. Winston–Salem, N.C.

"Abbott's Creek Primitive Baptist Church. Church Minute Book. Vol. 2, 1818–1874, 1886." Baptist Historical Collection, Wake Forest University.

Baptist State Convention of Texas. Session of 1860. Anderson: *Texas Baptist* Book and Job Power Press, 1860.

Baptist State Convention of Texas. Session of 1861. Houston: Texas Printing House, 1863.

Journal of the Proceedings of the Baptist State Convention, in Alabama, at its Twentieth Anniversary, at Marion, Perry County: Commencing on Saturday, November 16th, 1844. n.p., 1844.

Minutes of the Abbott's Creek Union Baptist Association, begun and held at Jamestown Meeting-House, Guilford County, N.C. Salem: Blum & Son, 1838.

Minutes of the Abbott's Creek Union Association, convened at Mount Tabor Meeting House, N.C. on the 22nd, 23rd, and 24th days of September, 1832. n.p., n.d.

Minutes of the Apostolic Baptist Association, Held at Valley Grove, Talbot County, from Fourth to the Seventh November, 1838. Columbus, Ga.: *Sentinel and Herald* Office, 1838.

Minutes of the Appomattox Baptist Association, Held at the Nottaway Church, on the 9th and 11th Days of August, 1845. Lynchburg: Taler, Townley & Statham, 1845.

Minutes of the Appomattox Baptist Association, Held in the Town of Farmville, August 6th and 7th, 1861. Richmond: H. K. Ellyson, 1861.

Minutes of the Baptist General Association of Virginia, Held in the City of Petersburg, June, 1861. Richmond: Macfarlane & Fergusson, 1863.

Minutes of the Bear Creek Baptist Association, convened in session, with the Grove-Spring Church (Union County, N.C.) on Saturday before the First Sunday in October, A.D. 1843. Charlotte: Office of the *Charlotte Journal,* 1844.

Minutes of the Bethel Baptist Association: at the Forty-First Anniversary Meeting, Convened at Cane-Creek Church, Union District (So. Carolina) October 2d, and continued till October 5th, 1830. n.p., 1830.

Minutes of the Bethel Baptist Association; at the Forty-Sixth Anniversary Meeting, Convened at Calvary Church, Chester District, S.C. n.p., 1830.

Minutes of the Buttehatcha Baptist Association. Held at South Carolina Meeting House, Pickens County, Alabama, Seventh and Eighth October, in the Year of our Lord, One Thousand Eight Hundred and Thirty One. Columbus: R. B. Mitchell, 1831.

Minutes of the Charleston Baptist Association, at their Ninety-Fourth Anniversary, held at High Hills Church, Sumter District, November 1, 1845 and Continued to Nov. 4, 1845. n.p., n.d.

Minutes of the County Line Baptist Association Begun and Held at Bush Arbour Meeting-House, Caswell County, N.C. On Saturday before the 3rd Lord's day in August 1835. Milton: *Spectator* Office, 1835.

Minutes of the Edgefield Baptist Association, convened at Mount Pleasant, S.C. on the 17th and continued to the 19th of October, 1835. Charleston: James S. Burges, 1835.

Minutes of the Eighteenth Annual Session of the Wetumpka Baptist Association, of the Primitive Order, held with Smyna Church, Coosa County, Alabama. From the 22nd to the 26th September. Wetumpka: *Spectator* Office, 1860.

Minutes of the Fifty-Fifth Anniversary of the Mississippi Baptist Association, Held with the Marts Hill Church, Amite County, Miss., October 12th and 14th, 1861. Jackson: *Mississippi Baptist* Book and Job Printing Office, 1861.

Minutes of the Fifty-Fifth Annual Session of the Chowan Baptist Association, Held with the Church at Sandy Run, Bertie Co., N.C., May 14–18, 1861. Raleigh: *Biblical Recorder* Office, 1861.

Minutes of the Fifty-Fifth Session of the Virginia Portsmouth Baptist Association Held at the Racoon Swamp Meeting House in Sussex County, May 23rd, 24th, 25th, & 26, 1845. Portsmouth, Va.: A. F. Cunningham, 1845.

Minutes of the Fifty-Fourth Anniversary of the Albemarle Baptist Association, Held in the Meeting House of the Free Union Church, Albemarle, August 16, 17, 18, 1845. Charlottesville: James Alexander, Printer, 1845.

Minutes of the First Anniversary of the Apostolic Baptist Association, of the Union Church, Marion Co., Ga., on the Fourth, Sixth and Seventh Days of November, 1837. Columbus: *Sentinel* Office, 1837.

"Minutes of the First Session of the Ebenezar Baptist Association Held at Fort

Dale Meetinghouse, Butler County, Ala. from the 7th to the 10th December Inclusive, A.D. 1838." Harwell G. Davis Special Collections, Samford University. Birmingham, Alabama.

Minutes of the Fortieth Annual Session of the Brier Creek Association, convened at Cool Spring Meeting House, Wilkes County, N.C. on Saturday before the 4th Lords Day in September, 1861. Salem: L. V. & E. T. Blum, 1861.

Minutes of the Forty-First Anniversary of the State Convention of the Baptist Denomination in S.C. held at Spartanburg, July 26th–28th, 1861. Columbia: *Southern Guardian* Steam-Power Press, 1861.

Minutes of the Fourteenth Annual Meeting of the Concord Baptist Association, Held at Liberty Church, Mecklenburg Co., Virginia, on Saturday, Lord's Day and Monday, August 16, 17 and 18, 1845. Petersburg: W. R. Drinkard, Printer, 1845.

Minutes of the Goshen Baptist Association; Held at Lyle's Church, Fluvanna County, Va. September 10–12, 1845. Richmond: Office of the *Religious Herald,* 1845.

Minutes of the Neuse Baptist Association, held at Fort Barnell Chapel, Craven County, N.C. on the 15, 16, & 17 days of October, 1836. n.p., 1836.

Minutes of the Neuse Baptist Association: held at Newbern N.C. on the 20th, 21st and 22nd days of October, A.D. 1838. Newbern: *Spectator* Office, 1838.

Minutes of the North Carolina Baptist State Convention, held in Raleigh, October 17–25, 1845. Raleigh: *Recorder* Office, 1846.

Minutes of the One Hundred and Ninth Session of the Charleston Baptist Association, held with the High Hills Baptist Church, November 17–19, 1860. Charleston: A. J. Burke, 1860.

Minutes of the Savannah River Baptist Association, at its Forty-Fourth Anniversary, held with the Beech Branch Church, S.C. November 22, 24, 25, and 26, 1845. Savannah: Office of P. G. Thomas, 1845.

Minutes of the Seventeenth Anniversary of the Pilgrim's Rest Association, of Old School United Baptists; Held with Five Mile Church, Greene County, Ala. Eutaw, Ala.: William H. Fowler, 1853.

Minutes of the Seventh Anniversary of the Choctaw Baptist Association, held with the Church at Wahalok, Kemper County, Mississippi on the 18th and 19th of October, 1845. Macon: A. & A. H. Marschall, 1845.

Minutes of the Sixteenth Annual Session of the Central Baptist Association, held with the Bethesda Church, Hinds County, Miss. Jackson: *Mississippi Baptist* Book and Job Printing Office, 1861.

Minutes of the State Convention of the Baptist Denomination in South Carolina, at its Twenty-Fourth Anniversary, held with the Darlington Baptist Church, commencing on the 7th, and ending on the 10th of December. n.p., n.d.

Minutes of the Tenth Annual Session of the Union Baptist Association, held at Fellowship Meeting House, Pickens County, Alabama, from 27th to 29th of September, 1845. Tuscaloosa: M. D. J. Slade, 1845.

Minutes of the Third Annual Session of the Rappahannock Baptist Association, held at Hermitage Church, Middlesex Co., on Saturday, Lord's Day and Monday, October 25, 26, 27, 1845. Richmond: H. K. Ellyson, 1845.

Minutes of the Thirteenth Annual Session of the Lookout Primitive Baptist Association held at Mt. Zion Church, Walker Co., Ga., on the 24th, 25th and 26th September, 1853. Jacksonville, Ala.: Office of the *Sunny South,* 1853.

Minutes of the Thirty-Eighth Anniversary of the Baptist Convention of the State of Georgia, held with the Baptist Church in Macon, April 20, 21, and 24, 1860. Macon: *Daily Telegraph* Stream Printing House, 1860.

Minutes of the Thirty-Eighth Annual Session of the Alabama Baptist State Convention, Held at Tuskegee, November 9–13, 1860. Tuskegee: Office of the *South Western Baptist,* 1860.

Minutes of the Thirty-Ninth Anniversary of the Baptist Convention of the State of Georgia, Held with the Baptist Church in Athens, April 26, 27th & 29, 1861. Macon: *Telegraph* Steam Printing House, 1861.

Minutes of the Thirty-Ninth Annual Session of the Ala. Baptist State Convention, Held at Marion, Nov. 8th, 9th, 10th, 11th, 12th, 1861. Tuskegee: Office of *South Western Baptist,* 1861.

Minutes of the Thirty-Third Annual Session of the Catawba River Baptist Association. Held with the Church at North Catawba, Burke Co., N.C. October 11–14, 1861. n.d., n.p.

Minutes of the Twelfth Anniversary of the Alabama Baptist State Convention. Held at Oakmulgee Meeting House, Perry County, Alabama, commencing on Saturday the 7th November, 1835. Greensborough: Smith and De Wolf, 1835.

Minutes of the Twelfth Annual Session of the Coosa River Association of Baptist Churches, Held at Big Spring Church, Shelby County, Alabama. n.p., 1845.

Minutes of the Twelfth Annual Session of the Louisiana Baptist State Convention, Held with Mt. Lebanon Church, Mt. Lebanon, La, June 29th–July 2nd 1860. Mt. Lebanon, La.: *Louisiana Baptist,* 1860.

Minutes of the Twenty-Fifth Anniversary of the Bethel Baptist Association, held with Union Church, Marengo Co., Ala. from the 4th to 6th October, inclusive, A.D. 1845. Macon: *Banner* Office, 1845.

Minutes of the Twenty-Fifth Annual Meeting of the Yalobusha Baptist Association, Held with the Providence Church, Carroll Co., Miss., Sept. 20th, 21st and 22nd, 1861. Grenada, Miss.: *Southern Rural Gentleman* Job Office, 1861.

Minutes of the Twenty-Ninth Annual Meeting of the Bethlehem Baptist Association, held with the Murder Creek Church, Conecuh County, Alabama, from the 27th to the 30th of September A.D. 1845. Claiborne: J. H. Curtis, 1845.

Minutes of the Twenty-Second Anniversary of the Ala. Baptist State Convention, Marion, Perry County, November 14–17, 1846. n.p., 1846.

Minutes of the Twenty-Third Anniversary of the Chickasaw Baptist Association, held with the Cherry Creek Church, Pontotoc Co., Miss. on the 13th, 14th, and 18th September, 1861. Jackson: *Mississippi Baptist* Book and Job Office, 1861.

Minutes of the Tyger River Baptist Association, convened at Head of Tyger Church, Greenville District, S.C., October 30, 1835. n.p., 1835.

Proceedings of the Fifth Annual Meeting of the Baptist State Convention, of North Carolina: Held at the Union Camp-Ground, Rowan County, October 30th–Nov. 3rd, 1835. Newbern: *Recorder* Office, 1835.

Proceedings of the Ninth Annual Meeting of the Convention of the Baptist Denomination of the State of Mississippi, held at Grenada, Yalobusha County, June 25, 1845. Jackson: *Southern Reformer* Office, 1845.

Proceedings of the Southern Baptist Convention at its Eighth Biennial Session, Held in the First Baptist Church, Savannah, GA, May 10th, 11th, 12th, and 13th, 1861. Richmond: MacFarlane and Fergusson, 1861.

Proceedings of the Southern Baptist Convention, Held in Augusta, Georgia. Richmond, Va.: H. K. Ellyson, 1845.

Proceedings of the Thirteenth Annual Meeting of the General Association of Virginia; held at the Second Baptist Church, Richmond, June 4–7, 1836. n.p., 1836.

Proceedings of the Twelfth Annual Session of the Central Baptist Association Held at Vicksburg, Mississippi, October 9, 10 and 12, 1857. Jackson: Book and Job Office of the *Mississippi Baptist,* 1857.

Proceedings of the Thirty-Second Annual Session of the Baptist State Convention of North Carolina, held with the Baptist Church in Raleigh, Nov. 13, 14, 15, 16, 17 and 18, 1861. Raleigh: *Biblical Recorder* Office, 1861.

Proceedings of the Twenty-Second Annual Meeting of the Baptist General Association of Virginia assembled at Lynchburg, Virginia, May 31st, 1845. n.p., n.d.

Proceedings of the Twenty-Fifth Session of the Mississippi Baptist State Convention, convened in Macon, Noxubee County, Miss. May 23rd, 1861 and Continuing Five Days. Jackson: *Mississippi Baptist* Book and Job Office, 1861.

Proceedings of the Twenty-Fourth Session of the Mississippi Baptist State Convention, convened in Natchez, Adams County, Miss. May 24th, 1860, and Continuing Five Days. Jackson: *Mississippi* Baptist Book and Job Office, 1860.

EPISCOPALIAN

Extracts from the Journal of the Twenty-Third Annual Convention of the Protestant Episcopal Church, in the Diocese of Louisiana, containing an extract from the Address of the Rt. Rev. Leonidas Polk, D.D., Bishop of the Diocese. New Orleans: *Bulletin* Book and Job Office, 1861.

Journal of the Proceedings of the Seventy-Second Annual Convention of the Protestant Episcopal Church in South Carolina, held in Trinity Church, Abbeville, on the 19th and 20th of June, 1861. Charleston: A. E. Miller, 1861.

Journal of the Thirty-Fifth Annual Convention of the Protestant Episcopal Church, in the Diocese of Mississippi held in Christ Church, Holly Springs, April 25, 26, and 27, 1861. Jackson: *Mississippian* Book and Job Office, 1861.

METHODIST

Minutes of the South Carolina Conference of the Methodist Episcopal Church for the Year 1832. Charleston: James S. Burges, 1832.

Minutes of the South Carolina Conference of the Methodist Episcopal Church for the Year 1834. Charleston: J. S. Burges, 1834.

Minutes of the South Carolina Conference of the Methodist Episcopal Church for the Year 1836. Charleston: J. S. Burges, 1836.

Minutes of the South Carolina Conference of the Methodist Episcopal Church for the Year 1839. Charleston: Burges & James, 1839.

Minutes of the South Carolina Conference of the Methodist Episcopal Church for the Year 1844. Charleston: Office of the *Southern Christian Advocate,* 1845.

"Minutes of the Virginia Annual Conferences, 1830–1840." Walter Hines Page Library Methodist Collection. Randolph–Macon College, Virginia.

PRESBYTERIAN

"East Hanover Presbytery Minutes, Vol. 2, 1835–1843." Historical Foundation of the Presbyterian and Reformed Churches, Inc. Montreat, N.C.

"Lexington Presbytery Minutes, Vol. 10, 1834–1841." Historical Foundation of the Presbyterian and Reformed Churches, Inc.

"Minutes of the South Alabama Presbytery, Vol. 4, 1835–1840." Historical Foundation of the Presbyterian and Reformed Churches, Inc.

"Records of Concord Presbytery, 1825–1836." Historical Foundation of the Presbyterian and Reformed Churches, Inc.

"Records of Flint River Presbytery, Vol. 1." Historical Foundation of the Presbyterian and Reformed Churches, Inc.

"Records of Amite Presbytery, Vol. 1, 1835." Historical Foundation of the Presbyterian and Reformed Churches, Inc.

"Records of the Harmony Presbytery, 1830–1848." Historical Foundation of the Presbyterian and Reformed Churches, Inc.

"Records of the Presbytery of Bethel, 1824–1849." Historical Foundation of the Presbyterian and Reformed Churches, Inc.

"Records of the Presbytery of Concord, Vol. 4, 1836–1846." Historical Foundation of the Presbyterian and Reformed Churches, Inc.

"Records of the Presbytery of Georgia, 1821–1840." Historical Foundation of the Presbyterian and Reformed Churches, Inc.

"Records of the Presbytery of North Alabama, 1825–1844." Historical Foundation of the Presbyterian and Reformed Churches, Inc.

Southern sermons and addresses

Address of the People of South Carolina assembled in Convention to the People of the Slaveholding States of the United States. Charleston: Evans & Cogswell, 1860.

Addresses at the Inauguration of the Rev. R. W. Baily, A.M. as President of Austin College. Houston: *Telegraph* Book and Job Establishment, 1859.

Addresses of the Rev. J. Thilman Hendrick, A.M., of Zion Church, Tennessee; and Hon. Sterling A.M. Wood, Florence, Alabama, Delivered at the Commencement of the Florence Synodical Female College, Lauderdale County, Alabama, June 16, 1859. Memphis: Steam Book Publishing House, 1859.

Adger, John B. *The Religious Instruction of the Colored Population. A Sermon preached by the Rev. John B. Adger, in the Second Presbyterian Church, Charleston, S.C. May 9th, 1847.* Charleston: T. W. Haynes, 1847.

Armstrong, George D. *"The good hand of our God upon us." A Thanksgiving Sermon preached on occasion of the Victory of Manassas, July 21st, 1861, in the Presbyterian Church, Norfolk, VA.* Norfolk: J.D. Ghiselin, Jr., 1861.

The Lesson of the Pestilence. A Discourse preached in the Presbyterian Church, Norfolk, Va., on Sabbath, December 2nd, 1855. Richmond: Charles H. Wynne, 1855.

Letters and Replies on Slavery. Three Letters to a Conservative by George D. Armstrong, D. D. of Virginia, and Three Conservative Replies, by C. Van Rensselaer, D. D. of New Jersey. Philadelphia: Joseph M. Wilson, Publisher, 1858.

Politics and the Pulpit: A Discourse preached in the Presbyterian Church. Norfolk, VA, on Thursday, November 27, 1856. Norfolk: J.D. Ghiselin, Jr., 1856.

Atkinson, Thomas. *Christian Duty in the Present Time of Trouble. A Sermon*

Preached at St. James Church, Wilmington, N.C. on the Fifth Sunday after Easter, 1861. Wilmington, N.C.: Fulton & Price, 1861.

National and Ecclesiastical Blessings. A Sermon, preached in St. Peter's Church, Baltimore, on Thursday, the 12th day of December. Baltimore: D. Brunner, 1845.

On the Causes of our National Troubles. A Sermon delivered in St. James Church, Wilmington, N.C. on Friday, the 4th of January, 1861. Wilmington: *Herald* Book and Job Office, 1861.

Axson, I.S.K. *Individual Responsibility: An Address before the Association for the Religious Instruction of the Negroes, in Liberty County, Georgia; delivered at the Annual Meeting, January 31, 1843.* Savannah: Thomas Purse, 1843.

Barnard, Frederick A.P. *Gratitude Due for National Blessings: A Discourse, delivered at Oxford, Mississippi, on Thanksgiving Day, November 20, 1856.* Memphis: *Bulletin* Company, 1857.

Barnwell, William H. *The Divine Government. A Sermon, for the Day of Thanksgiving, Humiliation & Prayer, Appointed by the Governor of South Carolina, November 21, 1851.* Charleston: Edward C. Councell, 1851.

Views upon the present Crisis. A Discourse, delivered in St. Peter's Church, Charleston, on the 6th of December, 1850, the Day of Fasting, Humiliation and Prayer, appointed by the Legislature of South Carolina. Charleston: E.C. Councell, 1850.

Barten, O.S. *A Sermon Preached in St. James Church, Warrenton, VA, on Fast Day June 13, 1861 by the Rector.* Richmond: *Enquirer* Book and Job Press, 1861.

Bascom, Henry B. *Methodism and Slavery: with other Matters in Controversy between the North and the South; being a review of the Manifesto of the Majority in reply to the Protest of the Minority, of the late General Conference of the Methodist E. Church, in the Case of Bishop Andrew.* Frankfort, Ky.: Hodges, Todd & Pruett, 1845.

Bell, George. *A Sermon, delivered in the Presbyterian Church, in Greensboro, Ala., on Sabbath, December 22, 1851.* Tuscaloosa: M. D. J. Slade, 1851.

Benjamin, Judah P. *Speech of Hon. J. P. Benjamin, of Louisiana on the Right of Secession. Delivered in the Senate of the United States, Dec. 31, 1860.* Washington, D.C.: L. Towers, 1861.

Booth, William. *The Writings of William A. Booth, M.D. During the Controversy upon Slavery. Which Ended in the Division of the Methodist Episcopal Church.* Sommerville, Tenn.: Reeves and Yancey, 1845.

Boyd, Andrew H. H. *Thanksgiving Sermon, delivered in Winchester, VA on Thursday, 29th November, 1860.* Winchester: *Winchester Virginian*, 1860.

Boyden, E. *The Epidemic of the Nineteenth Century.* Richmond: Charles H. Wynne, 1860.

Breckinridge, Robert J. *Fidelity in our Lot. The Substance of a Discourse preached by the Appointment of the General Assembly of the Presbyterian Church, at their Annual Meeting in the City of Nashville, Tennessee, in May 1855.* Philadelphia: Board of Missions, 1855.

Brookes, Iveson L. *A Defense of Southern Slavery Against the Attacks of Henry Clay and Alexander Campbell by a Southern Clergyman.* Hamburg, S.C.: Robinson and Carlisle, 1851.

A Defense of the South Against the Reproaches of and Incroachments of the North: In which Slavery is shown to be an Institution of God intended to form the basis of the best social state and the only safeguard to the permanence of a Republican Government. Hamburg, S.C.: *Republican* Office, 1850.

A Discourse, Investigating the Doctrine of Washing the Saints' Feet: Delivered at Monticello. Macon, Ga.: Rose & Slade, 1830.

Brownlow, William G. *A Sermon on Slavery. A Vindication of the Methodist Church, South: Her Position Stated.* Knoxville, Tenn.: Kinsloe & Rice, 1857.

Bulfinch, S. G. *The Benefits and Dangers Belonging to Seasons of Public Excitement: A Discourse, Delivered in the Unitarian Church at Charleston, S.C. on the Day of Humiliation and Prayer, January 31, 1833.* Charleston: J. S. Burges, 1833.

Butler, William C. *Sermon: Preached in St. John's Church, Richmond, Virginia, on the Sunday after the Battle at Manassas, July 21, 1861.* Richmond: Chas. H. Wynne, 1861.

Carnes, J. E. *Address, on the Duty of the Slave States in the Present Crisis, delivered in Galveston, December 12th, 1860.* Galveston, Tex.: *News* Book and Job Office, 1860.

Cater, Richard P. *A Discourse delivered in the Presbyterian Church at Pendleton Village, on the 31st January, 1833: A Day of Fasting, Humiliation and Prayer Appointed by the Convention of the Site of South Carolina.* Pendleton: *Messenger* Office, 1833.

Central Southern Rights Association of Virginia. *The Proceedings and Address of the Central Southern Rights Association of Virginia, to the Citizens of Virginia.* Richmond: Ritchies & Dunnavant, 1851.

Chadbourne, John S. *The Mortal and the Immortal: A Sermon, Preached in St. James Church, Baton Rouge, in improvement of the Character and Death of the Hon. Henry Clay.* New Orleans: New Orleans Office of the *Picayune*, 1852.

Clark, George H. *The Union. A Sermon, delivered in St. John's Church, Savannah, on Fast Day, November 28, 1860.* Savannah: Geo. N. Nichols, Printer, 1860.

Cobbs, Nicholas H. *Pastoral letter of the Rt. Rev. N. H. Cobbs, to the Clergy and Laity, of the Diocese of Alabama. May 5th, 1849.* Tuscaloosa: *Observer* Office, 1849.

Coit, J. C. *Discourse upon Government, Divine and Human, prepared by Appointment of the Presbytery of Harmony, and delivered before that body during its Sessions in Indiantown Church. Williamsburg District, S.C., April 1853.* Columbia: T. F. Greneker, 1853.

Eulogy on the Life, Character and Public Services of the Sen. John C. Calhoun, pronounced by appointment before the Citizens of Cheraw and its Vicinity on Wednesday, April 24, 1850. Columbia: A. S. Johnston, 1850.

Colton, Simeon. *An Address, Delivered before the Philomathesian & Euzelian Societies, in Wake Forest College, June 16, 1842.* Fayetteville, N.C.: Edward J. Hale, 1842.

Crane, William C. *The Effect of Classic Study upon the Advance of Mind. An Address delivered before the Philomathian and Hermenian Societies of Mississippi College on Thursday, August 7, 1856.* Memphis: *Eagle and Enquirer* Steam Presses, 1856.

Cummins, George D. *The African a Trust from God to the American. A Sermon delivered on the Day of National Humiliation, Fasting and Prayer in St. Peter's Church, Baltimore, January 4, 1861.* Baltimore: John D. Tay, 1861.

Cunningham, Hugh Blaire. *Two Sermons, delivered by the Rev. H. B. Cunningham, Pastor of the Congregations of Hopewell and Paw Creek, Mecklenburg County; NC.* Charlotte: *Hornets' Nest* Office, 1849.

Curry, J. L. M. *Perils and Duty of the South. Substance of a Speech delivered by Jabez L. M. Curry in Talledega, Alabama, November 26, 1860.* Washington, D.C.: L. Towers, 1860.

Cuthbert, Lucius. *The Scriptural Grounds for Secession from the Union. A Sermon, delivered by Rev. Lucius Cuthbert, Jr., at Aiken, S.C., Dec. 16, 1860.* Charleston: Welch, Harris & Co., 1861.

Dabney, Robert L. *The Christian's Best Motive for Patriotism. A Sermon: preached in the College Church, Hampden Sidney, Va, on the 1st of November, 1860.* Richmond: Chas. H. Wynne, 1860.

The World White to Harvest:–Reap; or it Perishes. A Sermon Preached for the Board of Foreign Missions of the Presbyterian Church, in New York, May 2, 1858. New York: Edward O. Jenkins, 1858.

Dana, William C. *A Sermon delivered in the Central Presbyterian Church, Charleston, S.C., November 21st, 1860, being the Day appointed by State Authority for Fasting, Humiliation, and Prayer.* Charleston: Steam Power Presses of Evans and Cogswell, 1860.

DeVeaux, T. L. *A Fast Day Sermon, preached in the Good Hope Church, Lowndes County, Alabama, Thursday, June 13th, 1861.* Wytheville, Ala.: D. A. St. Clair, 1861.

Dreher, Daniel I. *A Sermon Delivered by Rev. Daniel I. Dreher, pastor of St. James Church, Concord, N.C., June 13, 1861. Day of Humiliation and Prayer, as per Appointment of the President of the Confederate States of America.* Salisbury, N.C.: *Watchman* Office, 1861.

Dunwody, Samuel. *A Sermon Upon the Subject of Slavery.* Columbia, S.C.: S. Weir, 1837.

Eichelberger, L. *Inaugural Address Delivered in Saint Mark's Church, Edgefield District, S.C., November 15, 1852.* Columbia, S.C.: R. W. Gibbes, 1853.

Elliott, J. H. *The Bloodless Victory. A Sermon Preached in St. Michael's Church, Charleston, S.C. on Occasion of the taking of Fort Sumter.* Charleston: A. E. Miller, 1861.

Elliott, Stephen. *Address of the Rt. Rev. Stephen Elliott, D. D., to the Thirty-Ninth Annual Convention of the Protestant Episcopal Church in the Diocese of Georgia.* Savannah: Power Press of John M. Cooper & Company, 1861.

Annual Address before the Clariosophic and Euphradian Societies of the South Carolina College delivered December 4, 1859. Charleston: Walker, Evans & Co., 1860.

God's Presence with our Army at Manassas! A Sermon, preached in Christ Church, Savannah, on Sunday, July 28th, being the Day Recommended by the Congress of the Confederate States, to be observed as a Day of Thanksgiving, in commemoration of the Victory of Manassas Junction, on Sunday, the 21st of July, 1861. Savannah: W. Thorne Williams, 1861.

God's Presence with the Confederate States. A Sermon Preached in Christ Church, Savannah, on Thursday, the 13th June, being the Day Appointed at the Request of Congress, by the President of the Confederate States as a Day of Solemn Humiliation, Fasting and Prayer. Savannah: W. T. Williams, 1861.

The Little Foxes Spoiling the Vines: A Sermon preached before the Convention of the Episcopal Church of Georgia, on the First Friday in May, the day set apart by Legislative Enactment and Executive Proclamation as a Day of Fasting, Humiliation, and Prayer. Savannah: W. T. Williams, 1843.

The Silver Trumpets of the Sanctuary. A Sermon preached to the Pulaski Guards in Christ Church, Savannah, on the Second Sunday after Trinity. Savannah: Steam Press of John M. Cooper, 1861.

England, John. *Oration, delivered on the anniversary of the Literary and Philosophical Society of South Carolina on Wednesday on 9th of May, 1832*. Baltimore: J. Myres, 1832.

Fast Day Sermons: or The Pulpit on the State of the Country. New York: Rudd & Carleton, 1861.

Ferguson, Jesse B. *Address on the History, Authority and Influence of Slavery, by Rev. J. B. Ferguson, A. M., delivered on the First Presbyterian Church, Nashville, Tenn. 21st of November, 1850*. Nashville: John T. S. Fall, 1850.

Fugitt, James Preston. *Our Country and Slavery. A Friendly Word to the Rev. Francis L. Hawks, D.D., LL.D. and other Northern Clergymen*. Baltimore: Joseph Robinson, 1861.

Fuller, Richard. *Our Duty to the African Race. An Address delivered at Washington, D.C., January 21, 1851*. Baltimore: W. M. Innes, 1851.

Furman, Richard. *Rev. Dr. Richard Furman's Exposition of the Views of the Baptists, Relative to the Coloured Population in the United States in a Communication to the Governor of South Carolina*. 1822; reprint ed., Charleston: A. E. Miller, 1833.

Goulding, Thomas. *A Fast Day Sermon, for Thursday, January 31st, 1833. Columbia, S.C.* Columbia: *Telescope* Office, 1833.

Green, William M. *Funeral Discourse, on the Death of Rev. Stephen Patterson, Late Rector of Christ's Church, Vicksburg, Miss. delivered in that Church, December 4, 1853*. Vicksburg: *Whig* Book and Job Office, 1854.

Gregg, Alexander. *The Duties Growing out of It, and the Benefits to be Expected, from the Present War. A Sermon, preached in St. David's Church, Austin, on Sunday, July 7th, 1861*. Austin: Office of the *State Gazette*, 1861.

Hamilton, W. T. *The Duties of Masters and Slaves Respectively: or Domestic Servitude Sanctioned by the Bible: A Discourse, delivered in the Government Street Church, Mobile, Ala. on Sunday night December 15, 1844*. Mobile: F. A. Brooks, 1845.

Hayne, Robert Y. *Defence of the South. General Hayne, in Reply to Mr. Webster, of Massachusetts*. Charleston: A. E. Miller, 1830.

Hendrick, J. T. *Union and Slavery. A Thanksgiving Sermon, delivered in the Presbyterian Church, Clarksville, Tennessee, November 28th, 1850*. Clarksville, Tenn.: C. O. Foxen, 1851.

Hooper, William. *Fifty Years Since: An Address, Delivered before the Alumni of the University of North Carolina, on the 7th of June, 1859*. Raleigh: Holden & Wilson, *Standard* Office, 1859.

The Sacredness of Human Life, and American Indifference to its Destruction: An Address before the Literary Societies of Wake Forest College, June 10th, 1857. Raleigh, N.C.: Holden & Wilson, 1857.

Howard, C. W. *Life and Character of Oglethorpe. An Address delivered before the Literary Societies of the University of Georgia, Thursday, August 2, 1860*. Athens, Ga.: *Southern Banner* Power Press Print, 1860.

Howe, George. *An Appeal to the Young Men of the Presbyterian Church in the Synod of South Carolina and Georgia*. n.p., 1836.

Hunt, Benjamin Faneuil. *Speech of Hon. B. Faneuil Hunt of Charleston, Delivered in the House of Representatives of South Carolina, on Tuesday, December 18, 1850. On a bill to call a Convention of the State, to unite with the States of the South in action on the questions of federal usurpation.* n.p., 1850.

Jacobs, Ferdinand. *A Sermon, For the Times: Preached in Fairview Presbyterian Church, Perry County, Ala., on Thursday, June 13, 1861–The Day of Fasting and Prayer, appointed by the Confederate Authorities, in View of the National Exigencies.* n.p., 1861.

The Committing of Our Cause to God. A Sermon, preached in the Second Presbyterian Church, Charleston, South Carolina on Friday, 6th of December. Charleston: Edward C. Councell, 1851.

Jones, J. *The Southern Soldier's Duty. A Discourse Delivered by Rev. J. Jones to the Rome Light Guards, and Miller Rifles, in the Presbyterian Church of Rome, Ga., on Sabbath Morning, the 26th of May, 1861.* Rome: Steam Power Press of D. H. Mason, 1861.

Jordan, William H. *The Fragility of Human Life and Human Glory. A Sermon Preached at Island Creek Meeting House, Granville County, N.C. on the occasion of the Death of General Zachary Taylor.* Raleigh: *Raleigh Times* Office, 1850.

An Address Delivered before the Two Literary Societies of Wake Forest College on the 10th of June, 1847. Raleigh, N.C.: W. W. Holden, 1847.

Junkin, George, D.D. *An Apology for Collegiate Education, being the Baccalaureate Address, delivered on Commencement Day of Washington College, Lexington, VA. June 18th, 1851.* Lexington, Va.: n.p., 1851.

Kendrick, J. R. *Lessons from an Ancient Fast. A Discourse delivered in the Citadel Square Church, Charleston, S.C. on the occasion of the General Fast, Thursday, June 13, 1861.* Charleston: Steam Power Press of Evans & Cogswell, 1861.

Lacy, Drury. *A Thanksgiving Discourse, delivered in the Presbyterian Church, Raleigh, N.C., on Thursday, the 27th November, 1851.* Raleigh: Seaton Goles, 1851.

Leyburn, John. *National Mercies, Sins, and Duties. A Discourse, preached to the Congregation of the Presbyterian Church, Petersburg, Virginia, On Sabbath Morning, July 5th, 1846.* n.p., 1846.

Lipscomb, Andrew A. *Substance of a Discourse delivered before the Legislature of Georgia, on the Occasion of the Fast Day Appointed by his Excellency Joseph E. Brown, November 28, 1860.* Milledgeville: Boughton, Nisbet & Barnes, 1860.

Longstreet, Augustus B. *Fast Day Sermon: Delivered in the Washington Street Methodist Episcopal Church, Columbia, S.C., June 13, 1861.* Columbia: Townsend & North, 1861.

Lyon, James A. *Christianity and the Civil Laws: A Lecture on Christianity and the Civil Laws by Rev. James A. Lyon, D.D. of Columbus, Mississippi.* Columbus: *Mississippi Democrat* Print, 1859.

Manly, Basil. *Report on Collegiate Education, Made to the Trustees of the University of Alabama, July 1852.* Tuscaloosa: M. D. J. Slade, 1852.

McCaine, Alexander. *Slavery Defended from Scripture, against the Attacks of the Abolitionists, in a Speech delivered before the General Conference of the Methodist Protestant Church in Baltimore, 1842.* Baltimore: Wm. Woody, 1842.

McTyeire, H. N., Sturgis, C. F., and Holmes, A. T. *Duties of Masters to Servants:*

Three Premium Essays. 1851; reprint ed. Freeport, N.Y.: Books for Libraries Press, 1971.

Meade, William. *Addresses on the Day of Fasting and Prayer, appointed by the President of the Confederate States, June 13, 1861. Delivered at Christ Church, Millwood, VA.* Richmond: *Enquirer* Book and Job Press, 1861.

Pastoral Letter of the Right Rev. William Meade, Assistant Bishop of Virginia, to the Ministers, Members, and Friends of the Protestant Episcopal Church in the Diocese of Virginia, on the Duty of Affording Religious Instruction to Those in Bondage. 1834; reprint ed. Richmond: H. K. Ellyson, 1853.

Sermon Preached by Bishop Meade at the Opening of the Convention of the P. E. Church of Virginia in the City of Richmond. Richmond: Chas. H. Wynne, 1861.

[Mell, Patrick Hues.] *Slavery. A Treatise, showing that Slavery is neither a moral, political, nor social evil.* Penfield, Ga.: Benjamin Brantly, 1844.

Miles, James W. *The Discourse on the Occasion of the Funeral of the Hon. John C. Calhoun, delivered under the Appointment of the Joint Committee of the City Council and Citizens of Charleston, in St. Phillip's Church, April 26th, 1850.* Charleston, S.C.: John Russell, 1850.

The Relation between the Races at the South. Charleston, S.C.: Evans and Cogswell, 1861.

Mitchell, Arthur. *A Word of Scripture to North and South. A Sermon Delivered at the Third Presbyterian Church, Richmond, Virginia, Sunday, December 30th, 1860.* Richmond: MacFarlane & Fergusson, 1861.

Mitchell, J.C. *A Sermon delivered in the Government Street Church, on the National Fast Appointed by Jefferson Davis, President of these Confederate States, June 13, 1861.* Mobile, Ala.: Farrow & Dennett, 1861.

Moore, T. V. *God Our Refuge and Strength in this War. A Discourse before the Congregations of the First and Second Presbyterian Churches, on the day of Humiliation, Fasting, and Prayer, appointed by President Davis, Friday, November 15, 1861.* Richmond, Va.: W. Hargrave White, 1861.

Morey, Ira. *A Thanksgiving Sermon Preached in the Presbyterian Church, Greenville, Tenn., Thursday, November 30th, 1854.* Knoxville, Tenn.: John B. G. Kinsloe, 1855.

Morrison, R. H. *The Inaugural Address of the Rev. R. H. Morrison, D. D. pronounced at his Inauguration as President of Davidson College, North Carolina, August 2, 1838.* Philadelphia: William S. Martien, 1838.

Owens, W. A. *An Address to the People of Barnwell District, on Separate State Secession.* Charleston, S.C.: Steam Power Press of Walker & James, 1851.

Painter, H. M. *The Duty of the Southern Patriot and Christian in the Present Crisis. A Sermon preached in the First Presbyterian Church, Boonville, Mo. on Friday, January 4th, 1861, being the Day of the National Fast.* Boonville, Mo.: Caldwell & Stahl, 1861.

Palmer, Benjamin M. *The Rights of the South Defended in the Pulpits: by B. M. Palmer, D. D. and W. T. Leacock, D. D.* Mobile, Ala.: J. Y. Thompson, 1860.

The South: Her Peril and her Duty: A Discourse, delivered in the First Presbyterian Church, New Orleans, on Thursday, November 29, 1860. New Orleans: Office of the *True Witness and Sentinel,* 1860.

Pickens, Francis W. *Speech of Hon. F. W. Pickens, delivered before a Public Meeting of the People of the District held at Edgefield CH, S.C., July 7, 1851.* Edgefield, S.C.: *Advisor* Office, n.d.

Pierce, H. N. *Sermons Preached in St. John's Church, Mobile, on the 13th of June, 1861, the National Fast appointed by His Excellency Jefferson Davis, President of the Confederate States of America.* Mobile, Ala.: Farrow & Dennett, Book and Job Printers, 1861.

Pinckney, Charles C. *Nebuchadnezzar's Fault and Fall: A Sermon, preached at Grace Church, Charleston, S.C. on the 17th of February, 1861.* Charleston: A. J. Burke, 1861.

Pinney, Norman. *A Sermon, Preached July 5, 1835 in Christ's Church, Mobile.* Mobile, Ala.: McGuie and Brother, 1835.

Polk, Leonidas. *A Letter to the Right Reverend Bishops of Tennessee, Georgia, Alabama, Arkansas, Texas, Mississippi, Florida, South Carolina and North Carolina, from the Bishop of Louisiana.* New Orleans: B. M. Norman, 1856.

Porter, A. A. *Our Danger and Duty. A Discourse delivered in the Glebe-Street Presbyterian Church, on Friday, December 6th, 1850.* Charleston, S.C.: E. C. Councell, 1850.

Porter, R. K. *Christian Duty in the Present Crisis: The Substance of a sermon delivered in the Presbyterian church, in Waynesboro', Georgia ... December 9, 1860.* Savannah: Steam Press of J. M. Cooper & Company, 1860.

Pratt, N. A. *Perils of a Dissolution of the Union; A discourse, delivered in the Presbyterian Church of Roswell, on the Day of Public Thanksgiving. November 20, 1856.* Atlanta: C. R. Hanleiter & Co. Printers, 1856.

Prentiss, William O. *A Sermon Preached at St. Peter's Church, Charleston by the Rev. William O. Prentiss, on Wednesday, November 21, 1860, being a Day of Public Fasting, Humiliation and Prayer.* Charleston, S.C.: Evans & Cogswell, 1860.

Quarterman, Robert. *Motives and Encouragements. An Address before the Association for the Religious Instruction of the Negroes, in Liberty County, Georgia: Delivered at the Annual Meeting, January 23, 1844.* Savannah: Thomas Purse, 1844.

Randolph, A. M. *Address on the Day of Fasting and Prayer appointed by the President of the Confederate States, June 13, 1861. Delivered in St. George's Church, Fredericksburg, VA.* Fredericksburg: *Recorder* Job Office, 1861.

Read, C. H. *National Fast. A Discourse delivered on the Day of Fasting, Humiliation, and Prayer, appointed by the President of the United States, January 4, 1861.* Richmond: West & Johnson, 1861.

The Religious Instruction of our Colored Population: A Pastoral Letter from the Presbytery of Tombeckee to the Churches and People under Its Care. Columbia, S.C.: Steam Power Press of R. W. Gibbes, 1859.

Report of the Committee to whom was referred the subject of the Religious Instruction of the Colored Population of the Synod of South Carolina and Georgia, at its late session in Columbia, December 5th–9th, 1833. Charleston: Observer Office Press, 1834.

Resolutions and Address adopted by the Southern Convention, Held at Nashville, Tennessee, June 3rd to 12th, Inclusive, 1850: Together with a Preamble and Resolutions, Adopted November 18th, 1850. Columbia, S.C.: Steam Power Press of I. C. Morgan, 1850.

Rhett, Robert Barnwell. *Address to the People of Beaufort and Colleton Districts, upon the Subject of Abolition. January 15, 1838.* n.p., n.d.

Ross, F. A. *Position of the Southern Church in Relation to Slavery, as Illustrated in a Letter of Dr. F. A. Ross to Rev. Albert Barnes with an Introduction by a Constitutional Presbyterian.* New York: John A. Gray, 1857.

Scarburgh, George Baxter. *Address to the People of the County of Accomac.* n.p., n.d.

Scott, William Anderson. *Progress of Civil Liberty. A Thanksgiving Discourse: Pronounced in the Presbyterian Church, on Lafayette Square, New Orleans, on Thursday, 9th December, 1847, Being Thanksgiving Day.* New Orleans: Office of *The Daily Delta,* 1848.

Second Annual Report of the Missionary to the Negroes in Liberty County, GA. presented to the Association. Riceborough, January 1835. Charleston: *Observer* Office Press, 1835.

Seventh Annual Report of the Association for the Religious Instruction of the Negroes in Liberty County. GA, together with the Address to the Association by the President, the Rev. Josiah Spry Law. Savannah: Thomas Purse, Printer, 1842.

Sledd, R. N. *A Sermon, delivered in the Market Street M. E. Church, Petersburg, VA., before the Confederate Cadets, on the Occasion of their Departure for the Seat of War, Sunday, September 22, 1861.* Petersburg: A. F. Crutchfield & Co., 1861.

Smith, B. M. *An Inaugural Discourse; delivered in the Seminary Chapel, September 12, 1855.* Richmond: *Enquirer* Book and Job Press, 1855.

Smith, Whitefoord. *An Oration delivered before the Euphradian and Clariosophic Societies of the South Carolina College, on the 6th December, 1848.* Columbia, S.C.: John G. Bowman, 1849.

——— *God the Refuge of His People. A Sermon, delivered before the General Assembly of South Carolina, on Friday, December 6, 1850; being a Day of Fasting, Humiliation, and Prayer.* Columbia, S.C.: A. S. Johnston, 1850.

——— *National Sins: A Call to Repentance. A Sermon: preached on the National Fast, August 3, 1849, in Cumberland Church, Charleston, S.C.* Charleston: *Southern Christian Advocate,* 1849.

——— *The Discipline of the Methodist E. Church, South, in Regard to Slavery.* n.p., 1849.

——— *The Substance of an Address delivered to the Palmetto Regiment, South Carolina Volunteers, on Saturday, December 26, 1846.* n.p., n.d.

Smyth, Thomas. *The Battle of Fort Sumter: Its Mastery and Miracle: God's Mastery and Mercy. A Discourse preached on the Day of National Fasting, Thanksgiving and Prayer, in the First Presbyterian Church, Charleston, S.C. June 13, 1861.* Columbia, S.C.: *Southern Guardian* Steam Power Press, 1861.

Southern Education. Addresses delivered in the Chapel at Oakland College, on the day of Annual Commencement, June 29th, 1854. New Orleans: Office of the *Picayune,* 1854.

Stanton, Robert L. *Ungodly Nations Doomed: A Discourse Preached on the Occasion of the Annual Thanksgiving, November 29, 1849, recommended by the Governor of Louisiana.* New Orleans: William H. Toy, 1849.

Staunton, Benjamin F. *The Nation's Disease and Remedy, A Sermon delivered on the Occasion of the National Fast, May 14, 1841, in the Presbyterian Church of Farmville, Virginia.* Richmond: John B. Martin, 1841.

Stevens, William Bacon. *The Providence of God, in the Settlement and Protection of Georgia. A Sermon preached in Athens, on the 13th February, 1845, the Day set apart by Executive Proclamation for Prayer and Thanksgiving.* Athens, Ga.: *Whig* Office, 1845.

Stiles, William H. *An Address, delivered before the Georgia Democratic State Convention, assembled at Milledgeville, July 4th, 1856.* Atlanta: *Examiner* Office, 1856.

Stringfellow, Thornton. *A Brief Examination of Scripture Testimony on the Institution of Slavery.* Washington, D.C.: *Congressional Globe* Office, 1850.

Summers, Thomas O. *Christian Patriotism: A Sermon Preached in Cumberland St. M. E. Church, Charleston, S.C. on Friday, Dec. 6, 1850.* Charleston: C. Canning, 1850.

Taggart, Charles M. *The Virtue of Fasting and Prayer. A Discourse, preached on Thursday, Oct. 13, 1853, A Day of Fasting, Humiliation and Prayer, Appointed by the Governor of South Carolina.* Charleston: Steam Power Press of Walker & James, 1853.

Talmage, Samuel K. *Reasons for Public Thanksgiving. A Discourse delivered before the Legislature of Georgia, in the Representative Chamber, Milledgeville, on Thanksgiving Day, November 29, 1849.* Milledgeville: *Southern Recorder* Office, 1849.

Taylor, S. *Relation of Master and Servant, As Exhibited in the New Testament.* Richmond: T. W. White, Printer, 1836.

Thomas, James R. *An Address, Delivered Before the Society of Alumni on Randolph–Macon College, Va.* Richmond: Office of the *Christian Advocate,* 1841.

Thornwell, James H. *Judgments, A Call to Repentance. A Sermon Preached by Appointment of the Legislature in the Hall of the House of Representatives, Saturday, Dec. 9, 1854.* Columbia, S.C.: R. W. Gibbes & Co., 1854.

Thrasher, J. B. *Slavery a Divine Institution. A Speech Made before the Breckinridge and Lane Club, November 5th, 1860.* Port Gibson, Miss.: *Southern Reveille* Book and Job Office, 1861.

Townsend, John A. *The Doom of Slavery in the Union: Its Safety out of it.* Charleston, S.C.: Evans & Cogswell, 1860.

The Southern States. Their Present Peril, and their Certain Remedy. Why do they not Right Themselves? And so fulfil their Glorious Destiny. Charleston: Edward C. Councell, 1850.

Trippett, Reynolds. *A Fast Day Discourse by Rev. Reynolds Trippett, of the M.E. Church, South. Preached in the Court House Square, Richmond, La., Thursday, June 13th, 1861.* Vicksburg, Miss.: *Whig* Power Press Job Office, 1861.

Van Zandt, A. B. *God's Voice to the Nation: A Sermon occasioned by the Death of Zachary Taylor, President of the United States.* Petersburg, Va.: n.p., 1850.

The Claims of Virginia upon her Educated Sons: An Address delivered before the Union Society of Hampden Sidney College, June 13th, 1854. Petersburg, Va.: O. Ellyson, 1854.

Vedder, C. S. *"Offer unto God Thanksgiving": A Sermon delivered in the Summerville Presbyterian Church on Sunday, July 28, 1861.* Charleston: Steam Power Presses of Evans & Cogswell, 1861.

Vernor, W. H. *A Sermon, delivered before the Marshall Guards No. 1 on Sunday, May 5th, 1861 by Rev. W. H. Vernor at the Presbyterian Church, Lewisburg, Tennessee.* Lewisburg: n.p., 1860.

Verot, Augustine. *A Tract for the Times. Slavery and Abolitionism, being the Substance of a Sermon, Preached in the Church of St. Augustine, Florida, on the 4th Day of January, 1861, Day of Public Humiliation, Fasting, and Prayer.* [St. Augustine? 1861?]

Watkins, W. H. *The South, Her Position and Duty. A Discourse delivered at the Methodist Church, Natchez, Miss., January 4, 1861.* Natchez: *Natchez Daily Courier* Book and Job Office, 1861.

Wightman, John T. *The Glory of God, the Defense of the South. A Discourse delivered in the Methodist Episcopal Church, South, Yorkville, S.C., July 28, 1861, the Day of National Thanksgiving for the Victory at Manassas.* Portland, Me.: B. Thurston & Co., 1871.

[Wiley, Calvin H.] *A Sober View of the Slavery Question: By a Citizen of the South.* n.p., n.d.

Wilson, Joseph R. *Mutual Relation of Masters and Slaves as Taught in the Bible. A Discourse preached in the First Presbyterian Church, Augusta, Georgia, on Sabbath Morning, January 6, 1861.* Augusta, Ga.: Steam Press of *Chronicle & Sentinel*, 1861.

Winkler, E. T. *Duties of the Citizen Soldier. A Sermon, delivered in the First Baptist Church of Charleston, S.C. on Sabbath Morning, January 6th, 1861 before the Moultrie Guards.* Charleston: A. J. Burke, 1861.

Winn, T. S. *The Great Victory at Manassas Junction. God the Arbiter of Battles. A Thanksgiving Sermon, preached in the Presbyterian Church, at Concord, Greene County, Alabama, on the 28th day of July, 1861.* Tuscaloosa: J. F. Warren, 1861.

Northern sermons and addresses

Allen, B. R. *"The Constitution and the Union": A Sermon preached in the First Congregational Church in Marblehead, on the Occasion of the National Fast, January 4th, 1861.* Boston: J. H. Eastburn, 1861.

Atwood, E. S. *The Purse, the Knapsack, and the Sword. A Sermon delivered in the Congregational Church, Grantville, Mass., on Sunday, April 28, 1861.* Boston: Bazin & Chandler, 1861.

Barclay, Cuthbert C. *Sermon on the Times. A Sermon, Preached in the St. Thomas Church, Bethel, on the National Fast Day, January 4th, 1860.* New Haven, Conn.: Tuttle, Morehouse & Taylor, 1861.

Bartol, C. A. *The Duty of the Time. A Discourse Preached in the West Church Sunday Morning, April 28, 1861.* Boston: Walker, Wise & Co., 1861.

Benedict, A. D. *Our Republic, a Brotherhood. A Discourse delivered in St. John's Church Delhi, N.Y., on the National Fast Day, Jan. 4th, 1861.* Delhi, N.Y.: *Gazette* Print, 1861.

Bucher, T. P. *Union Fast Day Sermon, delivered in the United Presbyterian Church, Gettysburg, PA., Friday, January 4, A.D. 1861.* Gettysburg: H. C. Neinstedt, 1861.

Bulkley, C. H. A. *Removal of Ancient Landmarks: or the Causes and Consequences of Slavery Extension. A Discourse preached to the Second Congregational Church of West Winsted, CT., March 5th, 1854.* Hartford, Conn.: Case, Tiffany and Company, 1854.

Bushnell, Horace. *The Northern Iron. A Discourse delivered in the North Church, Hartford, on the Annual State Fast, April 14, 1854.* Hartford, Conn.: Edwin Hunt and Son, 1854.

   Politics under the Law of God. A Discourse delivered in the North Congregational Church, Hartford, on the Annual Fast of 1844. Hartford, Conn.: Edwin Hunt, 1844.

Chapin, E. H. *The Responsibilities of a Republican Government. A Discourse, preached Fast Day, April 8, 1841.* Boston: A. Tompkins, 1841.

Chase, Carlton. *A Discourse, delivered in Trinity Church, Claremont, January 4, 1861, being the day appointed by the President of the United States, for General Fasting and Prayer, on Account of the Distracted State of the Country.* Claremont, N.H.: George C. and Lemuel N. Ide, 1861.

Davis, Emerson. *A Thriving Town: A Sermon, Preached at the Annual Fast, April 6, 1837, in Westfield, Mass.* Springfield: Merriam, Wood & Co., 1837.

Dickinson, James T. *A Sermon, delivered in the Second Congregational Church, Norwich, on the fourth of July, 1834, at the Request of the Anti-Slavery Society of Norwich & Vicinity.* Norwich, Conn.: Published by the Anti-Slavery Society, 1834.

Dorr, Benjamin. *The American Vine. A Sermon Preached in Christ Church, Philadelphia, Friday, January 4, 1861, on occasion of the National Fast.* Philadelphia: Collins, Printer, 1861.

Dunning, Homer M. *Providential Design of the Slavery Agitation. A Sermon preached to the Congregational Church of Gloversville on the National Fast Day, January 4th, 1861.* Gloversville, N.Y.: A. Pierson, 1861.

Duryea, Joseph T. *Loyalty to Our Government: A Divine Command and a Christian Duty. A Sermon delivered in the Sixth-St. Presbyterian Church, Troy, Sabbath Morning, April 28, 1861.* Troy, N.Y.: A. W. Scribner & Company, 1861.

Dwight, William T. *Religion, the Only Preservative of National Freedom. A Discourse delivered in the Third Congregational Church of Portland; on the day of the annual Thanksgiving: December 1, 1836.* Portland, Me.: Arthur Shirley, 1836.

Fiske, John O. *A Sermon on the Present National Troubles, delivered in the Winter Street Church, January 4, 1861, The Day of the National Fast.* Bath, Me.: *Daily Times* Office, 1861.

Foot, Joseph I. *An Historical Discourse, delivered at West Brookfield, Mass., November 27, 1828, on the Day of the Annual Thanksgiving.* West Brookfield: Merriam & Cooke, 1843.

Foster, Daniel. *An Address on Slavery delivered in Danvers, Mass.* Boston: Bela Marsh, 1849.

Foster, Edin B. *The Rights of the Pulpit, and the Perils of Freedom. Two Discourses, preached in Lowell, Sunday, June 25th, 1854.* Lowell, Mass.: J. J. Judkins, 1854.

Frothingham, O. B. *The New Commandment: A Discourse delivered in the North Church, Salem, on Sunday, June 4, 1854.* Salem, Mass.: Printed at the *Observer* Office, 1854.

Fuller, Edward J. *A Fast Sermon, delivered April 7, 1836, before the Calvinistic Church and Society in Hardwick, Mass.* Brookfield, Mass.: E. and L. Merriam, Printers, 1836.

Furness, W. H. *A Sermon, delivered May 14, 1841 on the occasion of the National Fast recommended by the President.* Philadelphia: John C. Clark, 1841.

Gannett, Ezra S. *Relation of the North to Slavery. A Discourse preached in the Federal Street Meetinghouse, in Boston, on Sunday, June 11, 1854.* Boston: Crosby, Nichols & Company, 1854.

Goodrich, William H. *A Sermon, on the Christian Necessity of War; by William H. Goodrich, pastor of the First Presbyterian Church, Cleveland, preached April 21, 1861.* Cleveland: Fairbanks, Benedict & Co., Printers, *Herald* Office, 1861.

Gordon, William R. *The Peril of our Ship of State: A Sermon on the Day of Fasting and Prayer, January 4th, 1861*. New York: John A. Gray, 1861.

Green, Beriah. *Things for Northern Men to Do: A Discourse delivered Lord's Day Evening, July 17, 1836 in the Presbyterian Church, Whitesboro', N. Y.* New York, n.p. 1836.

Greenwood, F. W. P. *Prayer for the Sick. A Sermon Preached at King's Chapel, Boston, on Thursday, August 9, 1832, being the Fast Day Appointed by the Governor of Massachusetts, on Account of the Appearance of Cholera in the United States*. Boston: Leonard C. Bowles, 1832.

Grosvenor, Cyrus Pitt. *Address before the Anti-Slavery Society of Salem and the Vicinity, in the South Meeting House, in Salem, February 24, 1834*. Salem, Mass.: W & S. B. Ives, *Observer* Press, 1834.

Hamilton, L. *The Nebraska Offense. A Sermon, Preached in the Presbyterian Church, Ovid, June 4, 1854*. Ovid, N.Y.: Corydon Fairchild, 1854.

Helmer, C. D. *Two Sermons. I. Signs of Our National Atheism, II. The War Begun*. Milwaukee: Terry & Cleaver, 1861.

Hinckley, Frederic. *Freedom and Slavery; Our Present Relations and Duties. A Discourse, preached in the Church of the Savior, Hartford, Conn., July 9th, 1854, Being the Sunday Following the Anniversary of American Independence*. n.p., n.d.

Hopkins, Albert. *A Sermon delivered at Williamstown, Mass. on the Day of the Annual State Fast, March 28, 1839*. Troy, N.Y.: Stevenson and McCall, 1839.

Hopkins, Samuel. *A Sermon Preached on Fast Day, April 18, 1839*. Saco, Me.: S. L. Goodale, 1839.

Hovey, Horace C. *The National Fast. A Sermon, preached at Coldwater, Mich., January 4, 1861*. Coldwater, Mich.: *Republican* Print, 1861.

　Freedom's Banner. A Sermon preached to the Coldwater Light Artillery, and the Coldwater Zouve Cadets, April 28th 1861. Coldwater, Mich.: *Republican* Print, 1861.

Humphrey, Heman. *Death of President Harrison. A Discourse delivered in the Village Church in Amherst, Mass. on the Morning of the Annual State Fast. April 8, 1841*. Amherst: J. S. and C. Adams, 1841.

　Our Nation. A Discourse delivered at Pittsfield, Mass., January 4, 1861, on the Day of the National Fast. Pittsfield: Henry Chickering, 1861.

Ingersoll, George C. *A Sermon Preached on Fast Day, before the First Congregational Society, in Burlington, Vermont*. Burlington: Stillman Fletcher, 1843.

Johnson, Samuel. *The Crisis of Freedom. A Sermon, preached at the Free Church, in Lynn, on Sunday, June 11, 1854*. Boston: Crosby, Nichols & Co., 1854.

Leonard, Edwin. *A Discourse, delivered in the Second Evangelical Congregational Church, Milton, June 4, 1854*. Boston: George C. Rand, 1854.

Lincoln, Calvin. *A Sermon Preached on the Morning of the Annual Fast, April 3, 1834, before the First Congregational Society in Fitchburg, Mass.* n.p., 1834.

Lord, C. E. *Sermons on the Country's Crisis, delivered in Mount Vernon, N. H., April 28, 1861, by C. E. Lord, pastor of the Congregational Church*. Milford, N.H.: Boutwell's Newspaper, Book and Job Office, 1861.

Lord, John C. *Causes and Remedies of the Present Convulsions: A Discourse*. Buffalo, N.Y.: Joseph Warren & Co., 1861.

March, Daniel. *The Crisis of Freedom. Remarks on the Duty which all Christian Men and Good Citizens owe their country in the Present State of Public Affairs*. Nashua, N.H.: Dodge and Noyes, 1854.

Mason, J. K. *The Sword. A Sermon preached at Hampden, Me.* Bangor: Samuel S. Smith, 1861.

McCall, S. *Who Is Responsible for Public Calamities? A Sermon preached in the Congregational Church, in Old Saybrook, Conn., April 28, 1861.* New York: Hall, Clayton, & Co., 1861.

Mitchell, John. *A Sermon preached before the First Church and the Edwards Church, Northampton, on the Late Fast, September 1, 1837.* Northampton, Mass.: W. A. Hawley, 1837.

Morison, John H. *A Sermon preached in the First Congregational Church, Milton, June 4, 1854.* Boston: Benjamin H. Greene, 1854.

Nelson, J. *A Discourse on the Proposed Repeal of the Missouri Compromise: Delivered on Fast Day, April 6, 1854, in the First Congregational Church, in Leicester, Mass.* Worcester, Mass.: Edward R. Fiske, 1854.

Quint, Alonzo H. *The Christian Patriot's Present Duty. A Sermon addressed to the Mather Church and Society, Jamaica Plain, Mass., April 28, 1861.* Boston: Hollis & Gunn, 1861.

Rankin, J. E. *A Spurious Fear of God. A Discourse, delivered in St. Albans, VT, on the National Fast Day, January 4th 1861.* St. Albans, Vt.: Whiting and Davis, 1861.

Reed, Augustus B. *Historical Sermon delivered at Ware First Parish, on Thanksgiving Day, Dec. 2nd, 1830.* n.p., 1889.

Root, David. *The Abolition Cause eventually triumphant. A Sermon, delivered before the Anti-slavery Society of Haverhill, Mass.* Andover: Gould and Newman, 1836.

A Fast Sermon on Slavery, delivered April 2, 1835, to the Congregational Church & Society in Dover, N. H. Dover: Printed at the Enquirer Office, 1835.

Schuyler, Anthony. *Slaveholding as a Religious Question. A Sermon preached in Christ Church, Oswego, on the Evening of February 3, 1861.* n.p., n.d.

"Slavery and the Bible." *New Englander* 15 (February 1857): 102–34.

Smith, Matthew Hale. *Impiety in High Places, and Sympathy with Crime, A Curse to any People. A Sermon delivered before the First Church and Society in Nashua, N.H. on Sabbath, April 20, 1845, with Reference to the Annual State Fast.* Boston: S. N. Dickinson & Co., Printers, 1845.

Spear, Samuel T. *Two Sermons for the Times. Obedience to the Civil Authority; and Constitutional Government Against Treason.* New York: Nathan Lane & Co., 1861.

Staples, Nahor Augustus. *A Sermon on the "Irrepressible Conflict," preached by Rev. N. A. Staples on Thanksgiving Day, 1859.* Milwaukee, Wis.: Strickland & Co., 1859.

Stearns, William A. *Slavery, in its Present Aspects and Relations. A Sermon preached on Fast Day, April 6, 1854, at Cambridge, Mass.* Boston and Cambridge, Mass.: James Munroe and Company, 1854.

Swain, Leonard. *God in the Strife. A Sermon preached at the Central Congregational Church, Providence, R. I., April 28, 1861.* Providence: Knowles, Anthony & Co., 1861.

Thacher, George. *A Sermon delivered in the Congregational Church, Keokuk, Iowa, on the occasion of the late National Fast, January 4th, 1861.* Keokuk: Daily Gate City Office Print, 1861.

Thayer, Christopher. *A Discourse, delivered in the First Church, Beverley, at the Fast Observed in Massachusetts on Account of the Prevailing Cholera. August*

9, 1832. Salem, Mass.: Press of Foote & Brown, *Gazette and Mercury Office,* 1832.

Thompson, Joseph P. *The President's Fast; A Discourse upon Our National Crimes and Follies, preached in the Broadway Tabernacle Church, January 4, 1861.* New York: Thomas Neels, 1861.

Trapnell, Joseph. *A Word from the West. Our duty as American Citizens, in this, our Country's imminent Peril. A discourse delivered in St. John's Church, Keokuk, Iowa, on Friday January 4th, 1861.* Keokuk: Rees & Deloplaine, 1861.

Wadsworth, Charles. *Our Own Sins. A Sermon Preached in the Arch Street Church, on the Day of Humiliation and Prayer, appointed by the President of the United States, Friday, January 4th, 1861.* Philadelphia: King & Baird, 1861.

American Patriotism. A Sermon preached in the Arch Street Church, Sabbath Morning, April 28th, 1861. Philadelphia: J. W. Bradley, 1861.

Wallace, Cyrus W. *A Sermon on the Duty of Ministers to Oppose the Extension of American Slavery, preached in Manchester, N. H., Fast Day, April 3, 1857.* Manchester: Fisk & Gage, 1857.

Waterbury, Jared P. *Influence of Religion on National Prosperity: A Sermon, delivered in Portsmouth, N.H., April 1, 1830, Being the Annual Fast.* Portsmouth: John W. Shepard, 1830.

White, Isaac. *National Crisis. A Discourse delivered in the First Congregational Church in Nantucket, Massachusetts, May 5, 1861.* Boston: W. F. Brown, 1861.

White, Theodore F. *The "Godly Heritage." A Sermon, delivered on Thanksgiving Day, November 29, 1860, in the Church of the Puritans, New York.* New York: Thomas Holman, 1860.

Young, Joshua. *God Greater Than Man. A Sermon preached June 11th, After the Rendition of Anthony Burns, by Joshua Young, minister of the First Congregational Church, Burlington, VT.* Burlington: Samuel B. Nichols, 1854.

Miscellaneous primary sources

Adger, John B. *My Life and Times, 1810–1899.* Richmond, Va.: Presbyterian Committee of Publication, 1899.

Adger, John B., and Girardeau, John L., eds. *The Collected Writings of James Henley Thornwell, D.D., L.L.D.* Richmond, Va.: Presbyterian Committee of Publication, 1873.

Baker, Daniel. *The Life and Labours of Daniel Baker, D.D.* Philadelphia: William S. & Alfred Martien, 1858.

Blackburn, George A., comp. and ed. *The Life Work of John L. Girardeau, D.D.* Columbia, S.C.: The State Committee, 1916.

Broadus, John A. *Memoir of James Petigru Boyce, D.D., L.L.D., Late President of the Southern Baptist Theological Seminary, Louisville, KY.* New York: A. C. Armstrong and Son, 1893.

Caldwell, Joseph. *Autobiography of the Rev. Joseph Caldwell, D.D. L.L.D., First President of the University of North Carolina.* Chapel Hill: John B. Neathery, 1860.

Cassels, Samuel J. "Conscience – Its Nature, Office and Authority." *Southern Presbyterian Review* 6 (April 1853): 455–67.

Chesebrough, David B., ed. *"God Ordained This War": Sermons on the Sectional Crisis, 1830–1865.* Columbia, S.C.: University of South Carolina Press, 1991.

Clapp, Theodore. *Autobiographical Sketches and Recollections, during a Thirty-Five Years Residence in New Orleans.* Boston: Tompkins & Company, 1863.

Cross, Barbara, ed. *The Autobiography of Lyman Beecher, Vol. 2.* Cambridge, Mass.: Harvard University Press, 1961.

Dagg, John L. *Autobiography.* Rome, Ga.: J. F. Shaklin, 1886.

Duffy, John, ed. *Parson Clapp of the Strangers' Church of New Orleans.* Baton Rouge: Louisiana State University Press, 1957.

Dumond, Dwight L., ed. *Southern Editorials on Secession.* Originally published 1931; Gloucester, Mass.: Peter Smith, 1964.

Finney, Charles Grandison. *Lectures on Revivals of Religion by Charles Grandison Finney.* Ed. by William G. McLoughlin. Cambridge, Mass.: Harvard University Press, 1960.

Foote, William Henry. *Sketches of Virginia, Historical and Biographical.* 2nd ed. Philadelphia: Lippincott, 1856.

Fry, Rose W. *Recollections of the Rev. John McElhenney, D.D.* Richmond, Va.: Whittet & Shepperson, 1893.

Gillette, Walter Bloomfield. *Memoir of Rev. Daniel Holbrook Gillette, of Mobile, Alabama.* Philadelphia: Lippincott, 1846.

Griffith, H. P. *The Life and Times of Rev. John G. Landrum.* Philadelphia: H. B. Garner, 1885.

Hancock, Elizabeth H., ed. *Autobiography of John E. Massey.* New York and Washington: Neale Publishing Company, 1909.

Hutchison, John Russell. *Reminiscences, Sketches and Addresses selected from my Papers during a Ministry of Forty-Five Years in Mississippi, Louisiana and Texas.* Houston, Tex.: E. H. Cushing, 1874.

Jeter, Jeremiah Bell. *The Recollections of a Long Life.* Richmond: The *Religious Herald* Co., 1891.

Johnson, Thomas C. *The Life and Letters of Benjamin M. Palmer.* Richmond: Presbyterian Committee of Publication, 1906.

The Life and Letters of Robert Lewis Dabney. Edinburgh and Carlisle: 1903. The *Banner of Truth* Trust, 1977.

Mallory, Charles D. *Memoirs of Elder Jesse Mercer.* New York: Printed by John Gray, 1844.

Maxwell, William. *A Memoir of the Rev. John H. Rice, D.D.* Philadelphia: J. Whetham, 1835.

Miller, Samuel. *The Life of Samuel Miller, D.D., L.L.D.* Philadelphia: Claxton, Remser, and Heffelfenger, 1869.

Palmer, Benjamin M. *The Life and Letters of James Henley Thornwell, D.D., L.L.D.* Richmond: Whittet & Shepperson, 1875.

Richardson, Simon P. *The Light and Shadows of Itinerant Life: An Autobiography of Rev. Simon Peter Richardson, D.D. of the North Georgia Conference.* Nashville and Dallas: Publishing House Methodist Episcopal Church, South, 1901.

Robertson, A. T. *Life and Letters of John Albert Broadus.* Philadelphia: American Baptist Publication Society, 1901.

Sherwood, Julia. *Memoir of Adiel Sherwood, D.D. written by his Daughter.* Philadelphia: Grant and Faires, 1856.

Smith, William A. *Lectures on the Philosophy and Practice of Slavery.* Nashville: Stevenson and Evans, 1856.

Smyth, Thomas. *Autobiographical Notes, Letters and Reflections.* Charleston: Walker, Evans & Cogswell Company, 1914.

"The Province of Reason, Especially in Matters of Religion." *Southern Presbyterian Review* 7 (October 1853): 276–88.

Stanford, S. W. "Scripturalism versus Rationalism." *Southern Presbyterian Review* 5 (October 1851): 271–85.

Stratton, Joseph B., D.D. *Memorial of a Quarter Century Pastorate. A Sermon Preached on the Sabbaths, Jan 3rd and 17th, 1869 in the Presbyterian Church, Natchez, Miss.* Philadelphia: Lippincott, 1869.

Thomas, J. P., ed. *The Carolina Tribute to Calhoun.* Columbia, S.C.: Richard L. Bryan, 1857.

Wayland, Francis. *Elements of Moral Science.* Introduction by Joseph L. Blau. Cambridge, Mass.: Belknap Press, Harvard University Press, 1963.

Wightman, William M. *Life of William Capers, D.D. Including an Autobiography.* Nashville: Publishing House of the Methodist Episcopal Church, South, 1902.

Secondary sources

Books

Ahstrom, Sydney E. *A Religious History of the American People.* New Haven, Conn.: Yale University Press, 1972.

Allmendinger, David F. *Ruffin: Family and Reform in the Old South.* New York: Oxford University Press, 1990.

Amos, Harriet. *Cotton City: Urban Development in Antebellum Mobile.* University: University of Alabama Press, 1985.

Auer, J. Jeffrey, ed. *Antislavery and Disunion, 1858–1861: Studies in the Rhetoric of Compromise and Conflict.* New York and Evanston: Harper & Row, 1963.

Bailyn, Bernard. *The Ideological Origins of the American Revolution.* Cambridge, Mass.: Belknap Press, Harvard University Press, 1967.

Barnes, William Wright. *The Southern Baptist Convention, 1845–1953.* Nashville: Broadman Press, 1954.

Barney, William. *The Secessionist Impulse: Alabama and Mississippi in 1860.* Princeton, N.J.: Princeton University Press, 1974.

Bassett, John S. *Slavery in North Carolina.* Baltimore: Johns Hopkins University Press, 1899.

Bercovitch, Sacvan. *The American Jeremiad.* Madison: University of Wisconsin Press, 1978.

Berens, John F. *Providence and Patriotism in Early America, 1640–1815.* Charlottesville: University Press of Virginia, 1978.

Betts, Albert D. *History of South Carolina Methodism.* Columbia, S.C.: Advocate Press, 1952.

Bodo, John R. *The Protestant Clergy and Public Issues, 1812–1848.* Princeton, N.J.: Princeton University Press, 1954.

Boles, John B. *The Great Revival, 1787–1805: The Origins of the Southern Evangelical Mind.* Lexington: University Press of Kentucky, 1972.

Boles, John B., ed. *Masters & Slaves in the House of the Lord: Race and Religion in the American South, 1740–1870.* Lexington: University Press of Kentucky, 1988.

Bonner, James C. *Milledgeville: Georgia's Antebellum Capital*. Athens: University of Georgia Press, 1978.

Boucher, Chauncy S. *The Nullification Controversy in South Carolina*. Chicago: University of Chicago Press, 1916.

Boyd, Minnie Claire. *Alabama in the Fifties: A Social Study*. New York and London: Columbia University Press, 1931.

Bozeman, Theodore Dwight. *Protestants in an Age of Science: The Baconian Ideal and Antebellum American Religious Thought*. Chapel Hill: University of North Carolina Press, 1977.

Brown, Richard D. *Modernization: The Transformation of American Life, 1600–1865*. New York: Hill & Wang, 1976.

Bruce, Dickson D., Jr. *And They All Sang Hallelujah: Plain-Folk Camp-Meeting Religion, 1800–1845*. Knoxville: University of Tennessee Press, 1974.

Brumm, Ursula. *American Thought and Religious Typology*. John Hoaglund, trans. New Brunswick, N.J.: Rutgers University Press, 1970.

Bryson, Gladys. *Man and Society: The Scottish Inquiry of the Eighteenth Century*. Princeton, N.J.: Princeton University Press, 1945.

Bucke, Emory S., ed. *The History of American Methodism*. Vol. II. Nashville, Tenn.: Abington Press, 1964.

Buckley, Jerome H. *The Triumph of Time; A Study of the Victorian Concepts of Time, History, Progress and Decadence*. Cambridge, Mass.: Belknap Press, Harvard University Press, 1966.

Calhoon, Robert M. *Evangelicals and Conservatives in the Early South, 1740–1861*. Columbia: University of South Carolina Press, 1988.

Carpenter, Jesse T. *The South as a Conscious Minority, 1789–1861: A Study in Political Thought*. New York: New York University Press, 1930.

Cash, Wilbur J. *The Mind of the South*. New York: Knopf, 1941.

Caskey, Willie M. *Secession and Restoration of Louisiana*. Baton Rouge: Louisiana State University Press, 1938.

Channing, Steven. *Crisis of Fear: Secession in South Carolina*. New York: Simon and Schuster, 1970.

Cheshire, Joseph Blount. *The Church in the Confederate States: A History of the Protestant Episcopal Church in the Confederate States*. New York: Longmans, Green, and Co., 1912.

Clark, Erskine. *Wrestlin' Jacob: A Portrait of Religion in the Old South*. Atlanta: John Knox Press, 1979.

Cole, Charles C., Jr. *The Social Ideas of the Northern Evangelists: 1826–1860*. New York: Columbia University Press, 1954.

Cooper, William J., Jr. *The South and the Politics of Slavery, 1828–1856*. Baton Rouge and London: Louisiana State University Press, 1978.

Cotton, Gordon. *Of Primitive Faith and Order: A History of the Mississippi Baptist Church, 1780–1974*. Raymond, Miss.: Keith Press, 1974.

Cragg, Gerald R. *Reason and Authority in the Eighteenth Century*. Cambridge, Mass.: Harvard University Press, 1964.

Craven, Avery O. *The Growth of Southern Nationalism, 1848–1861*. Baton Rouge: Louisiana State University Press, 1953.

The Repressible Conflict, 1830–1861. University: Louisiana State University Press, 1939.

Crofts, Daniel W. *Reluctant Confederates: Upper South Unionists in the Secession Crisis*. Chapel Hill and London: University of North Carolina Press, 1989.

Davidson, James West. *The Logic of Millennial Thought: Eighteenth-Century New England*. New Haven, Conn.: Yale University Press, 1977.

Davis, David Brion. *The Problem of Slavery in the Age of Revolution, 1770–1823*. Ithaca, N.Y.: Cornell University Press, 1975.

Degler, Carl. *One Among Many: The Civil War in Comparative Perspective*. Gettysburg, Pa.: Gettysburg College, 1990.

Denman, Clarence P. *The Secession Movement in Alabama*. Originally published 1933. Reprint ed., New York: Books for Libraries Press, 1971.

Duffy, John, ed. *Parson Clapp of the Strangers' Church of New Orleans*. Baton Rouge: Louisiana State University Press, 1957.

Eaton, Clement. *Freedom of Thought in the Old South*. Durham, N.C.: Duke University Press,. 1940.

A History of the Old South. 3rd ed. New York: Macmillan, 1975.

The Mind of the Old South. Baton Rouge: Louisiana State University Press, 1964.

Eighmy, John Lee. *Churches in Cultural Captivity: A History of the Social Attitudes of Southern Baptists*. Knoxville: University of Tennessee Press, 1972.

Elkins, Stanley M. *Slavery: A Problem in American Institutional and Intellectual Life*. Chicago: University of Chicago Press, 1959.

Faust, Drew Gilpin. *A Sacred Circle: The Dilemma of the Intellectual in the Old South, 1840–1860*. Baltimore and London: Johns Hopkins University Press, 1977.

The Creation of Confederate Nationalism: Ideology and Identity in the Civil War South. Baton Rouge and London: Louisiana State University Press, 1988.

Faust, Drew Gilpin, ed. *The Ideology of Slavery: Proslavery Thought in the Antebellum South, 1830–1860*. Baton Rouge: Louisiana State University Press, 1981.

Filler, Louis. *The Crusade Against Slavery, 1830–1860*. New York: Harper & Row, 1960.

Flanders, Ralph. *Plantation Slavery in Georgia*. Originally published 1933. Reprint ed., Cos Cob, Conn.: John E. Edwards, 1967.

Fogel, Robert William. *Without Consent or Contract: The Rise and Fall of American Slavery*. New York: W. W. Norton, 1989.

Foner, Eric. *Free Soil, Free Labor, Free Men: The Ideology of the Republican Party before the Civil War*. New York: Oxford University Press, 1970.

Politics and Ideology in the Age of the Civil War. New York: Oxford University Press, 1980.

Foster, Charles I. *An Errand of Mercy: The Evangelical United Front, 1790–1837*. Chapel Hill: University of North Carolina Press, 1960.

Fredrickson, George M. *The Inner Civil War: Northern Intellectuals and the Crisis of the Union*. New York: Harper & Row, 1965.

Freehling, William W. *Prelude to Civil War: The Nullification Controversy in South Carolina, 1816–1836*. New York: Harper & Row, 1965.

The Road to Disunion, Volume I: Secessionists at Bay, 1776–1854. New York: Oxford University Press, 1990.

Genovese, Eugene D. *Roll, Jordan, Roll: The World the Slaves Made*. New York: Pantheon, 1975.

The Political Economy of Slavery: Studies in the Economy and Society of the Slave South. New York: Pantheon Books, 1965.

"Slavery Ordained of God": The Southern Slaveholders' View of Biblical History and Modern Politics, Gettysburg College: 24th Annual Robert Fortenbaugh Memorial Lecture, 1985.

The Slaveholders' Dilemma: Freedom and Progress in Southern Conservative Thought, 1820–1860. Columbia: University of South Carolina Press, 1992.

Gillespie, Neal C. *The Collapse of Orthodoxy: The Intellectual Ordeal of George Frederick Holmes.* Charlottesville: University Press of Virginia, 1972.

Godbold, Albea. *The Church College of the Old South.* Durham, N.C.: Duke University Press, 1944.

Goen, C. C. *Broken Churches, Broken Nation: Denominational Schisms and the Coming of the Civil War.* Macon, Ga.: Mercer University Press, 1985.

Revivalism and Separatism in New England, 1740–1800: Strict Congregationalists and Separate Baptists in the Great Awakening. New Haven, Conn.: Yale University Press, 1962.

Goldfield, David R. *Cotton Fields and Skyscrapers: Southern City and Region, 1607–1980.* Baton Rouge and London: Louisiana State University Press, 1982.

Grave, Selwyn A. *The Scottish Philosophy of Common Sense.* Oxford: Clarendon Press, 1960.

Greenberg, Kenneth S. *Masters and Statesmen: The Political Culture of American Slavery.* Baltimore and London: Johns Hopkins University Press, 1985.

Gregorie, Anne King. *History of Sumter County.* Sumter, S.C.: Library Board of Sumter County, 1954.

Gribbin, William. *The Churches Militant: The War of 1812 and American Religion.* New Haven, Conn.: Yale University Press, 1973.

Griffin, Clifford S. *Their Brothers' Keepers: Moral Stewardship in the United States, 1800–1865.* New Brunswick, N.J.: Rutgers University Press, 1960.

Hall, Peter Dobkin. *The Organization of American Culture, 1700–1900: Private Institutions, Elites, and the Origins of American Nationality.* New York: New York University Press, 1982.

Hamilton, Holman. *Prologue to Conflict: The Crisis and Compromise of 1850.* Originally published 1964; New York: W. W. Norton, 1966.

Handy, Robert T. *A Christian Nation: Protestant Hopes and Historical Realities.* New York: Oxford University Press, 1971.

Haroutunian, Joseph. *Piety Versus Moralism: The Passing of the New England Theology.* New York: Henry Holt, 1932.

Hatch, Nathan O. *The Sacred Cause of Liberty: Republican Thought and the Millennium in Revolutionary New England.* New Haven, Conn.: Yale University Press, 1977.

Hatch, Nathan O., and Noll, Mark A., eds. *The Bible in America: Essays in Cultural History.* New York: Oxford University Press, 1982.

Heimert, Alan. *Religion and the American Mind: From the Great Awakening to the Revolution.* Cambridge, Mass.: Harvard University Press, 1966.

Hoeveler, J. David. *James McCosh and the Scottish Intellectual Tradition: From Glasgow to Princeton.* Princeton, N.J.: Princeton University Press, 1981.

Holifield, E. Brooks. *The Gentlemen Theologians: American Theology in Southern Culture, 1795–1860.* Durham, N.C.: Duke University Press, 1978.

Holt, Michael. *The Political Crisis of the 1850s.* New York: Wiley, 1978.

Horsman, Reginald. *Josiah Nott of Mobile: Southerner, Physician, and Racial Theorist.* Baton Rouge and London: Louisiana State University Press, 1987.

Houghton, Walter. *The Victorian Frame of Mind. 1830–1870.* New Haven, Conn.: Yale University Press, 1957.

Houston, David F. *A Critical Study of Nullification in South Carolina.* New York: Longmans, Green, 1896.

Howe, Daniel Walker. *The Unitarian Conscience: Harvard Moral Philosophy, 1805–1861.* Cambridge, Mass.: Harvard University Press, 1970.

Howe, George. *History of the Presbyterian Church in South Carolina, Vol. 2.* Columbia, S.C.: Duffie & Chapman, 1870–1883.

Huggins, Maloy. *A History of North Carolina Baptists 1727–1932.* Raleigh: The General Board Baptist State Convention of North Carolina, 1967.

Isaac, Rhys. *The Transformation of Virginia, 1740–1790.* Chapel Hill, N.C.: Published for the Institute of Early American History and Culture, Williamsburg, by the University of North Carolina Press, 1982.

Jenkins, William Sumner. *Proslavery Thought in the Old South.* Chapel Hill: University of North Carolina Press, 1935.

Johnson, Guion Griffis. *Ante-Bellum North Carolina: A Social History.* Chapel Hill: University of North Carolina Press, 1937.

Johnson, Michael P. *Toward a Patriarchal Republic: The Secession of Georgia.* Baton Rouge: Louisiana State University Press, 1977.

Jones, John A. *A Complete History of Methodism as Connected with the Mississippi Conference of the Methodist Episcopal Church, South.* Vol. 2. Nashville, Tenn.: Publishing House of the Methodist Episcopal Church, South, 1908.

Jordan, Winthrop D. *White over Black: American Attitudes Toward the Negro, 1550–1812.* Originally published 1968; New York: W. W. Norton, 1977.

Kirkland, Thomas J., and Kennedy, Robert M. *Historic Camden. Part Two: The Nineteenth Century.* Columbia, S.C.: The *State* Company, 1926.

Klein, Rachel N. *Unification of a Slave State: The Rise of the Planter Class in the South Carolina Backcountry, 1760–1808.* Chapel Hill and London: Published for the Institute of Early American History and Culture, Williamsburg by the University of North Carolina Press, 1990.

Kuklick, Bruce. *Churchmen and Philosophers: From Jonathan Edwards to John Dewey.* New Haven, Conn., and London: Yale University Press, 1985.

Kuykendall, John W. *Southern Enterprize: The Work of National Evangelical Societies in the Antebellum South.* Westport, Conn.: Greenwood Press, 1982.

Lander, Ernest M., Jr. *Reluctant Imperialists: Calhoun, the South Carolinians and the Mexican War.* Baton Rouge: Louisiana State University Press, 1980.

Landrum, J. B. O. *History of Spartanburg County.* Atlanta: Franklin Printing and Publishing Company, 1900.

Lewis, Jan. *The Pursuit of Happiness: Family and Values in Jefferson's Virginia.* Cambridge: Cambridge University Press, 1983.

Locke, Mary S. *Antislavery in America from the Introduction of African Slaves to the Prohibition of the Slave Trade (1619–1808).* Originally published 1901; New York: Johnson Reprint Company, 1968.

Loveland, Anne C. *Southern Evangelicals and the Social Order, 1800–1860.* Baton Rouge: Louisiana State University Press, 1980.

Lowance, Mason. *The Language of Canaan: Metaphor and Symbol in New England from the Puritans to the Transcendentalists.* Cambridge, Mass., and London: Harvard University Press, 1980.

McCardell, John M. *The Idea of a Southern Nation: Southern Nationalists and Southern Nationalism, 1830–1860.* New York: W. W. Norton, 1979.

McCash, William B. *Thomas R. R. Cobb (1823–1862): The Making of a Southern Nationalist.* Macon, Ga.: Mercer University Press, 1983.

McColley, Robert. *Slavery and Jeffersonian Virginia.* Urbana: University of Illinois Press, 1964.

McKivigan, John. *The War Against Proslavery Religion: Abolitionism and the Northern Churches, 1830–1865.* Ithaca, N.Y., and London: Cornell University Press, 1984.

McLoughlin, William G. *Modern Revivalism: Charles Grandison Finney to Billy Graham.* New York: Ronald Press, 1959.

McPherson, James M. *Ordeal by Fire: The Civil War and Reconstruction.* New York: Knopf, 1982.

Marsden, George M. *The Evangelical Mind and the New School Presbyterian Experience: A Case Study of Thought and Theology in Nineteenth Century America.* New Haven, Conn.: Yale University Press, 1970.

Marszalek, John F., ed. *The Diary of Miss Emma Holmes, 1861–1865.* Baton Rouge: Louisiana State University Press, 1979.

Marty, Martin E. *Righteous Empire: The Protestant Experience in America.* New York: Dial Press, 1970.

Mathews, Donald G. *Religion in the Old South.* Chicago: University of Chicago Press, 1977.

Slavery and Methodism: A Chapter in American Morality, 1780–1845. Princeton, N.J.: Princeton University Press, 1965.

May, John A., and Faunt, Joan R. *South Carolina Secedes.* Columbia: University of South Carolina Press, 1960.

May, Robert A. *The Southern Dream of a Carribean Empire, 1854–1861.* Baton Rouge: Louisiana State University Press, 1973.

Mead, Sidney E. *Nathaniel William Taylor, 1786–1858: A Connecticut Liberal.* Chicago: University of Chicago Press, 1942.

Meyer, Donald H. *The Instructed Conscience: The Shaping of the American National Ethic.* Philadelphia: University of Pennsylvania Press, 1972.

Miller, Perry. *The Life of the Mind in America from the Revolution to the Civil War.* New York: Harcourt, Brace and World, 1966.

Montgomergy, Horace. *Cracker Parties.* Baton Rouge: Louisiana State University Press, 1950.

Mooney, Chase C. *Slavery in Tennessee.* Bloomington: Indiana University Press, 1957.

Moorhead, James H. *American Apocalypse: Yankee Protestants and the Civil War, 1860–1869.* New Haven, Conn.: Yale University Press, 1978.

Morgan, Edmund S. *American Slavery, American Freedom: The Ordeal of Colonial Virginia.* New York: W. W. Norton, 1975.

Morrison, Chaplain. *Democratic Politics and Sectionalism: The Wilmot Proviso Controversy.* Chapel Hill: University of North Carolina Press, 1967.

Nagel, Paul C. *One Nation Indivisible: The Union in American Thought, 1776–1861.* New York: Oxford University Press, 1964.

This Sacred Trust: American Nationality, 1798–1898. New York: Oxford University Press, 1971.

Noll, Mark A. ed. *Religion and American Politics: From the Colonial Period to the 1980s.* New York and Oxford: Oxford University Press, 1990.

Norwood, John Nelson. *The Schism in the Methodist Episcopal Church, 1844: A Study of Slavery and Ecclesiastical Politics.* Alfred, N.Y.: The Alfred Press, 1923.

Oakes, James. *The Ruling Race: A History of American Slaveholders*. New York: Knopf, 1982.

Parker, Franklin N., ed. *A Diary-Letter Written from the Methodist General Conference of 1844 by the Rev. W. J. Parks*. Atlanta: Emory University Library, 1944.

Pettit, Norman. *The Heart Prepared: Grace and Conversion in Puritan Spiritual Life*. New Haven, Conn., and London: Yale University Press, 1966.

Pierce, Alfred M. *A History of Methodism in Georgia, February 5, 1746–June 14, 1955*. Atlanta: Georgia Conference Historical Society, 1956.

Plumstead, A. W., ed. *The Wall and the Garden: Selected Massachusetts Election Sermons, 1670–1775*. Minneapolis: University of Minnesota Press, 1968.

Posey, Walter B. *The Baptist Church in the Lower Mississippi Valley, 1776–1845*. Lexington: University of Kentucky Press, 1957.

The Development of Methodism in the Old Southwest, 1783–1824. Originally published 1933. Reprint ed., Philadelphia: Porcupine Press, 1974.

Frontier Mission: A History of Religion West of the Appalachians to 1861. Lexington: University of Kentucky Press, 1966.

The Presbyterian Church in the Old Southwest, 1778–1838. Richmond, Va.: John Knox Press, 1952.

Religious Strife on the Southern Frontier. Baton Rouge: Louisiana State University Press, 1965.

Potter, David. *The Impending Crisis, 1848–1861*. New York: Harper & Row, 1976.

The South and the Sectional Conflict. Baton Rouge: Louisiana State University Press, 1968.

Pressly, Thomas J. *Americans Interpret Their Civil War*. Princeton, N.J.: Princeton University Press, 1954.

Putnam, Mary. *The Baptists and Slavery, 1840–1845*. Ann Arbor, Mich.: George Wohr, Publisher, 1913.

Raboteau, Albert. *Slave Religion: The "Invisible Institution" in the Antebellum South*. New York: Oxford University Press, 1978.

Rainwater, Percy Lee. *Mississippi: Storm Center of Secession, 1856–1861*. Originally published 1938. Reprint ed., New York: Da Capo Press, 1969.

Randall, James G. *Lincoln the Liberal Stateman*. New York: Dodd, Mead, 1947.

Reinders, Robert C. *End of an Era: New Orleans, 1850–1860*. Gretna, La.: Pelican Publishing, 1964.

Richards, I. A. *The Philosophy of Rhetoric*. New York: Oxford University Press, 1936.

Richards, Leonard. *"Gentlemen of Property and Standing": Anti-Abolition Mobs in Jacksonian America*. New York: Oxford University Press, 1970.

Riley, Benjamin F. *History of the Baptists of Alabama: From the Time of Their First Occupation of Alabama in 1809, until 1894*. Birmingham, Ala.: Roberts and Son, 1895.

Riley, Isaac Woodbridge. *American Philosophy: The Early Schools*. Originally published 1907. reprint ed. New York: Russell & Russell, 1958.

American Thought from Puritanism to Pragmatism. New York: Henry Holt, 1915.

Ryland, Garnett. *The Baptists of Virginia, 1699–1926*. Richmond: The Virginia Baptist Board of Missions and Education, 1955.

Scott, Donald M. *From Office to Profession: The New England Ministry, 1750–1850.* Philadelphia: University of Pennsylvania Press, 1978.

Sellers, Charles Grier. *James K. Polk, Jacksonian: 1795–1843.* Princeton, N.J.: Princeton University Press, 1957.

Sellers, James B. *Slavery in Alabama.* University: University of Alabama Press, 1950.

Sernett, Milton C. *Black Religion and American Evangelicalism: White Protestants, Plantation Missions, and the Flowering of Negro Christianity, 1787–1865.* Metuchen, N.J.: Scarecrow Press, 1975.

Shanks, Henry T. *The Secession Movement in Virginia, 1847–1861.* Originally published 1934. Reprint ed., New York: AMS Press, 1971.

Sherer, Lester B. *Slavery and the Churches in Early America, 1619–1819.* Grand Rapids, Mich.: William B. Eerdsman Publishing, 1975.

Shugg, Roger W. *Origins of Class Struggle in Louisiana.* Baton Rouge: Louisiana State University Press, 1934.

Silver, James W. *Confederate Morale and Church Propaganda.* New York: W. W. Norton, 1967.

Simkins, Francis B. *A History of the South.* 3rd ed. New York: Knopf, 1963.

Simpson, Lewis P. *The Dispossessed Garden: Pastoral and History in Southern Literature.* Athens: University of Georgia Press, 1975.

Mind and the American Civil War: A Meditation on Lost Causes. Baton Rouge and London: Louisiana State University Press, 1989.

Sitterson, J. Carlyle. *The Secession Movement in North Carolina.* Chapel Hill: University of North Carolina Press, 1939.

Sloan, Douglas. *The Scottish Enlightenment and the American College Ideal.* New York: Teachers College Press, Columbia University, 1971.

Smith, Elwyn A., ed. *The Religion of the Republic.* Philadelphia: Fortress Press, 1971.

Smith, H. Shelton. *In His Image, But ... Racism in Southern Religion, 1790–1910.* Durham, N.C.: Duke University Press, 1972.

Smith, Timothy. *Revivalism and Social Reform: American Protestantism on the Eve of the Civil War.* Nashville, Tenn.: Abington Press, 1957.

Somkin, Fred. *Unquiet Eagle: Memory and Desire in the Idea of American Freedom, 1815–1860.* Ithaca, N.Y.: Cornell University Press, 1967.

Sprague, William B. *Annals of the American Pulpit.* New York: Robert Carter & Brothers, 1858.

St. Amant, Penrose. *A History of the Presbyterian Church in Louisiana.* Richmond: Synod of Louisiana, Whittet & Shepperson, 1961.

Stampp, Kenneth M. *America in 1857: A Nation in Crisis.* New York and Oxford: Oxford University Press, 1990.

And the War Came: The North and the Secession Crisis, 1860–1861. Baton Rouge: Louisiana State University Press, 1950.

The Imperiled Union: Essays on the Background of the Civil War. New York: Oxford University Press, 1980.

Staudenraus, Phillip J. *The African Colonization Movement, 1816–1865.* New York: Columbia University Press, 1965.

Stewart, James B. *Holy Warriors: The Abolitionists and American Slavery.* New York: Hill & Wang, 1976.

Story, James. *A History of the Presbyterian Church in Georgia.* Elberton, Ga.: n.p., 1912.

Stroupe, Henry S. *The Religious Press in the South Atlantic States, 1802–1865.* Durham, N.C.: Duke University Press, 1956.

Sweet, William Warren. *Methodism in American History.* New York: The Methodist Book Concern, 1933.

———. *Religion on the American Frontier, Vol. 2: The Presbyterians, 1783–1840.* New York: Harper, 1936.

———. *Virginia Methodism: A History.* Richmond: Whittet & Shepperson, 1955.

Sydnor, Charles S. *The Development of Southern Sectionalism, 1819–1848.* Baton Rouge: Louisiana State University Press, 1934.

———. *Slavery in Mississippi.* New York: D. Appleton–Century Company, 1933.

Taylor, Joe. *Negro Slavery in Louisiana.* Baton Rouge: Louisiana Historical Association, 1963.

Taylor, Rosser H. *Ante–Bellum South Carolina: A Social and Cultural History.* Originally published 1942. Reprint ed., New York: Da Capo Press, 1970.

Taylor, William R. *Cavalier and Yankee: The Old South and the American National Character.* Originally published 1957. Reprint ed., Cambridge, Mass.: Harvard University Press, 1979.

Thomas, Emory M. *The Confederate Nation, 1861–1865.* New York: Harper & Row, 1979.

Thompson, Ernest Trice. *Presbyterians in the South, Vol. 1: 1607–1861.* Richmond, Va.: John Knox Press, 1963.

Thornton, J. Mills. *Politics and Power in a Slave Society: Alabama, 1800–1860.* Baton Rouge: Louisiana State University Press, 1978.

Tise, Larry E. *Proslavery: A History of the Defense of Slavery in America, 1701–1840.* Athens and London: University of Georgia Press, 1987.

Toon, Peter. *The Emergence of Hyper-Calvinism in English Nonconformity, 1689–1765.* London: The Olive Tree, 1967.

Tushnet, Mark. *The American Law of Slavery, 1810–1860.* Princeton, N.J.: Princeton University Press, 1981.

Tuveson, Ernest. *Redeemer Nation: The Idea of America's Millennial Role.* Chicago: University of Chicago Press, 1968.

Walther, Eric H. *The Fire-Eaters.* Baton Rouge and London: Louisiana State University Press, 1992.

Welter, Rush. *The Mind of America, 1820–1860.* New York: Columbia University Press, 1975.

Wilson, John F. *Pulpit in Parliament: Puritanism During the English Civil War, 1640–1648.* Princeton, N.J.: Princeton University Press, 1969.

Wiltse, Charles M. *John C. Calhoun: Nullifier, 1829–1839.* Indianapolis: Bobbs Merrill, 1949.

———. *John C. Calhoun: Sectionalist, 1840–1850.* Originally published 1951. Reprint ed., New York: Russell & Russell, 1968.

Woodward, C. Vann. *The Burden of Southern History.* Baton Rouge: Louisiana State University Press, 1960.

Wright, Benjamin. *American Interpretations of Natural Law: A Study in the History of Political Thought.* Cambridge, Mass.: Harvard University Press, 1931.

Wyatt-Brown, Bertram. *Southern Honor: Ethics and Behavior in the Old South.* New York: Oxford University Press, 1982.

———. *Yankee Saints and Southern Sinners.* Baton Rouge and London: Louisiana State University Press, 1985.

Articles

Ahlstrom, Sydney E. "The Romantic Religious Revolution and the Dilemmas of Religious History." *Church History* 46 (June 1977): 149–70.

"The Scottish Philosophy and American Theology." *Church History* 24 (September 1955): 257–72.

"Theology in America: A Historical Survey." In *Religion in American Life. Vol 1: The Shaping of American Religion,* edited by James Ward Smith and A. Leland Jamison. Princeton: Princeton University Press, 1961.

Akers, Charles. "Religion and the American Revolution: Samuel Cooper and the Brattle Street Church." *William and Mary Quarterly* Third Series 35 (July 1978): 477–98.

Allen, Carlos R., Jr. "David Barrow's Circular Letter of 1798." *William and Mary Quarterly* Third Series 20 (July 1963): 440–51.

Anesko, Michael. "So Discreet a Zeal: Slavery and the Anglican Church in Virginia, 1680–1730." *Virginia Magazine of History and Biography* 93 (July 1985): 247–78.

Bailor, Keith M. "John Taylor of Caroline: Continuity, Change, and Discontinuity in Virginia's Sentiments towards Slavery, 1790–1820." *Virginia Magazine of History and Biography* 75 (July 1967): 290–304.

Bailyn, Bernard. "Religion and Revolution: Three Biographical Studies." *Perspectives in American History* IV (1970): 83–169.

Bean, William. "Anti-Jeffersonianism in the Ante-Bellum South." *North Carolina Historical Review* 12 (April 1935): 103–24.

Bercovitch, Sacvan. "Typology in Puritan New England: The Williams–Cotton Controversy Reassessed." *American Quarterly* 19 (Summer 1967): 166–91.

Bergeron, Paul H. "The Nullification Controversy Revisited." *Tennessee Historical Quarterly* 35 (Fall 1976): 263–75.

Bestor, Arthur. "The Civil War as a Constitutional Crisis." *American Historical Review* 69 (January 1964): 327–53.

Bishop, Charles C. "The Proslavery Argument Reconsidered: James Henley Thornwell, Millennial Abolitionist." *South Carolina Historical Magazine* 73 (January 1972): 18–26.

Boles, John B. "Evangelical Protestantism in the Old South: From Religious Dissent to Cultural Dominance." In *Religion in the South,* edited by Charles Reagan Wilson. Jackson: University Press of Mississippi, 1985.

"Henry Holcombe, A Southern Baptist Reformer in the Age of Jefferson." *Georgia Historical Quarterly* 54 (Fall 1970): 381–407.

Bowman, Sherer D. "Antebellum Planters and Vormaz Junkers in Comparative Perspective." *American Historical Review* 85 (October 1980): 779–808.

Boyd, William M. "Southerners in the Anti-Slavery Movement, 1800–1830." *Phylon* 9 (1948): 153–63.

Bozeman, Theodore D. "Joseph LeConte: Organic Science and a 'Sociology for the South'." *Journal of Southern History* 39 (November 1973): 565–82.

"Science, Nature and Society: A New Approach to James Henley Thornwell." *Journal of Presbyterian History* 50 (Winter 1972): 306–25.

Bradbury, M. L. "Samuel Stanhope Smith: Princeton's Accommodation to Reason." *Journal of Presbyterian History* 48 (Fall 1970): 189–202.

Brantley, William H. "Alabama Secedes." *Alabama Review* 7 (July 1954): 165–185.

Bruce, Dickson D., Jr. "Religion, Society, and Culture in the Old South: A Comparative View." *American Quarterly* 26 (October 1974): 399–416.

Brugger, Robert J. "The Mind of the Old South: New Views." *Virginia Quarterly Review* (Spring 1980): 277–95.

Bryan, T. Conn. "The Secession of Georgia." *Georgia Historical Quarterly* 31 (June 1947): 89–111.

Butler, Jon. "Enlarging the Bonds of Christ: Slavery, Evangelism, and the Christianization of the White South, 1690–1790." In *The Evangelical Tradition in America*, edited by Leonard Sweet. Macon, Ga.: Mercer University Press, 1984.

Butterworth, John K. "Mississippi Unionism: The Case of the Rev. James A. Lyon." *Journal of Mississippi History* 1 (January 1939): 37–52.

Clive, John, and Bailyn, Bernard. "England's Cultural Provinces: Scotland and America." *William and Mary Quarterly* Third Series 11 (April 1954): 200–13.

Cole, Charles C. "Horace Bushnell and the Slavery Question." *New England Quarterly* 23 (March 1950): 19–30.

Crofts, Daniel W. "The Union Party of 1861 and the Secession Crisis." *Perspectives in American History* XI (1977–78): 327–79.

Crowther, Edward R. "Holy Honor: Sacred and Secular in the Old South." *Journal of Southern History* 58 (November 1992): 610–36.

Daniel, W. Harrison. "The Effects of the Civil War on Southern Protestantism." *Maryland Historical Magazine* 69 (Spring 1974): 44–63.

———. "Protestantism and Patriotism in the Confederacy." *Mississippi Quarterly* 24 (Spring 1971): 117–34.

———. "Southern Presbyterians in the Confederacy." *North Carolina Historical Review* 44 (Summer 1967): 231–55.

———. "Southern Protestantism and Secession." *The Historian* 29 (May 1967): 391–408.

———. "Southern Protestantism and the Negro, 1861–1865." *North Carolina Historical Review* 41 (Summer 1964): 338–59.

———. "Virginia Baptists, 1861–1865." *Virginia Magazine of History and Biography* 72 (January 1964): 94–114.

Davis, J. Treadwell. "The Presbyterians and the Sectional Conflict." *Southern Quarterly* 8 (January 1970): 117–35.

DesChamps, Margaret Burr. "Union or Division? South Atlantic Presbyterians and Southern Nationalism, 1820–1861." *Journal of Southern History* 20 (November 1954): 484–98.

Dodd, Dorothy, ed. "Edmund Ruffin's Account of the Florida Secession Convention, 1861." *Florida Historical Quarterly* 12 (October 1933): 67–76.

———. "The Secession Movement in Florida, 1850–1860," Part II. *Florida Historical Quarterly* 12 (October 1933): 45–66.

Dodd, William E. "The Social Philosophy of the Old South." *American Journal of Sociology* 23 (May 1918): 735–46.

Donald, David H. "American Historians and the Causes of the Civil War." *South Atlantic Quarterly* 59 (Summer 1960): 351–55.

Donnelly, William J. "Conspiracy or Popular Movement: The Historiography of Southern Support for Secession." *North Carolina Historical Review* 42 (Winter 1965): 70–84.

Essig, James D. "A Very Wintry Season: Virginia Baptists and Slavery, 1785–1797." *Virginia Magazine of History and Biography* 88 (April 1980): 170–85.

Ezell, John S. "A Southern Education for Southrons." *Journal of Southern History* 17 (August 1951): 304–27.

Farmer, James O., Jr. "Southern Presbyterians and Southern Nationalism: A Study in Ambivalence." *Georgia Historical Quarterly* 75 (Summer 1991): 275–94.

Faust, Drew Gilpin. "Evangelicalism and the Proslavery Argument: Reverend Thornton Stringfellow of Virginia." *Virginia Magazine of History and Biography* 85 (January 1977): 3–17.

"The Rhetoric and Ritual of Agriculture in Antebellum South Carolina." *Journal of Southern History* 45 (November 1979): 541–68.

Fehrenbacher, Don. "The Missouri Controversy and the Sources of Southern Separatism." *Southern Review* 14 (Autumn 1978): 653–67.

Finnie, Gordon. "The Antislavery Movement in the Upper South before 1840." *Journal of Southern History* 35 (August 1967): 319–42.

Freehling, William W. "The Editorial Revolution, Virginia, and the Coming of the Civil War: A Review Essay." *Civil War History* 16 (March 1969): 64–72.

"James Henley Thornwell's Mysterious Antislavery Moment." *Journal of Southern History* 57 (August 1991): 383–406.

Garson, Robert A. "Proslavery as Political Theory: The Examples of John C. Calhoun and George Fitzhugh." *South Atlantic Quarterly* 84 (Spring 1985): 197–212.

Genovese, Eugene D., and Fox-Genovese, Elizabeth. "Slavery, Economic Development and the Law: The Dilemma of Southern Political Economists, 1800–1860." *Washington and Lee Law Review* 41 (Winter 1984): 1–29.

"The Divine Sanction of Social Order: Religious Foundations of the Southern Slaveholders' World View." *Journal of the American Academy of Religion* 55 (Summer 1987): 211–34.

"The Religious Ideals of Southern Slave Society." *Georgia Historical Quarterly* 70 (Spring 1986): 2–16.

Goen, C. C. "Broken Churches, Broken Nation: Regional Religion and North–South Alienation in Antebellum America." *Church History* 52 (March 1983): 21–35.

"Jonathan Edwards: A New Departure in Eschatology." *Church History* 28 (March 1959): 25–40.

Govan, Thomas P. "Was the Old South Different?" *Journal of Southern History* 21 (November 1955): 447–56.

Graebner, Norman A. "1848: Southern Politics at the Crossroads." *The Historian* 25 (November 1962): 14–35.

Greenberg, Kenneth S. "Revolutionary Ideology and the Proslavery Argument: The Abolition of Slavery in Antebellum South Carolina." *Journal of Southern History* 42 (August 1976): 365–84.

Greene, Jack P. "'Slavery or Independence': Some Reflections on the Relationship Among Liberty, Black Bondage, and Equality in Revolutionary South Carolina." *South Carolina Historical Magazine* 80, no. 3 (1979): 193–214.

Haskell, Thomas L. "Capitalism and the Origins of the Humanitarian Sensibility, Part I." *American Historical Review* 90 (April 1985): 359–61.

"Capitalism and the Origins of the Humanitarian Sensibility, Part II." *American Historical Review* 90 (June 1985): 547–67.

Hayden, J. Carlton. "Conversion and Control: Dilemma of Episcopalians in Providing for the Religious Instruction of Slaves, Charleston, South Carolina,

1845–1860." *Historical Magazine of the Protestant Episcopal Church* 40 (June 1971): 143–71.

Hicken, Patricia. "Situation Ethics and Antislavery Attitudes in Virginia Churches." In *America, the Middle Period: Essays in Honor of Bernard Mayo,* edited by John B. Boles. Charlottesville: University Press of Virginia, 1973.

Hildebrand, Reginald F. "'An Imperious Sense of Duty': Documents Illustrating an Episode in the Methodist Reaction to the Nat Turner Revolt." *Methodist History* 19 (April 1981): 155–74.

Holifield, E. Brooks. "Mercersburg, Princeton, and the South: The Sacramental Controversy in the Nineteenth Century." *Journal of Presbyterian History* 54 (Summer 1976): 238–57.

Hutson, James L. "The Panic of 1857, Southern Economic Thought, and the Patriarchal Defense of Slavery." *The Historian* 46 (February 1984): 163–86.

Jackson, James C. "The Religious Education of the Negro in South Carolina Prior to 1850." *Historical Magazine of the Protestant Episcopal Church* 36 (March 1967): 35–61.

Johnson, Guion Griffis. "Revival Movements in Antebellum North Carolina." *North Carolina Historical Review* 10 (January 1933): 21–43.

Kerr, Harry P. "Politics and Religion in Colonial Fast and Thanksgiving Sermons, 1763–1783." *Quarterly Journal of Speech* 46 (December 1960): 372–82.

Kibler, Lillian A. "Unionist Sentiment in South Carolina in 1860." *Journal of Southern History* 4 (May 1938): 346–66.

Kolchin, Peter. "In Defense of Servitude: American Proslavery and Russian Proserfdom Arguments, 1790–1860." *American Historical Review* 85 (October 1980): 809–27.

Lane, Belden C. "Presbyterian Republicanism: Miller and the Eldership as an Answer to Lay–Clerical Tensions." *Journal of Presbyterian History* 56 (Winter 1978): 311–24.

Latner, Richard. "The Nullification Crisis and Republican Subversion." *Journal of Southern History* 43 (February 1977): 18–38.

Longton, William Henry. "The Carolina Ideal World: Natural Science and Social Thought in Ante Bellum South Carolina." *Civil War History* 20 (June 1974): 118–34.

Loveland, Anne C. "Evangelicalism and 'Immediate Emancipation' in American Antislavery Thought." *Journal of Southern History* 32 (May 1966): 172–88.

——— "Presbyterians and Revivalism in the Old South." *Journal of Presbyterian History* 57 (Spring 1979): 36–49.

——— "Richard Furman's 'Questions on Slavery.'" *Baptist History and Heritage* 10 (July 1975): 177–81.

Lowance, Mason. "Typology and the New England Way: Cotton Mather and the Exegesis of Biblical Types." *Early American Literature* 4 (1969): 15–37.

Luker, Ralph. "God, Men and the World of James Warley Miles, Charleston's Transcendentalist." *Historical Magazine of the Protestant Episcopal Church* 39 (June 1970): 101–39.

Luraghi, Raimondo. "The Civil War and the Modernization of American Society: Social Structure and Industrial Revolution in the Old South before and during the War." *Civil War History* 18 (September 1972): 230–51.

MacLear, James F. "'The True American Union' of Church and State: The Reconstruction of the Theocratic Tradition." *Church History* 28 (March 1959): 41–62.

McCrary, Peyton. "The Party of Revolution: Republican Ideas about Politics and Social Change, 1862–1867." *Civil War History* 30 (December 1984): 330–51.

McCrary, Peyton; Miller, Clark; and Baum, Dale. "Class and Party in the Secession Crisis: Voting Behavior in the Deep South, 1856–1861." *Journal of Interdisciplinary History* 8 (Winter 1978): 429–57.

McCurry, Stephanie. "The Two Faces of Republicanism: Gender and Proslavery Politics in Antebellum South Carolina." *Journal of American History* 78 (March 1992): 1245–64.

McLoughlin, William G. "Enthusiasm for Liberty: The Great Awakening as a Key to the Revolution." In *Preachers and Politicians: Two Essays on the Origins of the American Revolution.* Worcester, Mass.: American Antiquarian Society, 1977.

McPherson, James M. "Antebellum Southern Exceptionalism: A New Look at an Old Question." *Civil War History* 29 (September 1983): 230–45.

Maddex, Jack P., Jr. "Proslavery Millennialism: Social Eschatology in Antebellum Southern Calvinism." *American Quarterly* 31 (Spring 1979): 46–62.

" 'The Southern Apostacy' Revisited: The Significance of Proslavery Christianity." *Marxist Perspectives* (Fall 1979): 132–42.

"From Theocracy to Spirituality: The Southern Presbyterian Reversal on Church and State." *Journal of Presbyterian History* 14 (Winter 1970): 438–57.

Maier, Pauline. "The Road Not Taken: Nullification, John C. Calhoun, and the Revolutionary Tradition in South Carolina." *South Carolina Historical Magazine* 82 (January 1981): 1–19.

Mathews, Donald G. "Religion in the Old South: Speculations on Methodology." *South Atlantic Quarterly* 73 (Winter 1974): 34–53.

"The Second Great Awakening as an Organizing Process, 1780–1830: An Hypothesis." *American Quarterly* 21 (Spring 1969): 23–43.

Matthews, Albert. "Notes on the Proposed Abolition of Slavery in Virginia in 1785." *Publications of the Colonial Society of Massachusetts* 6 (February 1900): 370–80.

Mead, Sidney. "The Rise of the Evangelical Conception of the Ministry in America, 1607–1850." In *The Ministry in Historical Perspectives,* edited by H. Richard Neibuhr and Daniel Williams. New York: Harper, 1956.

Miller, Perry. "From the Covenant to the Revival." In *Nature's Nation.* Cambridge, Mass.: Harvard University Press, 1967.

Minter, David. "The Puritan Jeremiad as Literary Form." In *The American Puritan Imagination: Essays in Revaluation,* edited by Sacvan Bercovitch. London and New York: Cambridge University Press, 1974.

Monroe, Haskell. "Southern Presbyterians and the Secession Crisis." *Civil War History* 6 (December 1960): 351–60.

Moore, Edmund A. "Robert J. Breckinridge and the Slavery Aspect of the Presbyterian Schism of 1837." *Church History* 4 (December 1935): 282–94.

Moore, James T. "Secession and the States: A Review Essay." *Virginia Magazine of History and Biography* 94 (January 1986): 60–76.

Moorhead, James H. "Joseph Addison Alexander: Common Sense, Romanticism and Biblical Criticism at Princeton." *Journal of Presbyterian History* 53 (Spring 1975): 51–65.

Morrison, Alfred J. "The Virginia Literary and Evangelical Magazine, 1818–1828." *William and Mary Quarterly* First Series 19 (April 1911): 266–272.

Nash, A. E. Keir. "Fairness and Formalism in the Trials in the State Supreme Courts of the Old South." *Virginia Law Review* 56 (February 1970): 64–100.
——. "Reason of Slavery: Understanding the Judicial Role in the Peculiar Institution." *Vanderbilt Law Review* 32 (January 1979): 7–218.
Newmyer, Kent. "Harvard Law School, New England Legal Culture and the Antebellum Origins of American Jurisprudence." *Journal of American History* 74 (December 1987): 814–35.
Noll, Mark A. "The Image of the United States as a Biblical Nation, 1776–1865." In *The Bible in America: Essays in Cultural History,* edited by Nathan O. Hatch and Mark A. Noll. New York: Oxford University Press, 1982.
Oakes, James. "From Republicanism to Liberalism: Ideological Change and the Crisis of the Old South." *American Quarterly* 37 (Fall 1985): 551–72.
Ochenkowski, J. P. "The Origins of Nullification in South Carolina." *South Carolina Historical Magazine* 83 (April 1982): 121–53.
Olsen, Otto H. "Historians and the Extent of Slave Ownership in the Southern United States." *Civil War History* 18 (June 1972): 101–16.
Owen, Thomas M. "An Alabama Protest Against Abolitionism in 1835." *Gulf States Historical Magazine* 2 (July 1903): 26–34.
Paluden, Phillip S. "The American Civil War Considered as a Crisis in Law and Order." *American Historical Review* 77 (October 1972): 1013–34.
Parker, Harold. "The Independent Presbyterian Church and Reunion in the South, 1813–1863." *Journal of Presbyterian History* 50 (Summer 1972): 89–111.
Patton, James. "Facets of the South in the 1850s." *Journal of Southern History* 23 (February 1957): 3–24.
Phillipson, Nicholas. "The Scottish Enlightenment." In *The Enlightenment in National Context,* edited by Roy Porter and Mikulas Teich. Cambridge: Cambridge University Press, 1981.
——. "Culture and Society in the 18th Century Province: The Case of Edinburgh and the Scottish Enlightenment." In *The University in Society,* Vol. II, edited by Lawrence Stone. Princeton, N.J.: Princeton University Press, 1974.
Pocock, J. G. A. "Languages and Their Implications: The Transformation of the Study of Political Thought." In *Politics, Language, and Time.* New York: Atheneum, 1971.
Posey, Walter B. "The Baptists and Slavery in the Lower Mississippi Valley." *Journal of Negro History* 41 (April 1956): 117–30.
——. "The Slavery Question in the Presbyterian Church in the Old Southwest." *Journal of Southern History* 15 (August 1966): 311–24.
Purifoy, Lewis M. "The Southern Methodist Church and the Proslavery Argument." *Journal of Southern History* 32 (August 1966): 325–41.
Reilly, Timothy. "Slavery and the Southwestern Evangelist in New Orleans (1800–1860)." *Journal of Mississippi History* (November 1979): 301–18.
Roland, Charles P. "Louisiana and Secession." *Louisiana History* 19 (Fall 1978): 389–99.
Sandeen, Ernest. "The Princeton Theology: One Source of Biblical Literalism in American Protestantism." *Church History* 31 (September 1962): 307–21.
Schmidt, Fredrika, and Wilhelm, Barbara. "Early Proslavery Petitions in Virginia." *William and Mary Quarterly* First Series 30 (January 1973): 133–46.
Sellers, Charles G., Jr. "Who Were the Southern Whigs?" *American Historical Review* 59 (January 1954): 335–46.

Shalhope, Robert E. "Thomas Jefferson's Republicanism and Antebellum Southern Thought." *Journal of Southern History* 42 (November 1976): 529–56.

Shanks, Caroline. "The Biblical Anti-Slavery Argument, 1830–1840." *Journal of Negro History* 16 (April 1931): 132–46.

Silbey, Joel H. "The Civil War Synthesis in American Political History." In *New Perspectives on the American Past. Vol 1: 1607–1877,* edited by Stanley N. Katz and Stanley I. Kutler. Boston: Little, Brown, 1969.

Skinner, Quentin. "Some Problems in the Analysis of Political Thought and Action." *Political Theory* 2 (August 1974): 277–303.

Smith, Elwyn A. "The Doctrine of Imputation and the Presbyterian Schism of 1837–1838." *Journal of the Presbyterian Historical Society* 38 (September 1970): 129–51.

———. "The Role of the South in the Presbyterian Schism of 1837–1838." *Church History* 29 (March 1960): 44–63.

Smith, Harmon. "William Capers and William A. Smith, Neglected Advocates of the Pro-Slavery Moral Argument." *Methodist History* 3 (October 1964): 23–32.

Smith, H. Shelton. "The Church and the Social Order as Interpreted by James Henley Thornwell." *Church History* 7 (1938): 115–24.

Smylie, James H. "Clerical Perspectives on Deism: Paine's *Age of Reason* in Virginia," *Eighteenth Century Studies* 6 (Winter 1972): 202–20.

Snay, Mitchell. "American Thought and Southern Distinctiveness: The Southern Clergy and the Sanctification of Slavery." *Civil War History* 35 (December 1989): 311–28.

Sowle, Patrick. "The North Carolina Manumission Society, 1816–1834." *North Carolina Historical Review* 42 (Winter 1965): 47–69.

Staiger, C. Bruce. "Abolitionism and the Presbyterian Schism of 1837–38." *Mississippi Valley Historical Review* 36 (December 1949): 391–414.

Stewart, James B. "Evangelicalism and the Radical Strain in Southern Antislavery Thought During the 1820s." *Journal of Southern History* 39 (August 1973): 379–96.

Stout, Harry S. "Religion, Communications, and the Ideological Origins of the American Revolution." *William and Mary Quarterly* Third Series 34 (October 1977): 519–41.

Strickland, John Scott. "The Great Revival and Insurrectionary Fears in North Carolina: An Examination of Antebellum Southern Society and Slave Revolt Panics." In *Class, Conflict and Consensus: Antebellum Southern Communities Studies,* edited by Orville Vernon Burton and Robert C. McMath, Jr. Westport, Conn.: Greenwood Press, 1982.

Stromberg, Roland N. "History in the Eighteenth-Century." *Journal of the History of Ideas* 12 (April 1951): 295–304.

Sutton, Robert P. "Nostalgia, Pessimism and Malaise: The Doomed Aristocrat in Late-Jeffersonian Virginia." *Virginia Magazine of History and Biography* 76 (January 1968): 41–55.

Sweet, Leonard. "The Reaction of the Protestant Episcopal Church in Virginia to the Secession Crisis: October 1859–May 1861." *Historical Magazine of the Protestant Episcopal Church* 41 (June 1972): 139–51.

Thornton, J. Mills III. "The Ethic of Subsistence and the Origins of Southern Secession." *Tennessee Historical Quarterly* 48 (Summer 1989): 67–86.

Trevor-Roper, Hugh. "The Historical Philosophy of the Enlightenment." *Studies on Voltaire and the Eighteenth Century* 27 (1963): 1667–87.

Walters, Ronald. "The Erotic South: Civilization and Sexuality in American Abolitionism." *American Quarterly* 25 (May 1973): 177–201.

Wamble, Hugh. "Landmarkism: Doctrinaire Ecclesiology among Baptists." *Church History* 33 (December 1964): 429–47.

Watson, Harry L. "Conflict and Collaboration: Yeomen, Slaveholders and Politics in the Antebellum South." *Social History* 10 (October 1985): 273–98.

Wayne, Michael. "An Old South Morality Play: Reconsidering the Social Underpinnings of the Proslavery Ideology." *Journal of American History* 77 (December 1990): 838–63.

Weeks, Louis III. "John Holt Rice and the American Colonization Society." *Journal of Presbyterian History* 46 (1968): 26–41.

Wight, Willard E. "The Churches and the Confederate Cause." *Civil War History* 6 (December 1960): 361–73.

Wilson, Harold. "Basil Manly, Apologist for Slaveocracy." *Alabama Review* 15 (January 1962): 38–53.

Wooster, Ralph A. "The Secession of the Lower South: An Examination of Changing Interpretations." *Civil War History* 7 (June 1961): 117–27.

Wyatt-Brown, Bertram. "The Abolitionists' Postal Campaign of 1835." *Journal of Negro History* 50 (October 1965): 227–38.

"The Antimission Movement in the Jacksonian South: A Study in Regional Folk-Culture." *Journal of Southern History* 36 (November 1970): 501–30.

"God and Honor in the Old South." *Southern Review* 25 (Spring 1989): 283–96.

"The Ideal Typology and Ante-Bellum Southern History: A Testing of a New Approach." *Societas* 5 (Winter 1975): 1–29.

"Modernizing Southern Slavery: The Proslavery Argument Reinterpreted." In *Region, Race and Reconstruction: Essays in Honor of C. Vann Woodward,* edited by J. Morgan Kousser and James M. McPherson. New York: Oxford University Press, 1982.

"Proslavery and Antislavery Intellectuals: Class Concepts and Polemical Struggle." In *Antislavery Reconsidered: New Perspectives on the Abolitionists,* edited by Michael Fellman and Lewis Perry. Baton Rouge and London: Louisiana State University Press, 1979.

"Stanley Elkin's *Slavery:* The Antislavery Interpretation Reexamined." *American Quarterly* 25 (May 1973): 154–76.

Dissertations

Burich, Keith R. "The Primitive Baptist Schism in North Carolina: A Study of the Professionalization of the Baptist Ministry." M.A. thesis, University of North Carolina, Chapel Hill, 1973.

DesChamps, Margaret Burr. "The Presbyterian Church in the South Atlantic Church, 1801–1861." Ph.D. dissertation, Emory University, 1952.

Freehling, Alison H. G. "Drift Toward Dissolution: The Virginia Slavery Debates of 1831–1832." Ph.D. dissertation, University of Michigan, 1974.

Garber, Paul Leslie. "The Religious Thought of James Henley Thornwell." Ph.D. dissertation, Duke University, 1939.

Gardner, John C. "Winning the Lower South to the Compromise of 1850." Ph.D. dissertation, Louisiana State University and Agricultural and Mechanical College, 1974.

Jordan, Marjorie. "Mississippi Methodists and the Division of the Church over Slavery." Ph.D. dissertation, University of Southern Mississippi, 1972.

McCurry, Stephanie. "Defense of Their World: Gender, Class and the Yeomanry of the South Carolina Lowcountry, 1820–1860." Ph.D. dissertation, State University of New York at Binghamton, 1988.

Nelson, John Oliver. "The Rise of the Princeton Theology: A Genetic Study of American Presbyterianism until 1850." Ph.D. dissertation, Yale University, 1935.

Proctor, Emerson. "Georgia Baptists: Organization and Division: 1772–1840." M.A. thesis, Georgia Southern College, 1969.

Robertson, J. Dallas. "The Disruption of the Methodist Episcopal Church, 1844, and Its Effect in Virginia." Senior thesis, Randolph–Macon College, 1949.

Startup, Kenneth Moore. "Strangers in the Land: The Southern Clergy and the Economic Mind of the Old South." Ph.D. dissertation, Louisiana State University, 1983.

Tise, Larry Edward. "Proslavery Ideology: A Social and Intellectual History of the Defense of Slavery in America, 1790–1840." Ph.D. dissertation, University of North Carolina at Chapel Hill, 1975.

Touchstone, Donald B. "Planters and Slave Religion in the Deep South." Ph.D. dissertation, Tulane University, 1973.

Watkin, Robert N. "The Forming of the Southern Presbyterian Minister: From Calvin to the American Civil War." Ph.D. dissertation, Vanderbilt University, 1969.

Index